MW00444773

THE DIABETIC
COOKBOOK FOR BEGINNERS

*The Must-Have Guide For Newly Diagnosed.
A 28-Day Meal Plan With Over 500 Easy And
Healthy Recipes For Prediabetes And
Manage Type 2 Diabetes.*

© Copyright 2021 - All rights reserved.

The content contained within this book may not be reproduced, duplicated or transmitted without direct written permission from the author or the publisher. Under no circumstances will any blame or legal responsibility be held against the publisher, or author, for any damages, reparation, or monetary loss due to the information contained within this book. Either directly or indirectly.

Legal Notice:

This book is copyright protected. This book is only for personal use. You cannot amend, distribute, sell, use, quote or paraphrase any part, or the content within this book, without the consent of the author or publisher.

Disclaimer Notice:

Please note the information contained within this document is for educational and entertainment purposes only. All effort has been executed to present accurate, up to date, and reliable, complete information. No warranties of any kind are declared or implied. Readers acknowledge that the author is not engaging in the rendering of legal, financial, medical or professional advice. The content within this book has been derived from various sources. Please consult a licensed professional before attempting any techniques outlined in this book.

By reading this document, the reader agrees that under no circumstances is the author responsible for any losses, direct or indirect, which are incurred as a result of the use of information contained within this document, including, but not limited to, errors, omissions, or inaccuracies.

Table of Contents

Introduction

Diabetes and its complications affect millions of people around the world. The most common form is type 2 diabetes which afflicts over 30 million people in the United States alone.

Diabetes is a disease where your body cannot produce insulin, a hormone that helps it break down sugar. If you have diabetes, your blood glucose level may be too high or too low.

If your blood glucose level is too high, your body can destroy cells in your kidneys and eyes. As a result, you can develop cataracts and lose vision. If it stays too low, you can suffer diabetic ketoacidosis and coma.

During prediabetes, you may experience high blood sugar levels, but they do not cause long-term effects on your health. Because prediabetes is not a serious illness, it does not require a medical diagnosis. You should talk to your doctor if you have blood glucose levels higher than normal for your age and gender (200 mg./dl. for women and 140 mg./dl. for men). This is called prediabetes or impaired glucose tolerance (IGT).

Once you are diagnosed with diabetes, the best way to lower your blood glucose level is to eat healthy foods that are low in sugar and high in fiber, such as whole grains and vegetables. You may also eat less food containing refined sugar or fat. Some people find that taking insulin helps them to manage their condition better than controlling their appetite or keeps them from eating at all.

Diabetes is a disease that can threaten your life. It is a primary cause of heart attack, stroke, kidney failure, neuropathy, blindness, and poor circulation. Although it can be manageable in terms of symptoms and signs, it cannot be cured or prevented. This is why you need to learn how to control it first.

There are 2 types of diabetes. Type 1 is an autoimmune disorder that occurs when the immune system attacks cells in the pancreas causing them to die, which causes insulin deficiency. Type 2 is a metabolic disorder that happens when insulin is not able to do its job properly, which results in higher blood sugar levels.

- Type 1 is a disease in which the pancreas no longer produces enough of the hormone insulin. This results in glucose (sugar) not being able to enter the body's cells and to be used by your body. Type 1 diabetes can also cause other conditions, depending upon how long it has been present in your body. Type 1 diabetes tends to develop early in childhood or adolescence, although it can also occur at any age.

- Type 2 diabetes is a disease caused by the body's inability to make insulin or to use the insulin it does make effectively. An example of type 2 diabetes is when your body doesn't use insulin properly, even when consumed in large amounts by eating refined foods or sugary drinks. It isn't clear exactly why this occurs, but some researchers believe genetics is an important factor in developing type 2 diabetes.

A balanced diet is a very important part of maintaining a healthy lifestyle. For a diabetic, there is a very high risk of becoming obese due to poor nutrition alone. In addition to this, diabetes can cause many complications such as heart disease and kidney problems. The best way to keep your diabetes under control is through proper nutrition and weight management. A balanced diet works as an excellent starting point for both type 1 and type 2 diabetics.

Diabetic recipes are not only delicious, but they are also extraordinarily nutritious. course, that's not surprising if you consider what foods a diabetic is recommended to eat. The cornerstone of a diabetic diet is plenty of fresh vegetables, fruit, whole grains, legumes, and other low glycemic index food that will keep blood sugar stable and won't trigger cravings for unhealthy refined carbohydrates.

It's so important to remember when cooking for diabetics to emulate the same dietary plan. Most doctors today recommend that all diabetics who have been managing their disease for at least a year or so, begin eliminating refined carbohydrates (white flour products) and sugar, and gradually boost the number of high-fiber foods (vegetables, grains, beans) in the diet.

It should go without saying, of course, that diabetics who are deficient in vitamins or have other health problems that prevent them from achieving a healthy weight are advised to follow a special diet designed to promote full and healthy weight loss.

Diabetically Driven Diet

There's one dietary challenge that does not apply to diabetics. So many people are watching their weight that you may think that diabetics have to stay away from carbs and eat less food so that they can lose weight. Well, as we already know, eating less food is not an effective way to lose weight. As for refined carbohydrates like white flour products and sugars, they're not on the approved list for breakfast or snacks for a diabetic anyway. What about other carbs?

Diabetics can eat all the carbs they want, but they have to be the right kind of carbohydrate: complex carbohydrates. The glycemic index is a measure of how quickly foods turn into sugar in the body. So, eating foods with a high glycemic index (75 or higher) is not recommended for diabetics. The recommended sweetener for diabetics is stevia, an all-natural plant extract that's sweeter than sugar but doesn't raise blood sugar levels.

One of the reasons diabetics are urged to eat plenty of whole grains, legumes, fruits, and vegetables is because these foods contain fiber that is digested more slowly than simple carbohydrates. Fiber keeps blood sugar levels stable by slowing the absorption and digestion of sugars in the body. The more fiber you eat, the slower your blood sugar level rises and falls.

Foods that contain starch, like potatoes, bread, pasta, and rice are considered complex carbohydrates. They're low glycemic foods because they break down slowly in the body. If you eat a slice of whole wheat bread or a baked potato for breakfast or lunch, your blood sugar level will rise slowly over several hours and stay steady until your next snack or meal.

Good Carbs

Fruit and vegetable juices are also good choices for diabetics. These foods don't contain any fiber and therefore do not affect blood sugar levels. But they do contain a lot of vitamins, minerals, and other nutrients that are essential for good health. And, in terms of calories, fruit juices are very low in calories and as long as you're eating only an 8-oz. glass each time you'll hardly notice the difference between fruit juice and a soft drink or even water.

CHAPTER 1:

Beginners Guide

Diabetes is a disease that affects many people, both young and old alike. So how can you live a healthy life with this condition? What are the impact on your diet, your exercise regime, and your everyday life?

Eating healthily is an important part of diabetes management as it lowers blood sugar levels. This diabetic cookbook for beginners has all the recipes from appetizers to desserts, to help you eat the right way.

The guide helps you to make the best of a diet that is not the easiest. Here are some tips on how to get your body, mind, and soul into healthy habits when meal times are such a challenge.

Diabetes management requires a lot of planning and an excellent diet is a key to a healthy lifestyle. Following a nutritious diet means eating the right foods and avoiding empty calories. A healthy, balanced diet will help you lose weight and to avoid complications like heart disease.

But here are some things you should not eat if you suffer from diabetes:

- Sugary foods such as cakes, pastries, and sugary snacks like sweets should be avoided. You must replace them with healthier choices such as fruit or cereal bars.
- Skipping meals can raise blood sugar levels significantly. For this reason, it is important to eat regular meals.
- Fast food is a no-no because it is usually high in saturated fats and carbohydrates. A healthier alternative would be grilled fish or chicken and vegetables cooked in olive or sunflower oil and served with a yogurt sauce.
- High-fat dairy products should be avoided as they can dramatically increase blood sugar levels. Instead, choose low-fat dairy products such as cheese and yogurt or eat more beans and nuts.
- Sugary drinks like soda and fruit juice should be avoided, where possible. Choose water instead. If you do crave a drink then opt for something like diluted orange juice with a slice of lime, which is much healthier.
- When cooking for yourself, use olive oil in place of sunflower or vegetable oils.

Ensure and always keep your body hydrated by drinking lots of water. Don't drink too much, as you would with a hangover. A general rule of thumb is to drink at least 2-thirds of your body weight in oz., but you should check your doctor's advice before doing this.

Water is a very important part of a healthy lifestyle and it's easy to get carried away in the hot weather. It helps you to cool down.

If you can't make it to the supermarket for a shop every day, then try to buy some basics like tinned fish or tinned vegetables for convenience.

If you're concerned about the cost of eating healthily, then visit your local supermarket's website to plan your weekly shop. Compare prices and items between chains or supermarkets in your area.

Planning will help you to make sure that you don't get carried away with impulse purchases, too.

If you have diabetes, planning a healthy diet is essential for several reasons:

- It helps prevent complications such as heart disease and stroke.
- It helps you to lose weight.
- It makes sure that you get vitamins and minerals from the food that you eat.

Controlling your blood sugar levels is also very important when you're managing diabetes. Your body needs insulin to control the amount of sugar that is in your blood, as it's essential for your cells to use or store glucose for energy. The correct level of insulin is a key factor in controlling your blood sugar levels and stabilizing them.

A healthy diet is made up of plenty of carbohydrates foods to provide energy. Carbohydrates can be found in fruit and vegetables, as well as wholemeal bread, pasta, and rice. High-carb foods are not usually rich in nutrients.

They can also be used as a quick source of useful energy for the brain especially during exercise or when you're feeling tired.

These carbohydrates are found mainly in things like bread, sugar, and junk food such as cakes, biscuits, and pies. They should be avoided, as they are usually high in saturated fat and sugar, and can raise your blood sugar level dramatically.

Protein is essential for growth. It's found in meat, chicken, fish, eggs, and dairy products. Protein keeps you feeling fuller for longer. To get the most out of your diet, combine a carbohydrate meal with a small amount of protein like lean meat or fish to balance blood sugar levels and keep you feeling full until your next meal.

fats are also important for energy. Saturated fats can raise your bad cholesterol level, so try to avoid saturated fats like butter and palm oil. You should replace them with unsaturated fats like olive oil.

Unsalted nuts contain a lot of fat and can replace fatty snacks and foods, helping you to watch what you eat as well as giving you the nutrients that your body needs. Also, you can count on them when you're feeling hungry, as they can be very filling.

Vitamins and minerals are vital nutrients for good health. Your body needs vitamins and minerals to maintain a healthy immune system, for example. Vitamins are important co-enzymes that help your cells function correctly. Your body requires vitamins A, B1 (thiamin), B2 (riboflavin), B12, C, and E as well as the minerals iron and calcium to do this.

Minerals help to maintain a healthy immune system and to control your blood sugar levels. They are found in foods such as milk, green vegetables, fruit, and fish.

Eating a balanced diet will help you to stay fit, healthy, and strong. However, when you're managing diabetes it can be hard to eat the right food when you have an active lifestyle and work commitments.

Your doctor can advise you on what is safe for your condition. You should also consult a dietician to make sure that you get all the nutrients that you need.

If you are on medication, it's important to take it daily as prescribed by your doctor. If you stop taking your blood glucose-lowering tablets, your diabetes may not be under control and this could increase the risk of complications.

CHAPTER 2:

Practical Tips to Overcome and Control Panic, Anxiety, Fear and Start to Live Happy with Diabetes

Diabetes can be a dangerous disease with some of the long-term effects being dementia, heart attacks, and even cancer.

You can help reduce your chances of getting serious diabetic complications by following your doctor's advice, eating healthy foods, and keeping on top of your diabetes.

As a person living with type 1 or type 2 diabetes, you may be feeling the stress from juggling daily work life, family, and social commitments with taking care of your diabetes.

It is quite common to develop some sort of anxiety when you start managing a life-threatening illness like diabetes.

Your first step to overcoming anxiety about living with diabetes is learning as much as you can about it. Read a book, talk to your doctor or a diabetes specialist, and ask friends and family.

By reading something or hearing the views of those around you about the condition you are managing, you will be able to gain a better understanding of what it is all about. The more you learn and understand about diabetes, the better you will be able to manage it.

Being involved in the diabetes society and helping others also help in coping with diabetes.

The following are some tips that you can use to overcome the fear of living with diabetes. The more you read about them, the easier it will be for you to implement them in your daily routine.

Take Control of Your Life

By taking control of your diabetes, you can turn an unpleasant situation into a positive one. Staying in control will help you overcome the fear of living with diabetes that is slowly taking over your life.

Taking charge means learning everything you can about diabetes, eating healthy foods, and following whatever exercise plan your doctor has recommended. It also means learning how to manage stressful situations that come up in your daily routine and learning how to cope with them before they overwhelm you.

Live an Active Lifestyle

As a diabetic, you are more vulnerable to disease. Getting at least 30 minutes of activity daily helps keep your body fit and healthy. It also reduces various health risks that are associated with hypertension, heart disease, and various other conditions.

When you are physically active, you can improve your stamina and flexibility while strengthening your muscles and bones. If you have diabetes, being more physically active also lowers the risk of getting diabetic complications down the road.

Talk to Your Doctor

If you are afraid about your doctor will think you are crazy, then work through your fear by simply talking to him or her before you start. You may find out that there is little to worry about and that is better than the alternative.

Talking with your doctor is also a good way to help relieve the stress from living with diabetes.

Get Involved in the Diabetes Society

The more you are involved with the diabetes society, the less you will feel isolated and lonely. You will also be aware of what other people with diabetes are doing to help themselves and how they cope with their condition.

You may learn of some different methods that help manage your condition or ask for any suggestions that others have to offer. The more active you are in society, the better you will be able to cope with living with a chronic illness like diabetes.

Get Your Sleep

Not getting your 8 hours of sleep every night is going to make you feel more stressed and anxious. Being a little tired and groggy will not help you control anxiety related to living with diabetes because you will lack the mental alertness it takes to deal with stressful situations.

If you have a consistent sleep schedule it will be easier for you to manage your daily activities as well. It will also go a long way in helping you overcome the fear of living with diabetes when you are not exhausted all the time.

Find Something to Laugh About

You cannot let every little problem become overwhelming. Even though diabetes is a serious condition, it does not mean that you have to take yourself too seriously.

Learn to laugh about some of the little things that happen throughout your day. When you can laugh about some of the situations that come up, it will take a lot of stress off your shoulders and make you feel a lot better.

Manage Stress

You may have all the responsibilities that come with living with diabetes, you might find yourself having a hard time handling stress daily. Stress can lead to mental exhaustion which can contribute to anxiety if left unchecked.

If you can find ways to relax after a long day's work, it will ease the tension so that you do not feel the need to overreact emotionally.

Talk to Your Doctor Regularly

If you talk with your doctor frequently, you will know how he or she is progressing with treating the disease and whether any new things may be affecting your condition.

When you feel like talking about something stressful that has happened in your day, it is a good idea to take advantage of this. Your doctor may be able to provide insights that can help you avoid other stressful situations in the future.

CHAPTER 3:

Practical Tips to Help Diabetic People to Improve and Make Easier Their Daily Life

Today, the world has been undergoing a great change, and people have been facing numerous issues. One of the main problems these days is diabetes. This disease has affected many people, as it can be caused not only by genetic factors but also by consuming foods that contain too much sugar. However, despite all the problems that can occur with diabetes, one way to fight against it is by using practical tips for diabetic people to make their everyday life easier. In this practical guide, you will find a list of easy recipes that you can prepare in your own home, so you will not need to go out shopping for food very often.

You will also learn about ways to reduce your sugar intake and avoid consuming too many carbohydrates in your diet. Not only will you lose weight but you will also improve the quality of your skin and hair and improve the health of your heart. Besides, this guide will also help you to choose the best foods that contain less sugar and carbohydrates, such as vegetables and fruits. Not only can you eat these foods raw but you can also use them to prepare a delicious salad or even grilled fruits with honey.

Let's see how by using practical tips for diabetic people to make their everyday life easier they can easily prevent and fight against multiple health problems.

Practical Tips for Diabetic People Make Their Everyday Life Easier

Limit Your Consumption of the Most Common Sugars

"The percentage of glucose in fructose is about the same as that in sucrose, but the total fructose content per gram is approximately twice that of sucrose."

Fructose and sucrose are similar in their role in the body. But it is important to know for diabetic people to limit their consumption of them because these sugars can increase blood glucose levels too much.

Buy a Scale

To help you in keeping track of your food intake, you must buy a digital scale to measure the amounts of food you consume. After a few days, you can start weighing your portions and identifying those that are high in calories and sugar content.

Use Sugar Substitutes to Satisfy Your Sweet Tooth

Many diabetic people find that they cannot control their sugar intake because they are addicted to eating too much sweet. In this case, you can use artificial sweeteners instead of sugar. These substitute sugars contain fewer calories and carbohydrates than those found in real sugar, and they give a sweet taste without increasing blood glucose levels. Furthermore, these substitutes are safe to consume in large quantities and can also improve the health of your teeth and gums.

Avoid Fried Foods

Fried foods are full of carbohydrates and are one of the main causes of diabetes. If you cannot control your sugar intake, you should make a list of what you cannot eat at all. This includes foods that are deep-fried or cooked over high temperatures. Afterward, you must avoid eating them or at least choose to eat them only if they are prepared in a healthier way, such as when they are grilled with honey instead of oil.

Try to Eat Vegetables and Fruits Raw

To reduce your sugar intake, it is necessary to include in your diet more vegetables and fruits. But you should only eat them when they are raw. This way, you will avoid eating large quantities of sugar. However, do not use vinegar or lemon juice as a way to flavor them.

Eat Less Meat

Reducing the number of animal products in your diet is one of the best ways to improve your health. If you cannot control your sugar intake, you must avoid eating too much meat. This food has high sugar content and it also includes saturated fat.

Avoid Eggs and Dairy Products

This recommendation is important for diabetic people because these foods contain lactose, which can make them insulin-resistant and increase blood glucose levels.

Experiment with Different Types of Bread

Many people do not understand the importance of wheat and carbohydrates in their diet. Therefore, they may opt for sweet bread to obtain the taste they are searching for every day. However, this type of bread has high sugar content and can contain gluten, which is another problem for diabetic people. You should choose crusty bread that is not very flavorful to reduce your sugar intake.

Try to Eat Dairy Products Only in Moderation

Dairy products have many benefits for your health, but you should be careful about the amount of fat and carbohydrates they contain. This is why healthy diabetic people should only consume these foods in moderation. You should also remove most of the sugar from your diet so that you can control it better and avoid eating too much food containing sugar.

Eat Lots of Vegetables

Including vegetables and fruits in your diet is one of the best ways to lower blood glucose levels and make yourself healthier. But you should make sure that you include only those types of vegetables and fruits that do not contain a lot of sugar. For example, carrots and tomatoes are very healthy but are small in size so it does not pose a problem for diabetic people to control their intake.

Avoid Eating Sweet Foods

If you crave sweets, do not eat them because this food can cause sugar problems in your body. You can also use sweeteners instead of sugar for cooking purposes.

Use Healthier Fats

Instead of butter, you should try using olive oil for cooking because it contains less fat and Cholesterol: than butter. You can also add walnuts, salmon, or avocado to your diet because they are full of healthy fat that will not raise blood glucose levels. This way, you will be able to control the amount of fat you eat every day without compromising your health either.

Be Careful with Sugary Drinks

It can be hard to avoid sugary drinks in your diet. However, if you cannot control your sugar intake, you should try at least to consume them in moderation. This way, you will not have health problems caused by diabetes. You should also drink plain water instead of other types of sweetened liquids because they can also raise blood glucose levels and increase the risk of developing other diseases that are related to diabetes.

Avoid Artificial Sweeteners

If you cannot control your sugar intake, you should avoid going for these sweeteners because they can also increase your blood glucose levels. Try to reduce your consumption of these products. However, if you cannot do that, try to find other ways to reduce sugar. For example, you should try replacing sugar with a natural sweetener like honey or stevia.

Create a Healthy Eating Plan

Do you know that you should create a healthy eating plan for your diabetes? This means that you should come up with a nutritional meal plan so that you can follow it every day. This will improve your diet and make it healthier. You should also try to eat 3 meals and 2 snacks every day. This way, you will be able to prevent unhealthy eating habits from developing because this will make it difficult to overeat.

All these tips, help you live a healthier lifestyle and enjoy the same time as others without any complication.

CHAPTER 4:

Discover How to Overcome Diabetes and Regulate the Blood Sugar to Healthy Level

Diabetes is a disease where the normal production of insulin, a hormone, fails to function normally. As a result, the body can no longer regulate the level of glucose in the blood. This causes the blood sugar levels to rise rapidly and unpredictably to dangerous levels.

The great news is that diabetes can be managed easily and effectively by following a few simple steps. This Diabetes Cookbook for Beginners will guide you through all the possible scenarios and how you can manage them in case you or your loved one is diagnosed with diabetes. You will learn about methods to manage diabetes naturally and safely using what you already have on hand at home, without making any modifications or replacements.

Diabetes is a disease in which the body does not produce or properly use insulin. It is one of the most common disorders of people who are over the age of 40. The symptoms of diabetes can be controlled by diabetes self-management.

As you may know, there are 2 types of diabetes, type 1 and type 2. Type 1 diabetes is due to insufficient production of insulin by the pancreas, while type 2 diabetes is because the body does not use insulin effectively.

You are probably already aware that diabetes can be a challenge, but it doesn't have to be. With the right knowledge and the determination to overcome the condition, it is possible to regulate your blood sugar, which can greatly reduce your risk of complications.

The diagnosis of diabetes comes with a whole host of scary statistics and numbers. But there are some vital facts that you must know: the disease occurs at a rate of one in 3 among people over age 25; an estimated 25 percent of American adults have pre-diabetes; and one-third of diabetes cases develop this condition undiagnosed, according to the American Diabetes Association.

Once diagnosed, there are things that you can do to manage your condition: get regular checkups from your doctor; go for routine blood tests every 2–3 months; eat a healthy diet that includes more produce and fewer refined carbohydrates, and restrict alcohol consumption to less than 2 drinks per day.

Put those tips together with this knowledge of what foods are good for you and what foods may contribute to high blood sugar and you can create a sound plan for managing your condition. Doing so not only results in less risk for developing complications but also allows you to feel healthier overall. Not bad, considering all it takes is some extra effort.

You can control diabetes by following a healthy diet and regular exercise. It also helps to get annual check-ups from your doctor so that changes can be made in your lifestyle if needed. Here are some healthy dietary changes you can make to control your condition:

- Eat more foods with fiber for better digestion and control of blood sugar level. Foods rich in fibers include fruits, vegetables, whole grains, legumes, and beans. You can also choose dried beans instead of canned ones to provide additional fiber in your diet if possible.

- Consume foods rich in antioxidants to fight off free radicals that cause aging and damage to cells. Among other things, oranges, whole grains, dark green leafy vegetables, citrus fruits, and tea contain antioxidants.

- Avoid eating too much white sugar and flour products as they cause blood sugar levels to spike in the body. Instead, it is better to eat foods like dried beans; brown rice; and whole wheat pasta.

- When you need extra energy during the day, drink at least 8 oz. liquid every 2 hours to prevent hypoglycemia wherein low sugar in the blood causes dizziness or lightheadedness. You can choose liquid carbohydrates which are good options at this time as these carbohydrates to provide energy for the muscles when they are needed most such as during exercise or when you need extra energy during the day.

CHAPTER 5:

How to Equilibrate Diabetic Needs with Daily Life

It can be difficult to determine how much of a specific nutrient a diabetic person needs to take. For most diabetics, the answer is simple: no more than what they need to maintain their health. If they are not eating well, taking too much insulin, or ignoring their symptoms, they may require more insulin. But if they are eating a balanced diet and paying close attention to their blood glucose levels, they can probably get by with no more than 2–3 units of insulin per day.

Fats are a source of energy in diabetics, but fat comes only in 2 forms: saturated and unsaturated. People with diabetes who want to reduce their insulin needs should choose unsaturated fats over saturated fats because unsaturated fats do not raise blood glucose levels as much. Saturated fats like butter and lard are not useful for people with diabetes because they cause blood sugar levels to rise quickly.

The good news is that unsaturated fats are heart-healthy, and they keep the cholesterol levels in the blood from rising too high. They help lower total cholesterol levels and lower LDL ("bad") cholesterol levels. Vitamin E is also a component of both unsaturated and saturated fats, so unsaturated fats are necessary for health.

Diabetics should limit their saturated fats to less than 10% of their total caloric intake. Guidelines now suggest that a diabetic person should derive no more than 7% of their total caloric intake from saturated fats.

Many diabetics want to eat foods that contain a good deal of saturated fat and very little unsaturated fats. But they need to understand the connection between nutrient intake and diabetes control. To obtain an adequate amount of nutrition, they may have to accept a lower total fat intake.

Healthy and balanced nutrition can be the key to successful diabetes control for most diabetics.

The nutrients needed by diabetics can be found in the following food groups:

- Fruits, vegetables, grains, and beans are all excellent sources of carbohydrates (and they contain a lot of other nutrients as well).

- In a limited amount, margarine and shortening are acceptable choices because they provide healthy unsaturated fats.

- Fish oil is another excellent source of unsaturated fat. It's recommended that 65–75% of a diabetic's total fat intake comes from fish oil.

Since unsaturated fats are heart-healthy, diabetics should get most of their fat from unsaturated sources. Diabetics should be aware of the potential dangers of following tips that include a lot of meat, such as barbecued ribs, marinated chicken, and other sausages. When these meats are not cooked, they contain a high amount of unhealthy saturated fats. But when people follow safe cooking guidelines, they can include meats in their diet.

Most diabetics enjoy a wide variety of foods. Eating a variety of foods is healthy and recommended for all people.

If they would like to limit their fat intake, diabetics should get most of it from unsaturated sources such as fish oil or fat-free milk.

Controlling diabetes means making wise choices about carbohydrate intake, as well as other nutrients that are part of a healthy diet that meets the needs of all members of the family.

CHAPTER 6:

Help to Understand What Works Best for Their Life

We're all here for one thing: to live fuller, healthier lives. And for those living with diabetes, that often means balancing the demands of a challenging disease with a demanding lifestyle. Being a good caregiver is tough. But, armed with the right facts and the right tools, any diabetic can handle the daily challenges of diabetes better—things like counting carbs and measuring blood glucose levels. And that's when you can move forward.

How diabetes affects your life it's easy to get frustrated with the disease and its challenges. But any diabetic who has been living with the condition for any time knows that some of this frustration is a waste of precious energy and adds nothing to managing the condition.

It's important to keep the focus on the big picture—your lifelong quest to enjoy all life has to offer, even as you live with diabetes every day. Living with diabetes is a long-term process, not a short-term condition. You can be in control of the disease, but you have to get on board and take care of yourself first.

Living successfully with diabetes (type 1 or type 2) also means making the right lifestyle changes—like eating a diet that balances calories, carbs, fat, and nutrients. That's where good diabetic cookbooks can help. In short, for any diabetic diet to be effective, it must be:

1. **Diet-Adapted:** the right foods for you.
2. **Well-Balanced:** enough of the right foods to keep you healthy and satisfied.
3. **Nutritious:** plenty of vitamins, minerals, and fiber, in the form of fruits, vegetables, whole grains, and healthy fats.

For diabetics, that means relying on food that's good for you—not just to make you thinner or healthier—but to help keep your blood sugar levels stable. A diabetic diet focuses on maximizing your healthy eating and minimizing the unhealthy. Here's a list of the right foods for the type of diabetic you are:

- For Type 1 diabetes, the right foods include low-fat dairy products and meats (see our article), and whole grains.

- For Type 2 diabetes, try unrefined carbohydrates including potatoes, sweet potatoes, yams, and black beans.

- For both types of diabetes, legumes like beans (black or pinto), lentils, and peanuts are great sources of protein.

To meet your fiber needs, enjoy plenty of fruits and vegetables—they're the best sources of fiber.

For either type of diabetes, the right fat foods are fish like salmon or tuna, and cold-water fish oil supplements.

Whichever type of diabetes you have, there are great diabetic cookbooks available to help you learn how to enjoy these healthy foods without a lot of fuss or bother. Some great low-carb cookbooks can help you create meals with minimal carbs.

And if you or your loved ones are committed to a diabetic diet, it's time for you to get healthy, too:

- Exercise regularly.
- Stay away from alcohol and tobacco.
- And, talk to your doctor about your family medical history—if you have any family members with diabetes, you're more likely to develop the disease yourself. Be prepared to make a big change in your lifestyle.

CHAPTER 7:

Breakfast Recipes

Apple Cinnamon Scones

Preparation time: 5 minutes
Cooking time: 25 minutes
Servings: 16
Ingredients:

- 2 large eggs
- 1 apple, diced
- 1/4 cup+1/2 tbsp. margarine, melted and divided
- 1 tbsp. half-n-half
- 3 cups almond flour
- 1/3 cup+2 tsp. Splenda®
- 2 tsp. baking powder
- 2 tsp. cinnamon
- 1 tsp. vanilla
- 1/4 tsp. salt

Directions:

1. Heat oven to 325°F. Line a large baking sheet with parchment paper.
2. In a large bowl, whisk flour, 1/3 cup Splenda, baking powder, 1 1/2 tsp. cinnamon, and salt together. Stir in apple.
3. Add the eggs, 1/4 cup melted margarine, cream, and vanilla. Stir until the mixture forms a soft dough.
4. Divide the dough in half and pat it into 2 circles, about 1-inch thick, and 7–8 inches around.

5. In a small bowl, stir together the remaining 2 tsp. Splenda, and 1/2 tsp. cinnamon.
6. Brush the 1/2 tbsp. melted margarine over the dough and sprinkle with cinnamon mixture. Cut each into 8 equal pieces and place them on a prepared baking sheet.
7. Bake 20–25 minutes, or until golden brown and firm to the touch.

Nutrition:

- Calories: 176 Total Carbs: 12 g.
- Net Carbs: 9 g.
- Protein: 5 g.
- Fat: 12 g.
- Sugar: 8 g.
- Fiber: 3 g.

Apple Filled Swedish Pancake

Preparation time: 25 minutes
Cooking time: 20 minutes
Servings: 6
Ingredients:

- 2 apples, cored and thinly sliced
- 3/4 cup egg substitute
- 1/2 cup fat-free milk
- 1/2 cup sugar-free caramel sauce
- 1 tbsp. reduced-calorie margarine
- 1/2 cup flour
- 1`1/2 tbsp. brown sugar substitute
- 2 tsp. water
- 1/4 tsp. cinnamon
- 1/8 tsp. cloves
- 1/8 tsp. salt
- Nonstick cooking spray

Directions:

1. Heat oven to 400°F. Place margarine in cast-iron or ovenproof, skillet, and place in oven until margarine is melted.
2. In a medium bowl, whisk together flour, milk, egg substitute, cinnamon, cloves, and salt until smooth.
3. Pour batter in hot skillet and bake 20–25 minutes until puffed and golden brown.
4. Spray a medium saucepan with cooking spray. Heat over medium heat.
5. Add apples, brown sugar, and water. Cook, stirring occasionally until apples are tender and golden brown, about 4–6 minutes.
6. Pour the caramel sauce into a microwave-proof measuring glass and heat 30–45 seconds, or until warmed through.
7. To serve, spoon apples into pancake and drizzle with caramel. Cut into wedges.

Nutrition:

- Calories: 193
- Total Carbs: 25 g.
- Net Carbs: 23 g.
- Protein: 6 g.
- Fat: 2 g.
- Sugar: 12 g.
- Fiber: 2 g.

- 1 egg
- 1/4 cup skim milk
- 2 tbsp. margarine, divided
- 4 slices healthy loaf bread,
- 1 tbsp. Splenda® brown sugar
- 1 tsp. vanilla
- 1/4 tsp. cinnamon

Directions:

1. Melt 1 tbsp. margarine in a large skillet over med-high heat. Add apples, Splenda, and cinnamon and cook, stirring frequently, until apples are tender.
2. In a shallow dish, whisk together egg, milk, and vanilla.
3. Melt the remaining margarine in a separate skillet over med-high heat. Dip each slice of bread in the egg mixture and cook until golden brown on both sides.
4. Place 2 slices of French toast on plates, and top with apples. Serve immediately.

Nutrition:

- Calories: 394
- Total Carbs: 27 g.
- Net Carbs: 22 g.
- Protein: 10 g.
- Fat: 23 g.
- Sugar: 19 g.
- Fiber: 5 g.

3. Apple Topped French Toast

Preparation time: 10 minutes
Cooking time: 10 minutes
Servings: 2
Ingredients:

- 1 apple, peel and slice thin

Apple Walnut Pancakes

Preparation time: 15 minutes
Cooking time: 30 minutes
Servings: 18
Ingredients:

- 1 apple, peeled and diced

- 2 cup skim milk
- 2 egg whites
- 1 egg, beaten
- 1 cup flour
- 1 cup whole wheat flour
- 1/2 cup walnuts, chopped
- 2 tbsp. sunflower oil
- 1 tbsp. Splenda® brown sugar
- 2 tsp. baking powder
- 1 tsp. salt
- Nonstick cooking spray

Directions:

1. In a large bowl, combine dry ingredients.
2. In a separate bowl, combine egg whites, egg, milk, and oil and add to dry ingredients. Stir just until moistened. Fold in apple and walnuts.
3. Spray a large griddle with cooking spray and heat. Pour batter, 1/4 cup onto the hot griddle. Flip when bubbles form on top. Cook until the second side is golden brown. Serve with sugar-free syrup.

Nutrition:

- Calories: 120 Total Carbs: 15 g.
- Net Carbs: 13 g. Protein: 4 g.
- Fat: 5 g. Sugar: 3 g.
- Fiber: 2 g.

"Bacon" & Egg Muffins

Preparation time: 10 minutes
Cooking time: 15 minutes
Servings: 6
Ingredients:

- 1 1/4 cups frozen hash browns, thawed

- 1 cup egg substitute
- 2 turkey sausage patties, diced
- 2 tbsp. onion, finely diced
- 2 tbsp. turkey bacon, cooked and chopped
- 2 tbsp. Monterey Jack cheese, grated
- 1 tbsp. fat-free sour cream
- 1 garlic clove, finely diced
- 1 tsp. vegetable oil
- 1/4 tsp. salt
- 1/8 tsp. black pepper
- Cooking spray

Directions:

1. Heat oven to 400°F. Spray a 6 cup muffin pan with cooking spray.
2. Divide the hash browns evenly among the muffin cups, pressing firmly on the bottoms and up the sides.
3. In a large skillet, over medium heat, heat oil until hot. Add onion, and cook stirring frequently until tender.
4. Add garlic and sausage and cook for 1 minute.
5. Remove the skillet from heat and stir in sour cream.
6. In a medium bowl, beat egg substitute with salt and pepper. Pour egg mixture evenly over the potatoes.
7. Top with sausage mixture, bacon, and cheese. Bake 15–18 minutes, or until eggs are set. Serve immediately.

Nutrition:

- Calories: 165 Total Carbs: 13 g.
- Net Carbs: 12 g.
- Protein: 11 g.
- Fat: 7 g.
- Sugar: 1 g.
- Fiber: 1 g.

Berry Breakfast Bark

Preparation time: 10 minutes
Cooking time: 120 minutes
Servings: 6
Ingredients:

- 3–4 strawberries, sliced

- 1 1/2 cup plain Greek yogurt
- 1/2 cup blueberries
- 1/2 cup low-fat granola
- 3 tbsp. sugar-free maple syrup

Directions:
1. Line a baking sheet with parchment paper.
2. In a medium bowl, mix yogurt and syrup until combined. Pour into prepared pan and spread in a thin even layer.
3. Top with remaining ingredients. Cover with foil and freeze 2 hours or overnight.
4. To serve: slice into squares and serve immediately. If bark thaws too much it will lose its shape. Store any remaining bark in an airtight container in the freezer.

Nutrition:
- Calories: 69
- Total Carbs: 18 g.
- Net Carbs: 16 g.
- Protein: 7 g.
- Fat: 6 g.
- Sugar: 7 g.
- Fiber: 2 g.

Blueberry Cinnamon Muffins

Preparation time: 10 minutes
Cooking time: 30 minutes
Servings: 10
Ingredients:
- 3 eggs
- 1 cup blueberries
- 1/3 cup half-n-half

- 1/4 cup margarine, melted
- 1 1/2 cup almond flour
- 1/3 cup Splenda®
- 1 tsp. baking powder
- 1 tsp. cinnamon

Directions:
1. Heat oven to 350°F. Line 10 muffin cups with paper liners.
2. In a large mixing bowl, combine dry ingredients.
3. Stir in wet ingredients and mix well.
4. Fold in the blueberries and spoon evenly into the lined muffin pan.
5. Bake 25–30 minutes or they pass the toothpick test.

Nutrition:
- Calories: 194
- Total Carbs: 12 g.
- Net Carbs: 10 g.
- Protein: 5 g.
- Fat: 14 g.
- Sugar: 9 g.
- Fiber: 2 g.

Blueberry English Muffin Loaf

Preparation time: 15 minutes
Cooking time: 60 minutes
Servings: 12
Ingredients:
- 6 eggs beaten
- 1/2 cup almond milk, unsweetened
- 1/2 cup blueberries
- 1/2 cup cashew butter
- 1/2 cup almond flour
- 1/4 cup coconut oil
- 2 tsp. baking powder
- 1/2 tsp. salt
- Nonstick cooking spray

Directions:
1. Heat oven to 350°F. Line a loaf pan with parchment paper and spray lightly with cooking spray.

2. In a small glass bowl, melt cashew butter and oil together in the microwave for 30 seconds. Stir until well combined.
3. In a large bowl, stir together the dry ingredients. Add cashew butter mixture and stir well.
4. In a separate bowl, whisk the milk and eggs together. Add to flour mixture and stir well. Fold in blueberries.
5. Pour into the prepared pan and bake for 45 minutes, or until it passes the toothpick test.
6. Cook 30 minutes, remove from pan, and slice.

Nutrition:
- Calories: 162
- Total Carbs: 5 g.
- Net Carbs: 4 g.
- Protein: 6 g.
- Fat: 14 g.
- Sugar: 1 g.
- Fiber: 1 g.

Blueberry Stuffed French Toast

Preparation time: 15 minutes
Cooking time: 20 minutes
Servings: 8
Ingredients:
- 4 eggs
- 1 1/2 cup blueberries
- 1/2 cup orange juice
- 1 tsp. orange zest
- 16 slices bread,
- 3 tbsp. Splenda®, divided
- 1/8 tsp. salt
- Blueberry orange dessert sauce
- Nonstick cooking spray

Directions:
1. Heat oven to 400°F. Spray a large baking sheet with cooking spray.
2. In a small bowl, combine berries with 2 tbsp. of Splenda.
3. Lay 8 slices of bread on the work surface. Top with about 3 tbsp. of berries and place the second slice of bread on top. Flatten slightly.
4. In a shallow dish, whisk the remaining ingredients together. Carefully dip both sides of bread in egg mixture and place on prepared pan.
5. Bake 7–12 minutes per side, or until lightly browned.
6. Heat dessert sauce until warm. Plate the French toast and top with 1–2 tbsp. of the sauce. Serve.

Nutrition:
- Calories: 208
- Total Carbs: 20 g.
- Net Carbs: 18 g.
- Protein: 7 g.
- Fat: 10 g.
- Sugar: 14 g.
- Fiber: 2 g.

Breakfast Pizza

Preparation time: 10 minutes
Cooking time: 30 minutes
Servings: 8
Ingredients:
- 12 eggs
- 1/2 lb. breakfast sausage
- 1 cup bell pepper, sliced
- 1 cup red pepper, sliced
- 1 cup cheddar cheese, grated

- 1/2 cup half-n-half
- 1/2 tsp. salt
- 1/4 tsp. pepper

Directions:
1. Heat oven to 350°F.
2. In a large cast-iron skillet, brown sausage. Transfer to a bowl.
3. Add peppers and cook for 3–5 minutes or until they begin to soften. Transfer to a bowl.
4. In a small bowl, whisk together the eggs, cream, salt, and pepper. Pour into skillet. Cook for 5 minutes or until the sides start to set.
5. Bake 15 minutes.
6. Remove from oven and set it to broil. Top "crust" with sausage, peppers, and cheese. Broil 3 minutes, or until cheese is melted and starts to brown.
7. Let rest 5 minutes before slicing and serving.

Nutrition:
- Calories: 230
- Total Carbs: 4 g.
- Protein: 16 g.
- Fat: 17 g.
- Sugar: 2 g.
- Fiber: 0 g.

Cauliflower Breakfast Hash

Preparation time: 10 minutes
Cooking time: 20 minutes
Servings: 2
Ingredients:
- 4 cups cauliflower, grated
- 1 cup mushrooms, diced
- 3/4 cup onion, diced
- 3 slices bacon
- 1/4 cup sharp cheddar cheese, grated

Directions:
1. In a medium skillet, over med-high heat, fry bacon, set aside.
2. Add vegetables to the skillet and cook, stirring occasionally, until golden brown.

3. Cut bacon into pieces and return to skillet.
4. Top with cheese and allow it to melt. Serve immediately.

Nutrition:
- Calories: 155 Total Carbs: 16 g.
- Net Carbs: 10 g. Protein: 10 g.
- Fat: 7 g. Sugar: 7 g. Fiber: 6 g.

Cheese Spinach Waffles

Preparation time: 10 minutes
Cooking time: 20 minutes
Servings: 4
Ingredients:
- 2 strips bacon, cooked and crumbled
- 2 eggs, lightly beaten
- 1/2 cup cauliflower, grated
- 1/2 cup frozen spinach, chopped (squeeze water out first)
- 1/2 cup low-fat mozzarella cheese, grated
- 1/2 cup low-fat cheddar cheese, grated
- 1 tbsp. margarine, melted
- 1/4 cup reduced-fat Parmesan cheese, grated
- 1 tsp. onion powder
- 1 tsp. garlic powder
- Nonstick cooking spray

Directions:
1. Thaw spinach and squeeze out as much of the water as you, place it in a large bowl.
2. Heat your waffle iron and spray with cooking spray.
3. Add remaining ingredients to the spinach and mix well.
4. Pour small amounts on the waffle iron and cook like you would for regular waffles. Serve warm.

Nutrition:
- Calories: 186 Total Carbs: 2 g.
- Protein: 14 g. Fat: 14 g.
- Sugar: 1 g. Fiber: 0 g.

Cinnamon Apple Granola

Preparation time: 5 minutes
Cooking time: 35 minutes
Servings: 4
Ingredients:

- 1 apple, peel and finely diced
- 1/4 cup margarine, melted
- 1 cup walnuts or pecans
- 1 cup almond flour
- 3/4 cup coconut, flaked
- 1/2 cup sunflower seeds
- 1/2 cup hemp seeds
- 1/3 cup Splenda®
- 2 tsp. cinnamon
- 2 tsp. vanilla
- 1/2 tsp. salt

Directions:

1. Heat oven to 300°F. Line a large baking sheet with parchment paper.
2. Place the nuts, flour, coconut, seeds, Splenda, and salt in a food processor. Pulse until mixture resembles coarse crumbs but leave some chunks.
3. Transfer to a bowl and add apple and cinnamon. Stir in margarine and vanilla until well coated and the mixture starts to clump together.
4. Pour onto the prepared pan and spread out evenly. Bake 25 minutes, stirring a couple of times, until it starts to brown.
5. Turn the oven off and let the granola sit inside for 5–10 minutes. Remove from oven and cool completely, it will crisp up more as it cools. Store in an airtight container.

Nutrition:

- Calories: 360
- Total Carbs: 19 g.
- Net Carbs: 14 g.
- Protein: 10 g.
- Fat: 28 g.
- Sugar: 12 g.
- Fiber: 5 g.

Cinnamon Rolls

Preparation time: 15 minutes
Cooking time: 20 minutes
Servings: 6
Ingredients:

- 4 eggs
- 1 ripe banana
- 2/3 cup coconut flour
- 6 tbsp. honey, divided
- 6 tbsp. coconut oil, soft, divided
- 1 tsp. vanilla
- 1 tsp. baking soda
- 1/2 tsp. salt
- 1 tbsp.+1/2 tsp. cinnamon

Directions:

1. Heat oven to 350°F. Line a cookie sheet with parchment paper.
2. In a medium bowl, lightly beat eggs. Beat in the banana. Add 2 tbsp. honey, 2 tbsp. melted coconut oil, and vanilla and mix to combine.
3. Mix in flour, salt, baking soda, and 1/2 tsp. cinnamon until thoroughly combined. If the dough is too sticky add more flour, a little at a time.

4. Line a work surface with parchment paper and place dough on top. Place another sheet of parchment paper on top and roll out into a large rectangle.

5. In a small bowl, combine 2 tbsp. honey, 2 tbsp. coconut oil, and 1 tbsp. of cinnamon and spread on dough.

6. Roll up and cut into 6 equal pieces. Place on prepared pan and bake 15–30 minutes, or until golden brown.

7. Let cool for 10 minutes. Stir together the remaining 2 tbsp. of honey and coconut oil and spread over warm rolls. Serve.

Nutrition:
- Calories: 247
- Total Carbs: 23 g.
- Protein: 4 g.
- Fat: 17 g.
- Sugar: 20 g.
- Fiber: 1 g.

Coconut Breakfast Porridge

Preparation time: 2 minutes
Cooking time: 10 minutes
Servings: 4
Ingredients:
- 4 cup vanilla almond milk, unsweetened
- 1 cup coconut, unsweetened and grated
- 8 tsp. coconut flour

Directions:
1. Add coconut to a saucepan and cook over med-high heat until it is lightly toasted. Be careful not to let it burn.

2. Add milk and bring to a boil. While stirring, slowly add flour, cook, and stir until the mixture starts to thicken about 5 minutes.

3. Remove from heat, mixture will thicken more as it cools. Ladle into bowls, add blueberries, or drizzle with a little honey if desired.

Nutrition:
- Calories: 231
- Total Carbs: 21 g.
- Net Carbs: 8 g.
- Protein: 6 g.
- Fat: 14 g.
- Sugar: 4 g.
- Fiber 13 g.

Cottage Cheese Pancakes

Preparation time: 5 minutes
Cooking time: 5 minutes
Servings: 2
Ingredients:
- 1 cup low-fat cottage cheese
- 4 egg whites
- 1/2 cup oats
- 1 tbsp. Stevia®, raw, optional
- 1 tsp. vanilla
- Nonstick cooking spray

Directions:
1. Place all ingredients into a blender and process until smooth.

2. Spray a medium skillet with cooking spray and heat over medium heat.

3. Pour about 1/4 cup batter into a hot pan and cook until golden brown on both sides.
4. Serve with sugar-free syrup, fresh berries, or topping of your choice.

Nutrition:
- Calories: 250
- Total carbs: 25 g.
- Net Carbs: 23 g.
- Protein: 25 g.
- Fat: 4 g.
- Sugar: 7 g.
- Fiber: 2 g.

Crab & Spinach Frittata

Preparation time: 10 minutes
Cooking time: 30 minutes
Servings: 10
Ingredients:
- 3/4 lb. crabmeat
- 8 eggs
- 10 oz. spinach, frozen and thawed, squeeze dry
- 2 stalks celery, diced
- 2 cup half-n-half
- 1 cup Swiss cheese
- 1/2 cup onion, diced
- 1/2 cup red pepper, diced
- 1/4 cup mushrooms, diced
- 2 tbsp. margarine
- 1 cup bread crumbs
- 1/2 tsp. salt
- 1/4 tsp. pepper
- 1/4 tsp. nutmeg
- Nonstick cooking spray

Directions:
1. Heat oven to 375°F. Spray a large casserole or baking dish with cooking spray.
2. In a large bowl, beat eggs and half-n-half. Stir in crab, spinach, bread crumbs, cheese, and seasonings.
3. Melt butter in a large skillet over medium heat. Add celery, onion, red pepper, and mushrooms. Cook, stirring occasionally, until vegetables are tender, about 5 minutes. Add to egg mixture.
4. Pour mixture into prepared baking dish and bake 30–35 minutes, or until eggs are set and the top is light brown. Cool 10 minutes before serving.

Nutrition:
- Calories: 261 Total Carbs: 18 g.
- Net Carbs: 16 g. Protein: 14 g.
- Fat: 15 g.
- Sugar: 4 g.
- Fiber: 2 g.

Walnut and Oat Granola

Preparation time: 10 minutes
Cooking time: 30 minutes
Servings: 16
Ingredients:
- 4 cups oats, rolled
- 1 cup walnut pieces
- 1/2 cup pepitas

- 1/4 tsp. salt
- 1 tsp. cinnamon, ground
- 1 tsp. ginger, ground
- 1/2 cup coconut oil, melted
- 1/2 cup applesauce, unsweetened
- 1 tsp. vanilla extract
- 1/2 cup cherries, dried

Directions:

1. Preheat the oven to 350°F (180°C). Line a baking sheet with parchment paper.
2. In a large bowl, toss the oats, walnuts, pepitas, salt, cinnamon, and ginger.
3. In a large measuring cup, combine the coconut oil, applesauce, and vanilla. Pour over the dry mixture and mix well.
4. Transfer the mixture to the prepared baking sheet. Cook for 30 minutes, stirring about halfway through. Remove from the oven and let the granola sit undisturbed until completely cool. Break the granola into pieces, and stir in the dried cherries.
5. Transfer to an airtight container, and store at room temperature for up to 2 weeks.

Nutrition:

- Calories: 225 Fat: 14.9 g. Protein: 4.9 g.
- Carbs: 20.1 g. Fiber: 3.1 g.
- Sugar: 4.9 g. Sodium: 31 mg.

Crispy Pita with Canadian Bacon

Preparation time: 5 minutes
Cooking time: 15 minutes
Servings: 2
Ingredients:

- 1 (6-inch) whole-grain pita bread

- 3 tsp. extra virgin olive oil, divided
- 2 eggs
- 2 Canadian bacon slices
- 1/2 lemon juice
- 1 cup microgreens
- 2 tbsp. goat cheese, crumbled
- Freshly ground black pepper, to taste

Directions:

1. Heat a large skillet over medium heat. Cut the pita bread in half and brush each side of both halves with 1/4 tsp. of olive oil (using a total of 1 tsp. oil). Cook for 2–3 minutes on each side, then remove from the skillet.
2. In the same skillet, heat 1 tsp. of oil over medium heat. Crack the eggs into the skillet and cook until the eggs are set, 2–3 minutes. Remove from the skillet.
3. In the same skillet, cook the Canadian bacon for 3–5 minutes, flipping once.
4. In a large bowl, whisk together the remaining 1 tsp. of oil and lemon juice. Add the microgreens and toss to combine.
5. Top each pita half with half of the microgreens, 1 piece of bacon, 1 egg, and 1 tbsp. of goat cheese. Season with pepper and serve.

Nutrition:

- Calories: 251 Fat: 13.9 g.
- Protein: 13.1 g. Carbs: 20.1 g.
- Fiber: 3.1 g. Sugar: 0.9 g.
- Sodium: 400 mg.

Coconut and Chia Pudding

Preparation time: 5 minutes
Cooking time: 0 minutes
Servings: 2
Ingredients:

- 7 oz. (198 g.) light coconut milk
- 1/4 cup chia seeds
- 3–4 drops liquid Stevia
- 1 clementine
- 1 kiwi
- Coconut, shredded and unsweetened

Directions:

1. Start by taking a mixing bowl and adding in the light coconut milk. Add in the liquid stevia to sweeten the milk. Mix well.
2. Add the chia seeds to the milk and whisk until well-combined. Set aside.
3. Peel the clementine and carefully remove the skin from the wedges. Set aside.
4. Also, peel the kiwi and dice it into small pieces.
5. Take a glass jar and assemble the pudding. For this, place the fruits at the bottom of the jar; then add a dollop of chia pudding. Now spread the fruits and then add another layer of chia pudding.
6. Finish by garnishing with the remaining fruits and shredded coconut.

Nutrition:

- Calories: 486 Fat: 40.5 g.
- Protein: 8.5 g.
- Carbs: 30.8 g
- Fiber: 15.6 g.
- Sugar: 11.6 g.
- Sodium: 24 mg.

Blueberry Muffins

Preparation time: 10 minutes
Cooking time: 25 minutes
Servings: 18 muffins
Ingredients:

- 2 cups whole-wheat pastry flour
- 1 cup almond flour
- 1/2 cup sweetener, granulated
- 1 tbsp. baking powder
- 2 tsp. freshly grated lemon zest
- 3/4 tsp. baking soda
- 3/4 tsp. ground nutmeg
- Pinch sea salt
- 2 eggs
- 1 cup skim milk, at room temperature
- 3/4 cup 2 percent plain Greek yogurt
- 1/2 cup melted coconut oil
- 1 tbsp. freshly squeezed lemon juice
- 1 tsp. pure vanilla extract
- 1 cup fresh blueberries

Directions:

1. Preheat the oven to 350ºF (180ºC).
2. Line 18 muffin cups with paper liners and set the tray aside.
3. In a large bowl, stir together the flour, almond flour, sweetener, baking powder, lemon zest, baking soda, nutmeg, and salt.
4. In a small bowl, whisk together the eggs, milk, yogurt, coconut oil, lemon juice, and vanilla.
5. Add the wet ingredients to the dry ingredients and stir until just combined.
6. Fold in the blueberries without crushing them.
7. Spoon the batter evenly into the muffin cups. Bake the muffins until a toothpick inserted in the middle comes out clean, about 25 minutes.
8. Cool the muffins completely and serve.
9. Store leftover muffins in a sealed container in the refrigerator for up to 3 days or in the freezer for up to 1 month.

Nutrition:

- Calories: 166
- Fat: 9.1 g.
- Protein: 3.9 g.
- Carbs: 18.1 g.
- Fiber: 2.1 g.
- Sugar: 6.9 g.
- Sodium: 75 mg.

Apple and Bran Muffins

Preparation time: 10 minutes
Cooking time: 20 minutes
Servings: 18 muffins
Ingredients:

- 2 cups whole-wheat flour
- 1 cup wheat bran
- 1/3 cup granulated sweetener
- 1 tbsp. baking powder
- 2 tsp. ground cinnamon
- 1/2 tsp. ground ginger
- 1/4 tsp. ground nutmeg
- Pinch sea salt
- 2 eggs
- 1 1/2 cups skim milk, at room temperature
- 1/2 cup melted coconut oil
- 2 tsp. pure vanilla extract
- 2 apples, peeled, cored, and diced

Directions:

1. Preheat the oven to 350°F (180°C).
2. Line 18 muffin cups with paper liners and set the tray aside.
3. In a large bowl, stir together the flour, bran, sweetener, baking powder, cinnamon, ginger, nutmeg, and salt.
4. In a small bowl, whisk the eggs, milk, coconut oil, and vanilla until blended.
5. Add the wet ingredients to the dry ingredients, stirring until just blended.
6. Stir in the apples and spoon equal amounts of batter into each muffin cup.
7. Bake the muffins until a toothpick inserted in the center of a muffin comes out clean, about 20 minutes.
8. Cool the muffins completely and serve.
9. Store leftover muffins in a sealed container in the refrigerator for up to 3 days or in the freezer for up to 1 month.

Nutrition:

- Calories: 142
- Fat: 7.1 g.
- Protein: 4.1 g.
- Carbs: 19.1 g.
- Fiber: 3.1 g.
- Sugar: 6.1 g.
- Sodium: 21 mg.

Coconut and Berry Oatmeal

Preparation time: 10 minutes
Cooking time: 35 minutes
Servings: 6
Ingredients:

- 2 cups rolled oats
- 1/4 cup coconut, shredded and unsweetened
- 1 tsp. baking powder
- 1/2 tsp. ground cinnamon
- 1/4 tsp. sea salt
- 2 cups skim milk
- 1/4 cup melted coconut oil, plus extra for greasing the baking dish
- 1 egg

- 1 tsp. pure vanilla extract
- 2 cups fresh blueberries

For the garnish:
- 1/8 cup pecans, chopped
- 1 tsp. fresh mint leaves, chopped

Directions:
1. Preheat the oven to 350°F (180°C).
2. Lightly oil a baking dish and set it aside.
3. In a medium bowl, stir together the oats, coconut, baking powder, cinnamon, and salt.
4. In a small bowl, whisk together the milk, oil, egg, and vanilla until well blended.
5. Layer half the dry ingredients in the baking dish, top with half the berries, and then spoon the remaining half of the dry ingredients and the rest of the berries on top.
6. Pour the wet ingredients evenly into the baking dish. Tap it lightly on the counter to disperse the wet ingredients throughout.
7. Bake the casserole, uncovered, until the oats are tender, about 35 minutes.
8. Serve immediately, topped with pecans and mint.

Nutrition:
- Calories: 296
- Fat: 17.1 g.
- Protein: 10.2 g.
- Carbs: 26.9 g.
- Fiber: 4.1 g.
- Sugar: 10.9 g.
- Sodium: 154 mg.

Spanakopita Frittata
Preparation time: 10 minutes
Cooking time: 15 minutes
Servings: 4
Ingredients:
- 2 tbsp. extra virgin olive oil
- 1/2 sweet onion, chopped
- 1 red bell pepper, seeded and chopped
- 1/2 tsp. garlic, minced
- 1/4 tsp. sea salt

- 1/2 tsp. freshly ground black pepper
- 8 egg whites
- 2 cups spinach, shredded
- 1/2 cup low-sodium feta cheese, crumbled
- 1 tsp. chopped fresh parsley, for garnish

Directions:
1. Preheat the oven to 375°F (190°C).
2. Place a heavy ovenproof skillet over medium-high heat and add the olive oil.
3. Sauté the onion, bell pepper, and garlic until softened, about 5 minutes. Season with salt and pepper.
4. Whisk together the egg whites in a medium bowl, then pour them into the skillet and lightly shake the pan to disburse.
5. Cook the vegetables and eggs for 3 minutes, without stirring.
6. Scatter the spinach over the eggs and sprinkle the feta cheese evenly over the spinach.
7. Put the skillet in the oven and bake, uncovered, until cooked through and firm, about 10 minutes.
8. Loosen the edges of the frittata with a rubber spatula, and then invert it onto a plate.
9. Garnish with the chopped parsley and serve.

Nutrition:
- Calories: 146
- Fat: 10.1 g.
- Protein: 10.1 g.
- Carbs: 3.9 g.
- Fiber: 1 g.
- Sugar: 2.9 g.
- Sodium: 292 mg.

Ratatouille Egg Bake
Preparation time: 20 minutes
Cooking time: 50 minutes
Servings: 4
Ingredients:
- 2 tsp. extra virgin olive oil

- 1/2 sweet onion, finely chopped
- 2 tsp. minced garlic
- 1/2 small eggplant, peeled and diced
- 1 green zucchini, diced
- 1 yellow zucchini, diced
- 1 red bell pepper, seeded and diced
- 3 tomatoes, seeded and chopped
- 1 tbsp. chopped fresh oregano
- 1 tbsp. chopped fresh basil
- Pinch red pepper flakes
- Sea salt and freshly ground black pepper, to taste
- 4 large eggs

Directions:
1. Preheat the oven to 350°F (180°C).
2. Place a large ovenproof skillet over medium heat and add the olive oil.
3. Sauté the onion and garlic until softened and translucent, about 3 minutes. Stir in the eggplant and sauté for about 10 minutes, stirring occasionally. Stir in the zucchini and pepper and sauté for 5 minutes.
4. Reduce the heat to low and cover. Cook until the vegetables are soft, about 15 minutes.
5. Stir in the tomatoes, oregano, basil, and red pepper flakes, and cook 10 minutes more. Season the ratatouille with salt and pepper.
6. Use a spoon to create 4 wells in the mixture. Crack an egg into each well.
7. Place the skillet in the oven and bake until the eggs are firm about 5 minutes.
8. Remove from the oven. Serve the eggs with a generous scoop of vegetables.

Nutrition:
- Calories: 148
- Fat: 7.9 g.
- Protein: 9.1 g.
- Carbs: 13.1 g.
- Fiber: 4.1 g.
- Sugar: 7.1 g.
- Sodium: 99 mg.

Cottage Pancakes

Preparation time: 10 minutes
Cooking time: 20 minutes
Servings: 4
Ingredients:
- 2 cups low-fat cottage cheese
- 4 egg whites
- 2 eggs
- 1 tbsp. pure vanilla extract
- 1 1/2 cups almond flour
- Nonstick cooking spray

Directions:
1. Place the cottage cheese, egg whites, eggs, and vanilla in a blender and pulse to combine.
2. Add the almond flour to the blender and blend until smooth.
3. Place a large nonstick skillet over medium heat and lightly coat it with cooking spray.
4. Spoon 1/4 cup of batter per pancake, 4 at a time, into the skillet. Cook the pancakes until the bottoms are firm and golden, about 4 minutes.
5. Flip the pancakes over and cook the other side until they are cooked through about 3 minutes.
6. Remove the pancakes to a plate and repeat with the remaining batter.
7. Serve with fresh fruit.

Nutrition:
- Calories: 345 Fat: 22.1 g.
- Protein: 29.1 g. Carbs: 11.1 g.
- Fiber: 4.1 g. Sugar: 5.1 g.
- Sodium: 560 mg.

Greek Yogurt and Oat Pancakes

Preparation time: 5 minutes
Cooking time: 20 minutes
Servings: 4
Ingredients:

- 1 cup 2% plain Greek yogurt
- 3 eggs
- 1 1/2 tsp. pure vanilla extract
- 1 cup oats, rolled
- 1 tbsp. sweetener, granulated
- 1 tsp. baking powder
- 1 tsp. cinnamon, ground
- Pinch cloves, ground
- Nonstick cooking spray

Directions:

1. Place the yogurt, eggs, and vanilla in a blender and pulse to combine.
2. Add the oats, sweetener, baking powder, cinnamon, and cloves to the blender and blend until the batter is smooth.
3. Place a large nonstick skillet over medium heat and lightly coat it with cooking spray.
4. Spoon 1/4 cup of batter per pancake, 4 at a time, into the skillet. Cook the pancakes until the bottoms are firm and golden, about 4 minutes.
5. Flip the pancakes over and cook the other side until they are cooked through about 3 minutes.
6. Remove the pancakes to a plate and repeat with the remaining batter.
7. Serve with fresh fruit.

Nutrition:

- Calories: 244
- Fat: 8.1 g.
- Protein: 13.1 g.
- Carbs: 28.1 g.
- Fiber: 4 g.
- Sugar: 3 g.
- Sodium: 82 mg.

Apple and Pumpkin Waffles

Preparation time: 10 minutes
Cooking time: 20 minutes
Servings: 6
Ingredients:

- 2 1/4 cups whole-wheat pastry flour
- 2 tbsp. sweetener, granulated
- 1 tbsp. baking powder
- 1 tsp. cinnamon, ground
- 1 tsp. nutmeg, ground
- 4 eggs
- 11/4 cups pure pumpkin purée
- 1 apple, peeled, cored, and finely chopped
- 3 tbsp. Melted coconut oil, for cooking

Directions:

1. In a large bowl, stir together the flour, sweetener, baking powder, cinnamon, and nutmeg.
2. In a small bowl, whisk together the eggs and pumpkin.
3. Add the wet ingredients to the dry and whisk until smooth.
4. Stir the apple into the batter.
5. Cook the waffles according to the waffle maker manufacturer's directions, brushing your waffle iron with melted coconut oil, until all the batter is gone.
6. Serve immediately.

Nutrition:

- Calories: 232
- Fat: 4.1 g.
- Protein: 10.9 g.
- Carbs: 40.1 g.
- Fiber: 7.1 g.
- Sugar: 5.1 g.
- Sodium: 52 mg.

Buckwheat Crêpes

Preparation time: 20 minutes
Cooking time: 20 minutes
Servings: 5
Ingredients:

- 1 1/2 cups skim milk
- 3 eggs
- 1 tsp. extra virgin olive oil, plus more for the skillet
- 1 cup buckwheat flour
- 1/2 cup whole-wheat flour
- 1/2 cup 2% plain Greek yogurt
- 1 cup strawberries, sliced
- 1 cup blueberries

Directions:

1. In a large bowl, whisk together the milk, eggs, and 1 tsp. of oil until well combined.
2. Into a medium bowl, sift together the buckwheat and whole-wheat flours. Add the dry ingredients to the wet ingredients and whisk until well combined and very smooth.
3. Allow the batter to rest for at least 2 hours before cooking.
4. Place a large skillet or crêpe pan over medium-high heat and lightly coat the bottom with oil.
5. Pour about 1/4 cup of batter into the skillet. Swirl the pan until the batter completely coats the bottom.
6. Cook the crêpe for about 1 minute, and then flip it over. Cook the other side of the crêpe for another minute, until lightly browned. Transfer the cooked crêpe to a plate and cover with a clean dish towel to keep warm.
7. Repeat until the batter is used up; you should have about 10 crêpes.
8. Spoon 1 tbsp. of yogurt onto each crêpe and place 2 crêpes on each plate.
9. Top with berries and serve.

Nutrition:

- Calories: 330
- Fat: 6.9 g.
- Protein: 15.9 g.
- Carbs: 54.1 g.
- Fiber: 7.9 g.
- Sugar: 11.1 g.
- Sodium: 100 mg.

Mushroom Frittata

Preparation time: 10 minutes
Cooking time: 15 minutes
Servings: 4
Ingredients:

- 8 large eggs
- 1/2 cup skim milk
- 1/4 tsp. nutmeg, ground
- Sea salt and freshly ground black pepper, to taste
- 2 tsp. extra virgin olive oil
- 2 cups wild mushrooms, sliced (cremini, oyster, shiitake, Portobello, etc.)
- 1/2 red onion, chopped
- 1 tsp. garlic, minced
- 1/2 cup goat cheese, crumbled

Directions:

1. Preheat the broiler.
2. In a medium bowl, whisk together the eggs, milk, and nutmeg until well combined. Season the egg mixture lightly with salt and pepper and set it aside.
3. Place an ovenproof skillet over medium heat and add the oil, coating the bottom completely by tilting the pan.
4. Sauté the mushrooms, onion, and garlic until translucent, about 7 minutes.
5. Pour the egg mixture into the skillet and cook until the bottom of the frittata is set, lifting the edges of the cooked egg to allow the uncooked egg to seep under.
6. Place the skillet under the broiler until the top is set, about 1 minute.
7. Sprinkle the goat cheese on the frittata and broil until the cheese is melted, about 1 minute more.
8. Remove from the oven. Cut into 4 wedges to serve.

Nutrition:

- Calories: 227 Fat: 15.1 g.
- Protein: 17.1 g. Carbs: 5.1 g.
- Fiber: 0.9 g.
- Sugar: 4.1 g.
- Sodium: 224 mg.

Tropical Yogurt Kiwi Bowl

Preparation time: 5 minutes
Cooking time: 0 minutes
Servings: 2
Ingredients:

- 1 1/2 cups plain low-fat Greek yogurt
- 2 kiwis, peeled and sliced
- 2 tbsp. coconut flakes, shredded and unsweetened
- 2 tbsp. walnuts, halved
- 1 tbsp. chia seeds
- 2 tsp. honey, divided (optional)

Directions:

1. Divide the yogurt between 2 small bowls.
2. Top each serving of yogurt with half of the kiwi slices, coconut flakes, walnuts, chia seeds, and honey (if using).

Nutrition:

- Calories: 261
- Fat: 9.1 g.
- Protein: 21.1 g.
- Carbs: 23.1 g.
- Fiber: 6.1 g.
- Sugar: 14.1 g.
- Sodium: 84 mg.

Banana Crêpe Cakes

Preparation time: 5 minutes
Cooking time: 20 minutes
Servings: 4
Ingredients:

- Avocado oil cooking spray
- 4 oz. (113 g.) reduced-fat plain cream cheese, softened
- 2 medium bananas
- 4 large eggs
- 1/2 tsp. vanilla extract
- 1/8 tsp. salt

Directions:

1. Heat a large skillet over low heat. Coat the cooking surface with cooking spray, and allow the pan to heat for another 2–3 minutes.
2. Meanwhile, in a medium bowl, mash the cream cheese and bananas together with a fork until combined. The bananas can be a little chunky.
3. Add the eggs, vanilla, and salt, and mix well.
4. For each cake, drop 2 tbsp. of the batter onto the warmed skillet and use the bottom of a large spoon or ladle to

spread it thin. Let it cook for 7–9 minutes.

5. Flip the cake over and cook briefly for about 1 minute.

Nutrition:
- Calories: 176
- Fat: 9.1 g.
- Protein: 9.1 g.
- Carbs: 15.1 g.
- Fiber: 2.1 g.
- Sugar: 8.1 g.
- Sodium: 214 mg.

Tacos with Pico de Gallo

Preparation time: 5 minutes
Cooking time: 10 minutes
Servings: 4
Ingredients:
For the taco filling:
- Avocado oil cooking spray
- 1 medium green bell pepper, chopped
- 8 large eggs
- 1/4 cup sharp cheddar cheese, shredded
- 4 (6-inch) whole-wheat tortillas
- 1 cup fresh spinach leaves
- 1/2 cup *Pico de Gallo*
- Scallions, chopped, for garnish (optional)
- Avocado slices, for garnish (optional)

For the Pico de Gallo:
- 1 tomato, diced
- 1/2 large white onion, diced
- 2 tbsp. fresh cilantro, chopped
- 1/2 jalapeño pepper, stemmed, seeded, and diced
- 1 tbsp. lime juice, freshly squeezed
- 1/8 tsp. salt

Directions:
To Make the Taco Filling
1. Heat a medium skillet over medium-low heat. When hot, coat the cooking surface with cooking spray and put the pepper in the skillet. Cook for 4 minutes.
2. Meanwhile, whisk the eggs in a medium bowl, then add the cheese and whisk to combine. Pour the eggs and cheese into the skillet with the green peppers and scramble until the eggs are fully cooked for about 5 minutes.
3. Microwave the tortillas very briefly, about 8 seconds.
4. For each serving, top a tortilla with 1/4 of the spinach, eggs, and Pico de Gallo. Garnish with scallions and avocado slices (if using).

To Make the Pico de Gallo
1. In a medium bowl, combine the tomato, onion, cilantro, pepper, lime juice, and salt. Mix well and serve.

Nutrition:
- Calories: 277
- Fat: 12.1 g.
- Protein: 16.1 g.
- Carbs: 28.1 g.
- Fiber: 2.9 g.
- Sugar: 8.1 g.
- Sodium: 563 mg.

Portobello and Chicken Sausage Frittata

Preparation time: 10 minutes
Cooking time: 15 minutes
Servings: 4
Ingredients:
- Avocado oil cooking spray

- 1 cup Portobello mushrooms, roughly chopped
- 1 medium green bell pepper, diced
- 1 medium red bell pepper, diced
- 8 large eggs
- 3/4 cup half-and-half
- 1/4 cup almond milk, unsweetened
- 6 links maple-flavored chicken or turkey breakfast sausage, cut into 1/4-inch pieces

Directions:
1. Preheat the oven to 375°F (190°C).
2. Heat a large, oven-safe skillet over medium-low heat. When hot, coat the cooking surface with cooking spray.
3. Heat the mushrooms, green bell pepper, and red bell pepper in the skillet. Cook for 5 minutes.
4. Meanwhile, in a medium bowl, whisk the eggs, half-and-half, and almond milk.
5. Add the sausage to the skillet and cook for 2 minutes.
6. Pour the egg mixture into the skillet, then transfer the skillet from the stove to the oven, and bake for 15 minutes, or until the middle is firm and spongy.

Nutrition:
- Calories: 281
- Fat: 17.1 g.
- Protein: 20.9 g.
- Carbs: 10.1 g.
- Fiber: 2.1 g.
- Sugar: 7.1 g.
- Sodium: 445 mg.

Egg Salad Sandwiches

Preparation time: 10 minutes
Cooking time: 0 minutes
Servings: 4
Ingredients:
- 8 large hardboiled eggs
- 3 tbsp. plain low-fat Greek yogurt
- 1 tbsp. mustard
- 1/2 tsp. freshly ground black pepper

- 1 tsp. fresh chives, chopped
- 4 slices 100% whole-wheat bread
- 2 cups fresh spinach, loosely packed

Directions:
1. Peel the eggs and cut them in half.
2. In a large bowl, mash the eggs with a fork, leaving chunks.
3. Add the yogurt, mustard, pepper, and chives, and mix.
4. For each portion, layer 1 slice of bread with 1/4 of the egg salad and spinach.

Nutrition:
- Calories: 278
- Fat: 12.1 g.
- Protein: 20.1 g.
- Carbs: 23.1 g.
- Fiber: 2.9 g.
- Sugar: 3.1 g.
- Sodium: 365 mg.

Shrimp with Scallion Grits

Preparation time: 15 minutes
Cooking time: 20 minutes
Servings: 6–8
Ingredients:
- 1 1/2 cups fat-free milk
- 1 1/2 cups water
- 2 bay leaves
- 1 cup stone-ground corn grits
- 1/4 cup seafood broth
- 2 garlic cloves, minced
- 2 scallions, white and green parts, thinly sliced
- 1 lb. (454 g.) medium shrimp, shelled and deveined
- 1/2 tsp. dill, dried
- 1/2 tsp. smoked paprika
- 1/4 tsp. celery seeds

Directions:
1. In a medium stockpot, combine the milk, water, and bay leaves and bring to a boil over high heat.
2. Gradually add the grits, stirring continuously.

3. Reduce the heat to low, cover, and cook for 5–7 minutes, stirring often, or until the grits are soft and tender. Remove from the heat and discard the bay leaves.
4. In a small cast-iron skillet, bring the broth to a simmer over medium heat.
5. Add the garlic and scallions, and sauté for 3–5 minutes, or until softened.
6. Add the shrimp, dill, paprika, and celery seeds and cook for about 7 minutes, or until the shrimp is light pink but not overcooked.
7. Plate each dish with 1/4 cup of grits, topped with shrimp.

Nutrition:
- Calories: 198
- Fat: 1 g.
- Protein: 20.1 g.
- Carbs: 24.9 g.
- Fiber: 1 g.
- Sugar: 3.1 g.
- Sodium: 204 mg.

Breakfast Cheddar Zucchini Casserole
Preparation time: 10 minutes
Cooking time: 35 minutes
Servings: 12–15
Ingredients:
- Nonstick cooking spray
- 6 medium brown eggs
- 8 medium egg whites
- 1 green bell pepper, chopped
- 1/2 small yellow onion, chopped
- 1 zucchini, finely grated, with water pressed out
- 1 cup shredded reduced-fat cheddar cheese
- 1 tsp. paprika
- 1/2 tsp. garlic powder

Directions:
1. Preheat the oven to 350°F (180°C). Spray a large cast-iron skillet with cooking spray.

2. In a medium bowl, whisk the eggs and egg whites together.
3. Add the bell pepper, onion, zucchini, cheese, paprika, and garlic powder, mix well, and pour into the prepared skillet.
4. Transfer the skillet to the oven, and bake for 35 minutes. Remove from the oven, and let rest for 5 minutes before serving with Broccoli Stalk Slaw.

Nutrition:
- Calories: 79 Fat: 4.1 g.
- Protein: 8.1 g. Carbs: 2.1 g.
- Fiber: 1.1 g. Sugar: 1.2 g.
- Sodium: 133 mg.

Bulgur Porridge
Preparation time: 10 Minutes
Cooking time: 30 minutes
Servings: 2
Ingredients:
- 2/3 cup soy milk, unsweetened
- 1/3 cup bulgur, rinsed
- A pinch of salt
- 1 ripe banana, peeled and mashed
- 2 kiwis, peeled and sliced

Directions:
1. In a pan, add the soy milk, bulgur, and salt over medium-high heat and bring to a boil.
2. Adjust the heat to low and simmer for about 10 minutes.
3. Remove the pan of bulgur from heat and immediately, stir in the mashed banana.
4. Serve warm with the topping of kiwi slices.

Nutrition:
- Calories: 223 Total Fat: 2.3 g.
- Saturated Fat: 0.3 g.
- Cholesterol: 0 mg.
- Sodium: 126 mg.
- Total Carbs: 47.5 g.
- Fiber: 8.6 g.Sugar: 17.4 g.
- Protein: 7.1 g.

Turkey-Broccoli Brunch Casserole

Preparation time: 10 Minutes
Cooking time: 30 minutes
Servings: 6
Ingredients:

- 2 1/2 cups turkey breast, cubed and cooked
- 16 oz. broccoli, chopped and drained
- 1 1/2 cups of milk, fat-free
- 1 cup cheddar cheese, low-fat, shredded
- 10 oz. cream chicken soup, low-sodium and low-fat
- 8 oz. egg substitute
- 1/4 tsp. poultry seasoning
- 1/4 cup sour cream, low-fat
- 1/2 tsp. pepper
- 1/8 tsp. salt
- 2 cups seasoned stuffing cubes
- Cooking spray

Directions:

1. Bring together the egg substitute, soup, milk, pepper, sour cream, salt, and poultry seasoning in a big bowl.
2. Now stir in the broccoli, turkey, 3/4 cup of cheese, and stuffing cubes.
3. Transfer to a baking dish. Apply cooking spray.
4. Bake for 10 minutes. Sprinkle the remaining cheese.
5. Bake for another 5 minutes.
6. Keep it aside for 5 minutes. Serve.

Nutrition:

- Calories: 303
- Carbohydrates: 26 g.
- Fiber: 3 g.
- Sugar: 0.8 g.
- Cholesterol: 72 mg.
- Total Fat: 7 g.
- Protein: 33 g.

Cheesy Low-Carb Omelet

Preparation time: 10 Minutes
Cooking time: 30 minutes
Servings: 5
Ingredients:

- 2 whole eggs
- 1 tbsp. water
- 1 tbsp. butter
- 3 thin slices salami
- 5 fresh basil leaves
- 5 thin slices fresh ripe tomatoes
- 2 oz. fresh mozzarella cheese
- Salt and pepper as needed

Directions:

1. Take a small bowl and whisk in eggs and water
2. Take a nonstick Sauté pan and place it over medium heat, add butter and let it melt
3. Pour egg mixture and cook for 30 seconds
4. Spread salami slices on half of egg mix and top with cheese, tomatoes, basil slices
5. Season with salt and pepper according to your taste
6. Cook for 2 minutes and fold the egg with the empty half
7. Cover and cook on low for 1 minute
8. Serve and enjoy!

Nutrition:

- Calories: 451
- Fat: 36 g.
- Carbohydrates: 3 g.
- Protein: 33 g.

Apple and Cinnamon Pancake

Preparation time: 10 minutes
Cooking time: 30 minutes
Servings: 4
Ingredients:

- 1/4 tsp. cinnamon, ground
- 1 3/4 cups better baking mix
- 1 tbsp. oil
- 1 cup water
- 2 egg whites
- 1/2 cup sugar-free applesauce
- Cooking spray
- 1 cup plain yogurt
- Sugar substitute

Directions:

1. Blend the cinnamon and the baking mix in a bowl.
2. Create a hole in the middle and add the oil, water, egg, and applesauce.
3. Mix well.
4. Spray your pan with oil.
5. Place it on medium heat.
6. Pour 1/4 cup of the batter.
7. Flip the pancake and cook until golden.
8. Serve with yogurt and sugar substitute.

Nutrition:

- Calories: 231 Total Fat: 6 g.
- Saturated Fat: 1 g.
- Cholesterol: 54 mg.
- Sodium: 545 mg.
- Total Carbs: 37 g.
- Dietary Fiber: 4 g.
- Total Sugars: 1 g.
- Protein: 8 g.
- Potassium: 750 mg.

Guacamole Turkey Burgers

Preparation time: 10 minutes
Cooking time: 30 minutes
Servings: 3
Ingredients:

- 12 oz. turkey, ground
- 1 1/2 avocados
- 2 tsp. juice from a lime
- 1/2 tsp. cumin
- 1 red chili, chopped
- 1/2 tsp. garlic powder
- 1/2 tsp. onion powder
- 3 tsp. olive oil
- 1/2 tsp. salt

Directions:

1. Mix the turkey with cumin, chili, salt, garlic powder, and onion powder in a medium-sized bowl.
2. Create 3 patties
3. Pour 3 tsp. olive oil in a skillet and heat over medium heat.
4. Now cook your patties. Make sure that both sides are brown.
5. Make the guacamole in the meantime.
6. Mash together some garlic powder, juice from the lime, and avocados in a bowl.
7. Add salt for seasoning.
8. Serve the burgers with guacamole on the patties.

Nutrition:

- Calories: 316
- Carbohydrates: 9 g.
- Fiber: 8 g.
- Sugar: 0 g.
- Cholesterol: 80 mg.
- Total Fat: 21 g.
- Protein: 24 g.

Ham and Goat Cheese Omelet

Preparation time: 10 minutes
Cooking time: 30 minutes
Servings: 1
Ingredients:

- 1 slice ham, chopped

- 4 egg whites
- 2 tsp. water
- 2 tbsp. onion, chopped
- 1 tbsp. parsley, minced
- 2 tbsp. green pepper, chopped
- 1/8 tsp. pepper
- 2 tbsp. goat cheese, crumbled
- Cooking spray

Directions:
1. Whisk together the water, pepper, and egg whites in a bowl till everything blends well.
2. Stir in the green pepper, ham, and onion.
3. Now heat your skillet over medium heat after applying the cooking spray.
4. Pour in the egg white mix towards the edge.
5. As it sets, push the cooked parts to the center. Allow the uncooked portions to flow underneath.
6. Sprinkle the goat cheese to one side when there is no liquid egg.
7. Now fold your omelet in half.
8. Sprinkle the parsley.

Nutrition:
- Calories: 143
- Carbohydrates: 5 g.
- Fiber: 1 g.
- Sugar: 0.3 g.
- Cholesterol: 27 mg.
- Total Fat: 4 g.
- Protein: 21 g.

Cloud Bread

Preparation time: 10 minutes
Cooking time: 15 minutes
Servings: 10
Ingredients:
- 4 eggs, large, separated
- 1/2 tsp. garlic powder
- 1/2 tsp. cream of Tartar
- 1/2 tsp. sea salt
- 2 oz. cream cheese, low-fat
- 1 tsp. Italian seasoning

Directions:
1. Preheat the oven to 300°F.
2. Next, keep the egg whites in a large mixing bowl, and to this, spoon in the cream of tartar.
3. Whip it on high power until it turns to soft meringue peaks. Transfer to another bowl.
4. Place the cream of cheese into the large bowl and whip on high power to soften.
5. Stir in the egg one by one into the mixture and whisk it well each time before adding each egg. Repeat the procedure until the whole mixture becomes smooth.
6. Spoon in the Italian seasoning, salt, and garlic powder.
7. Gently fold the egg white into the mixture while maintaining the foamy texture.
8. Take 1/4 cup portion of the mixture to the greased baking sheet and spread to 4-inch circles. Leave ample space between each.
9. Finally, bake them for 15–20 minutes or until they golden on the outside and firm inside.
10. Cool for several minutes and then serve.

Tip: You can reduce the amount of garlic powder if desired.

Nutrition:
- Calories: 36
- Carbs: 1 g.
- Proteins: 2 g.
- Fat: 2 g.
- Sodium: 167 mg.

Cream Cheese Pancakes

Preparation time: 5 minutes
Cooking time: 10 minutes
Servings: 1
Ingredients:
- 1/2 tsp. cinnamon
- 2 oz. cream cheese
- 1 tsp. low-carb sweetener, granulated
- 2 eggs, large

Directions:

1. Place eggs, cream cheese, sweetener, and cinnamon in a high-speed blender and blend until combined well. Set it aside for 2 minutes.
2. Heat a large-sized skillet over medium heat.
3. When the skillet becomes hot, spoon 1/4 of the batter to it and spread it to a circle.
4. Cook for 2–3 minutes on each side or until cooked. Flip it. Cook the other side for 1 minute.
5. Repeat with the remaining batter and serve.

Tip: Serve it along with sugar-free syrup or berries.

Nutrition:

- Calories: 344 Kcal
- Carbs: 3 g.
- Protein: 17 g.
- Fat: 29 g.
- Sodium: 10 mg.

Bagels

Preparation time: 15 minutes
Cooking time: 15 minutes
Servings: 6
Ingredients:

- 1 tbsp. baking powder
- 1 1/2 cup almond flour, blanched
- 2 eggs, large, beaten
- 2 1/2 cup Mozzarella cheese, shredded
- 2 oz. cream cheese, cubed

Directions:

1. Preheat the oven to 400°F.
2. Combine almond flour and baking powder in a mixing bowl. Set aside.
3. Mix the mozzarella cheese and cream cheese in a large microwave-safe bowl and heat it for 2 minutes on high power. Stir halfway through and at the end.
4. Add the flour mixture and eggs to the cheese mixture and make dough out of it by kneading it quickly.
5. As the dough will be sticky, keep kneading it until it becomes smooth.
   Tip: If the dough seems too difficult to mix or is still sticky, you can microwave it again for another 15–20 seconds to make it soften.
6. Divide the dough into 6 portions and roll it into a long log.
7. Press the ends together of the long log to get the bagel shape. Arrange them on a parchment paper-lined baking sheet.
8. Finally, bake them for 12–14 minutes or until the bagels are firm and golden in color.

Tip: You can top it with sesame seeds if desired.

Nutrition:

- Calories: 360
- Carbs: 5 g.
- Protein: 21 g.
- Fat: 28 g.
- Sodium: 54 mg.

Granola Bars

Preparation time: 10 minutes
Cooking time: 15 minutes
Servings: 12
Ingredients:

- 1 cup pecans
- 1 cup almonds
- 1/3 cup sunflower seeds
- 1/2 cup golden flaxseed meal
- 1 cup hazelnuts
- 1/4 cup butter, melted
- 6 tbsp. erythritol
- 1 egg white, large
- 1/3 cup pumpkin seeds
- 1 tsp. vanilla extract

Directions:

1. Preheat the oven to 325°F.
2. Place hazelnuts and almonds in a food processor and process until the nuts get chopped.
3. Stir in the pecans and pulse again.
4. Add the pumpkin seeds, sunflower seeds, golden flaxseed, and erythritol to it. Pulse until everything mixes up. **Tip:** Don't over-process.
5. Pour the egg white into the processor. Mix the vanilla extract and butter in another bowl. Stir again.
6. Pulse a few times again and mix a little of the mixture from the bottom using a spatula. Pulse again until everything coats well. Everything should be a bit damp from the egg white mixture.
7. Transfer the mixture to a parchment paper-lined baking sheet and spread it across evenly.
8. Bake for 18 minutes or until browned slightly at the sides.
9. Cool completely before serving.

Tip: You can spoon a bit of salt if preferred.
Nutrition:

- Calories: 278 Carbs: 2 g.
- Protein: 7 g. Fat: 26 g. Sodium: 27 mg.

Pancakes

Preparation time: 5 minutes
Cooking time: 15 minutes
Servings: 6
Ingredients:

- 1/4 cup coconut flour
- 1 cup almond flour, blanched

- 8 tbsp. almond milk, unsweetened
- 2 tbsp. erythritol
- 1 1/2 tsp. vanilla extract
- 1 tsp. baking powder
- 6 eggs, large

Directions:

1. Place all the ingredients in a large mixing bowl until combined well.
2. Heat a medium-sized pan over medium-low heat.
3. Pat the pan with ghee and ladle a spoon of batter into the hot pan.
4. Form into circles and cover the pan.
5. Cook for a few minutes or until the bubbles start to appear.
6. Turn the pancake over and cook the other side or until slightly browned.
7. Serve and enjoy.

Tip: You can spoon a bit of salt if preferred.
Nutrition:

- Calories: 268
- Carbs: 3 g.
- Protein: 9 g.
- Fat: 23 g.
- Sodium: 15 mg.

Waffles

Preparation time: 10 minutes
Cooking time: 10 minutes
Servings: 2
Ingredients:

- 1/2 cup almond flour, blanched
- 1/4 cup almond milk, unsweetened
- 1 egg, large, separated
- 2 tbsp. butter

- 2 tbsp. erythritol
- 1/2 tsp. vanilla extract
- 1/2 tsp. baking powder
- 2 tbsp. nut butter of your choice
- 1/4 tsp. sea salt

Directions:

1. Preheat the waffle iron to high heat and grease it with oil.
2. Crack the egg into a bowl and whisk it until you get stiff peaks.
3. Mix almond flour, salt, erythritol, and baking powder in another bowl. Keep aside.
4. Melt butter and nut butter in a microwave-safe bowl.
5. Spoon this butter mixture into the flour mixture. Combine.
6. Once combined, stir in egg yolk, vanilla essence, and almond milk to it and give everything a good stir until you get a smooth mixture.
7. Fold the egg whites gently into the batter so that you get a fluffy and light mixture.
8. Pour half the batter into the waffle iron and close. Cook for 5 minutes or until the steam stops coming. Repeat with the remaining batter.
9. Serve and enjoy.

Tip: For a crisper waffle, you can toast it oven or toaster for a few minutes.

Nutrition:

- Calories: 401
- Carbs: 4 g.
- Protein: 13 g.
- Fat: 37 g.
- Sodium: 43 mg.

Gingerbread Oatmeal

Preparation time: 10 minutes
Cooking time: 15 minutes
Servings: 4
Ingredients:

- 1 cup oats, steel-cut
- 4 cups water
- 1/4 tsp. coriander, ground

- 11/2 tbsp. cinnamon, ground
- 1/4 tsp. ground cloves
- 1/4 tsp. ginger, fresh grated
- 1/4 tsp. allspice, ground
- 1/4 tsp. cardamom, ground
- A pinch of nutmeg, ground

Directions:

1. Heat a pan with the water over medium-high heat, add the oats, and stir. Add the coriander, cinnamon, cloves, ginger, allspice, cardamom, and nutmeg, stir, cook for 15 minutes, divide into bowls and serve.
2. Enjoy!

Nutrition:

- Calories: 188
- Fat: 3 g.
- Fiber: 6 g.
- Carbs: 13 g.
- Protein: 6 g.

Assorted Fresh Fruit Juice

Preparation time: 5 minutes
Cooking time: 0 minutes
Servings: 4
Ingredients:

- 1 cup ice shavings or crushed ice
- 1/4 cup frozen grapes, halved
- 1 apple, roughly chopped

Directions:

1. Add all ingredients into the blender.
2. Process until smooth.
3. Pour equal portions into glasses. Serve immediately.

Nutrition:

- Protein: 1.16 g. (2%)
- Potassium: (K) 367 mg. (8 %)
- Sodium: Na 3 mg. (0%)

Raspberry and Pineapple Smoothie (Dairy-Free)

Preparation time: 5 minutes
Cooking time: 0 minutes
Servings: 2
Ingredients:

- 1 can (8 oz.) pineapple tidbits, rinsed well, drained
- 1 small banana, overripe, roughly chopped
- 1/2 cup frozen raspberries
- 1/2 cup ice, crushed
- Stevia to taste
- 2 tbsp. cashew nuts

Directions:

1. Except for cashew nuts and stevia, combine the remaining ingredients in a deep microwave-safe bowl. Stir.
2. Microwave on the highest setting for 5–15 seconds. Keep a watchful eye on this. Stop the cooking process before milk bubbles out of the bowl.
3. Carefully remove the bowl from the microwave. Cool slightly for easier handling.
4. Stir in stevia if using. Sprinkle cashew nuts.

Nutrition:

- Protein: 3.1 g. (6%),
- Potassium: (K) 749 mg. (16 %)
- Sodium: (Na) 4 mg. (0%)

Mexican Frittata

Preparation time: 5 minutes
Cooking time: 30 minutes
Servings: 4
Ingredients:

- 1/2 cup almond milk
- 5 large eggs
- 1/4 cup onions, chopped
- 1/4 cup green bell pepper, chopped

Directions:

1. Preheat the oven to 400°F.
2. Using a large bowl, combine almond milk, eggs, onion, and green bell pepper. Whisk until all ingredients are well combined.
3. Transfer the mixture to a baking dish. Bake for 20 minutes. Serve.

Nutrition:

- Protein: 16.35 g. (30%)
- Potassium: (K) 243 mg. (5 %)
- Sodium: (Na) 216 mg. (14%)

Olive Oil and Sesame Asparagus

Preparation time: 5 minutes
Cooking time: 30 minutes
Servings: 4
Ingredients:

- 1/2 cup water
- 2 cups asparagus, sliced
- 1/2 tbsp. olive oil, add more for drizzling
- 1/8 tsp. red pepper flakes, crushed
- 1/2 tsp. sesame seeds

Directions:

1. In a large skillet, bring water to a boil.
2. Add in asparagus. Allow boiling for 2 minutes. Reduce the heat and cook for another 5 minutes. Drain asparagus and place it on a plate. Set aside.
3. Meanwhile, heat the olive oil. Tip in asparagus and red pepper flakes. Sauté for 3 minutes.

4. Remove from heat. Drizzle in more olive oil and sprinkle sesame seeds before serving.

Nutrition:

- Protein: 6.19 g. (11%)
- Potassium: (K) 547 mg. (12 %)
- Sodium: (Na) 9 mg. (1%)

CHAPTER 8:

Lunch Recipes

Spaghetti Squash and Chickpea Bolognese

Preparation time: 5 minutes
Cooking time: 25 minutes
Servings: 4
Ingredients:

- 1 (3–4 lb./1.4–1.8 kg.) spaghetti squash
- 1/2 tsp. cumin, ground
- 1 cup no-sugar-added spaghetti sauce
- 1 can (15 oz./425 g.) low-sodium chickpeas, drained and rinsed
- 6 oz. (170 g.) extra-firm tofu

Directions:

1. Preheat the oven to 400°F (205°C).
2. Cut the squash in half lengthwise. Scoop out the seeds and discard.
3. Season both halves of the squash with the cumin, and place them on a baking sheet cut-side down. Roast for 25 minutes.
4. Meanwhile, heat a medium saucepan over low heat, and pour in the spaghetti sauce and chickpeas.
5. Press the tofu between 2 layers of paper towels, and gently squeeze out any excess water.
6. Crumble the tofu into the sauce and cook for 15 minutes.

7. Remove the squash from the oven, and comb through the flesh of each half with a fork to make thin strands.
8. Divide the "spaghetti" into 4 portions, and top each portion with 1/4 of the sauce.

Nutrition:

- Calories: 276
- Fat: 7.1 g.
- Protein: 14.1 g.
- Carbs: 41.9 g.
- Fiber: 10.1 g.
- Sugar: 7 g.
- Sodium: 56 mg.

Zucchini and Pinto Bean Casserole

Preparation time: 15 minutes
Cooking time: 15 minutes
Servings: 4
Ingredients:

- 1 (6–7-inch) zucchini, trimmed
- 1 can (15 oz./425 g.) pinto beans or 1 1/2 cups Salt-Free No-Soak Beans, rinsed and drained
- 1 1/3 cups salsa
- 1 1/3 cups Mexican cheese blend, shredded
- Nonstick cooking spray

Directions:

1. Slice the zucchini into rounds. You'll need at least 16 slices.
2. Spray a 6-inch cake pan with nonstick spray.

3. Put the beans into a medium bowl and mash some of them with a fork.
4. Cover the bottom of the pan with about 4 zucchini slices. Add about 1/3 of the beans, 1/3 cup of salsa, and 1/3 cup of cheese. Press down. Repeat for 2 more layers. Add the remaining zucchini, salsa, and cheese. (There are no beans in the top layer.)
5. Cover the pan loosely with foil.
6. Pour 1 cup of water into the electric pressure cooker.
7. Place the pan on the wire rack and carefully lower it into the pot. Close and lock the lid of the pressure cooker. Set the valve to sealing.
8. Cook on "High Pressure" for 15 minutes.
9. When the cooking is complete, hit "Cancel" and allow the pressure to release naturally.
10. Once the pin drops, unlock and remove the lid.
11. Carefully remove the pan from the pot, lifting by the handles of the wire rack. Let the casserole sit for 5 minutes before slicing into quarters and serving.

Nutrition:
- Calories: 251
- Fat: 12.1 g.
- Protein: 16.1 g.
- Carbs: 22.9 g.
- Fiber: 7.1 g.
- Sugar: 4 g.
- Sodium: 1080 mg.

Eggplant-Zucchini Parmesan
Preparation time: 10 minutes
Cooking time: 120 minutes
Servings: 6
Ingredients:
- 1 medium eggplant, peeled and cut into 1-inch cubes
- 1 medium zucchini, cut into 1-inch pieces

- 1 medium onion, cut into thin wedges
- 1 1/2 cups store-bought light spaghetti sauce
- 2/3 cup reduced-fat Parmesan cheese, grated

Directions:
1. Place the vegetables, spaghetti sauce, and 1/3 cup Parmesan in the crockpot. Stir to combine. Cover and cook on "High" for 2–2 1/2 hours, or on "Low" for 4–5 hours.
2. Sprinkle the remaining Parmesan on top before serving.

Nutrition:
- Calories: 82
- Fat: 2.0 g.
- Protein: 5.1 g.
- Carbs: 12.1 g.
- Fiber: 5 g.
- Sugar: 7 g.
- Sodium: 456 mg.

Grilled Portobello and Zucchini Burger
Preparation time: 5 minutes
Cooking time: 10 minutes
Servings: 2
Ingredients:
- 2 large portabella mushroom caps
- 1/2 small zucchini, sliced
- 2 slices low-fat cheese
- 2 whole-wheat sandwich thins
- 2 tsp. roasted red bell peppers
- 2 tsp. olive oil

Directions:
1. Heat grill, or charcoal, to medium-high heat.
2. Lightly brush mushroom caps with olive oil. Grill mushroom caps and zucchini slices until tender, about 3–4 minutes per side.

3. Place on sandwich thin. Top with sliced cheese and roasted red bell pepper. Serve.

Nutrition:
- Calories: 178 Fat: 3.0 g.
- Protein: 15.1 g. Carbs: 26.1 g.
- Fiber: 8 g. Sugar: 3 g. Sodium: 520 mg.

Lemon Wax Beans

Preparation time: 5 minutes
Cooking time: 15 minutes
Servings: 4
Ingredients:
- 2 lb. (907 g.) wax beans
- 1/2 lemon juice
- 2 tbsp. extra virgin olive oil
- Sea salt and freshly ground black pepper, to taste

Directions:
1. Preheat the oven to 400°F (205°C).
2. Line a baking sheet with aluminum foil.
3. In a large bowl, toss the beans and olive oil. Season lightly with salt and pepper.
4. Transfer the beans to the baking sheet and spread them out.
5. Roast the beans until caramelized and tender, about 10–12 minutes.
6. Transfer the beans to a serving platter and sprinkle them with lemon juice.

Nutrition:
- Calories: 99 Fat: 7.1 g.
- Protein: 2.1 g.
- Carbs: 8.1 g.
- Fiber: 4.2 g.
- Sugar: 3.9 g.
- Sodium: 814 mg.

Wilted Dandelion Greens with Sweet Onion

Preparation time: 15 minutes
Cooking time: 12 minutes
Servings: 4
Ingredients:
- 1 Vidalia onion, thinly sliced
- 2 garlic cloves, minced
- 2 bunches dandelion greens, roughly chopped
- 1/2 cup low-sodium vegetable broth
- 1 tbsp. extra virgin olive oil
- Freshly ground black pepper, to taste

Directions:
1. Heat the olive oil in a large skillet over low heat.
2. Cook the onion and garlic for 2–3 minutes until tender, stirring occasionally.
3. Add the dandelion greens and broth and cook for 5–7 minutes, stirring frequently, or until the greens are wilted.
4. Transfer to a plate and season with black pepper. Serve warm.

Nutrition:
- Calories: 81
- Fat: 3.8 g.
- Protein: 3.1 g.
- Carbs: 10.7 g.
- Fiber: 3.8 g.
- Sugar: 2 g.
- Sodium: 72 mg.

Butter Cod with Asparagus

Preparation time: 5 minutes
Cooking time: 10 minutes
Servings: 4
Ingredients:
- 4 (4oz./113 g.) cod fillets
- 1/4 tsp. garlic powder
- 24 asparagus spears, woody ends trimmed
- 1/2 cup brown rice, cooked
- 1 tbsp. lemon juice, freshly squeezed

- 1/4 tsp. salt
- 1/4 tsp. freshly ground black pepper
- 2 tbsp. unsalted butter

Directions:
1. In a large bowl, season the cod fillets with garlic powder, salt, and pepper. Set aside.
2. Melt the butter in a skillet over medium-low heat.
3. Place the cod fillets and asparagus in the skillet in a single layer. Cook covered for 8 minutes, or until the cod is cooked through.
4. Divide the cooked brown rice, cod fillets, and asparagus among 4 plates. Serve drizzled with lemon juice.

Nutrition:
- Calories: 233 Fat: 8.2 g.
- Protein: 22.1 g. Carbs: 20.1 g.
- Fiber: 5.2 g.
- Sugar: 2.2 g.
- Sodium: 275 mg.

Creamy Cod Fillet with Quinoa and Asparagus

Preparation time: 5 minutes
Cooking time: 15 minutes
Servings: 4
Ingredients:
- 1/2 cup uncooked quinoa
- 4 (4 oz./113 g.) cod fillets
- 1/2 tsp. garlic powder, divided
- 24 asparagus spears, cut the bottom 1 1/2 inches off
- 1 cup half-and-half
- 1/4 tsp. salt
- 1/4 tsp. freshly ground black pepper
- 1 tbsp. avocado oil
- 2 cups water

Directions:
1. Put the quinoa in a pot of salted water. Bring to a boil. Reduce the heat to low and simmer for 15 minutes or until the quinoa is soft and has a white "tail."

Cover and turn off the heat. Let sit for 5 minutes.
2. On a clean work surface, rub the cod fillets with 1/4 tsp. of garlic powder, salt, and pepper.
3. Heat the avocado oil in a nonstick skillet over medium-low heat.
4. Add the cod fillets and asparagus to the skillet and cook for 8 minutes or until they are tender. Flip the cod and shake the skillet halfway through the cooking time.
5. Pour the half-and-half in the skillet, and sprinkle with remaining garlic powder. Turn up the heat to high and simmer for 2 minutes until creamy.
6. Divide the quinoa, cod fillets, and asparagus into 4 bowls and serve warm.

Nutrition:
- Calories: 258 Fat: 7.9 g.
- Protein: 25.2 g. Carbs: 22.7 g.
- Fiber: 5.2 g. Sugar: 3.8 g.
- Sodium: 410 mg.

Butter-Lemon Grilled Cod on Asparagus

Preparation time: 5 minutes
Cooking time: 9–12 minutes
Servings: 4
Ingredients:
- 1 lb. (454 g.) asparagus spears, ends trimmed
- 4 (4oz./113 g.) cod fillets, rinsed and patted dry
- 1 medium lemon juice and zest
- Cooking spray

- 1/4 tsp. black pepper (optional)
- 1/4 cup light butter with canola oil
- 1/4 tsp. salt (optional)

Directions:
1. Heat a grill pan over medium-high heat.
2. Spray the asparagus spears with cooking spray. Cook the asparagus for 6–8 minutes until fork-tender, flipping occasionally.
3. Transfer to a large platter and keep warm.
4. Spray both sides of fillets with cooking spray. Season with 1/4 tsp. black pepper, if needed. Add the fillets to the pan and sear each side for 3 minutes until opaque.
5. Meantime, in a small bowl, whisk together the light butter, lemon zest, and 1/4 tsp. salt (if desired).
6. Spoon and spread the mixture all over the asparagus. Place the fish on top and squeeze the lemon juice over the fish. Serve immediately.

Nutrition:
- Calories: 158 Fat: 6.4 g.
- Protein: 23.0 g. Carbs: 6.1 g.
- Fiber: 3.0 g. Sugar: 2.8 g.
- Sodium: 212 mg.

Lemon Parsley White Fish Fillets

Preparation time: 10 minutes
Cooking time: 10 minutes
Servings: 4
Ingredients:

- 4 (6 oz./170 g.) lean white fish fillets, rinsed and patted dry
- 2 tbsp. parsley, finely chopped
- 1/2 tsp. lemon zest

- 1/4 tsp. dill, dried
- 1 medium lemon, halved
- Cooking spray
- Paprika, to taste
- Salt and pepper, to taste
- 1/4 cup extra virgin olive oil

Directions:
1. Preheat the oven to 400°F (205°C). Line a baking sheet with aluminum foil and spray with cooking spray.
2. Place the fillets on the foil and scatter with the paprika. Season as desired with salt and pepper.
3. Bake in the preheated oven for 10 minutes or until the flesh flakes easily with a fork.
4. Meanwhile, stir together the parsley, lemon zest, olive oil, and dill in a small bowl.
5. Remove the fish from the oven to 4 plates. Squeeze the lemon juice over the fish and serve topped with the parsley mixture.

Nutrition:
- Calories: 283 Fat: 17.2 g.
- Protein: 33.3 g. Carbs: 1 g.
- Fiber: 0 g. Sugar: 0 g. Sodium: 74 mg.

Cilantro Lime Shrimp

Preparation time: 15 minutes
Cooking time: 8 minutes
Servings: 4
Ingredients:

- 1/2 tsp. garlic clove, minced

- 1 lb. (454 g.) large shrimp, peeled and deveined
- 1/4 cup fresh cilantro, chopped, or more to taste
- 1 lime, zested and juiced
- 1 tsp. extra virgin olive oil
- 1/4 tsp. salt
- 1/8 tsp. black pepper

Directions:

1. In a large heavy skillet, heat the olive oil over medium-high heat.
2. Add the minced garlic and cook for 30 seconds until fragrant.
3. Toss in the shrimp and cook for about 5–6 minutes, stirring occasionally, or until they turn pink and opaque.
4. Remove from the heat to a bowl. Add the cilantro, lime zest and juice, salt, and pepper to the shrimp, and toss to combine. Serve immediately.

Nutrition:

- Calories: 133
- Fat: 3.5 g.
- Protein: 24.3 g.
- Carbs: 1 g.
- Fiber: 0 g.
- Sugar: 0 g.
- Sodium: 258 mg.

Cajun Catfish

Preparation time: 5 minutes
Cooking time: 15 minutes
Servings: 4
Ingredients:

- 4 (8 oz./227 g.) catfish fillets
- 2 tsp. thyme
- 1/2 tsp. red hot sauce
- 2 tbsp. olive oil
- 2 tsp. garlic salt
- 2 tsp. paprika
- 1/2 tsp. cayenne pepper
- 1/4 tsp. black pepper
- Nonstick cooking spray

Directions:

1. Heat oven to 450°F (235°C). Spray a baking dish with cooking spray.
2. In a small bowl whisk together everything but catfish. Brush both sides of fillets, using all the spice mix.
3. Bake 10–13 minutes or until fish flakes easily with a fork. Serve.

Nutrition:

- Calories: 367
- Fat: 24.0 g.
- Protein: 35.2 g.
- Carbs: 0 g.
- Fiber: 0 g.
- Sugar: 0 g.
- Sodium: 70 mg.

Lamb and Mushroom Cheeseburgers

Preparation time: 15 minutes
Cooking time: 15 minutes
Servings: 4
Ingredients:

- 8 oz. (227 g.) grass-fed ground lamb
- 8 oz. (227 g.) brown mushrooms, finely chopped
- 1/4 cup goat cheese, crumbled
- 1 tbsp. fresh basil, minced
- 1/4 tsp. salt
- 1/4 tsp. freshly ground black pepper

Directions:

1. In a large mixing bowl, combine the lamb, mushrooms, salt, and pepper, and mix well.
2. In a small bowl, mix the goat cheese and basil.
3. Form the lamb mixture into 4 patties, reserving about 1/2 cup of the mixture in the bowl. In each patty, make an indentation in the center and fill with 1 tbsp. of the goat cheese mixture. Use the reserved meat mixture to close the burgers. Press the meat firmly to hold it together.
4. Heat the barbecue or a large skillet over medium-high heat. Add the burgers and cook for 5–7 minutes on each side, until cooked through. Serve.

Nutrition:

- Calories: 172
- Fat: 13.1 g.
- Protein: 11.1 g.
- Carbs: 2.9 g.
- Fiber: 0 g.
- Sugar: 1.0 g.
- Sodium: 155 mg.

Pulled Pork Sandwiches with Apricot Jelly

Preparation time: 5 minutes
Cooking time: 15 minutes
Servings: 4
Ingredients:

- 8 oz. (227 g.) store-bought pulled pork
- 1/2 cup green bell pepper, chopped
- 2 slices provolone cheese
- 4 whole-wheat sandwich thins
- 2 1/2 tbsp. apricot jelly
- Avocado oil cooking spray

Directions:

1. Heat the pulled pork according to the package directions.
2. Heat a medium skillet over medium-low heat. When hot, coat the cooking surface with cooking spray.
3. Put the bell pepper in the skillet and cook for 5 minutes. Transfer to a small bowl and set aside.
4. Meanwhile, tear each slice of cheese into 2 strips, and halves the sandwich thins so you have a top and bottom.
5. Reduce the heat to low, and place the sandwich thins in the skillet cut-side down to toast, about 2 minutes.
6. Remove the sandwich thins from the skillet. Spread 1/4 of the jelly on the bottom half of each sandwich thin, and then place 1/4 of the cheese, pulled pork, and pepper on top. Cover with the top half of the sandwich thin.

Nutrition:

- Calories: 250
- Fat: 8.1 g.
- Protein: 16.1 g.
- Carbs: 34.1 g.
- Fiber: 6.1 g.
- Sugar: 8.0 g.
- Sodium: 510 mg.

Parmesan Golden Pork Chops

Preparation time: 10 minutes
Cooking time: 25 minutes
Servings: 4
Ingredients:

- 4 bone-in, thin-cut pork chops
- 1/2 cup Parmesan cheese, grated
- 3 garlic cloves, minced
- 1/4 tsp. thyme, dried
- Nonstick cooking spray
- 2 tbsp. butter

- 1/4 tsp. salt
- Freshly ground black pepper, to taste

Directions:
1. Preheat the oven to 400°F (205°C). Line a baking sheet with parchment paper and spray with nonstick cooking spray.
2. Arrange the pork chops on the prepared baking sheet so they do not overlap.
3. In a small bowl, combine the butter, cheese, garlic, salt, thyme, and pepper. Press 2 tbsp. of the cheese mixture onto the top of each pork chop.
4. Bake for 18–22 minutes until the pork is cooked through and its juices run clear. Set the broiler to high, then broil for 1–2 minutes to brown the tops.

Nutrition:
- Calories: 333
- Fat: 16.1 g.
- Protein: 44.1 g.
- Carbs: 1.1 g.
- Fiber: 0 g.
- Sugar: 0 g.
- Sodium: 441 mg.

Chipotle Chili Pork

Preparation time: 4 hours 20 minutes
Cooking time: 20 minutes
Servings: 4
Ingredients:

- 4 (5 oz./142 g.) pork chops, about 1-inch thick
- 1 tbsp. chipotle chili powder
- 1 lime juice and zest

- 2 tsp. garlic, minced
- 1 tsp. cinnamon, ground
- 1 tbsp. extra virgin olive oil
- A pinch sea salt

Directions:
1. Combine all the ingredients, except for the lemon wedges, in a large bowl. Toss to combine well.
2. Wrap the bowl in plastic and refrigerate to marinate for at least 4 hours.
3. Preheat the oven to 400°F (205°C). Set a rack on a baking sheet.
4. Remove the bowl from the refrigerator and let sit for 15 minutes. Discard the marinade and place the pork on the rack.
5. Roast in the preheated oven for 20 minutes or until well browned. Flip the pork halfway through the cooking time.
6. Serve immediately.

Nutrition:
- Calories: 204 Fat: 9 g.
- Protein: 30 g. Carbs: 1 g.
- Fiber: 0 g. Sugar: 1.0 g.
- Sodium: 317 mg.

Pumpkin, Bean, and Chicken Enchiladas

Preparation time: 35 minutes
Cooking time: 20 minutes
Servings: 4
Ingredients:

- 2 tsp. olive oil

- 1/2 cup onion, chopped
- 1 jalapeno, seeded and chopped
- 1 can (15 oz.) pumpkin
- 1 1/2 cups water, more if needed
- 1 tsp. chili powder
- 1/2 tsp. salt
- 1/2 tsp. cumin, ground
- 1 cup canned no-salt-added red kidney beans, rinsed and drained
- 1 1/2 cups chicken breast, cooked and shredded
- 1/2 cup part-skim mozzarella cheese, shredded
- 8 (6-inch) whole-wheat tortillas, softened
- Salsa and lime wedges

Directions:

1. Lightly coat a 2-quart rectangular baking dish with cooking sprays and preheat the oven to 400°F.
2. In a saucepan, heat oil over medium heat. Add jalapeno and onion and stir-fry until onion is tender, for about 5 minutes. Stir in cumin, salt, chili powder, 1 1/2 cups water, and pumpkin and heat through. Add more water if needed.
3. Place beans in a bowl and mash slightly with a fork. Stir in 1/4 cup of the cheese, the chicken, and half of the pumpkin mixture.
4. Spoon 1/3 cup bean mixture onto each tortilla. Roll up tortillas. Place in the baking dish (seam sides down). Pour the remaining pumpkin mixture over enchiladas.
5. Bake, covered, for 15 minutes. Sprinkle with remaining ¼ cup cheese. Bake, uncovered until heated through, for about 10 minutes more.
6. Serve with salsa and lime wedges.

Nutrition:

- Calories: 357
- Fat: 8 g.
- Carbs: 44 g.
- Protein: 28 g.

Mu Shu Chicken

Preparation time: 20 minutes
Cooking time: 6 hours
Servings: 6
Ingredients:

- 1/2 cup hoisin sauce
- 2 tbsp. water
- 4 tsp. sesame oil, toasted
- 1 tbsp. cornstarch
- 1 tbsp. reduced-sodium soy sauce
- 3 garlic cloves, minced
- 1 pkg. (16 oz.) coleslaw mix (cabbage with carrots), shredded
- 1 cup carrots, coarsely shredded
- 12 oz. chicken thighs, boneless and skinless
- 6 (8-inch) whole wheat flour tortillas
- 3 Green onions chopped

Directions:

1. Combine the first 6 ingredients in a bowl (through garlic).
2. In a slow cooker, combine shredded carrots and coleslaw mix.
3. Cut chicken into 1/8-inch slices, cut each slice in half lengthwise. Place chicken on top of the cabbage mix. Drizzle with 1/4 cup of the hoisin mixture.
4. Heat tortillas according to package directions. Fill tortillas with a chicken mixture.
5. Top with green onions and serve.

Nutrition:

- Calories: 269 Fat: 8 g.
- Carbs: 34 g.
- Protein: 16 g.

Stove-Top Chicken, Macaroni, and Cheese

Preparation time: 10 minutes
Cooking time: 30 minutes
Servings: 5
Ingredients:

- 1 1/2 cups dried multigrain or elbow macaroni
- 12 oz. chicken breast halves, skinless, boneless and cut into 1-inch pieces,
- 1/4 cup onion, chopped
- 1 pkg. (6.5 oz.) light semisoft cheese with garlic and fine herbs
- 1 2/3 cups fat-free milk
- 1 tbsp. all-purpose flour
- 3/4 cup reduced-fat cheddar cheese, shredded
- 2 cups fresh baby spinach
- 1 cup cherry tomatoes, quartered
- Nonstick Cooking spray

Directions:

1. Cook macaroni according to package directions. Drain.
2. Meanwhile, coat a skillet with cooking spray. Heat skillet over medium-high heat.
3. Add onion and chicken until chicken is no longer pink, about 4–6 minutes. Stirring frequently. Remove from heat and stir in semisoft cheese until melted.
4. In a bowl, whisk together flour and milk until smooth. Gradually stir the milk mixture into the chicken mixture. Cook and stir until bubbly and thickened. Lower heat and gradually add cheddar cheese. Stirring until melted.
5. Add cooked macaroni cook and stir for 1–2 minutes or until heated through.
6. Stir in spinach. Top with cherry tomatoes and serve.

Nutrition:

- Calories: 369
- Fat: 12 g.
- Carbs: 33 g.
- Protein: 33 g.

Chicken Sausage Omelets with Spinach

Preparation time: 20 minutes
Cooking time: 10 minutes
Servings: 2
Ingredients:

- 2 cups fresh spinach
- 1/2 pkg. (7 oz.) frozen fully cooked chicken and maple breakfast sausage links, thawed and chopped
- 3 eggs, lightly beaten
- 2 tbsp. water
- 1/4 cup part-skim mozzarella cheese, shredded
- 2 green onions, green tops only, thinly sliced
- 1/2 cup grape tomatoes, quartered
- 1/4 cup fresh basil leaves, thinly sliced
- Nonstick cooking spray

Directions:

1. Coat a skillet with nonstick cooking spray. Heat over medium heat.
2. Add sausage and spinach. Cook until sausage is heated. Remove from the skillet.
3. In a bowl, whisk together the water and eggs. Add egg mixture to skillet and cook until egg is set and shiny.
4. Spoon spinach and sausage mixture over half of the omelet. Sprinkle with cheese and green onions. Fold the opposite side of the omelet over the sausage mixture.
5. Cook for 1 minute or until the filling is heated and the cheese is melted.
6. Transfer to a plate and cut in half. Transfer half of the omelet to a second plate.
7. Top with tomatoes and basil and serve.

Nutrition:

- Calories: 252 Fat: 16 g.
- Carbs: 5 g. Protein: 21 g.

Turkey Kabob Pitas

Preparation time: 25 minutes
Cooking time: 15 minutes
Servings: 4
Ingredients:

- 1 tsp. whole cumin seeds, lightly crushed
- 1 cup cucumber, shredded
- 1/3 cup Romaine tomato, seeded and chopped
- 1/4 cup red onion, slivered

- 1/4 cup radishes, shredded
- 1/4 cup fresh cilantro, snipped
- 1/4 tsp. black pepper
- 1 lb. turkey breast, cut into thin strips
- 1 recipe curry blend
- 1/4 cup plain fat-free Greek yogurt
- 4 (6-inch) whole-wheat pita bread rounds

Directions:

1. Soak wooden skewers in water for 30 minutes. Toast the cumin seeds for 1 minute and transfer them to a bowl. Add the next 6 ingredients to the bowl (through pepper). Mix.
2. In another bowl, combine curry blend and turkey. Stir to coat. Thread turkey onto skewers.
3. Grill kabobs, uncovered for 6–8 minutes or until turkey is no longer pink. Turning kabobs occasionally.
4. Remove turkey from skewers. Spread Greek yogurt on pita bread. Spoon cucumber mixture over yogurt. Top with grilled turkey.
5. Serve.

To make the curry blend

1. In a bowl, combine 2 tsp. olive oil, 1 tsp. curry powder, 1/2 tsp. each ground turmeric, ground cumin, and ground coriander, 1/4 tsp. ground ginger, and 1/8 tsp. salt and cayenne pepper.

Nutrition:

- Calories: 343 Fat: 6 g.
- Carbs: 40 g. Protein: 35 g.

Caribbean Fish with Mango-Orange Relish

Preparation time: 25 minutes
Cooking time: 15 minutes
Servings: 6
Ingredients:

- 2 1/2 lb. Fresh or frozen skinless barramundi, sea bass, or other whitefish fillets
- 3 navel oranges
- 1 large mango, chopped

- 3/4 cup red sweet pepper, roasted and chopped
- 2 tbsp. dry white wine
- 1 tbsp. fresh cilantro, snipped
- 1/4 tsp. salt
- 1/4 tsp. black pepper
- 1/3 cup all-purpose flour
- 2 tsp. cardamom, ground
- 1/4 cup butter
- Fresh chives, snipped

Directions:
1. For relish, juice one of the oranges. Peel and slice the remaining 2 oranges. Combine orange pieces, orange juice, and the next 4 ingredients (through cilantro).
2. Sprinkle fish with salt and pepper. In a dish, combine cardamom and flour. Dip fish in flour mixture, turning to coat.
3. Preheat the oven to 300°F. In a skillet, melt 2 tbsp. butter. Add half of the fish. Cook until fish is golden and flakes easily, about 6–8 minutes. Turning once.
4. Cook the remaining fish in the remaining 2 tbsp. Butter. Serve with relish and sprinkle with chives.

Nutrition:
- Calories: 343 Fat: 12 g.
- Carbs: 20 g. Protein: 37 g.

Lemon-Herb Roasted Salmon Sheet-Pan Dinner

Preparation time: 20 minutes
Cooking time: 15 minutes
Servings: 4
Ingredients:
- 1 lb. fresh or frozen skinless salmon fillet
- 2 tbsp. olive oil
- 1 1/2 tsp. oregano, dried and crushed
- 1/4 tsp. salt
- 1/8 tsp. black pepper
- 2 cups grape or cherry tomatoes, halved
- 2 cups broccoli florets
- 2 garlic cloves, minced
- 1 lemon juice
- 2 tbsp. fresh basil snipped
- 1 tbsp. fresh parsley, snipped
- 1 tbsp. honey (optional)

Directions:
1. Thaw salmon, if frozen. Preheat the oven to 400°F.
2. Line a baking pan with parchment paper.
3. Rinse fish and pat dry.
4. Place salmon in the prepared pan. Drizzle with 1 tbsp. oil and sprinkle with 3/4 tsp. oregano, salt, and pepper.
5. In a bowl, combine garlic, broccoli, tomatoes, and the remaining 1 tbsp. oil and 3/4 tsp. oregano. Sprinkle lightly with more salt and pepper. Toss to coat.
6. Place in the pan with salmon. Roast until salmon flakes, about 15–18 minutes.
7. Meanwhile, remove 1 tsp. zest and squeeze 3 tbsp. juice from lemon. In a small bowl, combine lemon juice and zest, and the remaining ingredients.
8. Spoon over salmon and vegetables before serving.

Nutrition:
- Calories: 276
- Fat: 14 g.
- Carb: 13 g.
- Protein: 25 g.

Cod With Eggplant Peperonata

Preparation time: 10 minutes
Cooking time: 25 minutes
Servings: 4
Ingredients:

- 4 (4 oz.) fresh or frozen cod fillets
- 1/2 medium sweet onion, thinly sliced
- 1 tbsp. olive oil
- 1 small eggplant, cut into 1-inch pieces
- 1 large yellow or red sweet pepper, thinly sliced
- 4 garlic cloves, minced
- 1 tsp. fresh rosemary, snipped
- 1/2 tsp. salt
- 1/4 tsp. black pepper
- 4 cups fresh spinach
- 1 cup water

Directions:

1. Thaw fish, if frozen. Rinse fish, pat dry with paper towels.
2. For eggplant peperonata, in a skillet, cook onion in hot oil for 5 minutes. Stirring occasionally.
3. Add the next 4 ingredients (through rosemary), and 1/4 tsp. salt. Cook until vegetables are very tender, about 10–12 minutes. Stirring occasionally. Remove peperonata from the skillet and keep warm.
4. Add 1-inch of water to the same skillet. Place a steamer basket in the skillet and bring the water to boil. Sprinkle cod with the remaining 1/4 tsp. salt and black pepper.
5. Add fish to the steamer basket. Cover and reduce heat to medium. Steam just until fish flakes, about 6–8 minutes.
6. Top spinach with fish and eggplant *peperonata*.

Nutrition:

- Calories: 189
- Fat: 5 g.
- Carb: 13 g.
- Protein: 23 g.

Parmesan-Crusted Cod with Garlicky Summer Squash

Preparation time: 20 minutes
Cooking time: 20 minutes
Servings: 4
Ingredients:

- 4 (5–6 oz.) fillets fresh or frozen skinless cod fillets
- 4 small zucchini or yellow summer squash, cut into 3/4 inch pieces
- 2 garlic cloves, minced
- 1/4 cup olive oil
- 1/4 tsp. salt
- 1/8 tsp. black pepper
- 1/4 cup panko breadcrumbs
- 1/4 cup Parmesan cheese, grated
- 2 tbsp. fresh parsley, snipped

Directions:

1. Preheat the oven to 350°F. In a baking pan, combine garlic and squash.
2. Drizzle with 2 tbsp. oil. Rinse and pat dry fish. Place in pan with squash. Sprinkle fish and squash with 1/8 tsp. of the salt and pepper.
3. In a bowl, combine parsley, cheese, panko, and the remaining 1/8 tsp. salt. Drizzle with the remaining 2 tbsp. oil and toss to coat.
4. Sprinkle on top of the fish. Press lightly.
5. Bake for about 20 minutes or until fish flakes. Sprinkle with additional parsley.
6. Serve.

Nutrition:

- Calories: 297 Fat: 16 g.
- Carb: 8 g. Protein: 29 g.

Fried Cauliflower Rice with Shrimp

Preparation time: 10 minutes
Cooking time: 10 minutes
Servings: 4
Ingredients:

- 8 oz. fresh or frozen medium shrimp, peeled and deveined

- 1 (2 lb.) head cauliflower, cut into florets
- 1 tsp. sesame oil, toasted
- 2 eggs, lightly beaten
- 1 tbsp. olive oil
- 4 tsp. fresh ginger, grated
- 4 garlic cloves, minced
- 2 cups Napa cabbage, chopped
- 1 cup carrots, coarsely shredded
- 1/2 tsp. sea salt
- 1/2 tsp. red pepper, crushed
- 1/3 cup green onions, sliced
- 2 tbsp. fresh cilantro, snipped
- 2 Lime wedges

Directions:

1. Thaw shrimp if frozen. Rinse shrimp and pat dry.
2. Pulse cauliflower in a food processor until rice size.
3. In a skillet, heat sesame oil over medium heat. Add eggs, stir gently until set. Remove eggs and cool slightly. Cut eggs into strips.
4. Heat the olive oil in the skillet over medium heat. Add garlic and ginger. Cook for 30 seconds.
5. Add carrots and cabbage and stir-fry until vegetables start to soften for about 2 minutes.
6. Add crushed red pepper, salt, and shrimp. Stir-fry for 2 minutes or until shrimp are opaque.
7. Add green onions and cooked egg. Stir-fry until heated through.
8. Shrink shrimp mixture with cilantro. Serve with lemon wedges.

Nutrition:

- Calories: 181
- Fat: 8 g.
- Carb: 14 g.
- Protein: 17 g.

Quick Scallop and Noodle Toss

Preparation time: 5 minutes
Cooking time: 10 minutes
Servings: 4
Ingredients:

- 12 fresh or frozen sea scallops
- 1 medium zucchini, trimmed
- 1/2 tsp. olive oil
- 2 tbsp. orange juice
- 2 tbsp. cider vinegar
- 1 tbsp. sesame oil, toasted
- 1 tsp. fresh ginger, grated
- 1/2 tsp. lime zest
- 1/2 tsp. sea salt
- 1 1/2 cups fresh baby spinach
- 1 cup cucumber, chopped
- 2/3 cups radishes, thinly sliced
- 1/4 tsp. black pepper
- 1 tbsp. olive oil
- 2 tbsp. sesame seeds, toasted

Directions:

1. Thaw scallops, if frozen. Cut zucchini into long, thin noodles.
2. Heat 1/2 tsp. olive oil in a skillet. Add zucchini noodles and stir-fry for 1 minute or until tender. Cool.
3. Meanwhile, in a bowl, combine the next 5 ingredients (through lime zest) and 1/4 tsp. salt. Stir in radishes, cucumber, spinach, and zucchini noodles.
4. Rinse scallops and pat dry. Sprinkle with remaining 1/4 tsp. salt and pepper.
5. Heat 1 tbsp. olive oil in the same skillet. Add the scallops and cook until opaque, about 3–5 minutes. Turning once.

6. Serve zucchini noodle mixture with scallops and sprinkle with sesame seeds.

Nutrition:
- Calories: 227 Fat: 10 g.
- Carb: 9 g. Protein: 24 g.

Monk-Fish Curry

Preparation time: 10 minutes
Cooking time: 20 minutes
Servings: 2
Ingredients:
- 1/2 lb. monk-fish
- 1 sweet yellow onion, thinly sliced
- 1/2 cup tomato, chopped
- 3 tbsp. strong curry paste
- 1 tbsp. oil or ghee

Directions:
1. Set the Instant Pot to sauté and add the onion, oil, and curry paste.
2. When the onion is soft, add the remaining ingredients and seal.
3. Cook on "Stew" for 20 minutes.
4. Release the pressure naturally.

Nutrition:
- Calories: 270 Carbs: 16 g.
- Sugar: 6 g.Fat: 11 g.
- Protein: 4 g.
- Glycemic Load: 12

Sweet and Sour Tuna

Preparation time: 10 minutes
Cooking time: 9 minutes
Servings: 4
Ingredients:
- 4 (6 oz.) tuna steaks, pat dried
- 1/2 cup low-sodium chicken broth

- 2 tbsp. yacon syrup
- 2 tbsp. balsamic vinegar
- 2 tbsp. kaffir lime leaves, minced
- 1 (1/2-inch) piece fresh ginger, minced
- Ground black pepper, as required

Directions:
1. In the pot of Instant pot, place all the ingredients and mix well.
2. Add the tuna steaks and mix with broth mixture.
3. Secure the lid and place the pressure valve in the "Seal" position
4. Press "Manual" and cook under "High Pressure" for about 6 minutes.
5. Press "Cancel" and carefully allow a "Quick" release.
6. Open the lid and with a slotted spoon, transfer the tuna steaks onto a plate.
7. Press "Sauté" and cook for about 2–3 minutes or until the sauce becomes slightly thick.
8. Press "Cancel" and pour the sauce over tuna steaks.
9. Serve immediately.

Nutrition:
- Calories: 329
- Fats: 7 g.
- Carbs: 3.3 g.
- Sugar: 1.8 g.
- Proteins: 5.1 g.
- Sodium: 97 mg.

Tuna and Cheddar

Preparation time: 10 minutes
Cooking time: 35 minutes
Servings: 2
Ingredients:
- 3 small cans tuna
- 1 lb. vegetables, finely chopped
- 1 cup low-sodium vegetable broth
- 1/2 cup cheddar, shredded

Directions:
1. Mix all the ingredients in your Instant Pot.
2. Cook on "Stew" for 35 minutes.

3. Release the pressure naturally.

Nutrition:

- Calories: 320 Carbs: 8 g. Sugar: 2 g.
- Fat: 11 g.Protein: 37 g.
- Glycemic Load: 4

Caribbean Chicken

Preparation time: 10 minutes
Cooking time: 6 hours
Servings: 6
Ingredients:

- 1 1/2 cups Goya® mojo criollo marinade (or another sauce by choice)
- 1 tbsp. curry powder
- 1 tsp. pepper
- 1 tsp. garlic powder
- 1 onion, sliced
- 8 chicken thighs

Directions:

1. In a small bowl, combine the spices.
2. Brush the mixture over the chicken.
3. Place the chicken thighs in your Slow Cooker and arrange the onion slices over.
4. Pour the marinade over—do NOT stir at this point.
5. Close the lid and cook for 6 hours on "Low."
6. Serve over rice or your preferred side dish and enjoy!

Nutrition:

- Calories: 210 Fats 10 g.
- Carbs 7 g.
- Protein 22 g.
- Fiber: 1 g.

Turkey with Gravy

Preparation time: 10 minutes
Cooking time: 5 hours
Servings: 12
Ingredients:

- 6 lb. turkey, bone-in
- 2 onions, chopped
- 3 carrots, sliced
- 3 celery ribs, chopped
- 1/4 cup whole-wheat flour
- 1/2 cup water
- 1/2 tsp. pepper
- 1/2 tsp. paprika
- 1 tsp. chicken seasoning
- 1 tsp. salt

Directions:

1. Combine the spices in a small bowl.
2. Massage the rub into the turkey meat.
3. Place the veggies at the bottom of your Slow Cooker.
4. Top with the turkey.
5. Put the lid on and cook for 6 hours on "Low."
6. Transfer the turkey to a cutting board.
7. Pour the cooking juices from the Slow Cooker into a saucepan.
8. Whisk the water and flour and add to the juices.
9. Cook over medium heat until thickened.
10. Slice the turkey and pour the gravy over.
11. Serve and enjoy!

Nutrition:

- Calories: 200 Total Fats 1 g.
- Carbs 2 g. Protein 43 g. Fiber: 0.5 g.

Deconstructed Philly Cheesesteaks

Preparation time: 10 minutes
Cooking time: 20 minutes
Servings: 4
Ingredients:

- 1 lb. lean beef, ground
- 5–6 mushrooms, halved
- 4 slices provolone cheese

- 3 green bell peppers, quartered
- 2 medium onions, quartered
- 1/2 cup low-sodium beef broth
- 1–2 tbsp. Worcestershire sauce
- 1 tsp. olive oil
- Salt and pepper, to taste

Directions:

1. Heat oven to 400°F.
2. Place vegetables in a large bowl and add oil. Toss to coat. Dump out onto a large baking sheet and bake 10–15 minutes, or until tender-crisp.
3. Place beef in a large skillet and cook over med-high heat until no longer pink. Drain off fat.
4. Add broth and Worcestershire. Cook, stirring occasionally until liquid is absorbed, about 5 minutes. Salt and pepper beef if desired. Top with sliced cheese, remove from heat and cover until cheese melts.
5. Divide vegetables evenly between 4 bowls. Top with beef and serve.

Nutrition:

- Calories: 388 Total Carbs: 15 g.
- Net Carbs: 12 g. Protein: 44 g.
- Fat: 16 g. Sugar: 9 g. Fiber: 3 g.

Beef and Broccoli Skillet

Preparation time: 10 minutes
Cooking time: 10 minutes
Servings: 4
Ingredients:

- 1 lb. lean beef, ground
- 3 cups cauliflower rice, cooked

- 2 cups broccoli, chopped
- 4 green onions, sliced
- 1 cup teriyaki sauce

Directions:

1. Cook beef in a large skillet over med-high heat until brown. Add the broccoli and white parts of the onion, cook, stirring for 1 minute.
2. Add the cauliflower and sauce and continue cooking until heated through and broccoli is tender-crisp about 3–5 minutes. Serve garnished with green parts of the onion.

Nutrition:

- Calories: 255
- Total Carbs: 9 g.
- Net Carbs: 6 g.
- Protein: 37 g.
- Fat: 7 g.
- Sugar: 3 g.
- Fiber: 3 g.

Balsamic Chicken and Vegetable Skillet

Preparation time: 10 minutes
Cooking time: 20 minutes
Servings: 4
Ingredients:

- 1 lb. chicken breasts, cut in 1-inch cubes
- 1 cup cherry tomatoes, halved
- 1 cup broccoli florets
- 1 cup baby Bella mushrooms, sliced
- 1 tbsp. fresh basil, diced

- 1/2 recipe homemade pasta, cooked and drain well
- 1/2 cup low-sodium chicken broth
- 3 tbsp. balsamic vinegar
- 2 tbsp. olive oil, divided
- 1 tsp. pepper
- 1/2 tsp. garlic powder
- 1/2 tsp. salt
- 1/2 tsp. red pepper flakes

Directions:

1. Heat oil in a large, deep skillet over med-high heat. Add chicken and cook until browned on all sides, 8–10 minutes.
2. Add vegetables, basil, broth, and seasonings. Cover, reduce heat to medium, and cook 5 minutes, or vegetables are tender.
3. Uncover and stir in cooked pasta and vinegar. Cook until heated through, 3–4 minutes. Serve.

Nutrition:

- Calories: 386
- Total Carbs: 11 g.
- Net Carbs: 8 g.
- Protein: 43 g.
- Fat: 18 g.
- Sugar: 5 g.
- Fiber: 3 g.

Russian Steaks with Nuts and Cheese

Preparation time: 10 minutes
Cooking time: 20 minutes
Servings: 4
Ingredients:

- 800 g. pork, minced
- 200 g. cream cheese
- 50 g. walnuts, peeled
- 1 onion
- Salt and Ground pepper to taste
- 1 egg
- 2 cups of Breadcrumbs
- 2 tbsp. Extra virgin olive oil

Directions:

1. Put the onion cut into quarters in the Thermo mix glass and select 5 seconds speed 5.
2. Add the minced meat, cheese, egg, salt, and pepper.
3. Select 10 seconds, speed 5, turn left.
4. Add the chopped and peeled walnuts and select 4 seconds, turn left, speed 5.
5. Pass the dough to a bowl.
6. Make Russian steaks and go through breadcrumbs.
7. Paint the Russian fillets with extra virgin olive oil on both sides with a brush.
8. Put in the basket of the air fryer, without stacking the Russian fillets.
9. Select 180°C, 15 minutes.

Nutrition:

- Calories: 1232
- Fat: 3.41 g.
- Carbs: 0 g.
- Protein: 20.99 g.
- Sugar: 0 g.
- Cholesterol: 63 mg.

Creamy Chicken Tenders

Preparation time: 10 minutes
Cooking time: 15 minutes
Servings: 4
Ingredients:

- 1 lb. chicken breast tenders
- 1 cup half-n-half
- 4 tbsp. margarine
- 2 tsp. garlic powder
- 2 tsp. chili powder

Directions:

1. In a small bowl, stir together seasonings with a little salt if desired. Sprinkle over chicken to coat.
2. Heat 2 tbsp. margarine in a large skillet over medium heat. Cook chicken until no longer pink, 3–4 minutes per side. Transfer to a plate.
3. Add half-n-half and stir, scraping up the brown bits from the bottom of the

skillet, and cook until it starts to boil. Reduce heat to med-low and simmer until sauce is reduced by half. Stir in the remaining margarine and add the chicken back to the sauce to heat through. Serve.

Nutrition:

- Calories: 281
- Total Carbs: 3 g.
- Protein: 24 g.
- Fat: 19 g.
- Sugar: 0 g.
- Fiber: 0 g.

Tangy Balsamic Beef

Preparation time: 10 minutes
Cooking time: 6–8 Hours
Servings: 8
Ingredients:

- 3–4 lb. beef roast, boneless
- 1/2 onion, finely diced
- 1 can low-sodium beef broth
- 1/2 cup balsamic vinegar
- 5 garlic cloves, finely diced
- 3 tbsp. honey (optional)
- 1 tbsp. lite soy sauce
- 1 tbsp. Worcestershire sauce
- 1 tsp. red chili flakes

Directions:

1. Place all ingredients, except the roast, into the crockpot. Stir well. Add roast and turn to coat.
2. Cover and cook on "Low" for 6–8 hours. When the beef is done, remove to a plate and shred, using 2 forks. Add it back to the sauce and serve.

Nutrition:

- Calories: 410
- Total Carbs: 9 g.
- Protein: 45 g.
- Fat: 20 g.
- Sugar: 7 g.
- Fiber: 0 g.

Sirloin Strips and "Rice"

Preparation time: 10 minutes
Cooking time: 30 minutes
Servings: 6
Ingredients:

- 1 1/2 lb. top sirloin steak, cut in thin strips
- 3 cups cauliflower rice, cook,
- 2 onions, thinly sliced
- 14 1/2 oz. tomatoes, diced and undrained
- 1/2 cup low-sodium beef broth
- 1/3 cup dry red wine
- 1 garlic clove, diced
- 1 bay leaf
- 2 tsp. olive oil, divided
- 1 tsp. salt
- 1/2 tsp. basil
- 1/2 tsp. thyme
- 1/4 tsp. pepper

Directions:

1. Sprinkle beef strips with salt and pepper.
2. Heat oil in a large skillet over medium heat. Add steak and cook, stirring frequently, just until browned. Transfer to a plate and keep warm.
3. Add remaining oil to the skillet along with the onion and cook until tender. Add the garlic and cook 1 minute more.
4. Stir in remaining ingredients, except the cauliflower, and bring to a boil. Reduce heat and simmer for 10 minutes.

5. Return the steak to the skillet and cook for 2–4 minutes until heated through and tender. Discard bay leaf and serve over cauliflower rice.

Nutrition:
- Calories: 278
- Total Carbs: 9 g.
- Net Carbs: 6 g.
- Protein: 37 g.
- Fat: 9 g.
- Sugar: 5 g.
- Fiber: 3 g.

Spicy BBQ Beef Brisket

Preparation time: 10 minutes
Cooking time: 5 Hours
Servings: 14
Ingredients:
- 3 1/2 lb. beef brisket
- 1/2 cup onion, finely diced
- 1 tsp. lemon juice
- 2 cups barbecue sauce
- 1 pct. Chili seasoning
- 1 tbsp. Worcestershire sauce
- 1 tsp. garlic, finely diced

Directions:
1. Cut the brisket in half and place it in the crockpot.
2. In a small bowl, combine the remaining ingredients, and pour over beef. Cover and cook on high heat 5–6 hours or until beef is fork-tender.
3. Transfer brisket to a bowl. Use 2 forks and shred. Add the meat back to the crockpot and stir to heat through. Serve as is or on buns.

Nutrition:
- Calories: 239 Total Carbs: 7 g.
- Protein: 34 g. Fat: 7 g. Sugar: 4 g.
- Fiber: 0 g.

Slow Cooker Lemon Chicken with Gravy

Preparation time: 10 minutes
Cooking time: 3 Hours
Servings: 4
Ingredients:
- 1 lb. chicken tenderloins
- 3 tbsp. fresh lemon juice
- 3 tbsp. margarine, cubed
- 2 tbsp. fresh parsley, diced
- 2 tbsp. fresh thyme, diced
- 1 tbsp. lemon zest
- 1/4 cup low-sodium chicken broth
- 2 garlic cloves, sliced
- 2 tsp. cornstarch
- 2 tsp. water
- 1/2 tsp. salt
- 1/2 tsp. white pepper

Directions:
1. Add the broth, lemon juice, margarine, zest, garlic, salt, and pepper to the crockpot, stir to combine. Add the chicken, cover, and cook on low heat for 2 1/2 hours.
2. Add the parsley and thyme and cook 30 minutes more, or chicken is cooked through.
3. Remove chicken to a plate and keep warm. Pour cooking liquid into a small saucepan and place over medium heat.
4. Stir water and cornstarch together until smooth. Add to saucepan and bring to a boil. Cook, stirring, 2 minutes or until thickened. Serve with chicken.

Nutrition:
- Calories: 303 Total Carbs: 2 g.
- Protein: 33 g.
- Fat: 17 g. Sugar: 0 g.
- Fiber: 0 g.

Ritzy Beef Stew

Preparation time: 10 minutes
Cooking time: 2 Hours
Servings: 6
Ingredients:

- 2 tbsp. all-purpose flour
- 1 tbsp. Italian seasoning
- 2 lb. (907 g.) beef top round, cut into 3/4-inch cubes
- 2 tbsp. olive oil
- 4 cups low-sodium chicken broth, divided
- 1 1/2 lb. (680 g.) cremini mushrooms, rinsed, stems removed, and quartered
- 1 large onion, coarsely chopped
- 3 garlic cloves, minced
- 3 medium carrots, peeled and cut into 1/2-inch pieces
- 1 cup frozen peas
- 1 tbsp. fresh thyme, minced
- 1 tbsp. red wine vinegar
- 1/2 tsp. freshly ground black pepper

Directions:

1. Combine the flour and Italian seasoning in a large bowl. Dredge the beef cubes in the bowl to coat well.
2. Heat the olive oil in a pot over medium heat until shimmering.
3. Add the beef to the single layer in the pot and cook for 2–4 minutes or until golden brown on all sides. Flip the beef cubes frequently.
4. Remove the beef from the pot and set aside, then add 1/4 cup of chicken broth to the pot.
5. Add the mushrooms and sauté for 4 minutes or until soft. Remove the mushrooms from the pot and set them aside.
6. Pour 1/4 cup of chicken broth in the pot. Add the onions and garlic to the pot and sauté for 4 minutes or until translucent.
7. Put the beef back to the pot and pour in the remaining broth. Bring to a boil.
8. Reduce the heat to low and cover. Simmer for 45 minutes. Stir periodically.
9. Add the carrots, mushroom, peas, and thyme to the pot and simmer for 45 more minutes or until the vegetables are soft.
10. Open the lid, drizzle with red wine vinegar, and season with black pepper. Stir and serve in a large bowl.

Nutrition:

- Calories: 250 Fat: 7 g.
- Protein: 25 g. Carbs: 24 g.
- Fiber: 3 g.
- Sugar: 5 g.
- Sodium: 290 mg.

Pork Trinoza Wrapped in Ham

Preparation time: 10 minutes
Cooking time: 20 minutes
Servings: 6
Ingredients:

- 6 pieces Serrano ham, thinly sliced

- 454 g. pork, halved, with butter and crushed
- 6 g. salt
- 1 g. black pepper
- 227 g. fresh spinach leaves, divided
- 4 slices Mozzarella cheese, divided
- 18 g. sun-dried tomatoes, divided
- 10 ml. olive oil, divided

Directions:
1. Place 3 pieces of ham on baking paper, slightly overlapping each other. Place 1 half of the pork in the ham. Repeat with the other half.
2. Season the inside of the pork rolls with salt and pepper.
3. Place half of the spinach, cheese, and sun-dried tomatoes on top of the pork loin, leaving a 13 mm. border on all sides.
4. Roll the fillet around the filling well and tie it with a kitchen cord to keep it closed.
5. Repeat the process for the other pork steak and place them in the fridge.
6. Select "Preheat" in the air fryer and press "Start/Pause."
7. Brush 5 ml. of olive oil on each wrapped steak and place them in the preheated air fryer.
8. Select "Steak." Set the timer to 9 minutes and press "Start/Pause."
9. Allow it to cool for 10 minutes before cutting.

Nutrition:
- Calories: 282 Fat: 23.41 g.
- Carbs: 0 g. Protein: 16.59 g.
- Sugar: 0 g. Cholesterol: 73 mg.

Mississippi Style Pot Roast

Preparation time: 10 minutes
Cooking time: 8 Hours
Servings: 8
Ingredients:
- 3 lb. chuck roast
- 6–8 *pepperoncini*

- 1 envelope au jus gravy mix
- 1 envelope ranch dressing mix

Directions:
1. Place roast in crockpot. Sprinkle both envelopes of mixes over top. Place the peppers around the roast.
2. Cover and cook on low 8 hours, or high 4 hours.
3. Transfer roast to a large bowl and shred using 2 forks. Add it back to the crockpot and stir. Remove the *pepperoncini*, chop, and stir back into the roast. Serve.

Nutrition:
- Calories: 379 Total Carbs: 3 g.
- Protein: 56 g. Fat: 14 g.
- Sugar: 1 g.
- Fiber: 0 g.

Spicy Grilled Turkey Breast

Preparation time: 10 minutes
Cooking time: 1 Hour 30 minutes
Servings: 14
Ingredients:
- 5 lb. turkey breast, bone-in
- 1 cup low-sodium chicken broth
- 1/4 cup vinegar
- 1/4 cup jalapeno pepper jelly
- 2 tbsp. Splenda® brown sugar
- 2 tbsp. olive oil
- 1 tbsp. salt
- 2 tsp. cinnamon
- 1 tsp. cayenne pepper
- 1/2 tsp. mustard, ground
- Nonstick cooking spray

Directions:

1. Heat grill to medium heat. Spray rack with cooking spray. Place a drip pan on the grill for indirect heat.
2. In a small bowl, combine Splenda® brown sugar with seasonings.
3. Carefully loosen the skin on the turkey from both sides with your fingers. Spread half the spice mix on the turkey. Secure the skin to the underneath with toothpicks and spread the remaining spice mix on the outside.
4. Place the turkey over the drip pan and grill for 30 minutes.
5. In a small saucepan, over medium heat, combine broth, vinegar, jelly, and oil. Cook and stir for 2 minutes until jelly is completely melted. Reserve 1/2 cup of the mixture.
6. Baste turkey with some of the jelly mixtures. Cook 1–1 hour 30 minutes, basting every 15 minutes until done when the thermometer reaches 170°F.
7. Cover and let rest 10 minutes. Discard the skin. Brush with reserved jelly mixture and slice and serve.

Nutrition:

- Calories: 314 Total Carbs: 5 g.
- Protein: 35 g. Fat: 14 g.
- Sugar: 5 g. Fiber: 0 g.

Stuffed Cabbage and Pork Loin Rolls

Preparation time: 10 minutes
Cooking time: 25 minutes
Servings: 4
Ingredients:

- 500 g. white cabbage

- 1 onion
- 8 pork tenderloin steaks
- 2 carrots
- 4 tbsp. soy sauce
- 50 g. olive oil
- 1/2 tsp. Salt
- 8 sheets of rice

Directions:

1. Put the chopped cabbage in the Thermo mix glass together with the onion and the chopped carrot.
2. Select 5 seconds, speed 5. Add the extra virgin olive oil. Select 5 minutes, Varoma® temperature, left turn, spoon speed.
3. Cut the tenderloin steaks into thin strips. Add the meat to the Thermomix glass. Select 5 minutes, Varoma® temperature, left turn, spoon speed. Without beaker
4. Add the soy sauce. Select 5 minutes, Varoma® temperature, left turn, spoon speed. Rectify salt. Let it cold down.
5. Hydrate the rice slices. Extend and distribute the filling between them.
6. Make the rolls, folding so that the edges are completely closed. Place the rolls in the air fryer and paint with the oil.
7. Select 10 minutes, 180°C.

Nutrition:

- Calories: 120
- Fat: 3.41 g.
- Carbs: 0 g.
- Protein: 20.99 g.
- Sugar: 0 g.
- Cholesterol: 65 mg.

Cheesy Chicken and Spinach

Preparation time: 10 minutes
Cooking time: 45 minutes
Servings: 6
Ingredients:

- 3 chicken breasts, boneless, skinless and halved lengthwise
- 6 oz. low-fat cream cheese, soft
- 2 cups baby spinach

- 1 cup mozzarella cheese, grated
- 2 tbsp. olive oil, divided
- 3 cloves garlic, finely diced
- 1 tsp. Italian seasoning
- Nonstick cooking spray

Directions:
1. Heat oven to 350°F. Spray a 9x13-inch glass baking dish with cooking spray.
2. Lay chicken breast cutlets in a baking dish. Drizzle 1 tbsp. oil over the chicken. Sprinkle evenly with garlic and Italian seasoning. Spread cream cheese over the top of the chicken.
3. Heat remaining tbsp. of oil in a small skillet over medium heat. Add spinach and cook until spinach wilts, about 3 minutes. Place evenly over cream cheese layer. Sprinkle mozzarella over top.
4. Bake 35–40 minutes, or until chicken is cooked through. Serve.

Nutrition:
- Calories: 363 Total Carbs: 3 g.
- Protein: 31 g.
- Fat: 25 g.
- Sugar: 0 g.
- Fiber: 0 g.

BBQ Chicken and Noodles

Preparation time: 10 minutes
Cooking time: 25 minutes
Servings: 4
Ingredients:
- 4 slices bacon, diced

- 1 chicken breast, boneless, skinless, cut into 1-inch pieces
- 1 onion, diced
- 1 cup low-fat cheddar cheese, grated
- 1/2 cup skim milk
- 14 1/2 oz. can tomatoes, diced
- 2 cups low-sodium chicken broth
- 1/4 cup barbecue sauce,
- 2 cloves garlic, finely diced
- 1/4 tsp. red pepper flakes
- 200 g Homemade noodles
- Salt and pepper, to taste

Directions:
1. Place a large pot over med-high heat. Add bacon and cook until crispy. Drain fat, reserving 1 tbsp.
2. Stir in chicken and cook until browned on all sides, 3–5 minutes.
3. Add garlic and onion and cook, stirring often, until onions are translucent, 3–4 minutes.
4. Stir in broth, tomatoes, milk, and seasonings. Bring to boil, cover, reduce heat and simmer for 10 minutes.
5. Stir in barbecue sauce, noodles, and cheese and cook until noodles are done and cheese has melted 2–3 minutes. Serve.

Nutrition:
- Calories: 331 Total Carbs: 18 g.
- Net Carbs: 15 g.
- Protein: 34 g.
- Fat: 13 g.
- Sugar: 10 g.
- Fiber: 3 g.

Homemade Flamingos

Preparation time: 10 minutes
Cooking time: 20 minutes
Servings: 4
Ingredients:
- 400 g. very thin pork fillets, sliced
- 2 eggs, boiled and chopped
- 100 g. Serrano ham, chopped

- 1 egg, beaten
- 2 cups Breadcrumbs

Directions:

1. Make a roll with the pork fillets. Introduce half-cooked egg and Serrano ham. So that the roll does not lose its shape, fasten with a string or chopsticks.
2. Pass the rolls through the beaten egg and then through the breadcrumbs until it forms a good layer.
3. Preheat the air fryer for a few minutes at 180°C.
4. Insert the rolls in the basket and set the timer for about 8 minutes at 180°C.

Nutrition:

- Calories: 482 Fat: 23.41 g.
- Carbs: 0 g.
- Protein: 16.59 g.
- Sugar: 0 g.
- Cholesterol: 173 mg.

Pesto Chicken

Preparation time: 10 minutes
Cooking time: 20 minutes
Servings: 6
Ingredients:

- 1 3/4 lbs. chicken breasts, skinless, boneless, and slice
- 1/2 cup mozzarella cheese, shredded
- 1/4 cup pesto

Directions:

1. Add chicken and pesto in a mixing bowl and mix until well coated.
2. Place in refrigerator for 2–3 hours.
3. Grill chicken over medium heat until completely cooked.
4. Sprinkle cheese over the chicken and serve.

Nutrition:

- Calories 303
- Fat: 13 g.
- Carbs: 1 g.
- Protein: 2 g.
- Sugar: 1 g.
- Cholesterol: 122 mg.

Breaded Chicken with Seed Chips

Preparation time: 10 minutes
Cooking time: 40 minutes
Servings: 4
Ingredients:

- 12 chicken breast fillets
- ¼ tsp. Salt
- 2 eggs
- 1 small bag of seed chips
- 2 cups Breadcrumbs
- 2 tbsp. Extra virgin olive oil

Directions:

1. Put salt into chicken fillets.
2. Crush the seed chips and when we have them fine, bind with the breadcrumbs.
3. Beat the 2 eggs.
4. Pass the chicken breast fillets through the beaten egg and then through the seed chips that you have tied with the breadcrumbs.
5. When you have them all breaded, paint with a brush of extra virgin olive oil.
6. Place the fillets in the basket of the air fryer without being piled up.
7. Select 170°F, 20 minutes.
8. Take out and put another batch, repeat temperature and time. So, until you use up all the steaks.

Nutrition:

- Calories: 242 Fat: 13 g.
- Carbs: 13.5 g. Protein: 18 g.
- Sugar: 0 g. Cholesterol: 42 mg.

Turkey Meatballs with Spaghetti Squash

Preparation time: 10 minutes
Cooking time: 35 minutes
Servings: 4
Ingredients:

- 1 lb. lean turkey, ground
- 1 lb. spaghetti squash, halved and seeds removed
- 2 egg whites

- 1/3 cup green onions, finely diced
- 1/4 cup onion, finely diced
- 2 1/2 tbsp. flat-leaf parsley, finely diced
- 1 tbsp. fresh basil, finely diced
- 14 oz. can no-salt-added tomatoes, crushed
- 1/3 cup soft whole-wheat breadcrumbs
- 1/4 cup low-sodium chicken broth
- 1 tsp garlic powder
- 1 tsp thyme
- 1 tsp oregano
- 1/2 tsp red pepper flakes
- 1/2 tsp whole fennel seeds

Directions:
1. In a small bowl, combine breadcrumbs, onion, garlic, parsley, pepper flakes, thyme, and fennel.
2. In a large bowl, combine turkey and egg whites. Add bread crumb mixture and mix well. Cover and chill for 10 minutes. Heat the oven to broil.
3. Place the squash, cut side down, in a glass baking dish. Add 3–4 tbsp. of water and microwave on high 10–12 minutes, or until fork-tender.
4. Make 20 meatballs from the turkey mixture and place them on a baking sheet. Broil 4–5 minutes, turn and cook 4 more minutes.
5. In a large skillet, combine tomatoes and broth and bring to a simmer over low heat. Add meatballs, oregano, basil, and green onions. Cook, stirring occasionally, 10 minutes or until heated through.
6. Use a fork to scrape the squash into "strands" and arrange it on a serving platter. Top with meatballs and sauce and serve.

Nutrition:
- Calories: 253 Total Carbs: 15 g.
- Net Carbs: 13 g.
- Protein: 27 g. Fat: 9 g.
- Sugar: 4 g.
- Fiber 2 g.

Spicy Lettuce Wraps

Preparation time: 10 minutes
Cooking time: 5 minutes
Servings: 6
Ingredients:
- 12 Romaine lettuce leaves
- 1 lb. chicken, ground
- 1/3 cup green onions, thinly sliced
- 2 tsp fresh ginger, grated
- 1/3 cup water chestnuts, finely diced
- 1/3 cup peanuts, chopped
- 2 cloves garlic, finely diced
- 3 tbsp. lite soy sauce
- 1 tbsp. cornstarch
- 1 tbsp. peanut oil
- 1/4 tsp red pepper flakes

Directions:
1. In a large bowl, combine chicken, ginger, garlic, and pepper flakes.
2. In a small bowl, stir together cornstarch and soy sauce until smooth.
3. Heat oil in a large skillet over med-high heat, add chicken, and cook, stirring, 2–3 minutes, or chicken is cooked through.
4. Stir in soy sauce and cook, stirring, until mixture starts to thicken, about 30 seconds.
5. Add water chestnuts, green onions, and peanuts and heat through.
6. Lay lettuce leaves out on a work surface. Divide filling evenly over them and roll up.

7. The filling can also be made ahead of time and reheated as needed. Serve warm with Chinese hot mustard for dipping,

Nutrition:
- Calories: 234
- Total Carbs: 13 g.
- Net Carbs: 12 g.
- Protein: 26 g.
- Fat: 12 g.
- Sugar: 6 g.
- Fiber: 1 g.

Slow Cooker Two-Bean Sloppy Joes

Preparation time: 10 minutes
Cooking time: 6 hours
Servings: 4
Ingredients:
- 1 can (15 oz.) low-sodium black beans
- 1 can (15 oz.) low-sodium pinto beans
- 1 can (15 oz.) no-salt-added diced tomatoes
- 1 medium green bell pepper, cored, seeded, and chopped
- 1 medium yellow onion, chopped
- 1/4 cup low-sodium vegetable broth
- 2 garlic cloves, minced
- 2 servings (1/4 cup) meal prep barbecue sauce or bottled barbecue sauce
- 1/4 tsp. salt
- 1/4 tsp. freshly ground black pepper
- 4 whole-wheat buns

Directions:
1. In a slow cooker, combine the black beans, pinto beans, diced tomatoes, bell pepper, onion, broth, garlic, meal prep barbecue sauce, salt, and black pepper. Stir the ingredients, then cover and cook on "Low" for 6 hours.
2. Into each of 4 containers, spoon 1 1/4 cups of sloppy add Joe mix. Serve with 1 whole-wheat bun.

Storage: Place airtight containers in the refrigerator for up to 1 week. To freeze, place freezer-safe containers in the freezer for up to 2 months. To defrost, refrigerate overnight. To reheat individual portions, microwave uncovered on high for 2–2 1/2 minutes. Alternatively, reheat the entire dish in a saucepan on the stovetop. Bring the sloppy joes to a boil, then reduce the heat and simmer until heated through 10–15 minutes. Serve with a whole-wheat bun.

Nutrition:
- Calories: 392
- Total Fat: 3 g.
- Saturated Fat: 0 g.
- Protein: 17 g.
- Total Carbs: 79 g.
- Fiber: 19 g.
- Sugar: 15 g.
- Sodium: 759 mg.

Lighter Eggplant Parmesan

Preparation time: 15 minutes
Cooking time: 35 minutes
Servings: 4
Ingredients:
- Nonstick cooking spray
- 3 eggs, beaten
- 1 tbsp. parsley, dried
- 2 tsp. oregano, ground
- 1/8 tsp. freshly ground black pepper
- 1 cup panko bread crumbs, preferably whole-wheat
- 1 large (about 2 lb.) eggplant
- 5 servings (2 1/2 cups) chunky tomato sauce or jarred low-sodium tomato sauce
- 1 cup part-skim Mozzarella cheese
- 1/4 cup Parmesan cheese, grated

Directions:
1. Preheat the oven to 450°F. Coat a baking sheet with cooking spray.
2. In a medium bowl, whisk together the eggs, parsley, oregano, and pepper.
3. Pour the panko into a separate medium bowl.
4. Slice the eggplant into 1/4-inch-thick slices. Dip each slice of eggplant into the egg mixture, shaking off the excess. Then

dredge both sides of the eggplant in the panko bread crumbs. Place the coated eggplant on the prepared baking sheet, leaving a 1/2-inch space between each slice.

5. Bake for about 15 minutes until soft and golden brown. Remove from the oven and set aside to slightly cool.

6. Pour 1/2 cup of chunky tomato sauce on the bottom of an 8x15-inch baking dish. Using a spatula or the back of a spoon spread the tomato sauce evenly. Place half the slices of cooked eggplant, slightly overlapping, in the dish, and top with 1 cup of chunky tomato sauce, 1/2 cup of mozzarella, and 2 tbsp. of grated parmesan. Repeat the layer, ending with the cheese.

7. Bake uncovered for 20 minutes until the cheese is bubbling and slightly browned.

8. Remove from the oven and allow cooling for 15 minutes before dividing the eggplant equally into 4 separate containers.

Nutrition:
- Calories: 333
- Total Fat: 14 g.
- Saturated Fat: 6 g.
- Protein: 20 g.
- Total Carbs: 35 g.
- Fiber: 11 g.
- Sugar: 15 g.
- Sodium: 994 mg.

Coconut-Lentil Curry

Preparation time: 15 minutes
Cooking time: 35 minutes
Servings: 4
Ingredients:
- 1 tbsp. olive oil
- 1 medium yellow onion, chopped
- 1 garlic clove, minced
- 1 medium red bell pepper, diced
- 1 can (15 oz.) green or brown lentils, rinsed and drained
- 2 medium sweet potatoes, washed, peeled, and cut into bite-size chunks (about 11/4 lb.)
- 1 can (15 oz.) no-salt-added diced tomatoes
- 2 tbsp. tomato paste
- 4 tsp. curry powder
- 1/8 tsp. cloves, ground
- 1 (15-oz.) can light coconut milk
- 1/4 tsp. salt
- 2 pieces whole-wheat naan bread, halved, or 4 slices crusty bread

Directions:
1. In a large saucepan over medium heat, heat the olive oil. When the oil is shimmering, add both the onion and garlic and cook until the onion softens and the garlic is sweet, for about 3 minutes.

2. Add the bell pepper and continue cooking until it softens, about 5 minutes more. Add the lentils, sweet potatoes, tomatoes, tomato paste, curry powder, and cloves, and bring the mixture to a boil. Reduce the heat to medium-low, cover, and simmer until the potatoes are softened about 20 minutes.

3. Add the coconut milk and salt, and return to a boil. Reduce the heat and simmer until the flavors combine for about 5 minutes.

4. Into each of 4 containers, spoon 2 cups of curry.

5. Enjoy each serving with half of a piece of naan bread or 1 slice of crusty bread.

Nutrition:
- Calories: 559
- Total Fat: 16 g.
- Saturated Fat: 7 g.
- Protein: 16 g.
- Total Carbs: 86 g.
- Fiber: 16 g.
- Sugar: 18 g.
- Sodium: 819 mg.

Stuffed Portobello with Cheese

Preparation time: 15 minutes
Cooking time: 25 minutes
Servings: 4
Ingredients:

- 4 Portobello mushroom caps
- 1 tbsp. olive oil
- 1/2 tsp. salt, divided
- 1/4 tsp. freshly ground black pepper, divided
- 1 cup baby spinach, chopped
- 1 1/2 cups part-skim ricotta cheese
- 1/2 cup part-skim Mozzarella cheese, shredded
- 1/4 cup Parmesan cheese, grated
- 1 garlic clove, minced
- 1 tbsp. parsley, dried
- 2 tsp. oregano, dried
- 4 tsp. unseasoned breadcrumbs, divided
- 4 servings (4 cups) roasted broccoli with shallots

Directions:

1. Preheat the oven to 375°F. Line a baking sheet with aluminum foil.
2. Brush the mushroom caps with olive oil, and sprinkle with 1/4 tsp. salt and 1/8 tsp. pepper. Put the mushroom caps on the prepared baking sheet and bake until soft, about 12 minutes.
3. In a medium bowl, mix the spinach, ricotta, mozzarella, parmesan, garlic, parsley, oregano, and the remaining 1/4 tsp. of salt and 1/8 tsp. of pepper.
4. Spoon 1/2 cup of cheese mixture into each mushroom cap, and sprinkle each with 1 tsp. of breadcrumbs. Return the mushrooms to the oven for an additional 8–10 minutes until warmed through.
5. Remove from the oven and allow the mushrooms to cool for about 10 minutes before placing each in an individual container. Add 1 cup of roasted broccoli with shallots to each container.

Nutrition:

- Calories: 419 Total Fat: 30 g.
- Saturated Fat: 10 g.
- Protein: 23 g.
- Total Carbs: 19 g.
- Fiber: 2 g.
- Sugar: 3 g.
- Sodium: 790 mg.

Lighter Shrimp Scampi

Preparation time: 15 minutes
Cooking time: 15 minutes
Servings: 4
Ingredients:

- 1 1/2 lb. large shrimp, peeled and deveined
- 1/4 tsp. salt
- 1/8 tsp. freshly ground black pepper
- 2 tbsp. olive oil
- 1 shallot, chopped
- 2 garlic cloves, minced
- 1/4 cup cooking white wine
- 1 tbsp. lemon juice
- 1/2 tsp. sriracha
- 2 tbsp. unsalted butter, at room temperature
- 1/4 cup fresh parsley, chopped
- 4 servings (6 cups) zucchini noodles with lemon vinaigrette

Directions:

1. Season the shrimp with salt and pepper.
2. In a medium saucepan over medium heat, heat the oil. Add the shallot and garlic, and cook until the shallot softens and the garlic is fragrant for about 3 minutes. Add the shrimp, cover, and cook until opaque, 2–3 minutes on each side. Using a slotted spoon, transfer the shrimp to a large plate.
3. Add the wine, lemon juice, and sriracha to the saucepan, and stir to combine. Bring the mixture to a boil, then reduce the heat and simmer until the liquid is reduced by about half, 3 minutes. Add the butter and stir until melted, about 3 minutes. Return the shrimp to the saucepan and toss to coat. Add the parsley and stir to combine.
4. Into each of 4 containers, place 1 1/2 cups of zucchini noodles with lemon vinaigrette, and top with 3/4 cup of scampi.

Nutrition:

- Calories: 364 Total Fat: 21 g.
- Saturated Fat: 6 g. Protein: 37 g.
- Total Carbs: 10 g. Fiber: 2 g.
- Sugar: 6 g. Sodium: 557 mg.

Maple-Mustard Salmon

Preparation time: 10 minutes+30 minutes marinating time
Cooking time: 20 minutes
Servings: 4
Ingredients:

- Nonstick cooking spray
- 1/2 cup 100% maple syrup
- 2 tbsp. Dijon mustard
- 1/4 tsp. salt
- 4 (5 oz.) salmon fillets
- 4 servings (4 cups) roasted broccoli with shallots
- 4 servings (2 cups) parsleyed whole-wheat couscous

Directions:

1. Preheat the oven to 400°F. Line a baking sheet with aluminum foil and coat with cooking spray.
2. In a medium bowl, whisk together the maple syrup, mustard, and salt until smooth.
3. Put the salmon fillets into the bowl and toss to coat. Cover and place in the refrigerator to marinate for at least 30 minutes and up to overnight.
4. Shake off excess marinade from the salmon fillets and place them on the prepared baking sheet, leaving a 1-inch space between each fillet. Discard the extra marinade.
5. Bake for about 20 minutes until the salmon is opaque and a thermometer inserted in the thickest part of a fillet reads 145°F. Into each of 4 resealable containers, place 1 salmon fillet, 1 cup of roasted broccoli with shallots, and 1/2 cup of parsleyed whole-wheat couscous.

Nutrition:

- Calories: 601 Total Fat: 29 g.
- Saturated Fat: 4 g. Protein: 36 g.
- Total Carbs: 51 g.Fiber: 3 g.
- Sugar: 23 g.Sodium: 610 mg.

Chicken Salad with Grapes and Pecans

Preparation time: 15 Minutes
Cooking time: 5 Minutes
Servings: 4
Ingredients:

- 1/3 cup unsalted pecans, chopped

- 10 oz. chicken breast or rotisserie chicken, finely chopped, cooked, skinless, and boneless
- 1/2 medium yellow onion, finely chopped
- 1 celery stalk, finely chopped
- 3/4 cup red or green seedless grapes, halved
- 1/4 cup light mayonnaise
- 1/4 cup nonfat plain Greek yogurt
- 1 tbsp. Dijon mustard
- 1 tbsp. parsley, dried
- 1/4 tsp. salt
- 1/8 tsp. freshly ground black pepper
- 1 cup romaine lettuce, shredded
- 4 (8-inch) whole-wheat pitas

Directions:

1. Heat a small skillet over medium-low heat to toast the pecans. Cook the pecans until fragrant, about 3 minutes. Remove from the heat and set aside to cool.
2. In a medium bowl, mix the chicken, onion, celery, pecans, and grapes.
3. In a small bowl, whisk together the mayonnaise, yogurt, mustard, parsley, salt, and pepper. Spoon the sauce over the chicken mixture and stir until well combined. Into each of 4 containers, place 1/4 cup of lettuce and top with 1 cup of chicken salad. Store the pitas separately until ready to serve.
4. When ready to eat, stuff the serving of salad and lettuce into 1 pita.

Nutrition:

- Calories: 418 Total Fat: 14 g.
- Saturated Fat: 2 g. Protein: 31 g.
- Total Carbs: 43 g. Fiber: 6 g.

Lemony Salmon Burgers

Preparation time: 10 Minutes
Cooking time: 10 Minutes
Servings: 4
Ingredients:

- 2 cans (3 oz.) pink salmon, boneless and skinless

- 1/4 cup panko breadcrumbs
- 4 tsp. lemon juice
- 1/4 cup red bell pepper
- 1/4 cup sugar-free yogurt
- 1 egg
- 2 (1 1/2 oz.) whole-wheat hamburger toasted buns

Directions:

1. Mix drained and flaked salmon, finely-chopped bell pepper, panko breadcrumbs.
2. Combine 2 tbsp. cup sugar-free yogurt, 3 tsp. fresh lemon juice, and egg in a bowl. Shape the mixture into 2 (3-inch) patties, bake on the skillet over medium heat 4–5 Minutes per side.
3. Stir together 2 tbsp. sugar-free yogurt and 1 tsp. lemon juice; spread over bottom halves of buns.
4. Top each with 1 patty, and cover with bun tops.
5. This dish is very mouth-watering!

Nutrition:

- Calories: 131
- Protein: 12
- Fat: 1 g
- Carbs: 19 g

Caprese Turkey Burgers

Preparation time: 10 Minutes
Cooking time: 10 Minutes
Servings: 4
Ingredients:

- 1/2 lb. 93% lean turkey, ground
- 2 (1 1/2 oz.) whole-wheat hamburger buns (toasted)
- 1/4 cup part-skim Mozzarella cheese, shredded
- 1 egg
- 1 large tomato
- 1 small garlic clove
- 4 large basil leaves
- 1/8 tsp. salt
- 1/8 tsp. pepper

Directions:

1. Combine turkey, white egg, minced garlic, salt, and pepper (mix until combined).
2. Shape into 2 cutlets. Put cutlets into a skillet; cook 5–7 minutes per side.
3. Top cutlets properly with cheese and sliced tomato at the end of cooking.
4. Put 1 cutlet on the bottom of each bun.
5. Top each patty with 2 basil leaves. Cover with bun tops.
6. My guests enjoy this dish every time they visit my home.

Nutrition:

- Calories: 180 Protein: 7 g.
- Fat: 4 g.
- Carbs: 20 g.

Lemon-Thyme Eggs

Preparation time: 10 Minutes
Cooking time: 5 Minutes
Servings: 4
Ingredients:

- 7 large eggs
- 1/4 cup mayonnaise (reduced-fat)
- 2 tsp. lemon juice
- 1 tsp. Dijon mustard
- 1 tsp. fresh thyme, chopped
- 1/8 tsp. cayenne pepper

Directions:

1. Bring eggs to a boil.
2. Peel and cut each egg in half lengthwise.
3. Remove yolks to a bowl. Add mayonnaise, lemon juice, mustard, thyme, and cayenne to egg yolks; mash to blend. Fill egg white halves with yolk mixture.
4. Chill until ready to serve.
5. Please your family with a delicious meal.

Nutrition:

- Calories: 40
- Protein: 10 g.
- Fat: 6 g.
- Carbs: 2 g.

Chicken with Caprese Salsa

Preparation time: 15 Minutes
Cooking time: 5 Minutes
Servings: 4
Ingredients:

- 3/4 lb. chicken breasts, boneless and skinless
- 2 big tomatoes
- 1/2 (8 oz.) ball fresh Mozzarella cheese
- 1/4 cup red onion
- 2 tbsp. fresh basil
- 1 tbsp. balsamic vinegar
- 2 tbsp. extra virgin olive oil, divided
- 1/2 tsp. salt, divided
- 1/4 tsp. pepper, divided

Directions:

1. Sprinkle cut in half lengthwise chicken with 1/4 tsp. salt and 1/8 tsp. pepper.
2. Heat 1 tbsp. olive oil, cook chicken for 5 Minutes.
3. Meanwhile, mix chopped tomatoes, diced cheese, finely chopped onion, chopped basil, vinegar, 1 tbsp. oil, and 1/4 tsp. salt and 1/8 tsp. pepper.
4. Spoon salsa over the chicken.
5. Chicken with Caprese Salsa is a nutritious, simple, and very tasty dish that can be prepared in a few minutes.

Nutrition:

- Calories: 210 Protein: 28 g.
- Fat: 17 g.
- Carbs: 0,1 g.

Balsamic-Roasted Broccoli

Preparation time: 10 Minutes
Cooking time: 15 Minutes
Servings: 4
Ingredients:

- 1 lb. broccoli
- 1 tbsp. extra virgin olive oil
- 1 tbsp. balsamic vinegar
- 1 garlic clove
- 1/8 tsp. salt
- Pepper to taste

Directions:

1. Preheat the oven to 450°F.
2. Combine broccoli, olive oil, vinegar, minced garlic, salt, and pepper; toss.
3. Spread broccoli on a baking sheet.
4. Bake 12–15 minutes.

Nutrition:

- Calories: 27
- Protein: 3 g.
- Fat: 0, 3 g.
- Carbs: 4 g.

Hearty Beef and Vegetable Soup

Preparation time: 10 Minutes
Cooking time: 30 Minutes
Servings: 4
Ingredients:

- 1/2 lb. lean beef, ground
- 2 cups beef broth
- 1 1/2 tbsp. vegetable oil (divided)
- 1 cup green bell pepper
- 1/2 cup red onion
- 1 cup green cabbage
- 1 cup frozen mixed vegetables
- 1/2 can tomatoes
- 1 1/2 tsp. Worcestershire sauce
- 1 small bay leaf
- 2 tsp. pepper
- 2 tbsp. ketchup

Directions:

1. Cook beef in 1/2 tbsp. hot oil for 2 minutes.
2. Stir in chopped bell pepper and chopped onion; cook for 4 minutes.
3. Add chopped cabbage, mixed vegetables, stewed tomatoes, broth, Worcestershire sauce, bay leaf, and pepper; bring to a boil.
4. Reduce heat to medium; cover, and cook for 15 minutes.
5. Stir in ketchup and 1 tbsp. oil, and remove from heat. Let stand 10 minutes.

Note: The right diet is an excellent diabetes remedy.

Nutrition:

- Calories: 170
- Protein: 17 g.
- Fat: 8 g.
- Carbs: 3 g.

Shrimp with Green Beans

Preparation time: 10 minutes
Cooking time: 2 minutes
Servings: 4
Ingredients:

- 3/4 lb. fresh green beans, trimmed
- 1 lb. medium frozen shrimp, peeled and deveined
- 2 tbsp. fresh lemon juice
- 2 tbsp. olive oil
- Salt and ground black pepper, as required
- 1 cup water

Directions:

1. Arrange a steamer trivet in the Instant Pot and pour a cup of water.
2. Arrange the green beans on top of the trivet in a single layer and top with shrimp.
3. Drizzle with oil and lemon juice.
4. Sprinkle with salt and black pepper.
5. Close the lid and place the pressure valve in the "Seal" position.
6. Press "Steam" and just use the default time of 2 minutes.
7. Press "Cancel" and allow a "Natural" release.
8. Open the lid and serve.

Nutrition:

- Calories: 223 Fat: 1 g.
- Carbs: 7.9 g.Sugar: 1.4 g.
- Protein: 27.4 g.Sodium: 322 mg.

Steamed Salmon

Preparation time: 50 minutes
Cooking time: 40 minutes
Servings: 4
Ingredients:

- 2 (150 g. each) salmon fillets

- 1 lemon, organic
- 200 g. asparagus
- 200 g. sugar snap peas
- 1 small Kohlrabi
- 1 sprig dill
- 4 tbsp. olive oil
- Salt and pepper to taste

Directions:
1. Rinse and blot salmon.
2. Wash the lemon, cut open, squeeze and drizzle on the salmon. Season the fish with salt and pepper.
3. Cut the lemon half into slices and set aside.
4. Peel the asparagus. Wash and clean the sugar snap peas. Peel kohlrabi.
5. Put the vegetables in a steamer. Put the salmon on top. Put 250 ml. water in a saucepan. Put the damper in. Heat the pot until it boils. Reduce temperature. Put the lid on and steam everything for 20–30 minutes.
6. Wash and chop the dill. Heat the oil.
7. Place salmon on a plate. Add the vegetables. Add the oil. Garnish with lemon wedges.

Nutrition:
- Calories: 503
- Carbs: 8 g.
- Protein: 34 g.
- Fat: 37 g.

Marinated Chicken Breast

Preparation time: 20 minutes (plus resting time overnight)
Cooking time: 20 minutes
Servings: 2
Ingredients:
- 500 g. chicken breast
- 2 tbsp. mustard
- 2 tbsp. honey (optional)
- 2 tbsp. oil
- 2 tbsp. soy sauce
- 4 garlic cloves

Directions:
1. Mix mustard, honey, olive oil, and soy sauce in a cup. Add salt and pepper.
2. Peel the garlic, cut into small pieces and add to the marinade.
3. Wash the chicken breast, pat dry with kitchen paper, and then place in a suitable container and cover with the marinade. Cover and chill overnight.
4. Remove the chicken breast from the marinade, dab with kitchen paper, and fry in a non-stick pan for 10 minutes without adding any fat.
5. Serve with seasonal oven vegetables.

Nutrition:
- Calories: 490
- Carbs: 50 g.
- Protein: 35 g.
- Fat: 15 g.

Salmon on Braised Tomatoes

Preparation time: 20 minutes
Cooking time: 20 minutes
Servings: 2
Ingredients:
- 4 salmon fillets
- 600 g. tomatoes
- 2 tbsp. olive oil
- 2 stalks basil
- 1 sprig thyme
- 200 g. rocket
- 2 tbsp. balsamic vinegar
- Salt and pepper to taste

Directions:
1. Rinse salmon, pat dry, and place in a steamer.
2. Fill a saucepan about 4 cm. with water, add salt, insert the insert, and put the lid on. Heat and steam the fish for 10 minutes.
3. Wash scald tomatoes and peel off the skin. Remove the seeds and then quarter the tomatoes. Wash and chop the basil and thyme and place in a pan with hot oil with the tomatoes. Add salt and pepper.

Warm everything up slightly.

4. Wash the rocket, sort, and chop. Put in a cup with olive oil, vinegar, and pepper.
5. Serve the tomatoes on a plate. Put salmon on top. Put the salad next to it and pour the dressing over it.

Nutrition:
- Calories: 410 Carbs: 6 g.
- Protein: 33 g. Fat: 28 g.

Fish with a Crispy Bonnet
Preparation time: 45 minutes
Cooking time: 30 minutes
Servings: 2
Ingredients:
- 2 (150 g. each) salmon fillets
- 1/4 zucchini
- 4 olives
- 3 tomatoes, pickled
- 1 slice crispbread
- 1 tsp. thyme, dried
- 1 tbsp. olive oil
- Salt and pepper to taste

Directions:
1. Preheat the oven to 160°F circulating air.
2. Rinse the fish, pat dry, season with salt and pepper, and place in an ovenproof dish.
3. Peel the zucchini and cut a quarter of it into small cubes.
4. Wash tomatoes. Remove stems and cut into small pieces. Chop the olives too.
5. Crumble crispbread and mix in a small bowl with salt, pepper, thyme, and olive oil. Stir in the vegetables. Mix everything well and then pour onto the fish. Put some olive oil on top.
6. Bake the fillet in the bacon for 20–30 minutes. Serve hot

Nutrition:
- Calories: 386
- Carbs: 15 g.
- Protein: 33 g.
- Fat: 22 g.

Turkey Breast on Vegetables
Preparation time: 15 minutes
Cooking time: 20 minutes
Servings: 2
Ingredients:
- 2 carrots
- 2 leeks
- 2 yellow peppers
- 2 red peppers
- 2 zucchini
- 2 tbsp. white wine vinegar
- 1 tsp. thyme, dried
- 200 g. turkey breast (smoked)
- 1 tbsp. rapeseed oil
- Salt and pepper to taste

Directions:
1. Wash the laugh and peppers. Cut the leek into small rings. Remove the stems and the casing edge from the peppers and then cut them into large pieces. Peel the carrots and zucchini and cut both into small pieces.
2. Put the oil in a pan and heat it. Add the vegetables and brown. Add the thyme and 4 tbsp. water. Simmer for 5–10 minutes and deglaze with the vinegar. Then remove the vegetables from the heat and season with salt and pepper.
3. Cut the turkey breast into 4 small pieces or cut into small pieces and then add to the vegetables. Serve like this.
4. Serve with whole-meal bread or rolls, depending on your taste.

Nutrition:
- Calories: 504
- Carbs: 28 g.
- Protein: 35 g.
- Fat: 24 g.

Spirred Egg with Crabs
Preparation time: 25 minutes
Cooking time: 30 minutes
Servings: 2
Ingredients:
- 80 g. frozen peas

- 100 g. crabs
- 2 spring onions
- 4 eggs
- 50 g. small cucumber
- 2 tbsp. milk
- 2 tsp. rapeseed oil
- 1 tsp. parsley
- Salt and pepper to taste

Directions:
1. Thaw the peas. Rinse the crabs and pat dry.
2. Wash and clean the spring onions and cut them into thin rings. Peel the cucumber cut lengthways. Remove the core casing with a spoon.
3. Beat the eggs, mix with the milk, and season with salt and pepper.
4. Heat the oil in a coated pan. Add the onions and cucumber and sauté everything for 1–2 minutes.
5. Put the egg over the vegetables and let both stand for 4 minutes. Turn the egg over with a spatula and bake again.
6. Put the crabs in the pan and fry them briefly. Serve on a plate and sprinkle with parsley.

Nutrition:
- Calories: 320
- Carbs: 13 g.
- Protein: 27 g.
- Fat: 17 g.

Pasta with Feta and Mince

Preparation time: 30 minutes
Cooking time: 30 minutes
Servings: 2
Ingredients:
- 1 small zucchini
- 10 cherry tomatoes
- 1 garlic clove
- 1 onion
- 1 tbsp. olive oil,
- 1 tbsp. basil
- 150 g. pea noodles

- 100 g. beef, ground
- 50 g. sheep cheese
- 100 ml. broth
- Salt and pepper to taste

Directions:
1. Peel the zucchini and cut it into 4 cm. pieces.
2. Wash the tomatoes. Peel and finely chop the onion and clove of garlic. Wash the basil.
3. Warm-up saltwater. Cook the peas and pasta until both are firm to the bite.
4. Prepare the vegetable stock.
5. Fry the onions and garlic in a pan with a little oil. Add the mince and fry. Always stir once. Add zucchini and fry. Later add the tomatoes and deglaze with the stock. Season with salt and pepper and season to taste.
6. Drain the pasta and add to the pan. Stir in. Crumble the sheep cheese over it. Likewise, the basil.

Nutrition:
- Calories: 491
- Carbs: 38 g.
- Protein: 31 g.
- Fat: 24 g.

Leek Noodles with Ham

Preparation time: 10 minutes
Cooking time: 20 minutes
Servings: 2
Ingredients:
- 300 g. leeks
- 50 g. pork ham
- 70 g. cocktail tomatoes
- 1/2 tbsp. olive oil
- 1 egg
- 50 g. cooking cream
- 1 tbsp. mustard
- 2 chives of garlic
- 300g pasta
- Salt and pepper to taste

Directions:
1. Wash the leek and cut it into 1 cm. strips.

Put on saltwater and add the leek. Blanch for 5 minutes. Then drain, quench and drain.

2. Dice the ham and fry in a pan without adding any fat. Take it out of the pan and put it aside on kitchen paper.

3. Wash the tomatoes and cut them in half. Peel the garlic and cut it into small pieces. Put these in the pan and brown. Add the leek and tomatoes.

4. Mix egg, cream, and mustard. Season with salt and pepper. Mix the mixture with the pasta. Take everything off the stove quickly. Serve and sprinkle with ham.

Nutrition:
- Calories: 290 Carbs: 10 g.
- Protein: 21 g. Fat: 18 g.

Zucchini Roll with Mince

Preparation time: 10 minutes
Cooking time: 20 minutes
Servings: 2
Ingredients:
- 2 zucchinis
- 1 onion
- 1 garlic clove
- 250 g. mixed meat, minced
- 2 tbsp. tomato pulp
- 100 g. sheep cheese
- 1 tsp. fresh rosemary
- Salt and pepper to taste
- 1 tbsp. oil

Directions:
1. Peel the zucchini and cut it into long, thin slices. Blanch with saltwater.
2. Peel and finely chop the onion and clove of garlic.
3. Fry the onions and garlic in a pan with a little oil. Add the mince and fry. Add the tomato paste. Mix well. Take the pan off the stove.
4. Wash the rosemary, shake dry, chop finely and pour over the mince. Season with salt and pepper. Crumble the cheese

and mix in.

5. Apply the minced meat mixture to the zucchini slices, roll up and hold with wooden skewers.

6. Fry the skewers in a pan with hot oil for 5 minutes. Always turn once.

Nutrition:
- Calories: 33 Carbs: 3 g.
- Protein: 18 g.Fat: 28 g.

Turkey Steak with Egg

Preparation time: 15 minutes
Cooking time: 15 minutes
Servings: 2
Ingredients:
- 1/2 scoop Mozzarella cheese
- 2 turkey schnitzel
- 1 tsp. butter
- 1 tbsp. coconut oil
- 4 eggs
- ¼ tsp. Salt
- ½ tsp. Pepper
- Some Paprika powder (noble sweet)

Directions:
1. Heat the oven. Set only 40°F!
2. Cut the Mozzarella cheese into strips.
3. Rinse turkey schnitzel, pat dry with kitchen paper, and dust with a little paprika powder. Heat the coconut oil in a pan. Add the schnitzel and fry for 3 minutes over medium heat. Then take it off the stove.
4. Place turkey escalope in an ovenproof dish. Season with salt and pepper. Place the Mozzarella strips on top and place them in the oven.
5. Put the butter in the pan. Put the eggs in the pan and season with salt and pepper.
6. Serve the turkey breast on a plate. Add 2 eggs each. Serve with a salad if you like.

Nutrition:
- Calories: 509 Carbs: 11 g.
- Protein: 54 g.
- Fat: 28 g.

Carrot Tagliatelle

Preparation time: 15 minutes
Cooking time: 20 minutes
Servings: 2
Ingredients:

- 40 g. frozen peas
- 250 g. carrots
- 100 g. shrimp or prawns
- 10 pine nuts
- 1/2 Sambal Oelek, knifepoint
- 1/2 tsp. rapeseed oil
- 1 tsp. chili sauce
- 1 tsp. pink peppercorns
- 1 cup water
- ½ tsp. salt

Directions:

1. Put on water. Add salt.
2. Thaw the peas. Peel the carrots, cut into thin strips and blanch them in salted water for 3 minutes. Then quench and drain.
3. Wash the prawns and pat dry. Roast the pine nuts in a pan without fat. Remove from heat and set aside.
4. Season the prawns or shrimp with sambal oelek and fry lightly in a pan with rapeseed oil. Add the chili sauce. Add the pine nuts, peas, and peppercorns. Stir well and cook for 4 minutes.

Nutrition:

- Calories: 330
- Carbs: 15 g.
- Protein: 29 g.
- Fat: 17 g.

Brokkoli-Putenschnitzel

Preparation time: 15 minutes
Cooking time: 15 minutes
Servings: 2
Ingredients:

- 180 g. turkey schnitzel
- 500 g. broccoli
- 1 red onion
- 200 g. cocktail tomatoes
- 75 g. Italian cheese, hard
- 2 eggs
- 2 tbsp. cooking cream
- 2 tbsp. olive oil
- Salt and pepper to taste

Directions:

1. Rinse turkey escalope, pat dry with kitchen paper, and season with salt and pepper.
2. Wash broccoli and cut into small florets.
3. Bring saltwater to a boil. Add the broccoli and blanch for 2 minutes, quench and drain.
4. Peel and dice the onion. Wash the tomatoes and cut them in 2.
5. Mix the eggs with cheese and cream in a bowl.
6. Heat the oil, add turkey schnitzel and fry for 3–4 minutes on each side.
7. Put the turkey out and sauté the onion in the pan. After 2 minutes add the broccoli and tomatoes and season with salt and pepper. Serve the vegetables and turkey schnitzel on a plate.

Nutrition:

- Calories: 500
- Carbs: 10 g.
- Protein: 38 g.
- Fat: 33 g.

Salmon with Chicory

Preparation time: 20 minutes
Cooking time: 10 minutes
Servings: 2
Ingredients:

- 1 chicory
- 1 tbsp. sunflower oil
- 200 g. frozen peas
- 50 g. cream
- 200 g. smoked salmon
- 3 parsley stalks
- 1 lemon
- Sea salt and Pepper to taste

Directions:

1. Wash the chicory, remove the stalk, and

then cut lengthways into 2 parts.

2. Heat the oil in a pan and fry the chicory for 5 minutes.
3. Wash parsley, shake dry, and chop finely.
4. Thaw the peas, cook in the boiling salt for 3 minutes, drain and drain. Pour into a blender jar. Add the cream, salt and pepper, and puree.
5. Put the puree on a slice of salmon. Roll up the fish and sprinkle with parsley.
6. Cut the lemon into small slices.
7. Serve the fish with chicory and lemon wedges. If desired, add a little horseradish to the plate.

Nutrition:
- Calories: 407
- Carbs: 15 g.
- Protein: 30 g.
- Fat: 25 g.

Baked Chicken

Preparation time: 45 minutes
Cooking time: 40 minutes
Servings: 2
Ingredients:
- 2 chicken breast fillets
- 225 g. spinach leaves, frozen
- 1 onion
- 1 tsp. rapeseed oil
- 100 g. sheep cheese
- 1 tbsp. ground Nutmeg
- Salt and pepper to taste

Directions:
1. Preheat the oven. Set 220°F and convection.
2. Thaw the spinach.
3. Wash the chicken breast, pat it dry, and season with salt and pepper.
4. Heat the oil in a pan and fry the turkey breast on both sides.
5. Peel the onion, dice it and then brown it in a pan with a little oil. Add the spinach and cook briefly. Season with salt, pepper, and grated nutmeg.
6. Place the chickens in a baking dish. Put

the spinach on top. Crumble the cheese into small pieces and place it on the turkey breast. Bake the chicken in the oven for 25–30 minutes.

Nutrition:
- Calories: 310
- Carbs: 3 g.
- Protein: 43 g.
- Fat: 14 g.

Salmon with Couscous

Preparation time: 20 minutes
Cooking time: 20 minutes
Servings: 2
Ingredients:
- 550 g. cauliflower
- 2 1/2 tsp. lemon juice
- 2 tbsp. olive oil
- 2 tbsp. walnuts, chopped
- 2 salmon fillets
- 1/2 bunch of dill
- Salt and pepper to taste

Directions:
1. Wash the cauliflower, remove the stalk and cut into small pieces. Chop the grain size with a lightning chopper or a food processor.
2. Heat oil in a pan, add cabbage and walnuts, and roast for 15 minutes. Season with salt and pepper. Keep warm in the oven.
3. Wash salmon, dab, and season with salt and pepper. Heat the remaining oil in the pan and add the salmon. Sauté for a short 2–4 minutes then cook over low heat for 3 minutes.
4. Wash the dill, shake it dry, chop it up and then mix it with the cauliflower.
5. Place the salmon on a plate and add the cauliflowers.

Nutrition:
- Calories: 610
- Carbs: 10 g.
- Protein: 42 g. Fat: 44 g.

Pointed Cabbage Pot

Preparation time: 40 minutes
Cooking time: 20 minutes
Servings: 2
Ingredients:

- 300 g. potatoes
- 240 g. carrots
- 400 g. cabbage, pointed
- 1 small onion
- 2 tsp. oil
- 500 ml. vegetable broth
- 20 g. sour cream
- 2 bunches of chives
- 3 strips of bacon

Directions:

1. Prepare the vegetable stock. Peel the potatoes and cut them into small cubes. Peel the carrots and dice them too. Clean the cabbage, remove the leaves and stalk and cut into small pieces. Peel and cut the onion.
2. Drain the bacon in a little oil. Fry the onion in it. Add the potatoes and carrots and roast them. Deglaze with the vegetable stock. Season with salt and pepper. Let the vegetable mixture simmer. Add the cabbage. Put on the lid and let everything cook for 15 minutes.
3. Wash and chop the chives and add to the vegetables. Add sour cream. Taste everything well.

Nutrition:

- Calories: 390
- Carbs: 35 g.
- Protein: 11 g.
- Fat: 22 g.

Egg and Ham Cocktail

Preparation time: 25 minutes
Cooking time: 20 minutes
Servings: 2
Ingredients:

- 200 g. tomatoes
- 4 eggs
- 2 tsp. mustard
- 2 (50 g. each) pickles
- 4 slices salmon ham
- 50 g. sour cream
- 150 g. whole milk yogurt
- 100 g. lettuce
- 1 whole-meal bread roll
- Salt and pepper to taste

Directions:

1. Wash the tomatoes. Remove stems. Hard boil the eggs for 10 minutes, quench, peel, and then cut into small slices.
2. Cut the salmon ham into small pieces. In a small bowl, mix the sour cream, about 4 tbsp. pickle water, yogurt, and mustard. Season with salt and pepper.
3. Wash the lettuce, shake it dry and cut into small pieces. Remove the stalk. Put the lettuce in a bowl. Add eggs and salmon ham. Chop the pickles and add to the salad. Also, add the tomatoes and the salad dressing. Mix everything well. Serve on a small plate.

Nutrition:

- Calories: 480
- Carbs: 33 g.
- Protein: 33 g.
- Fat: 22 g.

Crunchy Chicken Fingers

Preparation time: 10 minutes
Cooking time: 4 minutes
Servings: 2
Ingredients:

- 2 chicken breasts, medium-sized, cut in stripes
- 3 tbsp. Parmesan cheese
- 1/4 tbsp. fresh chives, chopped
- 1/3 cup breadcrumbs
- 1 egg white
- 2 tbsp. plum sauce, optional
- 1/2 tbsp. fresh thyme, chopped
- 1/2 tbsp. black pepper
- 1 tbsp. water

Directions:

1. Preheat the Air Fryer to 360°F. Mix the chives, Parmesan cheese, thyme, pepper, and breadcrumbs. In another bowl, whisk the egg white and mix it with the water. Dip the chicken strips into the egg mixture and the breadcrumb mixture. Place the strips in the air fryer basket and cook for 10 minutes. Serve with plum sauce.

Nutrition:

- Calories: 253
- Carbs: 31 g.
- Fat: 18 g.
- Protein: 28 g.

Polynesian Chicken

Preparation time: 10 minutes
Cooking time: 4 hours
Servings: 6 cups
Ingredients:

- 3 garlic cloves, minced
- 2 bell peppers, cut into 1/2-inch strips
- 1 can (20 oz.) pineapple chunks in juice, drained, with juice reserved
- 1 1/2 lb. chicken breasts, boneless, cut into 2-inch cubes
- 1/3 cup honey (optional)
- 2 tbsp. tapioca flour
- 3 tbsp. soy sauce low-sodium
- 1 tsp. ginger, ground

Directions:

1. Add reserved pineapple juice, 3 tbsp. soy sauce, 1/3 cup honey, 1 tsp. ground ginger and 3 minced cloves of garlic into a bowl; whisk well. Then add 2 tbsp. tapioca flour and whisk again until combined.
2. Add the chicken along with chunks of pineapple into a slow cooker.
3. Pour the mixture of pineapple juice over the chicken and cover the cooker.
4. Cook for 4–5 hours on "Low" until chicken is completely cooked through.
5. Then add strips of bell pepper in the last hour of cooking. Serve and enjoy!

Nutrition:

- Calories: 273
- Fat: 26 g.
- Total carbs: 37 g.
- Protein: 26 g.

Buffalo Chicken

Preparation time: 10 minutes
Cooking time: 30 minutes
Servings: 8
Ingredients:

- 2 celery stalks, diced
- 1 onion, medium-sized, chopped
- 100 ml. buffalo wing sauce
- 100 ml. chicken broth
- 21 kg. chicken breasts, frozen

Directions:

1. Add the celery, onions, buffalo wing sauce, chicken broth, and chicken to the Instant Pot. Cook frozen chicken on "High pressure" for 20 minutes. Turn the pressure valve to "Vent" to release all of the pressure.
2. Remove the chicken breasts from the pot, and shred them.
3. You can remove most of the liquid from the pot, or not.

Nutrition:

- Calories: 197
- Fat: 8 g.
- Carbs: 16 g.
- Protein: 14 g.

Chicken and Peanut Stir-fry

Preparation time: 10 minutes
Cooking time: 15 minutes
Servings: 4
Ingredients:

- 3 tbsp. lime juice
- 1/2 tsp. lime zest
- 4 garlic cloves, minced
- 2 tsp. chili bean sauce
- 1 tbsp. fish sauce
- 1 tbsp. water

- 2 tbsp. peanut butter
- 3 tsp. oil, divided
- 1 lb. chicken breast, sliced into strips
- 1 red sweet pepper, sliced into strips
- 3 green onions, sliced thinly
- 2 cups broccoli, shredded
- 2 tbsp. peanuts, chopped

Directions:
1. In a bowl, mix the lime juice, lime zest, garlic, chili bean sauce, fish sauce, water, and peanut butter.
2. Mix well.
3. In a pan over medium-high heat, add 2 tsp. oil.
4. Cook the chicken until golden on both sides.
5. Pour in the remaining oil.
6. Add the pepper and green onions.
7. Add the chicken, broccoli, and sauce.
8. Cook for 2 minutes.
9. Top with peanuts before serving.

Nutrition:
- Calories: 368 Total Fat: 11 g.
- Saturated Fat: 2 g.
- Cholesterol: 66 mg.
- Sodium: 556 mg.
- Total Carbs: 34 g.
- Dietary Fiber: 3 g.
- Total Sugars: 4 g.
- Protein: 32 g.
- Potassium: 482 mg.

Meatballs Curry
Preparation time: 10 minutes
Cooking time: 25 minutes
Servings: 6
Ingredients:
For Meatballs:
- 1 lb. lean chicken, ground
- 1 tbsp. onion paste
- 1 tsp. fresh ginger paste
- 1 tsp. garlic paste
- 1 green chili, chopped finely
- 1 tbsp. fresh cilantro leaves, chopped

- 1 tsp. coriander, ground
- 1/2 tsp. cumin seeds
- 1/2 tsp. red chili powder
- 1/2 tsp. turmeric, ground
- 1/8 tsp. salt

For Curry:
- 3 tbsp. olive oil
- 1/2 tsp. cumin seeds
- 1 (1-inch) cinnamon stick
- 2 onions, chopped
- 1 tsp. fresh ginger, minced
- 1 tsp. garlic, minced
- 4 tomatoes, chopped finely
- 2 tsp. coriander, ground
- 1 tsp. garam masala powder
- 1/2 tsp. nutmeg, ground
- 1/2 tsp. red chili powder
- 1/2 tsp. turmeric, ground
- Salt, as required
- 1 cup filtered water
- 3 tbsp. fresh cilantro, chopped

Directions:
1. For meatballs: in a large bowl, add all ingredients and mix until well combined.
2. Make small equal-sized meatballs from the mixture.
3. In a large deep skillet, heat the oil over medium heat and cook the meatballs for 3–5 minutes or until browned from all sides.
4. Transfer the meatballs into a bowl.
5. In the same skillet, add the cumin seeds and cinnamon stick and sauté for 1 minute.
6. Add the onions and sauté for 4–5 minutes.
7. Add the ginger and garlic and sauté for 1 minute.
8. Add the tomato and spices and cook, crushing with the back of a spoon for 2–3 minutes.
9. Add the water and meatballs and bring to a boil.
10. Now, reduce the heat to low and simmer for 10 minutes.

11. Serve hot with the garnishing of cilantro.

Nutrition:

- Calories: 196
- Total Fat: 11.4 g.
- Saturated Fat: 2.4 g.
- Cholesterol: 53 mg.
- Total Carbs 7.9 g.
- Sugar 3.9 g.
- Fiber: 2.1 g.
- Sodium: 143 mg.
- Potassium: 279 mg.
- Protein: 16.7 g.

Jerk Style Chicken Wings

Preparation time: 10 minutes
Cooking time: 25 minutes
Servings: 2–3
Ingredients:

- 1 g. thyme, ground
- 1 g. rosemary, dried
- 2 g. allspice
- 4 g. ginger, ground
- 3 g. garlic powder
- 2 g. onion powder
- 1 g. cinnamon
- 2 g. paprika
- 2 g. chili powder
- 1 g. nutmeg
- Salt to taste
- 30 ml. vegetable oil
- 0.5–1 kg. chicken wings
- 1 lime, juiced

Directions:

1. On the air fryer select "Preheat," set the temperature to 200°C, and press "Start/Pause."
2. Combine all spices and oil in a bowl to create a marinade.
3. Mix the chicken wings in the marinade until they are well covered.
4. Place the chicken wings in the preheated air fryer.
5. Select Chicken and press "Start/Pause." Be sure to shake the baskets in the middle of cooking.
6. Remove the wings and place them on a serving plate.
7. Squeeze fresh lemon juice over the wings and serve.

Nutrition:

- Calories: 240
- Fats: 15 g.
- Carbs: 5 g.
- Protein: 19 g.
- Sugars: 4 g.
- Cholesterol: 60 mg.

Italian Chicken

Preparation time: 10 minutes
Cooking time: 16 minutes
Servings: 4
Ingredients:

- 5 chicken thighs
- 1 tbsp. olive oil
- 1/4 cup Parmesan cheese, grated
- 1/2 cup sun-dried tomatoes
- 2 garlic cloves, minced
- 1 tbsp. thyme, chopped.
- 1/2 cup heavy cream
- 3/4 cup chicken stock
- 1 tsp. red pepper flakes, crushed
- 2 tbsp. basil, chopped
- Salt and black pepper to the taste

Directions:

1. Season chicken with salt and pepper, rub with half of the oil, place in your preheated air fryer at 350°F, and cook for 4 minutes.
2. Meanwhile; heat a pan with the rest of the oil over medium-high heat, add thyme, garlic, pepper flakes, sun-dried tomatoes, heavy cream, stock, Parmesan cheese, salt, and pepper; stir, bring to a simmer, take off the heat and transfer to a dish that fits your air fryer.
3. Add chicken thighs on top, introduce in your air fryer and cook at 320°F, for 12 minutes.

4. Divide among plates and serve with basil sprinkled on top.

Nutrition:
- Calories: 272
- Fat: 9 g.
- Fiber: 12 g.
- Carbs: 37 g.
- Protein: 23 g.

Coconut Chicken

Preparation time: 10 minutes
Cooking time: 4 hours
Servings: 6
Ingredients:
- 2 garlic cloves, minced
- Fresh cilantro, minced
- 1/2 cup light coconut milk
- 6 tbsp. sweetened coconut, shredded and toasted
- 2 tbsp. brown sugar
- 6 (about 1 1/2 lb.) chicken thighs, boneless, skinless
- 2 tbsp. reduced-sodium soy sauce
- 1/8 tsp. cloves, ground

Directions:
1. Mix brown sugar, 1/2 cup light coconut milk, 2 tbsp. soy sauce, 1/8 tsp. ground cloves and 2 minced cloves of garlic in a bowl.
2. Add 6 chicken boneless thighs into a Crockpot.
3. Now pour the mixture of coconut milk over the chicken thighs. Cover the cooker and cook for 4–5 hours on low.
4. Serve coconut chicken with cilantro and coconut; enjoy!

Nutrition:
- Calories: 201
- Fat: 10 g.
- Total carbs: 6 g.
- Protein: 21 g.

Spicy Lime Chicken

Preparation time: 10 minutes
Cooking time: 3 hours
Servings: 6
Ingredients:
- 3 tbsp. lime juice
- Fresh cilantro leaves
- 1 1/2 lb. (about 4) chicken breast halves, boneless, skinless
- 1 tsp. lime zest, grated
- 2 cups chicken broth
- 1 tbsp. chili powder

Directions:
1. Add chicken breast halves into a slow cooker.
2. Add 1 tbsp. chili powder, 3 tbsp. lime juice and 2 cups chicken broth in a small bowl; mix well and pour over the chicken.
3. Cover the cooker and cook for 3 hours on low. Once done, take the chicken out from the cooker and let it cool.
4. Once cooled, shred chicken by using forks and transfer back to the Crockpot.
5. Stir in 1 tsp. grated lime zest. Serve spicy lime chicken with cilantro and enjoy!

Nutrition:
- Calories: 132
- Fat: 3 g.
- Total carbs: 2 g.
- Protein: 23 g.

Crock-Pot Slow Cooker Ranch Chicken

Preparation time: 10 minutes
Cooking time: 4 hours
Servings: 4
Ingredients:
- 1 cup chive
- 1 cup onion cream cheese spread
- 1/2 tsp. freshly ground black pepper
- 4 chicken breasts, boneless
- 1 package (1-oz.) ranch dressing and seasoning mix
- 1/2 cup chicken stock, low-sodium

Directions:

1. Spray the Crock-pot slow cooker with cooking spray and preheat it.
2. Dry chicken with a paper towel and transfer it to the Crock-Pot slow cooker.
3. Cook each side, until the chicken is browned, for 4–5 minutes.
4. Add 1/2 cup low-sodium chicken stock, 1 package (1-oz.) ranch dressing and seasoning mix, 1 cup chive and onion cream cheese spread, and 1/2 tsp. freshly ground black pepper. Cover the Crock-Pot slow cooker and cook for 4 hours on "Low" or until the internal temperature reaches 165°F. Once cooked, take it out from the Crock-pot slow cooker.
5. Whisk the sauce present in the Crock-pot slow cooker until smooth. If you need thick sauce, then cook for 5–10 minutes, with frequent stirring.
6. Garnish chicken with sliced onions and bacon and serve.

Nutrition:

- Calories: 362
- Fat: 18.5 g.
- Total carbs: 9.7 g.
- Protein: 37.3 g.

Mustard Chicken with Basil

Preparation time: 10 minutes
Cooking time: 30 minutes
Servings: 4
Ingredients:

- 1 tsp. chicken stock
- 2 chicken breasts, skinless, boneless, halved
- 1 tbsp. basil, chopped
- Salt and black pepper
- 1 tbsp. olive oil
- 1/2 tsp. garlic powder
- 1/2 tsp. onion powder
- 1 tsp. Dijon mustard

Directions:

1. Press "Sauté" on the instant pot and add the oil. When it is hot, brown the chicken in it for 2–3 minutes.
2. Mix in the remaining ingredients and seal the lid to cook for 12 minutes at "High Pressure."
3. Natural release the pressure for 10 minutes, share into plates, and serve.

Nutrition:

- Calories: 34 g.
- Fat: 3.6 g.
- Carbs 0.7 g.
- Protein 0.3 g.
- Fiber: 0.1 g.

Chicken Chili

Preparation time: 10 minutes
Cooking time: 40 minutes
Servings: 6
Ingredients:

- 4 cups low-sodium chicken broth, divided
- 3 cups black beans, boiled, divided
- 1 tbsp. extra-virgin olive oil
- 1 large onion, chopped
- 1 jalapeño pepper, seeded and chopped
- 4 garlic cloves, minced
- 1 tsp. thyme, dried and crushed
- 11/2 tbsp. coriander, ground
- 1 tbsp. cumin, ground
- 1/2 tbsp. red chili powder
- 4 cups cooked chicken, shredded
- 1 tbsp. fresh lime juice
- 1/4 cup fresh cilantro, chopped

Directions:

1. In a food processor, add 1 cup of broth and 1 1/2 cup of black beans and pulse until smooth.
2. Transfer the beans puree into a bowl and set aside.
3. In a large pan, heat the oil over medium heat and sauté the onion and jalapeño for 4–5 minutes.
4. Add the garlic, spices, and sea salt and sauté for 1 minute.
5. Add the beans puree and remaining broth and bring to a boil.

6. Now, reduce the heat to low and simmer for 20 minutes.
7. Stir in the remaining beans, chicken, and lime juice and bring to a boil.
8. Now, reduce the heat to low and simmer for 5–10 minutes.
9. Serve hot with the garnishing of cilantro.

Nutrition:
- Calories: 356
- Total Fat: 7.1 g.
- Saturated Fat: 1.2 g.
- Cholesterol: 72 mg.
- Total Carbs 33 g.
- Sugar 2.7 g.
- Fiber: 11.6 g.
- Sodium: 130 mg.
- Potassium: 662 mg.
- Protein: 39.6 g.

Chicken with Cashew Nuts

Preparation time: 10 minutes
Cooking time: 30 minutes
Servings: 4
Ingredients:
- 1 lb. chicken cubes
- 2 tbsp. soy sauce
- 1 tbsp. corn flour
- 2 1/2 onion cubes
- 1 carrot, chopped
- 1/3 cup cashew nuts, fried
- 1 pepper, cut
- 2 tbsp. garlic, crushed
- 1/2 tbsp. salt
- 1/2 tbsp. white pepper

Directions:
1. Marinate the chicken cubes with 1/2 tbsp. white pepper, 1/2 tsp. salt, 2 tbsp. soya sauce, and add 1 tbsp. corn flour.
2. Set aside for 25 minutes. Preheat the air fryer to 380°F and transfer the marinated chicken. Add the garlic, the onion, the pepper, and the carrot; fry for 5–6 minutes. Roll it in the cashew nuts before serving.

Nutrition:
- Calories: 425
- Carbs: 25 g.
- Fat: 35 g.
- Protein: 53 g.

Grilled Tuna Steaks

Preparation time: 10 minutes
Cooking time: 10 minutes
Servings: 6
Ingredients:
- 6 (6 oz.) tuna steaks
- 3 tbsp. fresh basil, diced
- 4 1/2 tsp. olive oil
- 3/4 tsp. salt
- 1/4 tsp. pepper
- Nonstick cooking spray

Directions:
1. Heat grill to medium heat. Spray rack with cooking spray.
2. Drizzle both sides of the tuna with oil. Sprinkle with basil, salt, and pepper.
3. Place on grill and cook 5 minutes per side, tuna should be slightly pink in the center. Serve.

Nutrition:
- Calories: 343
- Total Carbs 0 g.
- Protein: 51 g.
- Fat: 14 g.
- Sugar 0 g.
- Fiber: 0 g.

Delicious Fish Tacos

Preparation time: 10 minutes
Cooking time: 8 minutes
Servings: 8
Ingredients:
- 4 tilapia fillets
- 1/4 cup fresh cilantro, chopped
- 1/4 cup fresh lime juice
- 2 tbsp. paprika
- 1 tbsp. olive oil

- Pepper
- Salt

Directions:

1. Pour 2 cups of water into the instant pot then place the steamer rack in the pot.
2. Place fish fillets on parchment paper.
3. Season fish fillets with paprika, pepper, and salt and drizzle with oil and lime juice.
4. Fold parchment paper around the fish fillets and place them on a steamer rack in the pot.
5. Seal pot with lid and cook on high for 8 minutes.
6. Once done, release pressure using quickly release. Remove lid.
7. Remove the fish packet from the pot and open it.
8. Shred the fish with a fork and serve.

Nutrition:

- Calories: 67
- Fat: 2.5 g.
- Carbs: 1.1 g.
- Sugar 0.2 g.
- Protein: 10.8 g.
- Cholesterol: 28 mg.

Shrimp Coconut Curry

Preparation time: 10 minutes
Cooking time: 20 minutes
Servings: 2
Ingredients:

- 1/2 lb. shrimp, cooked
- 1 onion, thinly sliced
- 1 cup coconut yogurt
- 3 tbsp. curry paste
- 1 tbsp. oil or ghee

Directions:

1. Set the Instant Pot to "Sauté" and add the onion, oil, and curry paste.
2. When the onion is soft, add the remaining ingredients and seal.
3. Cook on "Stew" for 20 minutes.
4. Release the pressure naturally.

Nutrition:

- Calories: 380 Carbs 13 g.
- Sugar 4 g.
- Fat: 22 g.
- Protein: 40 g.
- Glycemic Load: 14

Swordfish with Tomato Salsa

Preparation time: 10 minutes
Cooking time: 12 minutes
Servings: 4
Ingredients:

- 1 cup tomato, chopped
- 1/4 cup *tomatillo*, chopped
- 2 tbsp. fresh cilantro, chopped
- 1/4 cup avocado, chopped
- 1 garlic clove, minced
- 1 jalapeño pepper, chopped
- 1 tbsp. lime juice
- Salt and pepper to taste
- 4 swordfish steaks
- 1 garlic clove, sliced in half
- 2 tbsp. lemon juice
- 1/2 tsp. ground cumin

Directions:

1. Preheat your grill.
2. In a bowl, mix the tomato, tomatillo, cilantro, avocado, garlic, jalapeño, lime juice, salt, and pepper.
3. Cover the bowl with foil and put it in the refrigerator.
4. Rub each swordfish steak with sliced garlic.
5. Drizzle lemon juice on both sides.
6. Season with salt, pepper, and cumin.
7. Grill for 12 minutes or until the fish is fully cooked.
8. Serve with salsa.

Nutrition:

- Calories: 125 g. Fat: 27.2 g.
- Carbs: 13.6 g. Protein: 7 g.
- Cholesterol: 31 mg.

Shrimp Boil

Preparation time: 10 minutes
Cooking time: 15 minutes
Servings: 4
Ingredients:

- 8 oz. raw shrimp, unpeeled
- 8 oz. chicken sausage, small 1-inch pieces
- 8 oz. baby potatoes
- 1 leek, sliced
- 2 corns, cut into half
- 3 tbsp. lemon juice
- 10 cups water
- 1/4 cup Old Bay seasoning
- Melted butter (optional)
- 1 Lemon wedge

Directions:

1. Bring together the lemon juice, Old Bay seasoning, and water in your pot. Boil.
2. Include potatoes and cook for 5–7 minutes.
3. Add the sausage, shrimp, leek, and corn. Cook while stirring for another 5 minutes. The vegetables should be tender and the shrimp must be pink.
4. Now divide the vegetables, sausage, and shrimp with a spoon and tongs among the serving bowls.
5. Drizzle the cooking liquid equally.
6. Serve with lemon wedge and butter (optional).

Nutrition:

- Calories: 202 Carbs: 22 g.
- Fiber: 2 g.
- Sugar 0 g.
- Cholesterol: 109 mg.
- Total Fat: 5 g.
- Protein: 19 g.

Red Clam Sauce and Pasta

Preparation time: 10 minutes
Cooking time: 3 hours
Servings: 4
Ingredients:

- 1 onion, diced
- 1/4 cup fresh parsley, diced
- 2 cans (6 1/2 oz.) clams, chopped, undrained
- 14 (1/2 oz.) tomatoes, diced, undrained
- 6 oz. tomato paste
- 2 garlic cloves, diced
- 1 bay leaf
- 1 tbsp. sunflower oil
- 1 tsp. Splenda®
- 1 tsp. basil
- 1/2 tsp. thyme
- 1/2 homemade pasta, cooked, drain

Directions:

1. Heat oil in a small skillet over med-high heat. Add onion and cook until tender, add garlic and cook 1 minute more. Transfer to crockpot.
2. Add remaining ingredients, except pasta, cover, and cook on low 3–4 hours.
3. Discard bay leaf and serve over cooked pasta.

Nutrition:

- Calories: 223
- Total Carbs 32 g.
- Net Carbs 27 g.
- Protein: 12 g.
- Fat: 6 g.
- Sugar 15 g.
- Fiber: 5 g.

Air Fried Chicken Thighs

Preparation time: 10 minutes
Cooking time: 12 minutes
Servings: 2
Ingredients:

- 2 chicken thighs, boneless
- Salt and pepper to taste
- 1 tsp. rosemary, dried
- 1 tbsp. Worcestershire sauce
- 1 tbsp. oyster sauce
- 1 tsp. liquid stevia
- 2 garlic cloves, minced

Directions:

1. Add ingredients to a bowl and combine

well. Place the marinated chicken in the fridge for 1 hour.

2. Preheat your air fryer to 180°F for 3 minutes. Add marinated chicken to air fryer grill pan and cook for 12 minutes. Serve hot!

Nutrition:
- Calories: 270
- Total Fat: 17 g
- Carbs: 7 g.
- Protein: 20 g.

Chicken Cheese Fillet
Preparation time: 10 minutes
Cooking time: 15 minutes
Servings: 4
Ingredients:
- 2 chicken fillets, large
- 4 Gouda cheese slices
- 4 ham slices
- Salt and pepper to taste
- 1 tbsp. chives, chopped

Directions:
1. Preheat your air fryer to 180°F.
2. Cut chicken fillet into 4 pieces. Make a slit horizontally to the edge. Open the fillet and season with salt and pepper.
3. Cover each piece with chives and a cheese slice. Close fillet and wrap in a ham slice. Place wrap chicken fillet the into air fryer basket and cook for 15 minutes. Serve hot!

Nutrition:
- Calories: 386
- Total Fat: 21 g.
- Carbs: 14.3 g.
- Protein: 30 g

Pineapple Pizza
Preparation time: 10 minutes
Cooking time: 10 minutes
Servings: 3
Ingredients:
- 1 large whole-wheat tortilla

- 1/4 cup tomato pizza sauce
- 1/4 cup pineapple tidbits
- 1/4 cup Mozzarella cheese, grated
- 1/4 cup ham slice

Directions:
1. Preheat your air fryer to 300°F.
2. Place the tortilla on a baking sheet then spread pizza sauce over the tortilla. Arrange ham slice, cheese, pineapple over the tortilla. Place the pizza in the air fryer basket and cook for 10 minutes. Serve hot.

Nutrition:
- Calories: 80
- Total Fat: 2 g.
- Carbs: 12 g.
- Protein: 4 g.

Air Fryer Tortilla Pizza
Preparation time: 10 minutes
Cooking time: 7 minutes
Servings: 6
Ingredients:
- 1 large whole-wheat tortilla
- 1 tbsp. black olives
- Salt and pepper to taste
- 4 tbsp. tomato sauce
- 8 pepperoni slices
- 3 tbsp. sweet corn
- 1 medium tomato, chopped
- 1/2 cup Mozzarella cheese, grated

Directions:
1. Preheat your air fryer to 325°F.
2. Spread tomato sauce over tortilla. Add pepperoni slices, olives, corn, tomato, and cheese on top of the tortilla. Season with salt and pepper.
3. Place pizza in the air fryer basket and cook for 7 minutes. Serve and enjoy!

Nutrition:
- Calories: 110
- Total Fat: 5 g.
- Carbs: 10 g.
- Protein: 4 g.

Air Fried Pork Apple Balls

Preparation time: 10 minutes
Cooking time: 15 minutes
Servings: 8
Ingredients:

- 2 cups pork, minced
- 6 basil leaves, chopped
- 2 tbsp. cheddar cheese, grated
- 4 garlic cloves, minced
- 1/2 cup apple, peeled, cored, chopped
- 1 white onion, large, diced
- Salt and pepper to taste
- 2 tsp. Dijon Mustard
- 1 tsp. liquid Stevia

Directions:

1. Add the minced pork to a bowl then add diced onion and apple into a bowl and mix well.
2. Add the stevia, mustard, garlic, cheese, basil, salt, and pepper, and combine well. Make small round balls from the mixture and place them into the air fryer basket.
3. Cook at 350°F for 15 minutes. Serve and enjoy!

Nutrition:

- Calories: 64 kcal
- Total Fat: 2.05 g.
- Carbs: 2.23 g.
- Protein: 8.85 g

Stuffed Garlic Chicken

Preparation time: 10 minutes
Cooking time: 15 minutes
Servings: 2
Ingredients:

- 1/4 cup tomatoes, sliced
- 1/2 tbsp. garlic, minced
- 2 basil leaves
- Salsa for serving
- 1 Prosciutto slice
- 2 tsp. Parmesan cheese, freshly grated
- 2 chicken breasts, boneless
- Pepper and salt to taste

Directions:

1. Cut the side of the chicken breast to make a pocket. Stuff each pocket with tomato slices, garlic, grated cheese, and basil leaves. Cut a slice of prosciutto in half to form 2 equal size pieces.
2. Season chicken with salt and pepper and wrap each with a slice of prosciutto.
3. Preheat your air fryer to 325°F. Place the stuffed chicken breasts into the air fryer basket and cook for 15 minutes.
4. Serve chicken breasts with salsa.

Nutrition:

- Calories: 140 Kcal
- Protein: 18.81 g.
- Fat: 5.42 g.
- Carbs: 4.84 g.

Rosemary Citrus Chicken

Preparation time: 10 minutes
Cooking time: 15 minutes
Servings: 2
Ingredients:

- 1 lb. chicken thighs
- 1/2 tsp. fresh rosemary, chopped
- 1/8 tsp. thyme, dried
- 1/2 cup tangerine juice
- 2 tbsp. white wine
- 1 tsp. garlic, minced
- Salt and pepper to taste
- 2 tbsp. lemon juice

Directions:

1. Place the chicken thighs in a mixing bowl. In another bowl, mix tangerine juice, garlic, white wine, lemon juice, rosemary, pepper, salt, and thyme.
2. Pour the mixture over chicken thighs and place it in the fridge for 20 minutes.
3. Preheat your air fryer to 350°F, place your marinated chicken in the air fryer basket, and cook for 15 minutes. Serve hot and enjoy!

Nutrition:

- Calories: 473
- Total Fat: 17 g.
- Carbs: 7 g.
- Protein: 66 g.

Air Fried Garlic Popcorn Chicken

Preparation time: 10 minutes
Cooking time: 15 minutes
Servings: 6
Ingredients:

- 1 lb. chicken breasts, skinless, boneless, cut into bite-size chunks
- 1/4 tsp. garlic powder
- Salt and pepper to taste
- 1/4 tsp. paprika
- 1/4 cup buttermilk
- 1 tbsp. olive oil
- 1/2 cup flour, gluten-free
- 2 cups corn flakes
- 2 tbsp. Parmesan cheese, grated

Directions:

1. Preheat your air fryer to 350°F.
2. In a bowl, mix garlic, chicken, pepper, and salt. Add cornflakes, Parmesan cheese, pepper, paprika, and salt into the food processor and process mix until it forms a crumble.
3. In a shallow dish add flour. In another bowl add the crumbled cornflake mixture. Add chicken pieces to the flour and coat well. Drizzle buttermilk over the coated chicken pieces and mix well. Coat chicken pieces with cornflakes mixture.
4. Add coated chicken pieces onto a baking sheet and place them in the air fryer basket. Drizzle the olive oil over popcorn chicken.
5. Bake in the preheated air fryer for 15 minutes. Serve warm!

Nutrition:

- Calories: 235 Total Fat: 8 g.
- Carbs: 14 g. Protein: 23 g.

Macaroni Cheese Toast

Preparation time: 10 minutes
Cooking time: 5 minutes
Servings: 2
Ingredients:

- 1 egg, beaten

- 4 tbsp. Cheddar cheese, grated
- Salt and pepper to taste
- 1/2 cup macaroni and cheese
- 4 slices bread

Directions:

1. Spread the cheese and macaroni and cheese over the 2 bread slices.
2. Place the other bread slices on top of the cheese and cut diagonally.
3. In a bowl, beat egg and season with salt and pepper. Brush the egg mixture onto the bread.
4. Place the bread into the air fryer and cook at 300°F for 5 minutes.

Nutrition:

- Calories: 250
- Total Fat: 16 g.
- Carbs: 9 g.
- Protein: 14 g.

Cheese Burger Patties

Preparation time: 10 minutes
Cooking time: 15 minutes
Servings: 6
Ingredients:

- 1 lb. beef, ground
- 6 Cheddar cheese slices
- Pepper and salt to taste

Directions:

1. Preheat your air fryer to 390°F.
2. Season beef with salt and pepper. Make 6 round-shaped patties from the mixture and place them into the air fryer basket. Air fry the patties for 10 minutes.
3. Open the air fryer basket and place cheese slices on top of patties and place them into the air fryer with an additional cook time of 1 minute.

Nutrition:

- Calories: 253
- Total Fat: 14 g.
- Carbs: 0.4 g.
- Protein: 29 g.

Grilled Cheese Corn

Preparation time: 10 minutes
Cooking time: 15 minutes
Servings: 2
Ingredients:

- 2 whole corn on the cob, peel husks and discard silk
- 1 tsp. olive oil
- 2 tsp. paprika
- 1/2 cup feta cheese, grated

Directions:

1. Rub the olive oil over corn then sprinkle with paprika and rub all over the corn.
2. Preheat your air fryer to 300°F. Place the seasoned corn on the grill for 15 minutes.
3. Place corn on a serving dish then sprinkles with grated cheese over corn. Serve and enjoy!

Nutrition:

- Calories: 150
- Total Fat: 10 g.
- Carbs: 7 g.
- Protein: 7 g.

Air Fried Pita Bread Pizza

Preparation time: 10 minutes
Cooking time: 6 minutes
Servings: 3
Ingredients:

- 1 large pita bread
- 1 tsp. olive oil
- 7 pepperoni slices
- 1/4 cup sausage
- 1/2 tsp. garlic, minced
- 1 tbsp. pizza sauce
- 1/4 cup Mozzarella cheese, shredded
- 1 small onion, finely diced

Directions:

1. Spread the pizza sauce over the pita bread evenly.
2. Arrange pepperoni, onion, and sausage over pita bread. Sprinkle the top with garlic and cheese. Drizzle the pizza with

olive oil then place in the air basket.
3. Place on top of the trivet and air fry at 350°F for 6 minutes. Serve and enjoy!

Nutrition:

- Calories: 88 Kcal.
- Protein: 5.31 g.
- Fat: 3.73 g.
- Carbs: 8.32 g.

Eggplant Fries

Preparation time: 5 minutes
Cooking time: 15 minutes
Servings: 2–4
Ingredients:

- 2 large eggs
- 1/2 cup Parmesan cheese, grated
- 1/2 cup wheat germ, toasted
- 1 tsp. Italian seasoning
- 3/4 tsp. garlic salt
- 1 (about 1 1/4 lb.) medium eggplant
- Cooking spray
- 1 cup meatless pasta sauce, warmed

Directions:

1. Preheat air fryer to 400°F, in a shallow bowl, whisk eggs. In another shallow bowl, mix cheese, wheat germ, and seasonings.
2. Cut eggplant lengthwise into 1/2-inch thick slices. Dip eggplant in eggs, then coat with cheese mixture.
3. Spritz eggplant and the air fryer basket with cooking spray. Working in batches if needed, place eggplant in a single layer in the air fryer basket.
4. Cook until golden brown, for 10 minutes. Turn eggplant; spritz with additional cooking spray.
5. Continue cooking until golden brown, for 5 minutes. Serve immediately with pasta dipping sauce.

Nutrition:

- Calories: 242 Kcal
- Protein: 11.87 g.
- Fat: 9.13 g.
- Carbs: 30.04 g.

Raspberry Balsamic Smoked Pork Chops

Preparation time: 15 minutes
Cooking time: 15 minutes
Servings: 4–6
Ingredients:

- 2 eggs, large
- 1/4 cup milk
- 1 cup panko (Japanese bread crumbs)
- 1 cup pecans, finely chopped
- 4 pork chops, smoked bone-in (7 1/2 oz. each)
- 1/4 cup all-purpose flour
- 1/3 cup balsamic vinegar
- 2 tbsp. brown sugar
- 2 tbsp. raspberry jam, seedless
- 1 tbsp. orange juice concentrate, thawed frozen
- cooking spray

Directions:

1. Preheat air fryer to 400°F and spritz the air fryer basket with cooking spray. In a shallow bowl, whisk together eggs and milk.
2. In another shallow bowl, toss bread crumbs with pecans. Coat pork chops with flour and shakes off excess.
3. Dip in egg mixture, then in crumb mixture, patting to help adhere. Working in batches as needed, place chops in a single layer in the air fryer basket.
4. Spritz with cooking spray. Cook until golden brown, for 15 minutes, turning halfway through cooking and spritzing with additional cooking spray.
5. Remove and keep warm. Repeat with remaining chops. Meanwhile, place the remaining ingredients in a small saucepan; bring to a boil.
6. Cook and stir until slightly thickened, for 8 minutes. Serve with chops.

Nutrition:

- Calories: 222 Kcal
- Protein: 9.48 g. Fat: 14.75 g.
- Carbs: 13.78 g.

Pickles

Preparation time: 20 minutes
Cooking time: 15 minutes
Servings: 8–12
Ingredients:

- 32 dill pickle slices
- 1/2 cup all-purpose flour
- 1/2 tsp. salt
- 3 large eggs, lightly beaten
- 2 tbsp. dill pickle juice
- 1/2 tsp. cayenne pepper
- 1/2 tsp. garlic powder
- 2 cups panko (Japanese bread crumbs)
- 2 tbsp. fresh dill, snipped
- Cooking spray
- Ranch salad dressing, optional

Directions:

1. Preheat air fryer to 425°F and let pickles stand on a paper towel until liquid is almost absorbed, for 15 minutes.
2. Meanwhile, in a shallow bowl, combine flour and salt. In another shallow bowl, whisk eggs, pickle juice, cayenne, and garlic powder.
3. Combine panko and dill in a third shallow bowl. Dip pickles in flour mixture to coat both sides, shake off excess.
4. Dip in egg mixture, then in crumb mixture, patting to help coating adhere. Spritz pickles and the air fryer basket with cooking spray.
5. Working in batches if needed, place pickles in a single layer in the basket and cook until golden brown and crispy, for 10 minutes.
6. Turn pickles; spritz with additional cooking spray. Continue cooking until golden brown and crispy, for 10 minutes.
7. Serve immediately. If desired, serve with ranch dressing.

Nutrition:

- Calories: 57 Kcal Protein: 2.14 g.
- Fat: 1.67 g. Carbs: 8.75 g.

Garlic-Rosemary Brussels Sprouts

Preparation time: 5 minutes
Cooking time: 30 minutes
Servings: 2–4
Ingredients:

- 3 tbsp. olive oil - 2 garlic cloves, minced
- 1/2 tsp. salt
- 1/4 tsp. pepper
- 1 lb. Brussels sprouts, trimmed and halved
- 1/2 cup panko (Japanese bread crumbs)
- 1 1/2 tsp. fresh rosemary, minced

Directions:

1. Preheat the air fryer to 350°F and place the first 4 ingredients in a small microwave-safe bowl; microwave on high for 30 seconds.
2. Toss Brussels sprouts with 2 tbsp. oil mixture. Place all the Brussels sprouts in the fryer basket and cook for 5 minutes.
3. Stir sprouts. Continue to air-fry until sprouts are lightly browned and near desired tenderness, for 8 minutes longer, stirring halfway through cooking time.
4. Toss bread crumbs with rosemary and remaining oil mixture; sprinkle over sprouts.
5. Continue cooking until crumbs are browned and sprouts are tender, for 5 minutes. Serve immediately and Enjoy!

Nutrition:

- Calories: 154 Kcal Protein: 4.38 g.
- Fat: 10.64 g. Carbs: 13.13 g.

Air-Fried Asparagus

Preparation time: 5 minutes
Cooking time: 10 minutes
Servings: 2–4
Ingredients:

- 1/2 bunch of asparagus, with bottom 2 inches trimmed off
- Avocado or olive oil in an oil mister or sprayer
- Himalayan salt
- Black pepper

Directions:

1. Place trimmed asparagus spears in the air-fryer basket.
2. Spritz spears lightly with oil, and then sprinkle with salt and a tiny bit of black pepper.
3. Place basket inside air-fryer and bake at 400°F for 10 minutes. Serve immediately and Enjoy!

Nutrition:

- Calories: 154 Kcal
- Protein: 4.38 g.
- Fat: 10.64 g.
- Carbs: 13.13 g.

Roasted Asian Broccoli

Preparation time: 10 minutes
Cooking time: 20 minutes
Servings: 2–4
Ingredients:

- 1 lb. broccoli, cut into florets
- 1 1/2 tbsp. peanut oil
- 1 tbsp. garlic, minced
- Sea salt
- 2 tbsp. soy sauce, reduced-sodium
- 2 tsp. honey (or agave)
- 2 tsp. sriracha
- 1 tsp. rice vinegar
- 1/3 cup salted peanuts, roasted
- Fresh lime juice (optional)

Directions:

1. In a large bowl, toss the broccoli, peanut oil, garlic, and season with sea salt. Make sure the oil covers all the broccoli florets.
2. Spread the broccoli into the basket of

your air fryer, in a single layer, trying to leave a little bit of space between each floret.

3. Cook at 400°F until golden brown and crispy, for 15–20 minutes, stirring halfway.

4. While the broccoli and peanuts cook, mix the honey, soy sauce, sriracha, and rice vinegar in a small, microwave-safe bowl.

5. Once mixed, microwave the mixture for 10–15 seconds until the honey is melted and evenly incorporated.

6. Transfer the cooked broccoli to a bowl and add in the soy sauce mixture. Toss to coat and season to taste with a pinch more salt, if needed.

7. Stir in the peanuts and squeeze lime on top. Serve immediately and Enjoy!

Nutrition:
- Calories: 138 Kcal
- Protein: 6.43 g. Fat: 8.94 g.
- Carbs: 11.33 g.

Shrimp and Artichoke Skillet

Preparation time: 10 minutes
Cooking time: 10 minutes
Servings: 4
Ingredients:

- 1 1/2 cups shrimp, peel, devein
- 2 shallots, diced
- 1 tbsp. margarine
- 2 jars (12 oz.) artichoke hearts, drain, rinse
- 2 cups white wine
- 2 garlic cloves, finely diced

Directions:

1. Melt margarine in a large skillet over med-high heat. Add shallot and garlic and cook until they start to brown, stirring frequently.

2. Add artichokes and cook for 5 minutes. Reduce heat and add wine. Cook 3 minutes, stirring occasionally.

3. Add the shrimp and cook just until they turn pink. Serve.

Nutrition:
- Calories: 487
- Total Carbs 26 g.
- Net Carbs 17 g.
- Protein: 64 g.
- Fat: 5 g.
- Sugar 3 g.
- Fiber: 9 g.

Lemony Salmon

Preparation time: 5 minutes
Cooking time: 3 minutes
Servings: 3
Ingredients:

- 1 lb. salmon fillet, cut into 3 pieces
- 3 tsp. fresh dill, chopped
- 5 tbsp. fresh lemon juice, divided
- Salt and black pepper, as required

Directions:

1. Arrange a steamer trivet in Instant Pot and pour 1/4 cup of lemon juice.

2. Season the salmon with salt and black pepper evenly.

3. Place the salmon pieces on top of the trivet, skin side down, and drizzle with remaining lemon juice.

4. Now, sprinkle the salmon pieces with dill evenly.

5. Close the lid and place the pressure valve in the "Seal" position.

6. Press "Steam" and use the default time of 3 minutes.

7. Press "Cancel" and allow a "Natural" release.

8. Open the lid and serve hot.

Nutrition:
- Calories: 20
- Fats: 9.6 g.
- Carbs: 1.1 g.
- Sugar: 0.5 g.
- Protein: 29.7 g.
- Sodium: 74 mg.

Crab Curry

Preparation time: 10 minutes
Cooking time: 20 minutes
Servings: 2
Ingredients:

- 1/2 lb. crab, chopped
- 1 red onion, thinly sliced
- 1/2 cup tomato, chopped
- 3 tbsp. curry paste
- 1 tbsp. oil or ghee

Directions:

1. Set the Instant Pot to "Sauté" and add the onion, oil, and curry paste.
2. When the onion is soft, add the remaining ingredients and seal.
3. Cook on "Stew" for 20 minutes.
4. Release the pressure naturally.

Nutrition:

- Calories: 2
- Carbs: 11 g.
- Sugar: 4 g.
- Fat: 10 g.
- Protein: 24 g.
- Glycemic Load: 9

Citrus Salmon

Preparation time: 10 minutes
Cooking time: 7 minutes
Servings: 4
Ingredients:

- 4 (4 oz.) salmon fillets
- 1 cup low-sodium chicken broth
- 1 tsp. fresh ginger, minced
- 2 tsp. fresh orange zest, finely grated
- 3 tbsp. fresh orange juice
- 1 tbsp. olive oil
- Ground black pepper, as required

Directions:

1. In Instant Pot, add all ingredients and mix.
2. Close the lid and place the pressure valve in the "Seal" position.
3. Press "Manual" and cook under "High Pressure" for 7 minutes.

4. Press "Cancel" and allow a "Natural" release.
5. Open the lid and serve the salmon fillets with the topping of cooking sauce.

Nutrition:

- Calories: 190
- Fats: 10.5 g.
- Carbs: 1.8 g.
- Sugar: 1 g.
- Protein: 22 g.
- Sodium: 68 mg.

Herbed Salmon

Preparation time: 10 minutes
Cooking time: 3 minutes
Servings: 4
Ingredients:

- 4 (4 oz.) salmon fillets
- 1/4 cup olive oil
- 2 tbsp. fresh lemon juice
- 1 garlic clove, minced
- 1/4 tsp. oregano, dried
- Salt and ground black pepper, as required
- 4 sprigs fresh rosemary
- 4 slices lemon
- 1 ½ cups water

Directions:

1. For the dressing: in a large bowl, add oil, lemon juice, garlic, oregano, salt, and black pepper, and beat until well co combined.
2. Arrange a steamer trivet in the Instant Pot and pour 1 1/2 cups of water into Instant Pot.
3. Place the salmon fillets on top of the trivet in a single layer and top with

dressing.

4. Arrange 1 rosemary sprig and 1 lemon slice over each fillet.
5. Close the lid and place the pressure valve to the "Seal" position.
6. Press "Steam" and just use the default time of 3 minutes.
7. Press "Cancel" and carefully allow a "Quick" release.
8. Open the lid and serve hot.

Nutrition:
- Calories: 262
- Fats: 17 g.
- Carbs: 0.7 g.
- Sugar: 0.2 g.
- Protein: 22.1 g.
- Sodium: 91 mg.

Salmon in Green Sauce

Preparation time: 10 minutes
Cooking time: 12 minutes
Servings: 4
Ingredients:
- 4 (6 oz.) salmon fillets
- 1 avocado, peeled, pitted, chopped
- 1/2 cup fresh basil, chopped
- 3 garlic cloves, chopped
- 1 tbsp. fresh lemon zest, finely grated
- ½ cup water

Directions:
1. Grease a large piece of foil.
2. In a large bowl, add all ingredients except salmon and water, and with a fork, mash completely.

3. Place fillets in the center of foil and top with the avocado mixture evenly.
4. Fold the foil around fillets to seal them.
5. Arrange a steamer trivet in the Instant Pot and pour 1/2 cup of water.
6. Place the foil packet on top of the trivet.
7. Close the lid and place the pressure valve to the "Seal" position.
8. Press "Manual" and cook under "High Pressure" for minutes.
9. Meanwhile, preheat the oven to the broiler.
10. Press "Cancel" and allow a "Natural" release.
11. Open the lid and transfer the salmon fillets onto a broiler pan.
12. Broil for 3–4 minutes.
13. Serve warm.

Nutrition:
- Calories: 333
- Fats: 20.3 g.
- Carbs: 5.5 g.
- Sugar: 0.4 g.
- Protein: 34.2 g.
- Sodium: 79 mg.

Braised Shrimp

Preparation time: 5 minutes
Cooking time: 4 minutes
Servings: 4
Ingredients:
- 1 lb. large shrimp, frozen, peeled, deveined
- 2 shallots, chopped
- 3/4 cup chicken broth, low-sodium
- 2 tbsp. fresh lemon juice
- 2 tbsp. olive oil
- 1 tbsp. garlic, crushed
- Ground black pepper, as required

Directions:
1. In the Instant Pot, place oil and press "Sauté." Now add the shallots and cook for 2
2. minutes.
3. Add the garlic and cook for 1 minute.

4. Press "Cancel" and stir in the shrimp, broth, lemon juice, and black pepper.
5. Close the lid and place the pressure valve to the "Seal" position.
6. Press "Manual" and cook under "High Pressure" for 1 minute.
7. Press "Cancel" and carefully allow a "Quick" release.
8. Open the lid and serve hot.

Nutrition:
- Calories: 209
- Fats: 9 g.
- Carbs: 4.3 g.
- Sugar: 0.2 g.
- Protein: 26.6 g.
- Sodium: 293 mg.

Trout Bake

Preparation time: 10 minutes
Cooking time: 35 minutes
Servings: 2
Ingredients:
- 1 lb. trout fillets, boneless
- 1 lb. winter vegetables, chopped
- 1 cup fish broth, low-sodium
- 1 tbsp. mixed herbs
- Sea salt as desired

Directions:
1. Mix all the ingredients except the broth in a foil pouch.
2. Place the pouch in the steamer basket of your Instant Pot.
3. Pour the broth into the Instant Pot.
4. Cook on Steam for 35 minutes.
5. Release the pressure naturally.

Nutrition:
- Calories: 310
- Carbs: 14 g.
- Sugar: 2 g.
- Fat: 12 g.
- Protein: 40 g.
- Glycemic Load: 5

Sardine Curry

Preparation time: 5 minutes
Cooking time: 35 minutes
Servings: 2
Ingredients:
- 5 tins sardines in tomato
- 1 lb. vegetables, chopped
- 1 cup fish broth, low-sodium
- 3 tbsp. curry paste

Directions:
1. Mix all the ingredients in your Instant Pot.
2. Cook on "Stew" for 35 minutes.
3. Release the pressure naturally.

Nutrition:
- Calories: 320
- Carbs: 8 g.
- Sugar: 2 g.
- Fat: 16 g.
- Glycemic Load: 3

Swordfish Steak

Preparation time: 5 minutes
Cooking time: 35 minutes
Servings: 2
Ingredients:
- 1 lb. swordfish steak, whole
- 1 lb. Mediterranean vegetables, chopped
- 1 cup fish broth, low-sodium
- 2 tbsp. soy sauce

Directions:
1. Mix all the ingredients except the broth in a foil pouch.
2. Place the pouch in the steamer basket for your Instant Pot.
3. Pour the broth into the Instant Pot.

Lower the steamer basket into the Instant Pot.

4. Cook on "Steam" for 35 minutes.
5. Release the pressure naturally.

Nutrition:

- Calories: 270
- Carbs: 5 g.
- Sugar: 1 g.
- Fat: 10 g.
- Protein: 48 g.
- Glycemic Load: 1

Lemon Sole

Preparation time: 5 minutes
Cooking time: 5 minutes
Servings: 2
Ingredients:

- 1 lb. sole fillets, boned and skinned
- 1 cup low-sodium fish broth
- 2 sweet onions, shredded
- 1/2 lemon juice
- 2 tbsp. cilantro, dried

Directions:

1. Mix all the ingredients in your Instant Pot.
2. Cook on "Stew" for 5 minutes.
3. Release the pressure naturally.

Nutrition:

- Calories: 230
- Sugar: 1 g.
- Fat: 6 g.
- Protein: 46 g.
- Glycemic Load: 1

Tuna Sweetcorn Casserole

Preparation time: 5 minutes
Cooking time: 35 minutes
Servings: 2
Ingredients:

- 3 small tins of tuna
- 1/2 lb. sweetcorn kernels
- 1 lb. vegetables, chopped
- 1 cup low-sodium vegetable broth
- 2 tbsp. spicy seasoning

Directions:

1. Mix all the ingredients in your Instant Pot.
2. Cook on "Stew" for 35 minutes.
3. Release the pressure naturally.

Nutrition:

- Calories: 300
- Carbs: 6 g.
- Sugar: 1 g.
- Fat: 9 g.
- Glycemic Load: 2

Chili Shrimp

Preparation time: 5 minutes
Cooking time: 35 minutes
Servings: 2
Ingredients:

- 1 1/2 lb. shrimp, cooked
- 1 lb. stir fry vegetables
- 1 cup ready-mixed fish sauce
- 2 tbsp. chili flakes

Directions:

1. Mix all the ingredients in your Instant Pot.
2. Cook on "Stew" for 35 minutes.

3. Release the pressure naturally.

Nutrition:

- Calories: 270 Carbs: 6 g.
- Sugar: Fat: 8 g.
- Protein: 51 g.
- Glycemic Load: 2

Lemon Pepper Salmon

Preparation time: 10 minutes
Cooking time: 10 minutes
Servings: 4
Ingredients:

- 3 tbsps. ghee or avocado oil
- 1 lb. skin-on salmon filet
- 1 red bell pepper, julienned
- 1 green zucchini, julienned
- 1 carrot, julienned
- 3/4 cup water
- A few sprigs of parsley, tarragon, dill, basil, or a combination
- 1/2 lemon, sliced
- 1/2 tsp. black pepper
- 1/4 tsp. sea salt

Directions:

1. Add the water and the herbs into the bottom of the Instant Pot and put in a wire steamer rack making sure the handles extend upwards.
2. Place the salmon filet onto the wire rack, with the skin side facing down.
3. Drizzle the salmon with ghee, season with black pepper and salt, and top with the lemon slices.
4. Close and seal the Instant Pot, making sure the vent is turned to "Sealing."
5. Select the "Steam" setting and cook for 3 minutes.
6. While the salmon cooks, julienne the vegetables and set them aside.
7. Once done, quickly release the pressure, and then press the "Keep Warm/Cancel" button.
8. Uncover and wearing oven mitts, carefully remove the steamer rack with the salmon.

9. Remove the herbs and discard them.
10. Add the vegetables to the pot and put the lid back on.
11. Select the "Sauté" function and cook for 1–2 minutes.
12. Serve the vegetables with salmon and add the remaining fat to the pot.
13. Pour a little of the sauce over the fish and vegetables if desired.

Nutrition:

- Calories: 296,
- Carbs 8 g.
- Fat: 15 g.
- Protein: 31 g.
- Potassium: (K) 1084 mg.
- Sodium: (Na) 284 mg.

Mussels and Spaghetti Squash

Preparation time: 10 minutes
Cooking time: 35 minutes
Servings: 2
Ingredients:

- 1 lb. shelled mussels, cooked,
- 1/2 a spaghetti squash, to fit the Instant Pot
- 1 cup fish broth, low-sodium
- 3 tbsp. garlic, crushed
- Sea salt to taste

Directions:

1. Mix the mussels with garlic and salt. Place the mussels inside the squash.
2. Lower the squash into your Instant Pot.
3. Pour the broth around it, cook on "Stew" for minutes.
4. Release the pressure naturally.
5. Shred the squash, mixing the "spaghetti" with the mussels.

Nutrition:

- Calories: 2
- Carbs 7 g.
- Fat: 9 g.
- Protein: 24 g.
- Potassium: (K) 124.8 mg.
- Sodium: (Na) 462.6 mg.

Cod in White Sauce

Preparation time: 10 minutes
Cooking time: 5 minutes
Servings: 2
Ingredients:

- 1 lb. cod fillets
- 1 lb. swede and carrots, chopped
- 2 cups white sauce
- 1 cup peas
- 3 tbsp. black pepper

Directions:

1. Mix all the ingredients in your Instant Pot.
2. Cook on "Stew" for 5 minutes.
3. Release the pressure naturally.

Nutrition:

- Calories: 390
- Carbs: 10 g.
- Sugar: 2 g.
- Fat: 26 g.
- Glycemic Load: 5

Lemon Pepper and Dill Salmon

Preparation time: 5 minutes
Cooking time: 5 minutes
Servings: 4
Ingredients:

- 2 tbsp. butter
- 1 lb. salmon filet
- 1 lemon, sliced
- 3 sprigs thyme
- 1 sprig fresh dill
- 1 tsp. dill, chopped
- 1 lemon juice
- 1 lemon zest
- 1 tsp. sea salt
- 1/4 tsp. black pepper
- 1 cup water

Directions:

1. Add the butter, lemon zest, lemon juice, dill, salt, and pepper to a small mixing bowl. Mix well to form a compound butter.
2. Cut salmon into portion sizes, and place

dollops of the compound butter all around the salmon portions.

3. Pour 1 cup of water into the Instant Pot, along with some thyme and/or dill.
4. Place half of the salmon onto a standard trivet and insert this into the pot.
5. Season with more pepper, and then top the fish with 2 thin slices of lemon.
6. Place the second half of the fish onto a 3-inch trivet and insert it into the pot. Season with more black pepper, and then top the salmon again with 2 thin slices of lemon.
7. Close and lock the lid, cooking on "Manual, High Pressure" for 3 minutes.
8. Once done, quickly release the pressure.
9. Uncover, and serve immediately.

Nutrition:

- Calories: 224
- Carbs 3 g.
- Fat: 13 g.
- Protein: 22 g.
- Potassium: (K) 602 mg.
- Sodium: (Na) 581 mg.

Shrimp with Tomatoes and Feta

Preparation time: 10 minutes
Cooking time: 12 minutes
Servings: 6
Ingredients:

- 2 tbsp. butter
- 1 lb. shrimp, frozen
- 1 tbsp. garlic
- 1 1/2 cups white onion, chopped
- 14.5 oz. tomatoes, crushed
- 1 tsp. oregano, dried
- 1 tsp. sea salt
- 1/2 tsp. red pepper flakes, or to taste

To Serve:

- 1 cup feta cheese, crumbled
- 1/2 cup black olives, sliced
- 1/4 cup fresh parsley

Directions:

1. Select the "Sauté" function on your Instant Pot and once hot, add the butter.

2. Melt the butter and then add the garlic and red pepper flakes.
3. Next, add in the onions, tomatoes, salt, and oregano.
4. Add the frozen shrimp.
5. Set the Instant pot on "Manual," "High Pressure" setting for 1 minute.
6. Once done, release all the pressure and stir well to combine all the ingredients.
7. Allow to cool and then sprinkle with feta cheese, black olives, and parsley.
8. Serve with buttered French bread or rice.

Nutrition:
- Calories: 211
- Carbs 6 g.
- Fat: 11 g.
- Protein: 1 g.
- Potassium: (K) 148 mg.
- Sodium: (Na) 1468 mg.

Salmon with Sweet and Spicy Sauce

Preparation time: 5 minutes
Cooking time: 5 minutes
Servings: 4
Ingredients:
- 4 (5 oz.) salmon fillets
- 2 jalapeño peppers, seeded and chopped finely
- 2 tbsp. fresh parsley, chopped
- 2 tbsp. Yacon syrup
- 2 tbsp. hot water
- 3 garlic cloves, minced
- 3 tbsp. fresh lime juice
- 2 tbsp. olive oil
- 1 tsp. cumin, ground
- 1 tsp. paprika
- Salt and ground black pepper, as required

Directions:
1. Season the salmon fillets with salt and black pepper evenly.
2. Arrange a steamer trivet in the Instant Pot and pour 1 cup of water.
3. Place the salmon fillets on top of the trivet.
4. Close the lid and place the pressure valve to the "Seal" position.
5. Press "Steam" and just use the default time of minutes.
6. Press "Cancel" and carefully allow a "Quick" release.
7. Meanwhile, for the sauce: in a bowl, add the remaining ingredients and mix until well combined.
8. Open the lid and transfer the salmon fillets onto a serving plate.
9. Drizzle with sauce and serve.

Nutrition:
- Calories: 272
- Fats: 16.1 g.
- Carbs: 5 g.
- Sugar: 2.1 g.
- Protein: 28 g.
- Sodium: 252 mg.

Grilled Herbed Salmon with Raspberry Sauce and Cucumber Dill Dip

Preparation time: 10 minutes
Cooking time: 30 minutes
Servings: 4
Ingredients:
- 3 salmon fillets
- 1 tbsp. olive oil
- Salt and pepper to taste
- 1 tsp. fresh sage, chopped
- 1 tbsp. fresh parsley, chopped
- 2 tbsp. apple juice
- 1 cup raspberries
- 1 tsp. Worcestershire sauce
- 1 cup cucumber, chopped
- 2 tbsp. light mayonnaise
- 1/2 tsp. dill, dried

Directions:
1. Coat the salmon fillets with oil.
2. Season with salt, pepper, sage, and parsley.
3. Cover the salmon with foil.

4. Grill for 20 minutes or until the fish is flaky.
5. While waiting, mix the apple juice, raspberries, and Worcestershire sauce.
6. Pour the mixture into a saucepan over medium heat.
7. Bring to a boil and then simmer for 8 minutes.
8. In another bowl, mix the rest of the ingredients.
9. Serve salmon with raspberry sauce and cucumber dip.

Nutrition:

- Calories: 256
- Total Fat: 15 g.
- Saturated Fat: 3 g.
- Cholesterol: 68 mg.
- Sodium: 176 mg.
- Total Carbs: 6 g.
- Dietary Fiber: 1 g.
- Total Sugars: 5 g.
- Protein: 23 g.
- Potassium: 359 mg.

CHAPTER 9:

Dinner Recipes

Mustard-Crusted Sole

Preparation time: 5 minutes
Cooking time: 8–11 minutes
Servings: 4
Ingredients:

- 5 tsp. low-sodium yellow mustard
- 1 tbsp. lemon juice
- 4 (3 1/2 oz./99 g.) sole fillets
- 1/2 tsp. thyme, dried
- 1/2 tsp. marjoram, dried
- 1/8 tsp. freshly ground black pepper
- 1 slice low-sodium whole-wheat bread, crumbled
- 2 tsp. olive oil

Directions:

1. In a small bowl, mix the mustard and lemon juice. Spread this evenly over the fillets. Place them in the air fryer basket.
2. In another small bowl, mix the thyme, marjoram, pepper, breadcrumbs, and olive oil. Mix until combined.
3. Gently but firmly press the spice mixture onto the top of each fish fillet.
4. Bake at 320°F (160°C) for 8–11 minutes, or until the fish reaches an internal temperature of at least 145°F (63°C) on a meat thermometer, and the topping is browned and crisp. Serve immediately.

Nutrition:

- Calories: 143
- Fat: 4 g.
- Protein: 20 g.
- Carbs: 5 g.
- Fiber: 1 g.
- Sugar: 1 g.
- Sodium: 140 mg.

Almond Crusted Cod with Chips

Preparation time: 10 minutes
Cooking time: 11–15 minutes
Servings: 4
Ingredients:

- 2 russet potatoes, peeled, thinly sliced, rinsed, and patted dry
- 1 egg white
- 1 tbsp. lemon juice, freshly squeezed
- 1/3 cup ground almonds
- 2 slices low-sodium whole-wheat bread, finely crumbled
- 1/2 tsp. basil, dried
- 4 (4 oz./113 g.) cod fillets

Directions:

1. Preheat the oven to warm.
2. Put the potato slices in the air fryer basket and air fry at 390°F (199°C) for 11–15 minutes, or until crisp and brown. With tongs, turn the fries twice during cooking.
3. Meanwhile, in a shallow bowl, beat the egg white and lemon juice until frothy.
4. On a plate, mix the almonds, breadcrumbs, and basil.
5. One at a time, dip the fillets into the egg white mixture and then into the almond-bread crumb mixture to coat. Place the coated fillets on a wire rack to dry while the fries cook.
6. When the potatoes are done, transfer them to a baking sheet and keep warm in the oven on low heat.
7. Air fry the fish in the air fryer basket for 10–14 minutes, or until the fish reaches an internal temperature of at least 140°F (60°C) on a meat thermometer, and the

coating is browned and crisp. Serve immediately with the potatoes.

Nutrition:

- Calories: 248 Fat: 5 g.
- Protein: 27 g.
- Carbs: 25 g. Fiber: 3 g.
- Sugar: 3 g.
- Sodium: 131 mg.

Lemon Snapper with Fruit

Preparation time: 15 minutes
Cooking time: 9–13 minutes
Servings: 4
Ingredients:

- 4 (4 oz./113 g.) red snapper fillets
- 2 tsp. olive oil
- 3 nectarines, halved and pitted
- 3 plums, halved and pitted
- 1 cup red grapes
- 1 tbsp. lemon juice, freshly squeezed
- 1 tbsp. honey (optional)
- 1/2 tsp. thyme, dried

Directions:

1. Put the red snapper in the air fryer basket and drizzle with olive oil. Air fry at 390°F (199°C) for 4 minutes.
2. Remove the basket and add the nectarines and plums. Scatter the grapes overall.
3. Drizzle with lemon juice and honey and sprinkle with thyme.
4. Return the basket to the air fryer and air fry for 5–9 minutes more, or until the fish flakes when tested with a fork and the fruit is tender. Serve immediately.

Nutrition:

- Calories: 246
- Fat: 4 g.
- Protein: 25 g.
- Carbs: 28 g.
- Fiber: 3 g.
- Sugar: 24 g.
- Sodium: 73 mg.

Easy Tuna Wraps

Preparation time: 10 minutes
Cooking time: 4–7 minutes
Servings: 4
Ingredients:

- 1 lb. (454 g.) fresh tuna steak, cut into 1-inch cubes
- 1 tbsp. fresh ginger, grated
- 2 garlic cloves, minced
- 1/2 tsp. sesame oil, toasted
- 4 low-sodium whole-wheat tortillas
- 1/4 cup low-fat mayonnaise
- 2 cups Romaine lettuce, shredded
- 1 red bell pepper, thinly sliced

Directions:

1. In a medium bowl, mix the tuna, ginger, garlic, and sesame oil. Let it stand for 10 minutes, then transfer to the air fryer basket.
2. Air fry at 390°F (199°C) for 4–7 minutes, or until done to your liking and lightly browned.
3. Make wraps with tuna, tortillas, mayonnaise, lettuce, and bell pepper. Serve immediately.

Nutrition:

- Calories: 289
- Fat: 7 g.
- Protein: 31 g.
- Carbs: 26 g.
- Fiber: 1 g.
- Sugar: 1 g.
- Sodium: 135 mg.

Asian-Inspired Swordfish Steaks

Preparation time: 10 minutes
Cooking time: 6–11 minutes
Servings: 4
Ingredients:

- 4 (4 oz./113 g.) swordfish steaks
- 1/2 tsp. sesame oil, toasted
- 1 jalapeño pepper, finely minced
- 2 garlic cloves, grated
- 1 tbsp. fresh ginger, grated
- 1/2 tsp. Chinese 5-spice powder
- 1/8 tsp. black pepper, freshly ground
- 2 tbsp. lemon juice, freshly squeezed

Directions:

1. Place the swordfish steaks on a work surface and drizzle with the sesame oil.
2. In a small bowl, mix the jalapeño, garlic, ginger, 5-spice powder, pepper, and lemon juice. Rub this mixture into the fish and let it stand for 10 minutes. Put in the air fryer basket.
3. Roast at 380°F (193°C) for 6–11 minutes, or until the swordfish reaches an internal temperature of at least 140°F (60°C) on a meat thermometer. Serve immediately.

Nutrition:

- Calories: 188 Fat: 6 g.
- Protein: 29 g.
- Carbs: 2 g.
- Fiber: 0 g.
- Sugar: 1 g.
- Sodium: 132 mg.

Salmon with Fennel and Carrot

Preparation time: 15 minutes
Cooking time: 13–14 minutes
Servings: 2
Ingredients:

- 1 fennel bulb, thinly sliced
- 1 large carrot, peeled and sliced
- 1 small onion, thinly sliced
- 1/4 cup low-fat sour cream
- 1/4 tsp. pepper, coarsely ground
- 2 (5 oz./142 g.) salmon fillets

Directions:

1. Combine the fennel, carrot, and onion in a bowl and toss.
2. Put the vegetable mixture into a baking pan. Roast in the air fryer at 400°F (204°C) for 4 minutes or until the vegetables are crisp-tender.
3. Remove the pan from the air fryer. Stir in the sour cream and sprinkle the vegetables with the pepper.
4. Top with the salmon fillets.
5. Return the pan to the air fryer. Roast for another 9–10 minutes or until the salmon just barely flakes when tested with a fork.

Nutrition:

- Calories: 254
- Fat: 9 g.
- Protein: 31 g.
- Carbs: 12 g.
- Fiber: 3 g.
- Sugar: 5 g.
- Sodium: 115 mg.

Ranch Tilapia Fillets

Preparation time: 7 minutes
Cooking time: 17 minutes
Servings: 2
Ingredients:

- 2 tbsp. flour
- 1 egg, lightly beaten
- 1 cup cornflakes, crushed
- 2 tbsp. ranch seasoning
- 2 tilapia fillets
- Olive oil spray

Directions:

1. Place a parchment liner in the air fryer basket.
2. Scoop the flour out onto a plate; set it aside.
3. Put the beaten egg in a medium shallow bowl.
4. Place the cornflakes in a zip-top bag and crush with a rolling pin or another small, blunt object.

5. On another plate, mix to combine the crushed cereal and ranch seasoning.

6. Dredge the tilapia fillets in the flour, then dip in the egg, and then press into the cornflake mixture.

7. Place the prepared fillets on the liner in the air fryer in a single layer.

8. Spray lightly with olive oil, and air fry at 400°F (204°C) for 8 minutes. Carefully flip the fillets, and spray with more oil. Air fry for an additional 9 minutes, until golden and crispy, and serve.

Nutrition:
- Calories: 395
- Fat: 7 g.
- Protein: 34 g.
- Carbs: 49 g.
- Fiber: 3 g.
- Sugar: 4 g.
- Sodium: 980 mg.

Chilean Sea Bass with Green Olive Relish

Preparation time: 10 minutes
Cooking time: 10 minutes
Servings: 2
Ingredients:
- Olive oil spray
- 2 (6 oz./170 g.) Chilean sea bass fillets or other firm-fleshed white fish
- 3 tbsp. extra virgin olive oil
- 1/2 tsp. cumin, ground
- 1/2 tsp. kosher salt
- 1/2 tsp. black pepper
- ¹/3 cup pitted green olives, diced
- 1/4 cup onion, finely diced
- 1 tsp. capers, chopped

Directions:
1. Spray the air fryer basket with olive oil spray. Drizzle the fillets with olive oil and sprinkle with cumin, salt, and pepper. Place the fish in the air fryer basket. Bake at 325°F (163°C) for 10 minutes, or until the fish flakes easily with a fork.

2. Meanwhile, in a small bowl, stir together the olives, onion, and capers.

3. Serve the fish topped with the relish.

Nutrition:
- Calories: 366
- Fat: 26 g.
- Protein: 31 g.
- Carbs: 2 g.
- Fiber: 1 g.
- Sugar: 0 g.
- Sodium: 895 mg.

Ginger and Green Onion Fish

Preparation time: 15 minutes
Cooking time: 15 minutes
Servings: 2
Ingredients:
For the bean sauce:
- 2 tbsp. low-sodium soy sauce
- 1 tbsp. rice wine
- 1 tbsp. doubanjiang (Chinese black bean paste)
- 1 tsp. fresh ginger, minced
- 1 clove garlic, minced

For the vegetables and fish:
- 1 tbsp. peanut oil
- 1/4 cup green onions, julienned (white and green parts)
- 1/4 cup fresh cilantro, chopped
- 2 tbsp. fresh ginger, julienned
- 2 (6 oz./170 g.) white fish fillets, such as tilapia

Directions:
1. For the sauce: In a small bowl, combine all the ingredients and stir until well combined; set aside.

2. For the vegetables and fish: In a medium bowl, combine the peanut oil, green onions, cilantro, and ginger. Toss to combine.

3. Cut 2 squares of parchment large enough to hold one fillet and half of the vegetables. Place one fillet on each parchment square, top with the vegetables, and pour over the sauce. Fold

over the parchment paper and crimp the sides in small, tight folds to hold the fish, vegetables, and sauce securely inside the packet.

4. Place the packets in a single layer in the air fryer basket. Roast at 350°F (177°C) for 15 minutes.

5. Transfer each packet to a dinner plate. Cut open with scissors just before serving.

Nutrition:

- Calories: 237
- Fat: 9 g.
- Protein: 36 g.
- Carbs: 3 g.
- Fiber: 0 g.
- Sugar: 0 g.
- Sodium: 641 mg.

Asian Sesame Cod

Preparation time: 5 minutes
Cooking time: 7–9 minutes
Servings: 1
Ingredients:

- 1 tbsp. reduced-sodium soy sauce
- 2 tsp. honey (optional)
- 1 tsp. sesame seeds
- 6 oz. (170 g.) cod fillet
- Nonstick cooking spray

Directions:

1. In a small bowl, combine the soy sauce and honey.

2. Spray the air fryer basket with nonstick cooking spray, then place the cod in the basket, brush with the soy mixture, and sprinkle sesame seeds on top. Roast at 360°F (182°C) for 7–9 minutes or until opaque.

3. Remove the fish from the fryer and allow to cool on a wire rack for 5 minutes before serving.

Nutrition:

- Calories: 141
- Fat: 1 g.
- Protein: 26 g.

- Carbs: 7 g.
- Fiber: 1 g.
- Sugar: 6 g.
- Sodium: 466 mg.

Roasted Shrimp and Veggies

Preparation time: 12 minutes
Cooking time: 25–28 minutes
Servings: 3
Ingredients:
For the veggies:

- 1/2 tsp. salt
- 1/2 tsp. paprika
- 1/4 tsp. garlic powder
- 1/4 tsp. black pepper, ground
- 1/2 medium zucchini, diced
- 1 cup broccoli florets
- 1/2 sweet onion, cut into large chunks
- 1/2 red bell pepper, cut into large chunks
- 1 small carrot, thinly sliced
- 2 small red potatoes, diced
- 1 tbsp. olive oil
- 1 tbsp. white wine vinegar

For the shrimp:

- 1/2 lb. (227 g.) raw shrimp, peeled and deveined
- 1 tbsp. olive oil
- 1/4 tsp. salt
- 1/4 tsp. paprika
- 1/4 tsp. garlic powder
- 1/4 tsp. black pepper, ground
- 1 tbsp. lemon juice

Directions:
To make the veggies

1. In a small bowl, combine the salt, paprika, garlic powder, and pepper. Set aside.

2. In a large bowl, combine the zucchini, broccoli, onion, bell pepper, carrot, and red potatoes.

3. Drizzle the olive oil and white wine vinegar over the veggies, and sprinkle with spice mixture.

4. Transfer to the air fryer basket and roast at 400°F (204°C) for 15 minutes, or until the veggies are fork-tender.

To make the shrimps

1. In a large bowl, toss together the shrimp, olive oil, salt, paprika, garlic powder, and pepper.
2. Once the veggies are done roasting, transfer the shrimp mixture to the air fryer basket and roast at 350°F (177°C) for 10–13 minutes, or until the shrimp are browned.
3. Toss the shrimp with the roasted veggies and drizzle with the lemon juice before serving.

Nutrition:
- Calories: 129
- Fat: 5 g.
- Protein: 9 g.
- Carbs: 12 g.
- Fiber: 1 g.
- Sugar: 2 g.
- Sodium: 352 mg.

Lemon Scallops with Asparagus

Preparation time: 10 minutes
Cooking time: 7–10 minutes
Servings: 4
Ingredients:
- 1/2 lb. (227 g.) asparagus, ends trimmed and cut into 2-inch pieces
- 1 cup sugar snap peas
- 1 lb. (454 g.) sea scallops
- 1 tbsp. lemon juice
- 2 tsp. olive oil
- 1/2 tsp. thyme, dried
- A pinch of salt
- Freshly ground black pepper, to taste

Directions:
1. Place the asparagus and sugar snap peas in the air fryer basket. Air fry at 400°F (204°C) for 2–3 minutes or until the vegetables are just starting to get tender.

2. Meanwhile, check the scallops for a small muscle attached to the side, and pull it off and discard.
3. In a medium bowl, toss the scallops with lemon juice, olive oil, thyme, salt, and pepper. Place into the air fryer basket on top of the vegetables.
4. Air fry for 5–7 minutes, tossing the basket once during the cooking time until the scallops are just firm when tested with your finger and are opaque in the center, and the vegetables are tender. Serve immediately.

Nutrition:
- Calories: 163
- Fat: 4 g.
- Protein: 22 g.
- Carbs: 10 g.
- Fiber: 3 g.
- Sugar: 3 g.
- Sodium: 225 mg.

Fish Tacos

Preparation time: 15 minutes
Cooking time: 9–12 minutes
Servings: 4
Ingredients:
- 1 lb. (454 g.) white fish fillets, such as snapper
- 1 tbsp. olive oil
- 3 tbsp. lemon juice, freshly squeezed and divided
- 1 1/2 cups red cabbage, chopped
- 1/2 cup salsa
- 1/3 cup sour cream

- 6 whole-wheat tortillas
- 2 avocados, peeled and chopped

Directions:
1. Brush the fish with olive oil and sprinkle with 1 tbsp. of the lemon juice. Place in the air fryer basket and air fry at 400°F (204°C) for 9–12 minutes or until the fish just flakes when tested with a fork.
2. Meanwhile, combine the remaining 2 tbsp. lemon juice, cabbage, salsa, and sour cream in a medium bowl.
3. When the fish is cooked, remove it from the air fryer basket and break it into large pieces.
4. Let everyone assemble their taco combining the fish, tortillas, cabbage mixture, and avocados.

Nutrition:
- Calories: 547
- Fat: 27 g.
- Protein: 33 g.
- Carbs: 43 g.
- Fiber: 12 g.
- Sugar: 4 g.
- Sodium: 679 mg.

Spicy Cajun Shrimp
Preparation time: 7 minutes
Cooking time: 10–13 minutes
Servings: 2
Ingredients:
- 1/2 lb. (227 g.) shrimp, peeled and deveined
- 1 tbsp. olive oil
- 1 tsp. cayenne pepper, ground
- 1/2 tsp. Old Bay seasoning
- 1/2 tsp. paprika
- 1/8 tsp. salt
- 1/2 lemon juice

Directions:
1. In a large bowl, combine the shrimp, olive oil, cayenne pepper, Old Bay Seasoning, paprika, and salt; toss to combine.

2. Transfer to the air fryer basket and roast at 390°F (199°C) for 10–13 minutes, until browned.
3. Drizzle a bit of lemon juice over the shrimp before serving.

Nutrition:
- Calories: 159
- Fat: 7 g.
- Protein: 23 g.
- Carbs: 1 g.
- Fiber: 0 g.
- Sugar: 0 g.
- Sodium: 291 mg.

Bratwurst with Rosenkohl
Preparation time: 35 minutes
Cooking time: 20 minutes
Servings: 2
Ingredients:
- 400 g. Brussels sprouts
- 20 smoked bacon
- 2 onions
- 4 sausages
- ½ cup of powdered Milk
- 400 g. potatoes
- 1 tsp. Nutmeg
- 1 tbsp. Fat or butter
- A pinch of salt
- 3 cups water

Directions:
1. Wash the Brussels sprouts. Remove the outer and dark leaves. Cook the cabbage in boiling salted water for about 15–20 minutes. Drain the water.
2. Cut the bacon and leave it in a pan without fat.
3. Peel the onions, cut into rings and fry them with the sausages in the frying fat for about 10 minutes until crispy.
4. Peel the potatoes and boil them in salted water until they are firm to the bite. Pour off.
5. Put 8 tbsp. of water, milk, a pinch of salt in the pot with the potatoes, and mash

the potatoes to a pulp with the masher. Add some nutmeg to taste.

6. Mix the Brussels sprouts with the bacon and serve. Add the puree and sausages.

Nutrition:
- Calories: 560
- Carbs: 31 g.
- Protein: 25 g.
- Fat: 35 g.

General Tso's Chicken

Preparation time: 10 minutes
Cooking time: 15 minutes
Servings: 5
Ingredients:
- A pinch ground ginger
- 1 tsp. red pepper flakes
- Green onions, sliced for garnish
- 1/2 tsp. onion powder
- 1/4 tsp. sesame oil
- 2 tbsp. rice vinegar
- 2 tbsp. soy sauce
- 2 tbsp. chicken broth
- 3 tbsp. coconut oil
- 1 egg
- 1/2 cup almond flour
- 6 chicken breasts, boneless, skinless, and cubed

Directions:
1. Get out a bowl and whisk your soy sauce, rice vinegar, sesame oil, red pepper flakes, chicken broth, and ginger and onion powder before setting it to the side.
2. Get out a different bowl to whisk your eggs before placing that to the side as well.
3. Get out another shallow bowl for your almond flour.
4. Take your chicken and dip it into the almond flour, making sure it's coated on both sides, and then dip it into the egg mixture. Add it to the other mixture, and make sure it's well coated.

5. Get out a pan and heat your oil over medium heat. Add in the remaining soy sauce with a pinch of almond flour

6. Add in the chicken, and cook for 7 minutes. It should be browned and cooked all the way through. Serve with green onions.

Nutrition:
- Calories: 355
- Protein: 36 g.
- Fat: 22 g.
- Net Carbs: 1 g.

Balsamic Meatloaf

Preparation time: 10 minutes
Cooking time: 1 hour 10 minutes
Servings: 6
Ingredients:
- 1 tbsp. Italian seasoning
- 2 tbsp. Coconut oil
- Sea salt and black pepper to taste
- 1/4 cup balsamic vinegar
- 2 tbsp. tomato paste
- 2 garlic cloves, chopped
- 1 lb. beef, ground
- 1 yellow onion, chopped fine

Directions:
1. Heat your oven to 350°F, and then get out a 9x5-inch loaf pan using coconut oil.
2. Mix all ingredients, and then add them to your greased loaf pan. Cook for 15 minutes–1 hour. It should be cooked all the way through.
3. Allow it to cool for 10 minutes before slicing.

Nutrition:
- Calories: 163
- Protein: 24 g.
- Fat: 6 g.
- Net Carbs: 3 g.

Beef Pot Pie

Preparation time: 10 minutes
Cooking time: 55 minutes
Servings: 6
Ingredients:
For the crust:

- 1/4 cup coconut flour
- 3/4 cup butter
- 2 cups almond flour
- 8 tbsp. cold water
- 1/2 tsp. baking powder, gluten-free
- 1 pinch salt

For the filling:

- 3 garlic cloves, minced
- 1 onion, diced
- 1 1/2 lb. beef, ground
- 3/4 cup heavy cream
- 1 cup low-sodium beef broth
- 1/2 cup Mozzarella cheese, grated
- 1/2 cup Parmesan cheese, cubed
- 3 tbsp. olive oil
- 1/2 tsp. garlic powder
- Sea salt and black pepper, to taste

Directions:

1. Start by preparing your crust by adding your baking powder, salt, and flour in a food processor, processing until all clumps are gone. Add in your butter, and continue to pulse until it has a coarse sand consistency. Stream your cold water in with the processor running so that dough forms.

2. Transfer this to wax paper, and then flatten it to a 9-inch disk. Allow it to set in the fridge for 30 minutes.

3. Heat your oven to 350°F, and then heat your oil in a frying pan using medium heat.

4. Add your garlic and onion, cooking for 3 minutes.

5. Add in the beef, and season with salt and pepper. Cook until your beef is browned, and then mix in your beef broth and heavy cream. Add in your garlic powder, mixing well.

6. Reduce your heat to low, and allow it to simmer for 10 minutes. It should thicken.

7. Pour this into your pie dish, and top with the chilled crust as well as cheese. Bake for 30 minutes, and then allow it to cool for at least 5 minutes before serving.

Nutrition:

- Calories: 800
- Protein: 49 g.
- Fat: 64 g.
- Net Carbs: 7 g.

Lobster Bisque

Preparation time: 10 minutes
Cooking time: 2 hours and 5 minutes
Servings: 6
Ingredients:

- 1 tbsp. curry powder
- 1 cup heavy cream
- 2 garlic cloves, peeled and minced
- 6 cups vegetable broth

- 1 tbsp. tomato paste
- 1 onion, peeled and chopped
- 1 tsp. cayenne pepper
- 2 carrots, peeled and chopped
- 1/2 cup butter
- 2 tbsp. olive oil
- 2 lbs. lobster, shell on
- Sea salt and black pepper, to taste

Directions:
1. Remove the heads and shell from your lobster, chopping the meat gently.
2. Get out a stockpot and heat it over medium heat. Add in your carrots, garlic, butter, lobster, and onion. Cook for 5 minutes.
3. Add in your olive oil, seasoning, and tomato paste. Stir well, and then pour in your vegetable broth.
4. Allow it to simmer for 90 minutes, and then add in your heavy cream, sea salt, and black pepper. Blend with an immersion blender, and serve warm.

Nutrition:
- Calories: 486
- Protein: 32 g.
- Fat: 36 g.
- Net Carbs: 7 g.

Chicken Casserole
Preparation time: 10 minutes
Cooking time: 25 minutes
Servings: 4
Ingredients:
- 1 lb. chicken tenders
- 1 tbsp. oregano
- 1 tbsp. black pepper
- 1 cup cherry tomatoes, halved
- 1 cup Mozzarella cheese, shredded
- 2 tbsp. olive oil
- Sea salt to taste

Directions:
1. Start by heating your oven to 425°F, and then get out and grease a baking sheet

using coconut oil. Marinate your chicken in olive oil, oregano, and black pepper.
2. Transfer them to the baking dish topping with tomatoes and Mozzarella.
3. Bake for 25 minutes, and then season with salt before serving.

Nutrition:
- Calories: 282
- Protein: 34 g.
- Fat: 15 g.
- Net Carbs: 2 g.

Beef and Broccoli

Preparation time: 10 minutes
Cooking time: 15 minutes
Servings: 4
Ingredients:
- 1/4 cup cornstarch
- 1/2 tbsp. fresh ginger, grated
- 1/2 cup soy sauce, low-sodium
- 1 lb. flank steak, sliced thin
- 1 tbsp. garlic powder
- 2 cups broccoli florets
- 2 tbsp. peanut oil
- 2 tbsp. fish sauce
- 1/4 cup cabbage, shredded for garnish

Directions:
1. Place your beef in a bowl, and set it to the side.
2. Get out a different bowl and mix your fish sauce, cornstarch, soy sauce, garlic, and ginger. Pour half of this over your beef, and then get out a skillet.

3. Place your skillet over medium heat, heating a tbsp. of peanut oil. Add in your broccoli, and cook for 2 minutes. Place it on a serving plate.
4. Pour in your remaining peanut oil, adding in your beef. Cook for 1 minute per side, and then add in the rest of your sauce. Cook using high heat until it thickens, adding your broccoli back in. Stir to combine.
5. Serve topped with shredded cabbage.

Nutrition:
- Calories: 296
- Protein: 30 g.
- Fat: 15 g.
- Net Carbs: 11 g.

Garlic Shrimp

Preparation time: 10 minutes
Cooking time: 10 minutes
Servings: 3
Ingredients:
- 1 lb. shrimp, peeled, deveined, tails on
- 1 tsp. sesame oil
- 1 tbsp. soy sauce
- 2 tbsp. fish sauce
- 4 garlic cloves, peeled and chopped
- 2 green onions, chopped fine for garnish
- 1 tbsp. peanut oil

Directions:
1. Whisk your soy sauce, sesame oil, garlic, and cornstarch. Add fish sauce until smooth.
2. Get out a skillet, heating your peanut oil over medium heat. Once your oil is hot, add in your shrimp and cook for 5 minutes. Flip them halfway through, and then pour in your sauce mixture.
3. Simmer for 5 minutes to allow your sauce to thicken. Top with green onions before serving.

Nutrition:
- Calories: 185
- Protein: 22 g.
- Fat: 8 g.

- Net Carbs: 7 g.

Curried Shrimp

Preparation time: 10 minutes
Cooking time: 10 minutes
Servings: 4
Ingredients:
- 2 oranges, seedless and quartered
- 1 lb. shrimp, deveined
- 1 tbsp. curry powder
- 1 tbsp. coconut oil, melted
- 1/4 tsp. cinnamon
- Sea salt and black pepper, to taste
- ¼ cup Fresh cilantro, chopped for garnish

Directions:
1. Start by heating your skillet and melting your coconut oil over medium heat. Once your oil is hot, add in your shrimp, and cook for about 5 minutes. Add in your curry powder, cinnamon, salt, orange slices, and pepper next. Cook until your shrimp are pink and start to curl, and your oranges should be browned.
2. Serve your oranges and shrimp together. Garnish with cilantro.

Nutrition:
- Calories: 145
- Protein: 16 g.
- Fat: 5 g.
- Net Carbs: 8 g.

Chicken and Vegetable Stir Fry

Preparation time: 10 minutes
Cooking time: 30 minutes
Servings: 4
Ingredients:
- 1 tsp. cumin
- 1/4 tsp. turmeric
- 1/2 tsp. curry powder
- 1/2 tsp. red pepper flakes
- 1 eggplant, sliced into rounds
- 4 tbsp. olive oil
- 4 chicken breasts, boneless, skinless, and sliced into strips

- 1 red bell pepper, seeded and chopped
- 1 yellow bell pepper, seeded and chopped
- 1 onion, peeled and sliced
- 2 garlic cloves, crushed
- Rosemary, fresh to garnish
- Lettuce for garnish

Directions:
1. You need to start by making your marinade. Mix your cumin, curry powder, olive oil, red pepper flakes, and turmeric. Add in the chicken strips, and allow them to marinate for 30 minutes.
2. During this time chop your bell peppers, garlic, and eggplant before setting it to the side.
3. After your chicken has marinated, then get out the skillet and place it over medium heat. Cook your chicken for 5 minutes per side before adding in the vegetables. Cook until tender, and then serve with onion, rosemary, and lettuce.

Nutrition:
- Calories: 324
- Protein: 31 g.
- Fat: 18 g.
- Net Carbs: 6 g.

Blackened Salmon

Preparation time: 10 minutes
Cooking time: 35 minutes
Servings: 2
Ingredients:
- 2 salmon fillets
- 1 avocado
- 1 tbsp. blackening spice
- 1 tbsp. mayonnaise
- 1 cup lettuce
- A pinch sea salt

Directions:
1. Start by mashing the avocado and mixing it with your mayonnaise.
2. Preheat your grill, and rub your seasonings on the salmon fillet, and place

it on the grill. Cook for 5 minutes per side.
3. Top with lettuce and avocado sauce before serving warm.

Nutrition:
- Calories: 568
- Protein: 51 g.
- Fat: 38 g.
- Net Carbs: 1 g.

Cottage Pie

Preparation time: 10 minutes
Cooking time: 35 minutes
Servings: 6
Ingredients:
For the bottom layer:
- 1 1/2 lb. beef, ground
- 1 red onion, chopped
- 2 garlic cloves, minced
- 3 tomatoes, chopped
- 1/2 cup peas, frozen
- 1/2 tsp. cumin
- 1 cup beef stock, low-sodium
- 2 tbsp. olive oil
- Sea salt and black pepper, to taste

For the top layer:
- 1 1/2 heads cauliflower, chopped into florets
- 1/2 cup heavy cream
- 1/4 tsp. curry powder
- 1/4 cup Parmesan cheese, grated
- 3 tbsp. butter
- 5 tbsp. fresh chives, chopped fine
- Sea salt and black pepper, to taste

Directions:

1. Get out a large pan to steam your cauliflower for 10 minutes.
2. Drain, and then return it to the pot. Add your butter, curry powder, cheese, and heavy cream before seasoning with salt and pepper. Use an immersion blender to blend well.
3. Get out a frying pan, and then add in your olive oil. Place the pan over medium heat and cook your garlic and onion for 3 minutes before adding your tomatoes and peas. Cook over low heat for 5 minutes.
4. Add the ground beef, browning, and cooking all the way through. Stir in your cumin and stock, and then season with salt and pepper. Allow it to simmer until most of your liquid has evaporated.
5. Heat your oven's broiler, and put your filling in a baking dish, topped with the cauliflower puree.
6. Cook under the broiler for 5 minutes. Sprinkle with chives before serving warm.

Nutrition:

- Calories: 415
- Protein: 41 g.
- Fat: 23 g.
- Net Carbs: 7 g.

Coconut Shrimp Curry

Preparation time: 10 minutes
Cooking time: 2 hours 30 minutes
Servings: 4
Ingredients:

- 1 lb. shrimp
- 1/4 cup fresh cilantro, chopped
- 2 tsp. lemon garlic seasoning
- 1 tbsp. curry paste
- 15 oz. water
- 30 oz. coconut milk

Directions:

1. Add coconut milk, cilantro, lemon garlic seasoning, curry paste, and water to a crockpot and stir well.

2. Cover and cook on high for 2 hours.
3. Add shrimp, cover, and cook for 30 minutes longer.
4. Serve and enjoy.

Nutrition:

- Calories: 200
- Fat: 7.7 g.
- Carbs: 4.6 g.
- Sugar: 0 g.
- Protein: 26 g.
- Cholesterol: 239 mg.

Delicious Fish Curry

Preparation time: 10 minutes
Cooking time: 2 hours
Servings: 4
Ingredients:

- 1 lb. cod fish fillets
- 12 oz. carrots, cut into julienne strips
- 1 bell pepper, sliced
- 1 tsp. garlic powder
- 1 tsp. ginger, ground
- 1 tbsp. curry powder
- 3 tbsp. red curry paste
- 15 oz. coconut milk
- 1/2 tbsp. Pepper
- ¼ tsp. Salt

Directions:

1. Add coconut milk to a crockpot and whisk in curry powder, garlic powder, ground ginger, and curry paste.
2. Stir in carrots and bell peppers.
3. Place cod fillets in the sauce.
4. Cover and cook on "Low" for 2 hours.
5. Season with pepper and salt.
6. Serve and enjoy.

Nutrition:

- Calories: 232
- Fat: 6.5 g.
- Carbs: 14.1 g.
- Sugar: 5.2 g.
- Protein: 27.1 g.
- Cholesterol: 62 mg.

Lemon Dill Salmon

Preparation time: 10 minutes
Cooking time: 2 hours
Servings: 4
Ingredients:

- 1 lb. salmon fillet, skin-on
- 2 tbsp. fresh dill, chopped
- 1/2 lemon juice
- 1 1/2 cups vegetable stock
- 1 lemon, sliced
- ½ tsp. Pepper
- ¼ tsp. Salt

Directions:

1. Line a crockpot with parchment paper. Place lemon slices on the bottom of the crockpot and then place the salmon on top of the slices
2. Season salmon with pepper and salt.
3. Add lemon juice and stock to the crockpot.
4. Cover and cook on "Low" for 2 hours.
5. Serve and garnished with dill. Enjoy.

Nutrition:

- Calories: 162
- Fat: 7.7 g.
- Carbs: 2.9 g.
- Sugar: 1 g.
- Protein: 22.5 g.
- Cholesterol: 50 mg.

Rosemary Salmon

Preparation time: 10 minutes
Cooking time: 2 hours
Servings: 2
Ingredients:

- 8 oz. salmon
- 1/4 tsp. fresh rosemary, minced
- 2 tbsp. fresh lemon juice
- 1/3 cup water
- 1 tbsp. capers
- 1 fresh lemon, sliced

Directions:

1. Place salmon into a crockpot.

2. Pour lemon juice and water over the salmon.
3. Arrange lemon slices on top of the salmon.
4. Sprinkle with rosemary and capers.
5. Cover and cook on "Low" for 2 hours.
6. Serve and enjoy.

Nutrition:

- Calories: 164 Fat: 7.3 g.
- Carbs: 3.3 g. Sugar: 1.1 g.
- Protein: 22.6 g.Cholesterol: 50 mg.

Paprika Garlic Shrimps

Preparation time: 10 minutes
Cooking time: 50 minutes
Servings: 8
Ingredients:

- 2 lb. shrimps, peeled and deveined
- 1 tsp. paprika
- 5 garlic cloves, sliced
- 3/4 cup olive oil
- 1/4 tsp. red pepper flakes, crushed
- 1/4 tsp. black pepper
- 1 tsp. kosher s5
- alt

Directions:

1. Combine oil, red pepper flakes, black pepper, paprika, garlic, and salt in a crockpot.
2. Cover and cook on "High" for 30 minutes.
3. Open and add the shrimps; cover and cook on "High" for 10 minutes.
4. Open again and stir well. Cover and cook for 10 more minutes.
5. Serve and enjoy.

Nutrition:

- Calories: 301
- Fat: 20.9 g.
- Carbs: 2.6 g.
- Sugar: 0.1 g.
- Protein: 26 g.
- Cholesterol: 239 mg.

Simple Lemon Halibut

Preparation time: 10 minutes
Cooking time: 1 hour 30 minutes
Servings: 2
Ingredients:

- 12 oz. halibut fish fillet
- 1 tbsp. fresh lemon juice
- 1 tbsp. fresh dill
- 1 tbsp. olive oil
- 1/4 tsp. Pepper
- 1/8 tsp. Salt

Directions:

1. Place the fish fillet in the middle of a large sheet of aluminum foil. Season with pepper and salt.
2. In a small bowl, whisk together dill, oil, and lemon juice. Pour over the fish fillet.
3. Wrap foil around the fish fillet and make a packet.
4. Place the foil packet in a crockpot.
5. Cover and cook on "High" for 90 minutes.
6. Serve and enjoy.

Nutrition:

- Calories: 289 Fat: 11.2 g.
- Carbs: 1.1 g. Sugar: 0.2 g.
- Protein: 47 g. Cholesterol: 71 mg.

Crab Dip

Preparation time: 10 minutes
Cooking time: 3 hours
Servings: 24
Ingredients:

- 8 oz. imitation crab meat
- 1 tsp. paprika
- 2 tbsp. onion, chopped
- 8 oz. cream cheese
- 1/4 cup walnuts, chopped
- 1 tsp. hot sauce

Directions:

1. Place all ingredients, except paprika and walnuts, in a crockpot and stir well.
2. Sprinkle over the paprika and walnuts.
3. Cover and cook on "Low" for 3 hours.
4. Stir well and serve.

Nutrition:

- Calories: 53 Fat: 4.2 g.
- Carbs: 2.4 g.Sugar: 0.6 g.
- Protein: 1.8 g.Cholesterol: 12 mg.

Lemon Butter Tilapia

Preparation time: 10 minutes
Cooking time: 2 hours
Servings: 4
Ingredients:

- 4 tilapia fillets
- 1/4 tsp. lemon-pepper seasoning
- 3/4 cup fresh lemon juice
- 12 asparagus spears
- 2 tbsp. butter, divided

Directions:

1. Prepare 4 large sheets of aluminum foil.
2. Place a fish fillet on each sheet.
3. Sprinkle lemon pepper seasoning and lemon juice on top of fish fillets.
4. Add 1/2 tbsp. of butter on top of each fillet.
5. Arrange 3 asparagus spears on each fish fillet.
6. Fold foil around the fish fillet and make a packet.
7. Repeat with the remaining fish fillets.
8. Place fish fillet packets in a crockpot.
9. Cover and cook on high for 2 hours.
10. Serve and enjoy.

Nutrition:

- Calories: 112 Fat: 6.7 g.
- Carbs: 3.8 g. Sugar: 2.3 g.
- Protein: 10 g. Cholesterol: 37 mg.

Slow Cooker Mediterranean Salmon

Preparation time: 10 minutes
Cooking time: 6 hours
Servings: 4
Ingredients:

- 1 lb. salmon fillets
- 1 tbsp. Italian seasoning
- 1 tsp. onion powder
- 1 tsp. garlic powder
- 1 tbsp. olive oil
- 1/2 tsp. black pepper
- 1/2 onion, nicely chopped
- 3 garlic cloves, minced
- 1 red bell pepper
- 1 zucchini, quartered and sliced
- 1 chopped tomato
- Cooking oil, as required

Directions:

1. Take an oven-safe dish that fits perfectly inside a 6-quart slow cooker.
2. Spray some cooking oil inside the oven-safe dish.
3. In a medium bowl put half portion of the garlic powder, Italian seasoning, onion powder, olive oil, and black pepper. Combine the ingredients thoroughly.
4. Add the sliced garlic cloves, zucchini, onions, tomato, and bell pepper as well
5. Season the salmon fillets with the mix and place the fillets one by one into the bottom part of the oven-safe dish.
6. Season it with the remaining herbs, olive oil, and spices.
7. Gently toss it up with the vegetables to coat them thoroughly.
8. Cover up the oven-safe dish using a glass lid.
9. Place the dish correctly inside the slow cooker and cover the cooker.
10. Now low cook it for 6 hours.
11. Serve it with couscous or whole-grain pasta.

Nutrition:

- Calories: 225
- Carbs: 8.1 g.
- Protein: 23.5 g.
- Sugar: 4.1 g.
- Fat: 11.8 g.
- Dietary Fiber: 1.6 g.
- Cholesterol: 52 mg.
- Sodium: 59 mg.
- Potassium: 704 mg.

Baked Garlic Lemon Salmon

Preparation time: 5 minutes
Cooking time: 15 minutes
Servings: 4
Ingredients:

- 3 tbsp. lemon juice
- 4 medium-sized salmon fillets
- 1/4 cup unsalted butter, melted
- 2 garlic cloves, minced
- A handful of parsley, finely chopped
- Salt and pepper to taste

Directions:

1. Preheat the oven to 400°F (200°C). Line a baking dish or tray with tin foil; grease with some cooking spray.
2. Place the salmon fillets over the baking dish.
3. Add the butter, garlic, lemon juice, salt, and pepper to a mixing bowl. Mix well.
4. Brush the salmon fillets with the butter sauce, reserving some sauce.
5. Bake for around 15 minutes, or until the salmon is easy to flake. Bake for 2–3 minutes more if needed.
6. Brush with the reserved sauce and sprinkle some lemon juice on top.
7. Serve with chopped parsley on top.

Nutrition:

- Calories: 350Fat: 25 g.
- Total Carbs: 2 g. Sugar: 0.5 g.
- Protein: 28.5 g.
- Sodium: 68 mg.

Wholesome Broccoli Pork Chops

Cooking time: 10 minutes
Preparation time: 10–15 minutes
Servings: 4
Ingredients:

- 1 1/2 tbsp. canola oil (divided)
- 1/4 tsp. red pepper flakes, crushed
- 1 clove garlic, minced
- 1 lb. pork loin chops, boneless and divided into 4 equal parts
- 2 cups broccoli florets
- 2 tbsp.+1 tsp. reduced-sodium soy sauce
- 2 tbsp. water
- 3 tbsp. rice wine vinegar
- 2 tbsp. cilantro, chopped

Directions:

1. Add the water, soy sauce, vinegar, red pepper, garlic, and 1 tbsp. of the canola oil to a mixing bowl. Mix well.
2. Add the pork chops and combine well.
3. Refrigerate for 20–30 minutes to marinate.
4. Steam the broccoli florets over boiling water for 5 minutes; drain and set aside.
5. Heat the remaining 1/2 tbsp. of canola oil over medium heat in a medium saucepan or skillet.
6. Add the pork chops (reserve the marinade) and stir-cook for 4–5 minutes until evenly brown. Transfer the chops to a serving platter.
7. In another saucepan, boil the reserved marinade.
8. Cover and simmer the mixture over low heat for about 2–3 minutes until it thickens.
9. Pour it over the pork chops; top with chopped cilantro and serve with cooked broccoli on the side.

Nutrition:

- Calories: 235 Fat: 13 g.
- Total Carbs: 5 g. Sugar: 1 g.
- Protein: 23 g.
- Sodium: 480 mg.

Herbed Chicken Meal

Preparation time: 5 minutes
Cooking time: 25 minutes
Servings: 6
Ingredients:

- 3 cloves garlic
- 3 large chicken breasts, boneless, skinless
- 3 tbsp. rosemary
- 3 tbsp. butter, melted
- 1 1/2 tbsp. olive oil
- 1 tsp. salt
- 1 cup dry vermouth
- 1/2 cup red wine vinegar
- 3/4 tsp. pink peppercorns

Directions:

1. Divide the chicken breasts into halves and pat dry with paper towels.
2. Heat the butter and olive oil over medium heat in a medium saucepan or skillet.
3. Add the garlic and stir cook for 30 seconds until softened.
4. Add the chicken breasts and stir-cook for 1–2 minutes until evenly brown.
5. Add the salt and vinegar; stir the mixture.
6. Cover and simmer over low heat for about 5 minutes.
7. Add the rosemary and vermouth; stir and simmer the mixture uncovered for about 10 minutes until the chicken is tender and well cooked. Transfer the chicken to serving plates.

8. Add the peppercorns and simmer the mixture for 4–5 minutes.
9. Pour the mixture over the chicken and serve warm.

Nutrition:
- Calories: 187
- Fat: 11.5 g
- Total Carbs: 1 g.
- Sugar: 0 g.
- Protein: 16.5 g.
- Sodium: 183 mg.

Avocado Orange Salmon

Preparation time: 10 minutes
Cooking time: 15 minutes
Servings: 8
Ingredients:
- 3 cups watercress, roughly chopped
- 3 tbsp. cucumbers, finely chopped
- 4 (4–6 oz. each) Alaska salmon fillets, rinsed and dried
- 1/4 cup avocado oil, divided
- 2 oranges, peeled, segmented, and discard membranes
- 1 tsp. white wine vinegar
- Salt and pepper, to taste
- 1/2 avocado, pitted, peeled, and sliced
- 2 cups mixed greens
- 1/4 cup walnuts
- 2 tbsp. apple cider vinegar
- 1 pinch smoked paprika

Directions:
1. Heat 3 tbsp. of avocado oil over medium heat in a medium saucepan or skillet.

2. Add the salmon and brown evenly for 3–4 minutes.
3. Flip the salmon and season with salt and pepper; cook for 3–4 more minutes until opaque. Divide onto serving plates.
4. Add the watercress, cucumber, smoked paprika, mixed greens and orange segments to a mixing bowl; mix well.
5. Add the remaining oil, white wine vinegar, salt, and pepper.
6. Add the mixture to the serving plates beside the salmon; top with apple cider vinegar, avocado, and walnuts.

Nutrition:
- Calories: 382
- Fat: 38 g.
- Total Carbs: 7 g.
- Sugar: 0 g.
- Protein: 46 g.
- Sodium: 160 mg.

Mediterranean Chicken Breasts

Preparation time: 5 minutes
Cooking time: 35 minutes
Servings: 4
Ingredients:
- 4 (4 oz.) chicken breasts, boneless and skinless
- 2 tbsp. lemon juice
- 1 tbsp. olive oil
- 1 garlic clove, minced
- 1/2 tsp. garlic powder
- 1/4 tsp. pepper
- 1 (15 oz.) can artichoke hearts, drained and chopped
- 1/3 cup low-sodium, fat-free chicken broth,
- 3 tbsp. Parmesan cheese, grated
- Cooking spray

Directions:
1. Preheat the oven to 350°F (175°C). Grease a baking pan or dish with some cooking spray.
2. Place the chicken breasts in a plastic bag and lb. them to 1/2 inch thick.

3. Pour the lemon juice over the chicken breasts and season with garlic powder and pepper.
4. Place the chicken breasts in the baking pan and bake for about 25 minutes.
5. Heat the olive oil over medium heat in a medium saucepan or skillet.
6. Add the garlic and stir cook for 1 minute until softened.
7. Add the artichoke hearts; stir-cook for about 3 minutes.
8. Add the chicken broth and simmer for 5 minutes. Mix in the cheese until it melts.
9. Pour the artichoke mixture over chicken breasts and bake for 10 more minutes until the chicken is cooked to perfection. Serve warm.

Nutrition:
- Calories: 215
- Fat: 7 g.
- Total Carbs: 9 g.
- Sugar: 1 g.
- Protein: 28 g.
- Sodium: 340 mg.

Crunchy Crusted Salmon
Preparation time: 5–10 minutes
Cooking time: 12–15 minutes
Servings: 4
Ingredients:
- 2 slices whole-wheat bread, torn into pieces
- 4 tsp. honey (optional)
- 2 tsp. canola oil
- 3 tbsp. walnuts, finely chopped
- 4 (4 oz.) salmon fillets
- 4 tsp. Dijon mustard
- 1/2 tsp. thyme, dried
- Cooking spray

Directions:
1. Preheat the oven to 400°F (200°C). Grease a baking sheet with some cooking spray.
2. Place the salmon over the baking sheet.

3. Combine the mustard and honey in a bowl. Brush the salmon with the honey mixture.
4. Add the bread pieces to a blender or food processor and blend to make fine crumbs.
5. Add the crumbs and walnuts to a mixing bowl. Mix well.
6. Add the thyme and canola oil; combine again.
7. Press the mixture over the salmon and bake for 12–15 minutes until the topping is evenly brown and the salmon is easy to flake.
8. Serve warm.

Nutrition:
- Calories: 295
- Fat: 17 g.
- Total Carbs: 13 g.
- Sugar: 7 g.
- Protein: 22 g.
- Sodium: 243 mg.

Italian Pork Chops
Preparation time: 5 minutes
Cooking time: 25 minutes
Servings: 4
Ingredients:
- 4 garlic cloves, sliced
- 4 thick pork chops, fat trimmed
- 1 small yellow onion, cut into rings
- 1/2 cup low-fat mozzarella cheese
- 1 (28 oz.) can tomatoes, diced
- 1 tsp. paprika
- 1 tsp. oregano, dried
- 1 chicken bouillon cube
- Salt and pepper to taste
- Cooking spray

Directions:
1. Preheat the oven to 400°F (200°C). Grease a baking pan with some cooking spray.
2. Season the pork chops with salt and pepper.

3. Grease a medium saucepan or skillet with cooking spray and heat it over medium heat.
4. Add the pork chops and stir-cook for 2 minutes per side until evenly brown.
5. Add the garlic and onion rings and stir-cook for 1–2 minutes until softened.
6. Add the spices, tomato, and bouillon cube; simmer for 2–3 minutes.
7. Pour in the tomato sauce.
8. Add the mixture to the baking pan, top with the cheese, and bake for about 20 minutes until the top is golden brown.
9. Let cool slightly and serve warm.

Note: You can store leftovers in an airtight container in the refrigerator for up to 3–4 days. Simply reheat in a saucepan and serve.

Nutrition:
- Calories: 405
- Fat: 17 g.
- Total Carbs: 16 g.
- Sugar: 7.5 g.
- Protein: 43.5 g.
- Sodium: 1275 mg.

Mushroom Chicken Mania

Preparation time: 10 minutes
Cooking time: 20 minutes
Servings: 4
Ingredients:
- 10 oz. white button mushrooms, sliced
- 1/4 tsp. pepper
- 1/3 cup balsamic vinegar

- 1/2 cup low-sodium, fat-free chicken broth
- 1-lb. chicken breasts, boneless, skinless
- 1 tbsp. olive oil
- 1/4 cup all-purpose flour
- 1 tbsp. low-fat margarine
- Cooking spray

Directions:
1. Add the chicken breasts to a plastic bag and lb. to flatten with your palm.
2. Coat them evenly with flour.
3. Grease a medium saucepan or skillet with some cooking spray and heat it over medium heat.
4. Add the chicken breasts and brown evenly for 4–5 minutes on each side. Set aside.
5. Melt the margarine in the pan, add mushrooms and pepper, and stir-cook for 4–5 minutes until softened.
6. Add the balsamic vinegar, chicken broth and boil the mixture until the sauce thickens.
7. Cover and simmer over low heat for about 2 minutes.
8. Add the chicken and simmer for 5 more minutes.
9. Serve warm.

Nutrition:
- Calories: 240
- Fat: 9 g.
- Total Carbs: 12 g.
- Sugar: 4 g.
- Protein: 27 g
- Sodium: 150 mg.

Tomato Steak Kebabs

Preparation time: 10–15 minutes
Cooking time: 10 minutes
Servings: 4
Ingredients:
- 1 tsp. Dijon mustard
- 1 lb. top sirloin steak, cut into 1-inch cubes
- 1/4 cup balsamic vinaigrette

- 2 cups cherry tomatoes
- 1/4 cup barbecue sauce
- Cooking spray

Directions:
1. Add the barbecue sauce, vinaigrette, and mustard to a mixing bowl; mix well. Set aside 1/4 of the mixture.
2. Add the beef and coat well.
3. Take 4 metal or soaked wooden skewers and thread them alternately with tomatoes and beef pieces.
4. Preheat the grill to medium-high heat. Grease the grill rack with cooking spray.
5. Grill the skewers for 6–8 minutes until the beef is tender. When 3–4 minutes remain, begin basting frequently with the reserved mixture.

Nutrition:
- Calories: 194
- Fat: 7 g.
- Total Carbs: 7 g.
- Sugar: 5 g.
- Protein: 25 g.
- Sodium: 288 mg.

Baked Broccoli Chicken

Preparation time: 10 minutes
Cooking time: 45 minutes
Servings: 4
Ingredients:

- 1 tsp. vegetable oil
- 4 medium chicken fillets, chopped
- 1 medium onion, finely chopped
- 1 (10.5 oz.) can chicken or mushroom soup
- 1 lb. broccoli florets, boiled and drained
- 1 tsp. curry powder
- 2 oz. brown breadcrumbs
- 2 oz. low-fat cheddar cheese, grated
- 1/2 cup skimmed milk
- Salt and pepper to taste
- Cooking spray

Directions:
1. Preheat the oven to 425°F (220°C). Grease a baking dish or casserole dish with some cooking spray.
2. Heat the oil over medium heat in a medium saucepan or skillet.
3. Add the onion and stir-cook until softened and translucent.
4. Add the chicken pieces; stir-cook for 10 minutes until evenly brown. Set aside.
5. Add the chicken or mushroom soup, milk, salt, pepper and curry powder to a mixing bowl. Mix well.
6. Arrange the chicken mixture and broccoli in the baking dish; pour the soup mixture on top.
7. Top with the crumbs and cheddar cheese.
8. Bake for about 30 minutes until the top is evenly brown.
9. Slice and serve warm.

Nutrition:
- Calories: 332 Fat: 9 g.
- Total Carbs: 15 g.
- Sugar: 6 g.
- Protein: 44.5 g.
- Sodium: 700 mg.

Baked Creamed Chicken

Preparation time: 5 minutes
Cooking time: 25 minutes
Servings: 4
Ingredients:

- 5 oz. low-fat cream cheese

- 20–40 basil leaves (more or less to taste)
- 4 chicken breasts, boneless, skinless
- 5 1/2 oz. prosciutto, finely sliced
- Pepper to taste

Directions:

1. Preheat the oven to 375°F (190°C).
2. Arrange the prosciutto slices on a piece of aluminum foil so they overlap slightly. Spread the cream cheese over them and set aside for 15 minutes.
3. Place the basil leaves on top.
4. Wrap the prosciutto slices around the chicken breasts. Season with pepper.
5. Place them over a baking sheet.
6. Bake for 25–30 minutes until the chicken is tender.
7. Let cool slightly, slice, and serve warm.

Note: You can store leftovers in an airtight container in the refrigerator for up to 3–4 days. Simply reheat in the oven and serve.

Nutrition:

- Calories: 294
- Fat: 11.5 g.
- Total Carbs: 3 g.
- Sugar: 2.5 g.
- Protein: 38.5 g.
- Sodium: 934 mg.

Pork Mushroom Stew

Preparation time: 10 minutes
Cooking time: 90 minutes
Servings: 5
Ingredients:

- 1 can (16 oz.) unsalted tomato sauce
- 2 cups carrots, sliced
- 1 medium green pepper, chopped
- 1/2 lb. mushrooms, sliced
- 1 tsp. basil, dried
- 1/2 tsp. rosemary, dried and crushed
- 1 lb. lean boneless pork, cut into 1-inch cubes
- 1 cup onion, chopped
- 1/2 cup water
- 1/4 tsp. pepper

Directions:

1. Grease a large cooking pot or Dutch oven with some cooking oil and heat it over medium heat.
2. Add the pork and stir-cook to brown evenly.
3. Add the onion, seasonings, water, and tomato sauce; stir.
4. Bring to a boil, cover, and simmer over low heat for about 60 minutes until the pork is tender.
5. Add the other ingredients; combine and cook for 30 more minutes until the veggies are tender.
6. Serve warm.

Nutrition:

- Calories: 201
- Fat: 7 g.
- Total Carbs: 15 g.
- Sugar: 0 g.
- Protein: 18 g.
- Sodium: 644 mg.

Beef Korma Curry

Preparation time: 10 minutes
Cooking time: 17–20 minutes
Servings: 4
Ingredients:

- 1 lb. (454 g.) sirloin steak, sliced
- 1/2 cup yogurt
- 1 tbsp. curry powder
- 1 tbsp. olive oil
- 1 onion, chopped
- 2 garlic cloves, minced
- 1 tomato, diced
- 1/2 cup frozen baby peas, thawed

Directions:

1. In a medium bowl, combine the steak, yogurt, and curry powder. Stir and set aside.
2. In a metal bowl, combine the olive oil, onion, and garlic. Bake at 350°F (177°C) for 3–4 minutes or until crisp and tender.
3. Add the steak along with the yogurt and the diced tomato. Bake for 12–13

minutes or until the steak is almost tender.

4. Stir in the peas and bake for 2–3 minutes or until hot.

Nutrition:

- Calories: 299
- Fat: 11 g.
- Protein: 38 g.
- Carbs: 9 g.
- Fiber: 2 g.
- Sugar: 3 g.
- Sodium: 100 mg.

Chicken Fried Steak

Preparation time: 15 minutes
Cooking time: 12–16 minutes
Servings: 4
Ingredients:

- 4 (6 oz./170 g.) beef cube steaks
- 1/2 cup buttermilk
- 1 cup flour
- 2 tsp. paprika
- 1 tsp. garlic salt
- 1 egg
- 1 cup soft breadcrumbs
- 2 tbsp. olive oil

Directions:

1. Place the cube steaks on a plate or cutting board and gently lb. until they are slightly thinner. Set aside.
2. In a shallow bowl, combine the buttermilk, flour, paprika, garlic salt, and egg until combined.

3. On a plate, combine the breadcrumbs and olive oil and mix well.
4. Dip the steaks into the buttermilk batter to coat, and let sit on a plate for 5 minutes.
5. Dredge the steaks in the breadcrumbs. Pat the crumbs onto both sides to coat the steaks thoroughly.
6. Air fry the steaks at 350°F (177°C) for 12–16 minutes or until the meat reaches 160°F (71°C) on a meat thermometer and the coating is brown and crisp. You can serve this with heated beef gravy.

Nutrition:

- Calories: 631
- Fat: 21 g.
- Protein: 61 g.
- Carbs: 46 g.
- Fiber: 2 g.
- Sugar: 3 g.
- Sodium: 358 mg.

Lemon Greek Beef and Vegetables

Preparation time: 10 minutes
Cooking time: 9–19 minutes
Servings: 4
Ingredients:

- 1/2 lb. (227 g.) 96% lean ground beef
- 2 medium tomatoes, chopped
- 1 onion, chopped
- 2 garlic cloves, minced
- 2 cups fresh baby spinach
- 2 tbsp. lemon juice, freshly squeezed
- 1/3 cup low-sodium beef broth
- 2 tbsp. crumbled low-sodium feta cheese

Directions:

1. In a baking pan, crumble the beef. Place in the air fryer basket. Air fry at 370°F (188°C) for 3 to 7 minutes, stirring once during cooking until browned. Drain off any fat or liquid.
2. Swell the tomatoes, onion, and garlic into the pan. Air fry for 4–8 minutes more, or until the onion is tender.

3. Add the spinach, lemon juice, and beef broth.
4. Air fry for 2–4 minutes more, or until the spinach is wilted.
5. Sprinkle with feta cheese and serve immediately.

Nutrition:
- Calories: 98
- Fat: 1 g.
- Protein: 15 g.
- Carbs: 5 g.
- Fiber: 1 g.
- Sugar: 2 g.
- Sodium: 123 mg.

Country-Style Pork Ribs

Preparation time: 5 minutes
Cooking time: 20–25 minutes
Servings: 4
Ingredients:
- 12 country-style pork ribs, trimmed of excess fat
- 2 tbsp. cornstarch
- 2 tbsp. olive oil
- 1 tsp. dry mustard
- 1/2 tsp. thyme
- 1/2 tsp. garlic powder
- 1 tsp. marjoram, dried
- A pinch salt
- Freshly ground black pepper, to taste

Directions:
1. Place the ribs on a clean work surface.
2. In a small bowl, combine the cornstarch, olive oil, mustard, thyme, garlic powder,

marjoram, salt, and pepper, and rub into the ribs.
3. Abode the ribs in the air fryer basket and roast at 400°F (204°C) for 10 minutes.
4. Carefully turn the ribs using tongs and roast for 10–15 minutes or until the ribs are crisp and register an internal temperature of at least 150°F (66°C).

Nutrition:
- Calories: 579
- Fat: 44 g.
- Protein: 40 g.
- Carbs: 4 g.
- Fiber: 0 g.
- Sugar: 0 g.
- Sodium: 155 mg.

Lemon Pork Tenderloin and Honey

Preparation time: 5 minutes
Cooking time: 10 minutes
Servings: 4
Ingredients:
- 1 (1 lb./454 g.) pork tenderloin, cut into 1/2-inch slices
- 1 tbsp. olive oil
- 1 tbsp. lemon juice, freshly squeezed
- 1 tbsp. honey (optional)
- 1/2 tsp. lemon zest, grated
- 1/2 tsp. marjoram, dried
- A pinch salt
- Freshly ground black pepper, to taste

Directions:
1. Put the pork tenderloin slices in a medium bowl.
2. In a minor bowl, combine the olive oil, lemon juice, honey, lemon zest, marjoram, salt, and pepper. Mix.
3. Pour this marinade over the tenderloin slices and massage gently with your hand to work it into the pork.

4. Place the pork in the air fryer basket and roast at 400°F (204°C) for 10 minutes or until the pork registers at least 145°F (63°C) using a meat thermometer.

Nutrition:

- Calories: 208
- Fat: 8 g.
- Protein: 30 g.
- Carbs: 5 g.
- Fiber: 0 g.
- Sugar: 4
- Sodium: 104 mg.

Dijon Pork Tenderloin

Preparation time: 10 minutes
Cooking time: 12–14 minutes
Servings: 4
Ingredients:

- 1 lb. (454 g.) pork tenderloin, cut into 1-inch slices
- A Pinch of salt
- Freshly ground black pepper, to taste
- 2 tbsp. Dijon mustard
- 1 garlic clove, minced
- 1/2 tsp. basil, dried
- 1 cup soft breadcrumbs
- 2 tbsp. olive oil

Directions:

1. Slightly lb. the pork slices until they are about 3/4 inch thick. Sprinkle with salt and pepper on both sides.
2. Coat the pork with the Dijon mustard and sprinkle with garlic and basil.
3. On a plate, combine the breadcrumbs and olive oil and mix well. Coat the pork slices with the bread crumb mixture, patting, so the crumbs adhere.
4. Place the pork in the air fryer basket, leaving a little space between each piece. Air fry at 390°F (199°C) for 12–14 minutes or until the pork reaches at least 145°F (63°C) on a meat thermometer and the coating is crisp and brown. Serve immediately.

Nutrition:

- Calories: 336 Fat: 13 g.
- Protein: 34 g. Carbs: 20 g.
- Fiber: 2 g.
- Sugar: 2 g.
- Sodium: 390 mg.

Air Fryer Pork Satay

Preparation time: 15 minutes
Cooking time: 9–14 minutes
Servings: 4
Ingredients:

- 1 (1 lb./454 g.) pork tenderloin, cut into 1 1/2-inch cubes
- 1/4 cup minced onion
- 2 garlic cloves, minced
- 1 jalapeño pepper, minced
- 2 tbsp. lime juice, freshly squeezed
- 2 tbsp. coconut milk
- 2 tbsp. unsalted peanut butter
- 2 tsp. curry powder

Directions:

1. In a medium bowl, mix the pork, onion, garlic, jalapeño, lime juice, coconut milk, peanut butter, and curry powder until well combined. Let position for 10 minutes at room temperature.
2. With a slotted spoon, remove the pork from the marinade. Reserve the marinade.
3. Thread the pork onto about 8 bamboo or metal skewers. Air fry at 380°F (193°C) for 9–14 minutes, brushing once with the reserved marinade until the pork reaches at least 145°F (63°C) on a meat thermometer. Discard any remaining marinade. Serve immediately.

Nutrition:

- Calories: 195 Fat: 7 g.
- Protein: 25 g. Carbs: 7 g.
- Fiber: 1 g. Sugar: 3 g.
- Sodium: 65 mg.

Pork Burgers with Red Cabbage Slaw

Preparation time: 20 minutes
Cooking time: 7–9 minutes
Servings: 4
Ingredients:

- 1/2 cup Greek yogurt
- 2 tbsp. low-sodium mustard, divided
- 1 tbsp. lemon juice, freshly squeezed
- 1/4 cup red cabbage, sliced
- 1/4 cup carrots, grated
- 1 lb. (454 g.) lean pork, ground
- 1/2 tsp. paprika
- 1 cup baby lettuce greens, mixed
- 2 small tomatoes, sliced
- 8 small low-sodium whole-wheat sandwich buns, cut in half

Directions:

1. In a lesser bowl, syndicate the yogurt, 1 tbsp. mustard, lemon juice, cabbage, and carrots; mix and refrigerate.
2. In a medium bowl, combine the pork, remaining 1 tbsp. mustard, and paprika. Form into 8 small patties.
3. Lay the patties into the air fryer basket. Air fry at 400°F (204°C) for 7–9 minutes, or until the patties register 165°F (74°C) as tested with a meat thermometer.
4. Assemble the burgers by placing some of the lettuce greens on a bun bottom. Top with a tomato slice, the patties, and the cabbage mixture. Add the bun top and serve immediately.

Nutrition:

- Calories: 473
- Fat: 15 g.
- Protein: 35 g.
- Carbs: 51 g.
- Fiber: 8 g.
- Sugar: 8 g.
- Sodium: 138 mg.

Greek Lamb Pita Pockets

Preparation time: 15 minutes
Cooking time: 5–7 minutes
Servings: 4
Ingredients:

For the dressing:

- 1 cup plain Greek yogurt
- 1 tbsp. lemon juice
- 1 tsp. dill weed, dried and crushed
- 1 tsp. oregano, ground
- 1/2 tsp. salt

For the meatballs:

- 1/2 lb. (227 g.) lamb, ground
- 1 tbsp. onion, diced
- 1 tsp. parsley, dried
- 1 tsp. dill weed, dried and crushed
- 1/4 tsp. oregano
- 1/4 tsp. coriander
- 1/4 tsp. cumin, ground
- 1/4 tsp. salt
- 4 pita halves

For the suggested toppings:

- Red onion, slivered
- Seedless cucumber, thinly sliced
- Feta cheese, crumbled
- Black olives, sliced
- Fresh peppers, chopped

Directions:

1. Stir dressing ingredients together and refrigerate while preparing lamb.
2. Combine all meatball ingredients in a large bowl and stir to distribute seasonings.

3. Shape the meat mixture into 12 small meatballs, rounded or slightly flattened if you prefer.
4. Air fry at 390°F (199°C) for 5–7 minutes, until well done. Remove and drain on paper towels.
5. To serve, pile meatballs and your choice of toppings in pita pockets and drizzle with dressing.

Nutrition:
- Calories: 270
- Fat: 14 g.
- Protein: 18 g.
- Carbs: 18 g.
- Fiber: 2 g.
- Sugar: 2 g.
- Sodium: 618 mg.

Fried Green Beans with Pecorino Romano

Preparation time: 15 minutes
Cooking time: 10 minutes
Servings: 3
Ingredients:
- 2 tbsp. buttermilk
- 1 egg
- 4 tbsp. cornmeal
- 4 tbsp. tortilla chips, crushed
- 4 tbsp. Pecorino Romano cheese, finely grated
- Coarse salt and crushed black pepper, to taste
- 1 tsp. smoked paprika
- 12 oz. green beans, trimmed

Directions:
1. In a light bowl, whisk together the buttermilk and egg.
2. In a separate bowl, combine the cornmeal, tortilla chips, Pecorino Romano cheese, salt, black pepper, and paprika.
3. Incline the green beans in the egg mixture, then, in the cornmeal/cheese mixture. Place the green beans in the lightly greased cooking basket.
4. Cook in the preheated Air Fryer at 390°F for 4 minutes. Shake the basket and cook for a further 3 minutes.
5. Taste, adjust the seasonings, and serve with the dipping sauce if desired. Bon appétit!

Nutrition:
- Calories: 340 Fat: 9.7 g.
- Carbs: 50.9 g. Protein: 12.8 g.
- Sugar: 4.7 g.

Spicy Glazed Carrots

Preparation time: 20 minutes
Cooking time: 10 minutes
Servings: 3
Ingredients:
- 1 lb. carrots, cut into matchsticks
- 2 tbsp. peanut oil
- 1 tbsp. agave syrup
- 1 jalapeño, seeded and minced
- 1/4 tsp. dill
- 1/2 tsp. basil
- Salt and white pepper to taste

Directions:
1. Jolt by warming your Air Fryer to 380°F.
2. Toss all ingredients together and place them in the Air Fryer basket.
3. Prepare for 15 minutes, pulsating the basket halfway through the cooking time. Transfer to a serving platter and enjoy!

Nutrition:
- Calories: 162 Fat: 9.3 g.
- Carbs: 20.1 g. Protein: 1.4 g.
- Sugar: 12.8 g.

Corn on the Cob with Herb Butter

Preparation time: 15 minutes
Cooking time: 10 minutes
Servings: 2
Ingredients:

- 2 ears new corn, shucked and cut into halves
- 2 tbsp. butter, room temperature
- 1 tsp. garlic, granulated
- 1/2 tsp. fresh ginger, grated
- Sea salt and pepper, to taste
- 1 tbsp. fresh rosemary, chopped
- 1 tbsp. fresh basil, chopped
- 2 tbsp. fresh chives, roughly chopped
- Cooking spray

Directions:

1. Spritz the corn with cooking spray. Cook at 395°F for 6 minutes, turning them over halfway through the cooking time.
2. For the time being, mix the butter with granulated garlic, ginger, salt, black pepper, rosemary, chives and basil.
3. Spread the butter mixture all over the corn on the cob. Cook in the preheated Air Fryer for an additional 2 minutes. Bon appétit!

Nutrition:

- Calories: 239
- Fat: 13.3 g.
- Carbs: 30.2 g.
- Protein: 5.4 g.
- Sugar: 5.8 g.

Rainbow Vegetable Fritters

Preparation time: 20 minutes
Cooking time: 10 minutes
Servings: 2
Ingredients:

- 1 zucchini, grated and squeezed
- 1 cup corn kernels
- 1/2 cup green peas, canned
- 4 tbsp. all-purpose flour
- 2 tbsp. fresh shallots, minced

- 1 tsp. fresh garlic, minced
- 1 tbsp. peanut oil
- Sea salt and pepper, to taste
- 1 tsp. cayenne pepper
- Cooking spray

Directions:

1. In a mixing bowl, thoroughly combine all ingredients until everything is well incorporated.
2. Shape the mixture into patties. Spritz the Air Fryer carrier with cooking spray.
3. Cook in the preheated Air Fryer at 365°F for 6 minutes. Fit them over and cook for a further 6 minutes
4. Serve immediately and enjoy!

Nutrition:

- Calories: 215 Fat: 8.4 g.
- Carbs: 31.6 g.
- Protein: 6 g.
- Sugar: 4.1 g.

Mediterranean Vegetable Skewers

Preparation time: 30 minutes
Cooking time: 10 minutes
Servings: 4
Ingredients:

- 2 medium-sized zucchinis, cut into 1-inch pieces
- 2 red bell peppers, cut into 1-inch pieces
- 1 green bell pepper, cut into 1-inch pieces
- 1 red onion, cut into 1-inch pieces
- 2 tbsp. olive oil
- Sea salt, to taste
- 1/2 tsp. black pepper, preferably freshly cracked
- 1/2 tsp. red pepper flakes

Directions:

1. Soak the wooden skewers in water for 15 minutes.
2. Thread the vegetables on skewers; drizzle olive oil all over the vegetable skewers; sprinkle with spices.

3. Cook in the preheated Air Fryer at 400°F for 13 minutes. Serve warm and enjoy!

Nutrition:

- Calories: 138
- Fat: 10.2 g.
- Carbs: 10.2 g.
- Protein: 2.2 g.
- Sugars: 6.6 g.

Mediterranean Style Beans and Vegetables

Preparation time: 15 minutes
Cooking time: 8 hours
Servings: 2
Ingredients:

- 1/2 cup great northern beans, drained and rinsed
- 1/2 cup red beans, drained and rinsed
- 1 tsp. garlic, minced
- 1 small onion, chopped
- 1 carrot, thinly sliced
- 1 stick celery, thinly sliced
- 1/2 cup green beans, cleaned and cut fresh
- 1 chopped red chili peppers, or to taste
- 1 tbsp. tomato paste
- 1 bay leaves
- Sea salt to taste
- Freshly cracked black pepper, to taste

Directions:

1. Place everything straight into your crockpot and cook covered on the low setting for 8 hours, or until tender. Remove the bay leaf and serve

Nutrition:

- Calories; 195.4
- Total Fat: 0.8 g.
- Saturated Fat: 0.2 g.
- Sodium: 25.9 mg.
- Carbs: 37.1 g.
- Fiber: 10.9 g.
- Protein: 12.3 g.

Spicy Vegetarian Chili

Preparation time: 10 minutes
Cooking time: 4 hours
Servings: 2
Ingredients:

- 1/2 cup farro
- 1 small onion, diced
- 1 garlic clove, minced
- 1 chipotle chili in adobo sauce, chopped
- 1/2 cup dark red kidney beans, drained
- 1/2 cup light red kidney beans, drained
- 1/2 cup tomato sauce
- 1/2 cup tomatoes, diced
- 2 tbsp. green chilies, chopped
- 1 cup vegetable stock
- 1/2 cup beer or vegetable broth
- 1 tsp. chili powder
- 1/2 tbsp. cumin, ground
- Sea salt to taste
- Freshly ground black pepper to taste

Directions:

1. Place everything in your crockpot and cook, covered, on "High" for 4 hours or low for 8 hours
2. Taste it and adjust the seasoning
3. Serve garnished with extra toppings if desired
4. Optional toppings you may wish to use are shredded cheese, olives, sun-dried tomatoes, sun-dried eggplant, crushed tortilla chips, thinly-sliced green onions, pickles, sour cream, salsa, etc.

Nutrition: Calories: 234 Total Fat: 2.6 g. Saturated Fat: 0.3 g. Sodium: 687 mg. Carbs: 42.2 g. Fiber: 8.8 g. Protein: 12.4 g.

Heavenly Vegan White Bean Stew

Preparation time: 20 minutes
Cooking time: 10 hours
Servings: 2
Ingredients:

- 1/2 lb. white beans
- 1 small carrot, diced
- 1 small celery stalk
- 1 small onion, diced
- 1 garlic clove, minced
- 1 bay leaf
- 1/2 tsp. rosemary, dried
- 1/2 tsp. thyme, dried
- 1/2 tsp. oregano, dried
- 3–6 cups fresh drinking water
- 1 tbsp. sea salt, more or less to taste
- Freshly ground white pepper, to taste
- 1/2 cup tomatoes, diced
- 2–3 cups (or more) green leafy green vegetables (kale, chard, spinach), roughly chopped
- Couscous, polenta for serving

Directions:

1. Place the soaked beans in your crockpot, covered with the water
2. Cook, covered, for 8–10 hours on low
3. Then add the carrots, onion, celery, garlic, bay leaf, and dried herbs
4. Cook, covered, on low for 4–7
5. When the beans are tender, add the tomatoes, salt, and pepper to taste
6. Add the greens about 15 minutes before serving
7. They can be served hot, warm, or cold over couscous, polenta, or bread

Nutrition:

- Calories: 336
- Total Fat: 0.9 g.
- Saturated Fat: 0.2 g.
- Sodium: 136 mg.
- Carbs: 65.7 g.
- Fiber: 16.4 g.
- Protein: 233 g.

Exotic Curried Vegetable and Chickpea Casserole

Preparation time: 15 minutes
Cooking time: 8 hours
Servings: 2
Ingredients:

- 1/2 cup cauliflower, cut into bite-sized florets
- 1 small onion, diced
- 1 small green pepper, diced
- 1 small red pepper, diced
- 1 small potato, diced
- 2.5 oz. baby spinach
- 1 tsp. fresh ginger, grated
- 1 garlic clove, minced
- 1 cup low-sodium vegetable stock
- 1/2 cup chickpeas, drained and rinsed
- 1/2 cup tomatoes with the juices, diced
- 1/2 cup coconut milk
- 1 tsp. curry powder more or less to taste
- a dash cayenne pepper or to taste
- 1 tbsp. sea salt, divided
- 1/4 tsp. freshly ground black pepper

Directions:

1. Place everything except the spinach and coconut milk in your crockpot and stir it to mix thoroughly.
2. Cook, covered, on "High" for 4 hours.
3. Then stir in the coconut milk.
4. Add the spinach and let it wilt in the residual heat.
5. Check and adjust the seasoning if necessary.
6. Serve over couscous or orzo pasta.

Nutrition:

- Calories: 261
- Total Fat: 5.1 g.
- Sat Fat: 1 g.
- Carbs: 44.6 g.
- Fiber: 11.5 g.
- Cholesterol: 13.1 mg.
- Sodium: 978.9 mg.
- Protein: 12.5 g.

Fabulous Vindaloo Vegetables

Preparation time: 15 minutes
Cooking time: 6 hours
Servings: 2
Ingredients:

- 1 garlic clove
- 1 tsp. fresh ginger, chopped
- 1 pitted date, coarsely chopped
- 1/2 tsp. coriander, ground
- 1/4 tsp. cumin, ground
- 1/4 tsp. dry mustard
- A dash cayenne pepper or to taste
- 1/2 tsp. turmeric powder
- A dash cardamom, ground
- 1 tbsp. white wine vinegar
- 1 small onion, diced
- 1 small carrot, thinly sliced
- 1/2 cup cauliflower florets
- 1/2 cup kidney beans, cooked
- 2 oz. tomato paste
- 1 small zucchini, cut into 1/4-inch-thick slices
- 1 small green or red pepper, seeded and diced
- Sea salt to taste
- Freshly ground black pepper to taste
- 1/2 cup frozen green peas, thawed
- 1 cup fresh water

Directions:

1. Blend the tomato paste, vinegar, garlic, water, ginger, date, and coriander along with the other spices until smooth, then set it aside. Place the kidney beans, cauliflower, zucchini, pepper, onions, and carrots in your crockpot and stir in the date garlic mixture to combine.
2. Cook, covered, on "Low" for 6 hours or 4 hours on "High."
3. Add the peas and let them heat through before serving.

Nutrition:

- Calories: 159 Total Fat: 1 g.
- Sodium: 464 mg. Carbs: 32.6 g.
- Fiber: 10 g. Protein: 9 g.

Italian, Vegan Casserole with Quinoa

Preparation time: 20 minutes
Cooking time: 5 hours
Servings: 2
Ingredients:

- 3/4 cup chickpeas, soaked and dried
- 1 medium potato
- 2 medium carrots
- 1 small onion
- 1 cup quinoa, cooked

For the sauce:

- 1 tsp. red peppers, crushed
- 2 tsp. paprika
- 1 tbsp. miso
- 1 tbsp. tamari or soy sauce
- 1 tbsp. mirin
- 1 tbsp. pomegranate molasses
- 1 tbsp. balsamic vinegar
- 1 garlic clove, crushed
- 1 tbsp. sesame oil
- 1 spring onion, sliced
- 1/4 cup toasted almonds, sliced

Directions:

1. Wash and slice the carrots, onions, and potatoes into bite-sized pieces.
2. Place everything except the quinoa, chickpeas spring onions, and sliced almonds in your crockpot and stir to combine.
3. Cook, covered, for 6 hours on "High."

4. Serve the casserole over the cooked quinoa garnished with sliced spring onions, chickpeas and almonds.

Nutrition:

- Calories: 602
- Total Fat: 11.2 g.
- Saturated Fat: 1.4 g.
- Sodium: 770 mg.
- Carbs: 106 g.
- Fiber: 18.2 g.
- Protein: 22.5 g.

Homely Healthy Baked Beans

Preparation time: 10 minutes
Cooking time: 8 hours
Servings: 2
Ingredients:

- 1/2 lb. dry beans, soaked overnight or for 8 hours
- 1 small onion, diced
- 1 stalk celery, diced
- 2 garlic cloves, minced
- 1/2 cup tomatoes, crushed
- 1 cup water
- 1/4 cup olive oil
- 1/2 tbsp. oregano, ground
- 1/2 a tbsp. thyme, ground
- 1 bay leaf
- 1 tbsp. sea salt

Directions:

1. Place everything in your crockpot and cook, covered, on "Low" for 7–8 hours.
2. Serve with feta cheese, freshly baked bread, or on toast.

Nutrition:

- Calories: 149
- Total Fat: 1.1 g.
- Saturated Fat: 0.2 g.
- Sodium: 751 mg.
- Carbs: 39.5 g.
- Fiber: 19.4 g.
- Protein: 12.8 g.

Dreamy Kale and Cannellini Casserole with Farro

Preparation time: 15 minutes
Cooking time: 6 hours
Servings: 2
Ingredients:

- 1 cup vegetable stock or broth
- 1/2 cup fire-roasted tomatoes, unsalted
- 1/2 cup farro, rinsed
- 1 small onion, coarsely chopped
- 1 medium carrot, thinly sliced
- 1 stalk celery, diced
- 1 garlic clove, crushed
- 1/2 tsp. red pepper, crushed
- 1/4 tsp. sea salt
- 2 cups fresh green kale, coarsely chopped
- 1/2 a cup cannellini beans, rinsed and drained
- 1 tbsp. fresh lemon juice
- 1/4 cup feta cheese, crumbled
- A hand full of chopped fresh basil or parsley

Directions:

1. Place the farro, stock, tomatoes, onions, celery, carrots, garlic, crushed red pepper, and salt in your crockpot and cook, covered on "High" for 2 hours.
2. Stir in the beans, kale, and lemon juice, then continue cooking, covered for about another hour.
3. Serve with a sprinkling of parsley, cheese, or fresh basil.

Nutrition:

- Calories: 274
- Fat: 4 g.
- Cholesterol: 11 mg.
- Sodium: 691 mg.
- Carbs: 46 g.
- Fiber: 9 g.
- Protein: 14 g.

Delightful Ratatouille

Preparation time: 15 minutes
Cooking time: 3 hours
Servings: 2
Ingredients:

- 1 small eggplant cut into inch cubes
- 1 medium ripe tomato, chopped
- 1 medium zucchini, sliced
- 1 small onion, chopped
- 1 small sweet green pepper, chopped
- 1 small sweet yellow pepper, chopped
- 1 small sweet red pepper, chopped
- 2 tbsp. green olives, pitted
- 2 tbsp. black olives, pitted
- 1 tbsp. tomato paste
- 1 tbsp. fresh basil, minced
- 1/2 tsp. cracked black pepper
- 2 tsp. olive oil

Directions:

1. Place everything in your crockpot and cook covered on "High" for 4 hours or "Low" for 7 hours.

Nutrition:

- Calories: 127 Total Fat: 7 g.
- Saturated Fat: 1 g. Carbs: 15 g.
- Protein: 3 g. Fiber: 4 g. Sodium: 488 g.

Amazing Vegetable Lasagna

Preparation time: 20 minutes
Cooking time: 4 hours
Servings: 2
Ingredients:

- 3 oz. baby spinach, chopped and drained
- 1 garlic clove, minced
- 1 tbsp. fresh oregano, minced
- 1/2 cup tomatoes, diced
- 1/2 cup marinara sauce
- 1/2 box lasagna noodles
- 6 oz. ricotta cheese
- 1 cup Mozzarella cheese
- 2 tbsp. Parmesan cheese
- 1/4 tsp. black pepper
- 1/4 tsp. red pepper flakes
- 1 tbsp. chopped parsley

Directions:

1. Combine the ricotta, Parmesan, pepper, pepper flakes, garlic, oregano in one bowl. Combine the diced tomatoes. Marinara sauce and parsley in another bowl. Place a little sauce mixture on the bottom of your crockpot.
2. Add a layer of noodles and half of the baby spinach. Add 1/3 of the ricotta mixture and 1/3 of the mozzarella.
3. Then a layer of the tomato sauce.
4. Add a layer of noodles and repeat finishing with the last of the cheeses on top.

Nutrition:

- Calories: 350 Total Fat: 19 g.
- Saturated Fat: 10 g. Cholesterol: 55 mg.
- Sodium: 840 mg. Carbs: 29 g. Fiber: 6 g.
- Protein: 19 g.

Garlic, Herb, and Mushroom Surprise

Preparation time: 5 minutes
Cooking time: 4 hours
Servings: 2
Ingredients:

- 12 oz. cremini mushrooms

- 2 garlic cloves, minced
- 2 small mild green chilies
- 2 small mild red chilies
- 1/4 tsp. basil, dried
- 1/4 tsp. oregano, dried
- 1/4 tsp. thyme, dried
- 1 bay leaf
- 1/2 cup vegetable stock
- 1 tbsp. unsalted butter
- 1 tbsp. fresh parsley, chopped

Directions:
1. Place everything except the butter in your crockpot and cook covered on "Low" for 4 hours.
2. During the last 15 minutes of cooking time stir in the butter, then serve with parsley.

Nutrition:
- Calories: 120
- Total Fat: 8 g.
- Saturated Fat: 4.5 g.
- Cholesterol: 20 mg.
- Sodium: 450 mg.
- Carbs: 9 g.
- Fiber: 2 g.
- Protein: 6 g.

Amazing Greek *Gigantes* in Tomato Sauce

Preparation time: 10 minutes
Cooking time: 8 hours
Servings: 2
Ingredients:
- 1/2 lb. dry *gigantes* beans, soaked overnight
- 1 onion, peeled and chopped
- 1 garlic clove, diced
- 1/2 cup tomatoes, diced
- 1/4 cup sun-dried tomatoes
- 1 cup vegetable stock
- 1 bay leaf
- 1/2 tsp. oregano, dried
- 1/4 tsp. thyme dried

- 1 pinch of red pepper flakes
- Sea salt to taste
- 1 tbsp. extra virgin olive oil
- Crusty bread, black pepper, and some more olive oil for serving

Directions:
1. Place all the ingredients into your crockpot and cook covered for 8 hours on "Low" or 4 hours on "High."
2. Taste and add salt or pepper if required.
3. This dish can be a whole meal or an accompaniment.
4. Garnish with freshly ground black pepper and a drizzle of olive oil.

Nutrition:
- Calories 182
- Total Fat: 9.1 g.
- Saturated Fat: 1.6 g.
- Cholesterol: 2 mg.
- Sodium: 568 mg.
- Carbs: 23.4 g.
- Fiber: 6.8 g.
- Protein: 4.7 g.

Magic Whole Stuffed Squash

Preparation time: 20 minutes
Cooking time: 8 hours
Servings: 2
Ingredients:
- 1 small ripe winter squash or butternut squash that fits whole in your crockpot
- 1 small onion, diced
- 1 small red pepper, diced
- 1 small green pepper, diced
- 1 small carrot, diced
- 1 stalk celery, diced

- 1/2 cup tomatoes, diced
- 1 bunch green leafy vegetables, chopped
- 1/4 cup pine nuts
- 1/8 tsp. ginger, ground
- 1/8 tsp. cinnamon, ground
- 1/8 tsp. coriander, ground
- 1/8 tsp. cumin, ground
- Sea salt and black pepper to taste

Directions:

1. Slice the top from the pumpkin to make a lid and scoop out the seeds and stringy bits.
2. Place all the ingredients inside the pumpkin and put the top back on, then place it in your crockpot and cook it covered on "Low" for 8 hours or until soft and tender.

Nutrition:

- Calories: 231
- Total Fat: 1.3 g.
- Saturated Fat: 0.2 g.
- Sodium: 92 mg.
- Carbs: 56.5 g.
- Fiber: 10.2 g.
- Protein: 6 g.

Coconut Quinoa Curry

Preparation time: 20 minutes
Cooking time: 4 hours
Servings: 2
Ingredients:

- 1 cup sweet potato, chopped
- 1 cup broccoli florets
- 1 small onion, chopped
- 1/2 cup chickpeas, drained and rinsed
- 1/2 cup tomatoes, diced
- 1 cup coconut milk
- 1/4 cup quinoa
- 1 garlic clove, minced
- 1/2 tbsp. ginger, minced
- 1 tsp. turmeric, grated
- 1 tsp. tamari sauce
- 1/4 tsp. chili flakes

Directions:

1. Place everything in your crockpot and stir then cook covered for 4 hours on "High" and serve when the sweet potatoes are tender.

Nutrition:

- Calories: 507
- Total Fat: 32 g.
- Saturated Fat: 26 g.
- Sodium: 380 mg.
- Carbs: 50 g.
- Fiber: 11 g.
- Protein: 13 g.

Refried Beans

Preparation time: 10 minutes
Cooking time: 51 minutes
Servings: 4
Ingredients:

- 1 cup white beans, rinsed and drained
- 1 medium onion, chopped
- 1 jalapeño pepper, minced
- 3 cups water
- 2 garlic cloves, chopped
- 1 bay leaf
- 1/4 cup olive oil
- Salt and ground black pepper, as required

Directions:

1. In the pot of Instant Pot, place the beans, garlic, bay leaf, and water and stir to combine.
2. Close the lid and place the pressure valve in the "Seal" position.
3. Press "Manual" and cook under "High Pressure" for about 40 minutes.
4. Press "Cancel" and allow a "Natural" release.
5. Open the lid and transfer the bean mixture into a large bowl.
6. With paper towels, then pat dries the pot.
7. In the Instant Pot, place oil and press "Sauté." Now add the onion and jalapeño and cook for about 4–5 minutes.

8. Add the salt and black pepper and cook for about 1–2 minutes.
9. Stir in the beans mixture and with a potato masher, mash the mixture slightly.
10. Cook for about 4 minutes or until the desired thickness of chili.
11. Press "Cancel" and serve hot.

Nutrition:
- Calories: 182
- Fat: 12.7 g.
- Carbs: 13.8 g.
- Sugar: 1.8 g.
- Protein: 4.5 g.
- Sodium: 72 mg.

Red Kidney Beans with Spinach

Preparation time: 15 minutes
Cooking time: 20 minutes
Servings: 4
Ingredients:
- 1 cup red kidney beans, soaked overnight, and drained
- 1 cup onion, finely chopped
- 1/2 cup homemade tomato puree
- 1 1/4 cups water
- 2 cups fresh spinach, chopped
- 2 tbsp. olive oil
- 1 tsp. garlic, finely minced
- 1 tsp. fresh ginger, finely minced
- 1 tsp. coriander, ground
- 1/2 tsp. turmeric, ground
- 1 tsp. red chili powder
- Salt, as required

Directions:
1. In the Instant Pot, place oil and press "Sauté." Now add the onion and cook for about 2 minutes.
2. Add the ginger and garlic and cook for about 30 seconds.
3. Add the tomato puree and spices and cook for about 30 seconds.
4. Press "Cancel" and stir in the remaining ingredients except for spinach.
5. Close the lid and place the pressure valve in the "Seal" position.

6. Press "Manual" and cook under and "High Pressure" for about 14 minutes.
7. Press "Cancel" and allow a "Natural" release.
8. Open the lid and press "Sauté."
9. Stir in spinach and lemon juice and cook for about 2–3 minutes.
10. Press "Cancel" and serve hot.

Nutrition:
- Calories: 141
- Fat: 7.3 g.
- Carbs: 15.9 g.
- Sugar: 2.9 g.
- Protein: 5.4 g.
- Sodium: 75 mg.

Spicy Black Beans

Preparation time: 15 minutes
Cooking time: 32 minutes
Servings: 8
Ingredients:
- 2 cups black beans, dried, soaked overnight, and drained
- 1 cup yellow onion, finely chopped
- 1 cup green bell pepper, seeded and chopped finely
- 1/4 cup fresh cilantro, chopped roughly
- 3 cups water
- 3 tbsp. olive oil
- 4 garlic cloves, finely chopped
- 1/2 tbsp. cumin, ground
- 1/4 tbsp. coriander, ground
- 1/2 tsp. turmeric, ground

- Salt and ground black pepper, as required
- 3 tbsp. fresh lemon juice

Directions:

1. In the Instant Pot, place oil and press "Sauté." Now add the bell pepper and onion and cook for about 4–5 minutes.
2. Add the garlic, cilantro, and spices; cook for about 2 minutes.
3. Press "Cancel" and stir in the beans, water, salt, and black pepper.
4. Close the lid and place the pressure valve in the "Seal" position.
5. Press "Manual" and cook under and "High Pressure" for about 25 minutes.
6. Press "Cancel" and allow a "Natural" release.
7. Open the lid and stir in lemon juice.
8. Serve immediately.

Nutrition:

- Calories: 144
- Fat: 6.2 g.
- Carbs: 17.6 g.
- Sugar: 2.3 g.
- Protein: 15.8 g.
- Sodium: 33 mg.

Simple Brown Rice

Preparation time: 5 minutes
Cooking time: 22 minutes
Servings: 4
Ingredients:

- 1 cup brown basmati rice, rinsed
- 1 1/4 cups water
- 1 tbsp. olive oil
- Salt, as required

Directions:

1. In the pot of Instant Pot, place all ingredients and mix well.
2. Close the lid and place the pressure valve in the "Seal" position.
3. Press "Manual" and cook under "High Pressure" for about 22 minutes.
4. Press "Cancel" and allow a "Natural" release for about 10 minutes. Then allow a "Quick" release.

5. Open the lid and with a fork, fluff the rice.
6. Serve warm.

Nutrition:

- Calories: 202
- Fat: 4.8 g.
- Carbs: 36.2 g.
- Sugar: 0 g.
- Protein: 3.6 g.
- Sodium: 41 mg.

Spicy Mixed Greens

Preparation time: 15 minutes
Cooking time: 9 minutes
Servings: 6
Ingredients:

- 2 medium onions, chopped
- 1 lb. mustard leaves, rinsed
- 1 lb. fresh spinach, rinsed
- 2 tbsp. olive oil
- 4 garlic cloves, minced
- 1 (2-inch) piece fresh ginger, minced
- 1 tsp. cumin, ground
- 1 tsp. coriander, ground
- 1/2 tsp. red chili powder
- 1/2 tsp. turmeric, ground
- Salt and ground black pepper, as required

Directions:

1. In the Instant Pot, place oil and press "Sauté." Now add the onion, garlic, ginger, and spices and cook for about 2–3 minutes.
2. Add the greens and cook for about 2 minutes.
3. Press "Cancel" and stir well.
4. Close the lid and place the pressure valve in the "Seal" position.
5. Press "Manual" and cook under "High Pressure" for about 4 minutes.
6. Press "Cancel" and allow a "Natural" release.
7. Open the lid and with an immersion blender, puree the mixture until smooth.

8. Serve immediately.

Nutrition:
- Calories: 98
- Fat: 5.3 g.
- Carbs: 11 g.
- Sugar: 3.2 g.
- Protein: 4.8 g.
- Sodium: 110 mg.

Zucchini with Tomatoes

Preparation time: 15 minutes
Cooking time: 11 minutes
Servings: 8
Ingredients:
- 6 medium zucchinis, roughly chopped
- 1 lb. cherry tomatoes
- 2 small onions, roughly chopped
- 2 tbsp. fresh basil, chopped
- 1 cup water
- 1 tbsp. olive oil
- 2 garlic cloves, minced
- Salt and ground black pepper, as required
- 1 tbsp. fresh ginger ground

Directions:
1. In the Instant Pot, place oil and press "Sauté." Now add the onion, garlic, ginger, and spices and cook for about 3–4 minutes.
2. Add the zucchinis and tomatoes and cook for about 1–2 minutes.
3. Press "Cancel" and stir in the remaining ingredients except for basil.

4. Close the lid and place the pressure valve in the "Seal" position.
5. Press "Manual" and cook under "High Pressure" for about 5 minutes.
6. Press "Cancel" and allow a "Natural" release.
7. Open the lid and transfer the vegetable mixture onto a serving platter.
8. Garnish with basil and serve.

Nutrition:
- Calories: 57
- Fat: 2.1 g.
- Carbs: 9 g.
- Sugar: 4.8 g.
- Protein: 2.5 g.
- Sodium: 39 mg.

Sweet and Sour Brussels Sprout

Preparation time: 15 minutes
Cooking time: 4 minutes
Servings: 6
Ingredients:
- 2 lb. Brussels sprouts, trimmed
- 2 tbsp. yacon syrup
- 3 tbsp. fresh lemon juice
- 2 tbsp. olive oil
- Salt and ground black pepper, as required

Directions:
1. In the pot of Instant Pot, place all ingredients and stir to combine.
2. Close the lid and place the pressure valve in the "Seal" position.

3. Press "Manual" and cook under "High Pressure" for about 4 minutes.
4. Press "Cancel" and carefully allow a "Quick" release.
5. Open the lid and stir the mixture well.
6. Serve immediately.

Nutrition:
- Calories: 115
- Fat: 5.3 g.
- Carbs: 15 g.
- Sugar: 4.6 g.
- Protein: 5.2 g.
- Sodium: 69 mg.

Garlicky Broccoli

Preparation time: 15 minutes
Cooking time: 5 minutes
Servings: 6
Ingredients:
- 1 lb. broccoli florets
- 1 jalapeño pepper, finely chopped
- 2 tbsp. olive oil
- 2 garlic cloves, chopped
- 1/4 tsp. red pepper flakes, crushed
- Salt and ground black pepper, as required

Directions:
1. Arrange a trivet in the Instant Pot and pour 1 cup of water.
2. Place the broccoli florets on top of the trivet in a single layer.
3. Close the lid and place the pressure valve in the "Seal" position.
4. Press "Manual" and cook under "High Pressure" for about 3–5 minutes.
5. Press "Cancel" and carefully allow a "Quick" release.
6. Meanwhile, heat the oil in a frying pan over medium heat and sauté the garlic, jalapeño pepper, and red pepper flakes for about 1 minute.
7. Stir in the salt and black pepper and remove from the heat.
8. Open the lid of the Instant Pot and transfer the broccoli onto a serving platter.
9. Drizzle with the garlic mixture and serve immediately.

Nutrition:
- Calories: 102
- Fat: 7.4 g.
- Carbs: 8.3 g.
- Sugar: 2.1 g.
- Proteins: 3.3 g.
- Sodium: 76 mg.

Spicy Cauliflower Rice

Preparation time: 10 minutes
Cooking time: 14 minutes
Servings: 4
Ingredients:
- 1 cup water
- 1 medium head cauliflower, chop into large pieces
- 2 tbsp. fresh parsley, chopped
- 2 tbsp. olive oil
- 1/2 tsp. parsley, dried
- 1/4 tsp. cumin, ground
- 1/4 tsp. paprika
- 1/4 tsp. turmeric, ground
- Salt, as required

Directions:
1. Arrange a steamer trivet in the Instant Pot and pour 1 cup of water.
2. Place the cauliflower pieces on top of the trivet.
3. Close the lid and place the pressure valve in the "Seal" position.
4. Press "Manual" and cook under "High Pressure" for about 10 minutes.
5. Press "Cancel" and carefully allow a "Quick" release.
6. Open the lid and transfer the cauliflower onto a plate.
7. Remove the water from Instant Pot.
8. With paper towels, then pat dries the pot.
9. In the Instant Pot, place oil and press "Sauté." Now add the cooked cauliflower and with a spoon, break into smaller chunks.
10. Add the parsley and spices and cook for about 1–2 minutes.

11. Press "Cancel" and serve hot.

Nutrition:
- Calories: 79
- Fat: 7.2 g.
- Carbs: 3.9 g.
- Sugar: 1.6 g.
- Protein: 1.4 g.
- Sodium: 60 mg.

Baked Eggs with Kale

Preparation time: 5 minutes
Cooking time: 20 minutes
Servings: 4
Ingredients:
- 2 tsp. olive oil
- 1 oz. shallots, diced
- 3 cups kale
- 4 large eggs
- Salt and ground pepper to taste
- 1 oz. blue cheese
- 1 oz. mascarpone
- 3 garlic cloves, minced
- 1 oz. coconut, grated
- 1 tbsp. ghee
- 1 stick butter

Directions:
1. Preheat the oven to 400°F. Grease 4 ramekins with olive oil. Heat a large pan over medium heat. Add ghee and shallots and cook for 2 minutes.
2. Add kale, salt, pepper, water and boil until the kale wilts—about 3 minutes.

Mix in blue cheese, mascarpone and remove from the heat.
3. Divide the wilted kale evenly into the 4 ramekins and make a depression in the middle of each. Drop an egg into the depression in each dish and season with grated coconut, minced garlic, salt, and pepper.
4. Place the ramekins on a baking sheet and bake until the whites are set and the yolks are firm around the edges, but still soft in the middle—about 15 minutes. Serve immediately.

Nutrition:
- Calories: 120
- Protein: 5.33 g.
- Fat: 8.97 g.
- Carbs: 5.09 g.

Mushroom Meal

Preparation time: 5 minutes
Cooking time: 10 minutes
Servings: 1
Ingredients:
- 1 egg
- 6 oz. mushrooms
- 2 oz. sweet potato, cubed,
- 1 oz. red bell pepper
- 1 tbsp. ghee
- Salt and pepper to taste
- 1 tbsp. fresh sage

Directions:
1. In a small pan, sauté the mushrooms with ghee and season with salt, pepper. Keep aside.
2. Roast the bacon, sweet potato cubes, and red bell pepper and keep aside. In the same pan, make an omelet with the egg and garnish with freshly chopped sage.
3. Finally, place all items on a serving plate and enjoy.

Nutrition:
- Calories: 215 Protein: 16.57 g.
- Fat: 10.83 g. Carbs: 17.04 g.

Salmon with Mint Paste

Preparation time: 10 minutes
Cooking time: 15 minutes
Servings: 2
Ingredients:

- 1 lb. salmon fillets
- 3 tbsp. (see step #1 below) mint paste
- 1/2 tsp. mustard
- 1/4 tsp. thyme
- 1 tbsp. ghee
- Salt and pepper to taste

Directions:

1. Preheat the oven to 350°F. Place macadamia nuts, mint, maple syrup, your spices, and mustard in the food processor and make a paste.
2. Heat a pan and add ghee. Sear the salmon fillets on each side for about 3 minutes. Add the mint paste to the top of each salmon fillet.
3. Once they are seared, transfer them to the oven and bake for about 10 minutes. Serve with some fresh baby kale and smoked paprika to add extra flavor.

Nutrition:

- Calories: 357
- Protein: 47.29 g.
- Fat: 16.35 g.
- Carbs: 2.23 g.

Chicken Pumpkin *Zoodles*

Preparation time: 10 minutes
Cooking time: 15 minutes
Servings: 2
Ingredients:

- 3 1/2 oz. chicken breast
- 1 tbsp. olive oil
- 1 tbsp. ghee
- 1/2 tsp. curry powder
- 1 stalk spring onion
- 1 garlic clove
- 1 large egg
- 1 oz. sprouts
- 3 1/2 oz. pumpkin
- 1 tsp. soy sauce
- 1/2 tsp. fish sauce
- 1/4 tsp. pepper
- 1 tsp. lime juice
- 1 green chili pepper
- 1 tbsp. cilantro
- Salt and pepper to taste

Directions:

1. Season the chicken with curry powder, salt, and pepper and set aside.
2. Prepare the sauce by combining the soy sauce and fish sauce.
3. Finely chop the spring onion and garlic. Make *zoodles* out of pumpkin (use a spiralizer)
4. Fry the seasoned chicken with olive oil until brown.
5. In a pan, melt ghee and sauté the chopped spring onion until fragrant. Add the garlic and egg to the pan.
6. Add sprouts and zoodles and mix everything well
7. Together and continue cooking until the sprouts and zoodles are tender.
8. Cut the fried chicken into pieces. Add the chicken to the pan and squeeze some lemon juice on top. Garnish with cilantro. Enjoy.

Nutrition:

- Calories: 435
- Protein: 22.97 g.
- Fat: 23.94 g.
- Carbs: 18.3 g.

Pepperoni and Cauliflower "Rice"

Preparation time: 10 minutes
Cooking time: 10 minutes
Servings: 4
Ingredients:

- 1 lb. riced cauliflower
- 8 1/2 oz. pepperoni
- 3 oz. jalapeño peppers
- 1 red chili, dried

- 1 tbsp. fresh turnip greens
- 1 tbsp. fresh rosemary
- 2 tbsp. olive oil
- 2 tbsp. ghee
- Salt and pepper to taste

Directions:

1. Grate cauliflower and make "rice" from it. Set aside.
2. Slice pepperoni, jalapeño peppers, and dried red chili and keep aside.
3. Place a large skillet over medium heat add the olive oil and ghee. When ghee is hot, add peppers, chili, turnip greens, and pepperoni. Cook until slightly browned.
4. Add the cauliflower "rice" and cook for 10 minutes, season with salt, pepper. Add finely chopped rosemary and enjoy the flavors.

Nutrition:

- Calories: 400
- Protein: 16.72 g.
- Fat: 33.38 g.
- Carbs: 8.92 g.

Salmon Wraps

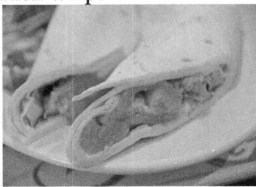

Preparation time: 15 minutes
Cooking time:
Servings: 2
Ingredients:

- 3 large eggs
- 3 1/2 oz. avocado
- 2 oz. smoked salmon
- 2 tbsp. fresh dill
- 2 tbsp. spring onion

- 2 oz. Mascarpone cheese
- 1 tbsp. ghee
- Salt and pepper to taste

Directions:

1. Whisk eggs, salt, and pepper in a small bowl. Add mascarpone cheese with chopped dill and keep aside.
2. Place a pan over medium heat and add ghee. When ghee is hot, add egg mixture and cook for 1 minute. Flip over and cook for 1 minute longer.
3. Meanwhile, slice the smoked salmon and avocado and set aside. Slide the unfolded omelet onto a plate, add sliced salmon, spring onion and avocado, and fold into a wrap.

Nutrition:

- Calories: 324
- Protein: 17.5 g.
- Fat: 23.56 g.
- Carbs: 14.02 g.

Dandelion Omelet

Preparation time: 10 minutes
Cooking time: 37 minutes
Servings: 4
Ingredients:

- 1 tbsp. ghee
- 1 oz. onion
- 10 oz. dandelion greens
- 8 large eggs
- 1 tsp. sea salt
- 2 oz. goat cheese
- 1 oz. Mascarpone
- 1/2 tsp. black pepper

Directions:

1. Preheat the oven to 350°F and place a pan over medium heat. Add ghee and when it is hot, add onion and cook until it becomes soft.
2. Add dandelion greens and cook for 2 minutes. Place aside. In a bowl, mix eggs, goat cheese, mascarpone, salt, pepper and add to dandelion mixture.

3. Using a blender, blend the mixture and pour it into a pan. Put the pan in the preheated oven for 30 minutes and enjoy.

Nutrition:

- Calories: 145
- Protein: 7.42 g.
- Fat: 9.54 g.
- Carbs: 8.64 g.

Broiled Shrimp with Garlic and Herb Potatoes

Preparation time: 10 minutes
Cooking time: 40–45 minutes
Servings: 2
Ingredients:

- 2 cups medium shrimp
- 1 tbsp. olive oil
- 1 tsp. red pepper flakes
- 1 tsp. orange peel
- 1 tsp. garlic powder
- 1/3 tsp. pepper
- 1/2 tbsp. lemon juice
- 1 can slice potatoes
- 1/2 cup spinach
- 1 tbsp. Asiago or Parmesan cheese
- 1/2 tbsp. no salt garlic and herb seasoning
- 1/2 cup evaporated milk
- 1 cup Italian breadcrumbs

Directions:

1. Preheat the oven to 350°F and prepare 8x8-inch baking dish. In a large bowl mix together potatoes, spinach, cheese, seasoning, and milk; place in dish and top with breadcrumbs. Bake, cover for 20 minutes, uncover and bake 10 more minutes.
2. In separate bowl mix shrimp, oil, red pepper flakes, garlic powder, pepper, and orange peel. Lay in a single layer on a broiling sheet covered with tin foil and broil for 5–8 minutes. Due to the differences in ovens, it is important to maintain close supervision over the shrimp to prevent burning.

Nutrition:

- Calories: 160
- Carbs: 5 g.
- Protein: 22 g.
- Fat: 8 g.

Broiled Cod and Linguine

Preparation time: 10 minutes
Cooking time: 10 minutes
Servings: 4
Ingredients:

- 8 cups linguine
- 1 tbsp. olive oil
- 4 tsp. lemon juice
- 2 tsp. garlic powder
- 2 tsp. onion powder
- 2 tsp. basil, dried
- 1/4 tsp. oregano, dried
- 4 fillets Cod Fish
- 2 cups water

Directions:

1. With the oven set to broil cover a broiling pan with tin foil and place 4 fillets on the sheet. In small bowl mix olive oil, lemon juice, onion powder, garlic powder, basil, and oregano; stir and pour over each fillet. Broil 8–10 minutes.
2. While waiting for fish to cook start a pot of boiling water and when ready start cooking pasta following the directions on the package.

3. When ready drain but do not rinse and transfer to plate.

Nutrition:
- Calories: 140
- Carbs: 30 g.
- Protein: 35 g.
- Fat: 5 g.

Mush-Li Stir Fry

Preparation time: 10 minutes
Cooking time: 20 minutes
Servings: 6
Ingredients:
- 1 8 oz. tub mushrooms, sliced
- 1 green onion or scallion, diced
- 1/2 cup matchstick carrots
- 1 tbsp. slivered almonds, peanuts, or cashews
- Soy sauce (optional)
- 2 cup broccoli florets
- 2 tbsp. water
- Cooking spray

Directions:
1. Over high heat cook broccoli in skillet or wok coated with cooking spray. Add 2 tbsp. water and cover but stir frequently until broccoli is crisp. Remove broccoli and add mushrooms and scallions.
2. Cook carrots the same way as you did the broccoli, until crisp and tender. Approximately 2–3 minutes. When ready remove from burner and mix together with broccoli, cover with nuts, and any other toppings or additions.

Nutrition:
- Calories: 60 Carbs: 8 g.
- Protein: 5 g. Fat: 3 g.

Herbed Shells and Ciabatta

Preparation time: 10 minutes
Cooking time: 40 minutes
Servings: 6
Ingredients:
- 1 tbsp. Oil
- 6 large pasta shells
- 1 (15 oz.) tub ricotta cheese
- 1 can no-salt tomatoes, stewed
- 1/2 tbsp. parsley
- 1 basil leaf, finely chopped or 1 tsp. dried basil
- 1/2 tbsp. oregano or 1 tsp. dried oregano
- 1 tsp. thyme
- 1 cup Asiago cheese
- 1 pkg. ciabatta rolls

Directions:
1. Preheat the oven to 350°F and coat 8x8-inch casserole dish with baking spray. Cook pasta shells according to package and arrange side by side in dish; evenly fill each shell with ricotta. In a bowl mix together tomatoes, parsley, basil, oregano, and thyme; evenly spread over shells. Sprinkle with cheese.
2. Cook uncovered for 30 minutes. Cut in 2 each roll and paint each slice with olive oil; broil 3–5 minutes.

Nutrition:
- Calories: 236 Carbs: 35 g.
- Protein: 16 g. Fat: 6 g.

Tuna or Cod Tacos and Homemade Salsa

Preparation time: 10 minutes
Cooking time: 10 minutes
Servings: 8
Ingredients:
- 8 (6-inch) low-sodium tortillas
- 2 tuna steaks or 2 cod fillets

- 2 tbsp. fish seasoning or blackening seasoning

For the salsa:
- 1 can tomatoes, diced
- 1/2 cucumber, diced
- 1/2 stalk celery, diced
- 1 tbsp. lemon juice
- 1/2 tsp. torn basil leaves

Directions:
1. Place steaks or fillets on coated broiler pan and cover with seasoning. Broil 5–8 minutes on each side.
2. In a medium-sized bowl stir together tomatoes, cucumber, celery, basil, and lemon juice; warm tortillas in the oven for 3–5 minutes.

Nutrition:
- Calories: 420 Carbs: 54 g.
- Protein: 28 g. Fat: 11 g.

Jasmine Meatball Curry

Preparation time: 10 minutes
Cooking time: 20 minutes
Servings: 2
Ingredients:
- 1 cup jasmine rice (enough for 2 people)
- 2 cups water
- 3 tsp. olive oil
- 1 lb. turkey, ground
- 1/3 cup parsley
- 1 tsp. Italian seasonings
- 1 packet beef broth
- 1 can tomatoes, diced

- 1 tbsp. curry paste
- 1 can low-sodium green beans
- 1 chive garlic

Directions:
1. Following package directions make 1 cup (enough for 2 servings) jasmine rice. In a large mixing bowl add parsley, Italian seasonings, and turkey and gently mix. Form into 12 meatballs.
2. Heat the oil in a large skillet over medium-high heat. Add the meatballs, reduce the heat to medium and cook for 4–6 minutes. Push the meatballs to the side of the pan; add garlic and cook, stirring, for 1 minute. Add the beef broth, tomatoes, and curry paste. Make sure all meatballs are thoroughly coated and cook for 10 more minutes. Remove from heat and put on a plate over rice. Sprinkle beans over the dish.

Nutrition:
- Calories: 409
- Carbs: 37 g.
- Protein: 52 g.
- Fat: 5 g.

Mexi-Chicken Casserole

Preparation time: 10 minutes
Cooking time: 25 minutes
Servings: 4
Ingredients:
- 1 tbsp. olive oil
- 1 cup brown rice
- 1/2 can black beans, rinsed and drained
- 1/2 cup whole kernel corn, low-sodium
- 1 cup spinach
- 4 cups water
- 2 cups shredded Mexican blend cheese, or Monterey and Colby Jack cheeses.
- 1 cup chicken, shredded

For the marinade:
- 2 tbsp. olive oil
- 3 tsp. chili powder
- Marinade 4 hours up to 24 hours before cooking.

Directions:

1. In a large pot over high heat add oil, uncooked rice, black beans, corn, spinach, and water. Constantly stirring, let come to a boil. Once it comes to a boil turn heat down to low and cover. In skillet warm chicken over medium-high heat for approximately 5–10 minutes or cook until pieces are no longer pink. Add chicken to pot with rice and mix well. Rice mixture should show signs of "cooking." If not add more water one tbsp. at a time and turn up the heat. Once the rice is cooked up and heat can be lowered back to low sprinkle with cheese and stir well. Wait 1 minute and serve.

Nutrition:

- Calories: 272
- Carbs: 21 g
- Protein: 19 g.
- Fat: 7 g.

Marinated Tuna and Roasted Kale Salad

Preparation time: 10 minutes
Cooking time: 30–35 minutes
Servings: 2
Ingredients:

- 2 tuna steaks

For the marinade for tuna:

- 3 tsp. olive or canola oil
- 1/2 tbsp. garlic, minced (about 2–3 cloves)
- 1 tbsp. orange or pineapple juice
- 1 tsp. basil, dried

For the salad:

- 4–6 cups kale leaves
- 2 cups chickpeas or garbanzo beans
- 6 cherry tomatoes, sliced
- 1 stalk celery, chopped
- 1 tbsp. almonds or pistachios
- 1/4 cup bell peppers
- 4 tbsp. olive oil

- 1 tbsp. basil
- 1/2 tbsp. ginger
- 1/4 tsp. pepper

Directions:

1. In large bowl mix kale, tomatoes, celery, nuts, and peppers in a bowl then spread out on a baking sheet. Drizzle with olive oil. Cook approximately 8–10 minutes. Let cool and place back into the bowl where all ingredients including beans, basil, and ginger are mixed.
2. Marinate tuna 5–10 minutes before cooking. Prepare broiler pan or grill. Over high heat grill or broil on each side for 3–5 minutes.

Note: Bell peppers taste the same regardless of color. Color differences only reflect a difference in the seeds and the time spent in the soil but nothing else. So, the color of the peppers should accommodate the dish.

Nutrition:

- Calories: 287
- Carbs: 17 g.
- Protein: 33 g.
- Fat: 11 g.

Chicken with Black Beans and Corn

Preparation time: 10 minutes
Cooking time: 30 minutes
Servings: 2
Ingredients:

- 1 tbsp. vegetable oil
- 4 chicken breast halves, boneless and skinless
- 1 (10 oz.) can diced tomatoes with green chili peppers
- 1 (15 oz.) can black beans, rinsed and drained
- 1 (8.75 oz.) can whole kernel corn, drained
- 1 pinch ground cumin

Directions:
1. In a large skillet, heat oil over medium-high heat. Brown chicken breasts on both sides.
2. Add tomatoes with green chili peppers, beans, and corn. Reduce heat and let simmer for 25–30 minutes or until chicken is cooked through and juices run clear.
3. Add a dash of cumin and serve.

Nutrition:
- Calories: 310
- Fat: 6 g.
- Carbs: 28 g.
- Protein: 35 g.

Baked Tilapia with Lemon
Preparation time: 10 minutes
Cooking time: 40 minutes
Servings: 2
Ingredients:
- 4 (4 oz.) fillets tilapia
- 2 tsp. butter
- 1/4 tsp. seasoning to taste (your choice)
- 1/2 tsp. garlic salt, or to taste
- 1 lemon, sliced
- 1 (16 oz.) pkg. frozen cauliflower with broccoli and red pepper

Directions:
1. Preheat the oven to 375°F. Grease a 9x13-inch baking dish.
2. Place the tilapia fillets in the bottom of the baking dish and dot them with butter. Season with Old Bay seasoning and garlic salt.
3. Top each one with 1 or 2 slices of lemon. Arrange the frozen mixed vegetables around the fish, and season lightly with salt and pepper.
4. Cover the dish and bake for 25–30 minutes in the preheated oven, until vegetables are tender and fish flakes easily with a fork.

Nutrition:
- Calories: 172
- Fat: 4 g.
- Carbs: 7 g.
- Protein: 25 g.

Dijon Chicken
Preparation time: 10 minutes
Cooking time: 55 minutes
Servings: 4
Ingredients:
- 6 chicken breast halves, boneless and skinless
- Salt and pepper to taste
- 1/2 cup honey (optional)
- 1/2 cup mustard, prepared
- 1 tsp. basil, dried
- 1 tsp. paprika
- 1/2 tsp. parsley, dried

Directions:
1. Preheat the oven to 350°F.
2. Sprinkle chicken breasts with salt and pepper to taste, and place in a lightly greased 9x13-inch baking dish.
3. In a small bowl, combine the honey, mustard, basil, paprika, and parsley. Mix well. Pour 1/2 of this mixture over the chicken, and brush to cover.
4. Bake in the preheated oven for 30 minutes. Turn chicken pieces over and brush with the remaining 1/2 of the honey mustard mixture.
5. Bake for an additional 10–15 minutes, or until chicken is no longer pink and juices run clear. Let cool 10 minutes before serving.

Nutrition:
- Calories: 232 Fat: 4 g.
- Carbs: 25 g. Protein: 26 g.

Parmesan Chicken Breasts
Preparation time: 10 minutes
Cooking time: 45 minutes
Servings: 2
Ingredients:
- 2 tbsp. olive oil

- 1 garlic clove, minced
- 1 cup dry breadcrumbs
- 2/3 cup Parmesan cheese, grated
- 1 tsp. basil leaves, dried
- 1/4 tsp. ground black pepper
- 6 chicken breast halves, boneless and skinless

Directions:

1. Preheat the oven to 350°F (175°C). Lightly grease a 9x13-inch baking dish.
2. In a bowl, blend the olive oil and garlic. In a separate bowl, mix the breadcrumbs, Parmesan cheese, basil, and pepper.
3. Dip each chicken breast in the oil mixture, then in the bread crumb mixture. Arrange the coated chicken breasts in the prepared baking dish, and top with any remaining bread crumb mixture.
4. Bake 30 minutes in the preheated oven, or until chicken is no longer pink and juices run clear.

Nutrition:

- Calories: 281 Fat: 11 g.
- Carbs: 14 g.
- Protein: 30 g.

Mediterranean Spinach and Tomato Pasta

Preparation time: 15 minutes
Cooking time: 50 minutes
Servings: 4
Ingredients:

- 1 cup vegetable broth
- 12 sun-dried tomatoes, dehydrated
- 1 pkg. (8 oz.) penne pasta, uncooked
- 2 tbsp. pine nuts
- 1 tbsp. olive oil
- 1/4 tsp. red pepper flakes, crushed
- 1 garlic clove, minced
- 1 bunch fresh spinach, rinsed and torn into bite-size pieces
- 1/4 cup Parmesan cheese, grated
- 1 cup water

Directions:

1. In a small saucepan, bring the broth to a boil. Remove from heat. Place the sun-dried tomatoes in the broth for 15 minutes, or until softened. Drain, reserving the broth, and coarsely chop.
2. Bring a large pot of lightly salted water to a boil. Place penne pasta in the pot, cook for 9–12 minutes, until al dente, and drain.
3. Place the pine nuts in a skillet over medium heat. Cook and stir until lightly toasted.
4. Heat the olive oil and red pepper flakes in a skillet over medium heat, and sauté the garlic for 1 minute, until tender. Mix in the spinach, and cook until almost wilted. Pour in the reserved broth, and stir in the chopped sun-dried tomatoes. Continue cooking for 2 minutes, or until heated through.
5. In a large bowl, toss the cooked pasta with the spinach and tomato mixture and pine nuts. Serve with Parmesan cheese.

Nutrition:

- Calories: 340
- Fat: 9 g.
- Carbs: 52 g.
- Protein: 15 g.

Vegetarian Chili

Preparation time: 10 minutes
Cooking time: 40 minutes
Servings: 4
Ingredients:

- 1 tbsp. vegetable oil
- 1 cup onions, chopped
- 3/4 cup carrots, chopped
- 3 garlic cloves, minced
- 1 cup green bell pepper, chopped
- 1 cup red bell pepper, chopped
- 3/4 cup celery, chopped
- 1 tbsp. chili powder
- 1 1/2 cups fresh mushrooms, chopped
- 1 can (28 oz.) whole peeled tomatoes

with liquid, chopped

- 1 can (19 oz.) kidney beans with liquid
- 1 can (11 oz.) whole kernel corn, undrained
- 1 tbsp. cumin, ground
- 1 1/2 tsp. oregano, dried
- 1 1/2 tsp. basil, dried

Directions:

1. Heat oil in a large saucepan over medium heat. Sauté onions, carrots, and garlic until tender. Stir in green pepper, red pepper, celery, and chili powder. Cook until vegetables are tender, about 6 minutes.
2. Stir in mushrooms, and cook for 4 minutes. Stir in tomatoes, kidney beans, and corn.
3. Season with cumin, oregano, and basil. Bring to a boil, and reduce heat to medium. Cover, and simmer for 20 minutes, stirring occasionally.

Nutrition:

- Calories: 155
- Fat: 3 g.
- Carbs: 29 g.
- Protein: 7 g. per 1/8 of recipe

Pasta with Spinach

Preparation time: 10 minutes
Cooking time: 17 minutes
Servings: 8
Ingredients:

- 1 box whole wheat penne
- 1/4 cup Parmesan cheese, grated
- 2 tbsp. olive oil
- 1 red bell pepper, chopped
- 6 garlic cloves, minced
- Dash of red pepper flakes
- 1 bag fresh spinach
- Salt and pepper to taste

Directions:

1. First, prepare the pasta in a pot of boiling salted water for 10 minutes.
2. Drain the pasta and set it aside.
3. Heat the olive oil in a skillet the sauté the

red bell pepper and garlic for 5 minutes.
4. Next, season with salt and pepper. Add the cooked pasta and the spinach.
5. Stir for 2 minutes
6. Serve topped with Parmesan cheese.

Nutrition:

- Calories: 247.9
- Protein: 8.3 g.
- Carbs: 42.1 g.
- Sugar: 2.3 g.
- Fat: 5.1 g.

Pasta with Tomato Sauce

Preparation time: 10 minutes
Cooking time: 15 minutes
Servings: 8
Ingredients:

- 1/4 cup olive oil
- 1 cup mushrooms, sliced
- 16 oz. penne pasta
- 4 garlic cloves, minced
- 4 tomatoes, seeded and diced
- 3 tbsp. roasted red peppers, chopped
- 1/4 cup black olives, sliced
- 1/4 cup fresh basil, chopped
- Salt and pepper to taste
- 1/4 cup parmesan cheese, grated

Directions:

1. First, prepare the pasta according to directions, 10 minutes.
2. Drain and set aside.

3. Heat the olive oil in a large skillet and sauté the mushrooms and garlic for 5 minutes.
4. Next, transfer the pasta to a bowl and toss with the mushrooms, garlic, tomatoes, roasted red peppers, and black olives.
5. Add the basil. Then, season with salt and pepper.
6. Top with grated parmesan cheese.

Nutrition:
- Calories: 255
- Protein: 10.1 g.
- Carbs: 45.8 g.
- Sugar: 3.1 g.
- Fat: 6.1 g.

Black Beans Burgers

Preparation time: 15 minutes
Cooking time: 10 minutes
Servings: 4
Ingredients:
- 15 oz. black beans, drained and mashed
- 1/4 cup onions, chopped
- 2 eggs, beaten
- 2 tsp. garlic cloves, minced
- 2 carrots, grated
- 1 tsp. flaxseeds
- 2 tbsp. chili sauce
- 1/2 tsp. paprika
- Salt and pepper to taste
- 3/4 cup Panko breadcrumbs

Directions:
1. Preheat the oven to 350°F.

2. Coat a baking sheet with non-stick spray.
3. Combine the ingredients in a bowl.
4. Create 4 burgers and place them on a baking sheet.
5. Bake for 10 minutes.

Nutrition:
- Calories: 268
- Protein: 12.5 g.
- Carbs: 49.9 g.
- Sugar: 3.8 g.
- Fat: 1.8 g.

No Worries Meatloaf

Preparation time: 10 minutes
Cooking time: 55 minutes
Servings: 8
Ingredients:
- 1 1/2 cups ketchup, sugar-free
- 1 1/2 cups turkey, ground
- 1 green bell pepper, chopped
- 1 onion, small, chopped
- 1 garlic clove, minced
- 1/3 cup Panko breadcrumbs
- 3 mushrooms, diced
- 1 egg, beaten
- 3/4 tsp. Italian seasoning
- Salt and pepper to taste

Directions:
1. Preheat the oven to 325°F.
2. Coat a loaf pan with non-stick spray.
3. Combine all ingredients in a bowl but use only half the ketchup.
4. Transfer the mixture to the loaf pan.
5. Bake for 40 minutes.
6. Top with the remaining ketchup and bake for 15 minutes.

Nutrition:
- Calories: 150
- Protein: 10.1 g.
- Carbs: 22.1 g.
- Sugar: 4.7 g.
- Fat: 3.9 g.

Hawaiian Chicken

Preparation time: 15 minutes
Cooking time: 18 minutes
Servings: 4
Ingredients:

- 4 cubed chicken breast halves

Marinade:

- 1 1/4 cups liquid amino
- 2 tbsp. apple cider vinegar
- 3 tbsp. Truvia brown sugar substitute

Chicken:

- 1 green bell pepper, chopped
- 1 red bell pepper, chopped
- 1 orange bell pepper, chopped
- 1 onion, chopped
- 2 1/2 cups pineapple chunks without liquid.
- 1 cup mushrooms, sliced
- Dash of red pepper flakes

Directions:

1. Combine the marinade ingredients. Then, toss with the chicken.
2. Marinade for 1 hour.
3. Add the marinade, to a large skillet.
4. Stir in the remaining ingredients except for the chicken and bring the sauce to a simmer.
5. Simmer for 10 minutes—the peppers should be soft.
6. Add the chicken pieces and cook for 8 minutes, until done.
7. Serve over rice.

Nutrition:

- Calories: 299 Protein: 32.8 g.
- Carbs: 36 g. Sugar: 8 g. Fat: 1.8 g.

Yakisoba Chicken

Preparation time: 10 minutes
Cooking time: 7 minutes
Servings: 6
Ingredients:

- 1/3 cup tonkatsu sauce
- 3 garlic cloves, minced
- 1 tsp. ginger, grated
- 4 chicken breast halves, cubed
- 1/4 cup chicken broth
- 1/4 cup liquid amino
- 1 onion, sliced
- 1 1/2 cups cabbage, chopped
- 1 large carrot, chopped
- 1 cup bamboo shoots, chopped
- 1 cup sprouts
- 2 tsp. rice wine vinegar
- 1 cup soba noodles, cooked

Directions:

1. Heat the tonkatsu sauce in a skillet.
2. Stir the garlic and ginger for 1 minute.
3. Stir in the chicken, chicken broth, and liquid amino and brown for 1 minute.
4. Transfer the ingredients to a bowl and keep warm.
5. Add all remaining ingredients to the skillet except the soba noodles
6. Stir the vegetable for 3 minutes.
7. Add the chicken mixture back into the skillet along with the cooked noodles and stir for 2 minutes.

Nutrition:

- Calories: 301.2
- Protein: 29.8 g.
- Carbs: 39.7 g.
- Sugar: 2.8 g.
- Fat: 4.7 g.

Slow Cooker Chicken Creole

Preparation time: 10 minutes
Cooking time: 4 minutes
Servings: 6
Ingredients:

- 6 chicken breast halves

- Salt and pepper to taste
- 2 tbsp. Creole seasoning or to taste
- 2 cups sugar-free tomatoes, stewed with liquid
- 1 cup chicken broth
- 1 cup Rotel® tomatoes
- 3 tbsp. tomato paste
- 2 stalks celery, diced
- 1 red pepper, diced
- 4 garlic cloves, minced
- 1 onion, sliced
- 1 cup mushrooms, sliced
- 2 jalapeño pepper, seeded and chopped
- 1–2 tsp. hot sauce

Directions:
1. Transfer the chicken to a slow cooker.
2. Sprinkle with salt, pepper, and Creole seasoning.
3. Add the tomatoes (including liquid), chicken broth, Rotel® tomatoes, tomato paste, celery, red bell pepper, garlic, onion, mushrooms, jalapeño pepper, and the hot sauce. Stir well.

Nutrition:
- Calories: 199.3 Protein: 30.1 g.
- Carbs: 13.5 g. Sugar: 4.7 g.
- Fat: 2.1 g.

Salmon Cakes

Preparation time: 10 minutes
Cooking time: 8 minutes per batch
Servings: 10
Ingredients:

- 2 cups potatoes, thawed frozen, shredded
- 3 eggs, beaten
- Salt and pepper to taste
- 1/2 tsp. oregano
- 1/2 tsp. basil
- 1/2 tsp. lemon pepper
- 1/2 lb. salmon or 3 cans of salmon, cooked
- 3 tbsp. onions, chopped
- 3/4 cup Panko breadcrumbs
- 1/2 cup mayonnaise, fat-free
- 1 tbsp. sriracha sauce

Directions:
1. Once the frozen potatoes are thawed, press as much moisture out of them as possible.
2. Transfer the potatoes to a bowl.
3. Add the eggs, salt, pepper, oregano, basil, and lemon pepper, and mix thoroughly.
4. Stir in the flaked salmon, onion, and breadcrumbs.
5. Create 10 crab cake patties.
6. Heat the oil in a skillet. Fry the patties for 4 minutes on each side.
7. Drain on a paper towel.
8. Combine the mayonnaise and sriracha sauce for dipping.

Nutrition:
- Calories: 136.8
- Protein: 9.1 g.
- Carbs: 16.3 g.
- Sugar: 3 g.
- Fat: 1.5 g.

Orange Tilapia

Preparation time: 10 minutes
Cooking time: 8 minutes
Servings: 4
Ingredients:

- 2 tbsp. olive oil
- 4 tilapia fillets
- 1/2 tsp. Old Bay seasoning
- Salt and pepper to taste
- 1/2 tsp. lemon basil

- 5 tbsp. juice from a fresh orange
- 3 tbsp. juice from a fresh lemon

Directions:

1. Heat the oil in a skillet.
2. Season the tilapia with Old Bay seasoning, salt, pepper, and lemon basil.
3. Top with the orange and lemon juices.
4. Cook for 8 minutes. The fish should be flaky

Nutrition:

- Calories: 135.7
- Protein: 18.1 g.
- Carbs: 8 g.
- Sugar: 3 g.
- Fat: 3.9 g.

Crusted Red Snapper

Preparation time: 5 minutes
Cooking time: 14 minutes
Servings: 4
Ingredients:

- 1 lb. red snapper fillets
- 1/4 cup Parmesan cheese, grated
- 1/3 cup Panko breadcrumbs
- Salt and pepper to taste
- 3 tbsp. olive oil
- 2 tbsp. mayonnaise, fat-free
- 1/2 tsp. garlic powder

Directions:

1. Preheat the oven to 450°F.
2. Combine all ingredients except the red snapper and the olive oil.
3. Coat the fish with the mixture and transfer to a baking dish.
4. Drizzle the fish with olive oil.
5. Bake for 14 minutes. The fish should be flaky.

Nutrition:

- Calories: 215
- Protein: 28.2 g.
- Carbs: 8 g.
- Sugar: 3.2 g.
- Fat: 7.9 g.

Crusted Tilapia

Preparation time: 5 minutes
Cooking time: 10 minutes
Servings: 4
Ingredients:

- 1 lb. tilapia fillets
- 1/3 cup Panko breadcrumbs
- 1/4 cup walnuts, crushed
- 2 tsp. lemon juice
- Salt and pepper to taste
- 5 tbsp. milk
- 3 tbsp. olive oil

Directions:

1. Preheat the oven to 500°F.
2. Combine the Panko, walnuts, lemon juice, salt, and pepper in a dish.
3. Pour the milk into a second dish.
4. Coat the fillets first with milk, then the Panko mix.
5. Transfer the coated fillets to a baking pan.
6. Top the fish with some olive oil
7. Bake for 10 minutes.

Nutrition:

- Calories: 229 Protein: 25 g.
- Carbs: 10 g. Sugar: 6 g.
- Fat: 11.8 g.

Lemon and Garlic Chicken

Preparation time: 10 minutes
Cooking time: 5 hours
Servings: 6
Ingredients:

- 2 lb. chicken breast, boneless and skinless

- 3 tbsp. lemon Juice
- 2 tbsp. butter
- 3 garlic cloves, minced
- 1 tbsp. chicken bouillon granules
- 1/4 cup water
- Salt and pepper, to taste

Directions:
1. Turn on your Slow Cooker and place the butter inside.
2. When melted, add the garlic and chicken, and gently cover the chicken with the buttery and garlicky mixture.
3. Place the chicken inside.
4. Combine the water, lemon, and bouillon granules, and pour over the chicken.
5. Season with salt and pepper.
6. Put the lid on and cook for 5 hours on "LOW."
7. Serve and enjoy!

Nutrition:
- Calories: 190
- Fat: 4 g.
- Carbs: 1 g.
- Protein: 21 g.
- Fiber: 0 g.

Cheesy Tomato Chicken

Preparation time: 10 minutes
Cooking time: 8 hours 15 minutes
Servings: 4
Ingredients:
- 1 1/2 lb. chicken breast, boneless and skinless
- 28 oz. canned tomatoes, diced
- 3 cups Mozzarella cheese, shredded
- 1/2 cup Kalamata olives, chopped
- 1 tsp. basil
- 1/4 tsp. oregano
- Salt and pepper, to taste

Directions:
1. Combine the chicken and tomato sauce in your Slow Cooker.
2. Put the lid on and cook for 8 hours on "LOW."
3. Open the chicken and shred the chicken

within the pot.
4. Add the remaining ingredients.
5. Stir well to combine.
6. Cook on "HIGH" for 15 more minutes.
7. Serve as desired and enjoy!

Nutrition:
- Calories: 241
- Fats: 7 g.
- Carbs 4 g.
- Protein: 25 g.
- Fiber: 1 g.

Peanut-Chicken Pitas

Preparation time: 10 minutes
Cooking time: 25 minutes
Servings: 4
Ingredients:
- 4 (4 oz.) chicken breasts, boneless and skinless
- 2 tsp. fresh ginger, minced
- 1 garlic clove, minced
- 1/4 tsp. kosher salt
- 2 tsp. canola oil
- 4 (6-inch) whole-wheat pita breads, warmed and halved
- 1 cup alfalfa sprouts
- 4 radishes, thinly sliced
- 1/2 hothouse (English) cucumber, thinly sliced
- 1 recipe Peanut Sauce
- 2 tbsp. dry-roasted peanuts, unsalted, chopped

Directions:
1. Sprinkle the chicken with ginger, garlic, and salt.
2. Heat a large skillet over medium heat. Add the oil and tilt the pan to coat the bottom evenly. Add the chicken and cook until the juices run clear, for 4 minutes on each side. Transfer the chicken to a cutting board and thinly slice.
3. Fill the pita bread halves evenly with the alfalfa sprouts, then with the sliced chicken. Top evenly with the radishes

and cucumbers. Drizzle each half evenly with the sauce and sprinkle with peanuts. Serve at once.

Nutrition:

- Calories: 413
- Carbs: 32 g.
- Fat: 16 g.
- Saturated Fat: 2 g.
- Cholesterol: 63 mg.
- Fiber: 5 g.
- Protein: 33 g.
- Sodium: 578 mg.

Leeks Braised in White Wine

Preparation time: 10 minutes
Cooking time: 30 minutes
Servings: 4
Ingredients:

- 4 medium leeks, cut in half lengthwise, sliced into 3-inch slices
- 1 tbsp. extra virgin olive oil
- 1 tsp. kosher salt
- 1/2 cup dry white wine
- 1 tsp. lemon juice
- Pinch of freshly ground pepper

Directions:

1. Submerge the sliced leeks in a large bowl of cold water, lift them out, and drain them in a colander. Repeat, using freshwater, until no grit remains in the bottom of the bowl. Drain the leeks well.
2. Heat a large nonstick skillet over medium-high heat. Add the oil and tilt the pan to coat the bottom evenly. Add the leeks and salt and cook, stirring often, until the leeks are wilted, about 5 minutes.
3. Add the wine and bring it to a boil. Reduce the heat to low, cover, and simmer, stirring occasionally, until the leeks are very tender for 30 minutes. Remove from the heat and stir in the lemon juice and pepper. Spoon the leeks into a serving dish and serve hot or warm.

Nutrition:

- Carbs: 13 g.
- Calories: 110
- Fat: 4 g.
- Saturated Fat: 1 g.
- Cholesterol: 0 mg.
- Fiber: 2 g.
- Protein: 1 g.
- Sodium: 298 mg.

Fresh Salmon Burgers

Preparation time: 15 minutes
Cooking time: 10 minutes
Servings: 4
Ingredients:

- 1 lb. salmon fillets, skinless, cut into 1-inch pieces
- 1/4 cup dry breadcrumbs, plain
- 1 large egg white
- 2 tbsp. fresh Italian parsley, chopped
- 2 tbsp. scallion, chopped
- 2 tbsp. lemon juice
- 1/4 tsp. kosher salt
- 1/4 tsp. freshly ground pepper
- 2 tsp. canola oil
- 2 whole-wheat English muffins, split and toasted
- Cucumber slices
- Thinly sliced green or napa cabbage

Directions:

1. Place the salmon in a food processor and pulse until coarsely chopped. Add the breadcrumbs, egg white, parsley, scallion, lemon juice, salt, and pepper, and pulse until well blended. Shape into 4 patties.

2. Heat a large nonstick skillet over medium heat. Add the oil and tilt the pan to coat the bottom evenly. Add the burgers and cook, turning once, until well browned and opaque in the centers, 3–4 minutes on each side.

3. To serve, place each burger on half an English muffin and top with the cucumber and cabbage.

Nutrition:

- Carbs: 21 g.
- Calories: 314
- Fat: 12 g.
- Saturated Fat: 2 g.
- Cholesterol: 72 mg.
- Fiber: 3 g.
- Protein: 31 g.
- Sodium: 353 mg.

Baked Chicken with Artichokes and Tomatoes

Preparation time: 10 minutes
Cooking time: 10 minutes
Servings: 4
Ingredients:

- 4 (6 oz.) chicken breasts, bone-in skin-on
- 1/4 tsp. kosher salt
- 1/8 tsp. freshly ground pepper
- 2 tsp. extra virgin olive oil
- 1 cup chicken stock or chicken broth, low-sodium
- 1 can (14 oz.) artichoke hearts, drained
- 4 small plum tomatoes, halved
- 2 garlic cloves, minced
- 2 tbsp. fresh Italian parsley, chopped

Directions:

1. Preheat the oven to 375°F.
2. Gently loosen but do not detach the skin from the chicken breasts. Rub the salt and pepper over the breast underneath the skin. Heat a large ovenproof skillet over medium-high heat. Add the oil and tilt the pan to coat the bottom evenly. Place the chicken in the skillet, skin side down, and cook, turning once until both sides are well browned for 6 minutes.

3. Add the stock to the skillet. Place the artichokes, tomatoes, and garlic around the chicken. Transfer the skillet to the oven and bake until the juices of the chicken run clear for 30 minutes.

4. Transfer the chicken to 4 plates. Stir the parsley into the vegetables in the skillet. Divide the vegetables evenly among the plates. Remove the skin before eating.

Nutrition:

- Carbs: 9 g.
- Calories: 213
- Fat: 5 g.
- Saturated Fat: 1 g.
- Cholesterol: 72 mg.
- Fiber: 1 g.
- Protein: 30 g.
- Sodium: 386 mg.

Spanish Braised Chicken with Tomatoes and Peppers

Preparation time: 10 minutes
Cooking time: 40 minutes
Servings: 4
Ingredients:

- 4 (6 oz.) chicken thighs, skinned
- 2 tsp. smoked paprika, divided
- 1/2 tsp. kosher salt
- 2 tsp. extra virgin olive oil
- 1 red or yellow bell pepper, thinly sliced
- 1 small onion, halved lengthwise, thinly sliced
- 2 garlic cloves, minced
- 1 can (14 1/2 oz.) tomatoes, diced, no-salt-added
- 2/3 cup dry sherry
- 1/2 cup chicken stock or chicken broth, low-sodium
- 1 tbsp. tomato paste, no-salt-added
- 2 tbsp. fresh Italian parsley, chopped
- 1 tsp. sherry vinegar or white wine vinegar

Directions:

1. Sprinkle the chicken with 1 tsp. the paprika and the salt. Heat a large deep skillet over medium-high heat. Add the oil and tilt the pan to coat the bottom evenly. Add the chicken and cook until well browned, about 3 minutes on each side. Transfer to a plate.
2. Add the bell pepper and onion to the skillet and cook, stirring often, until softened, 5 minutes. Add the garlic and cook, stirring constantly, until fragrant, 30 seconds. Add the tomatoes, sherry, stock, tomato paste, and remaining 1 tsp. paprika and bring to a boil.
3. Return the chicken to the skillet, reduce the heat to low, cover, and simmer for 20 minutes. Uncover and cook until the sauce is slightly thickened, about 10 minutes. Stir in the parsley and vinegar. Divide the chicken among 4 plates. Spoon the sauce evenly over the chicken and serve at once.

Nutrition:

- Carbs: 11 g.
- Calories: 211
- Fat: 6 g.
- Saturated Fat: 1 g.
- Cholesterol: 81 mg.
- Fiber: 3 g.
- Protein: 21 g.
- Sodium: 292 mg.

Polenta-Topped Casserole   Ratatouille

Preparation time: 15 minutes
Cooking time: 20 minutes
Servings: 4
Ingredients:

- 3 tsp. extra virgin olive oil, divided
- 1 medium onion, chopped
- 1 large yellow or red bell pepper, chopped
- 1 (about 1 1/4 lb.) medium eggplant, cut into 1/2-inch pieces
- 2 garlic cloves, minced
- 1 can (14 1/2 oz.) tomatoes, diced, no-salt-added
- 3/4 tsp. kosher salt, divided
- 1/4 tsp. freshly ground pepper, divided
- 2 tbsp. fresh basil, chopped or 1 tsp. dried basil
- 2 cups vegetable stock or vegetable broth, low-sodium
- 1/2 cup fine-grind yellow cornmeal
- 1/2 cup (2 oz.) plus 2 tbsp. fontina, shredded, divided

Directions:

1. Preheat the oven to 375°F. Brush an 8-inch square baking dish with 1 tsp. of the oil.
2. Heat a large nonstick skillet over medium heat. Add the remaining 2 tsp. oil and tilt the pan to coat. Add the onion, bell pepper, eggplant, and garlic and cook, covered, stirring occasionally, until the vegetables are softened, 6–8 minutes. Add the tomatoes, 1/4 tsp. the salt, and 1/8 tsp. the ground pepper and cook, covered, stirring occasionally, until the vegetables are tender, about 5 minutes. Stir in the basil and spoon the mixture into the prepared baking dish.
3. Combine the stock, remaining 1/2 tsp. salt, and remaining 1/8 tsp. ground pepper in a medium saucepan and bring to a boil over medium-high heat.
4. Slowly sprinkle the cornmeal into the stock, whisking constantly. Reduce the heat and cook, stirring constantly, until the polenta is thickened, about 3 minutes. Remove from the heat and stir in 1/2 cup of the fontina.
5. Spoon the polenta over the vegetables in the baking dish. Sprinkle the polenta with the remaining 2 tbsp. fontina. Bake until the casserole is hot and the cheese melts for 15 minutes. Let stand 5 minutes before serving. Spoon the casserole evenly onto 4 plates and serve at once.

Nutrition:

- Carbs: 32 g.
- Calories: 239
- Fat: 10 g.
- Saturated Fat: 4 g.
- Cholesterol: 20 mg.
- Fiber: 8 g.
- Protein: 9 g.
- Sodium: 466 mg.

Carb Choices: 2
Exchanges:

- Starch: 1
- Vegetables: 3
- Protein: 1
- Fat: 1/2

Swiss Chard with Raisins and Pine Nuts

Preparation time: 10 minutes
Cooking time: 15 minutes
Servings: 4
Ingredients:

- 12 oz. Swiss chard
- 2 tbsp. pine nuts
- 2 tsp. extra virgin olive oil
- 1 medium red onion, halved and thinly sliced
- 1/4 cup golden raisins
- 1/4 cup chicken stock or chicken broth or water, low-sodium
- 1/4 tsp. kosher salt
- Pinch of freshly ground pepper
- 1/2 tsp. red wine vinegar

Directions:

1. Cut the stems away from the tender leaves of the chard. Chop the stems and thinly slice the leaves, keeping the stems and leaves separate. Set aside.
2. Place the pine nuts in a large nonstick skillet and toast over medium heat, stirring frequently, until lightly browned and fragrant. Transfer to a plate to cool.
3. Increase the heat under the skillet to medium-high. Add the oil and tilt the pan to coat the bottom evenly. Add the chard stems and onion and cook, stirring often, until softened, 5 minutes. Add the chard leaves, raisins, stock, salt, and pepper. Cover and cook, stirring frequently, until the chard is tender, for 6–8 minutes. Remove from the heat and stir in the vinegar and pine nuts. Spoon the Swiss chard into a serving dish and serve at once.

Nutrition:

- Carbs: 14 g.
- Calories: 88
- Fat: 3 g.
- Saturated Fat: 0 g.
- Cholesterol: 0 mg.
- Fiber: 3 g.
- Protein: 3 g.
- Sodium: 303 mg.

Grilled Vegetable and Goat Cheese Sandwiches

Preparation time: minutes
Cooking time: minutes
Servings: 6
Ingredients:

- 3 tbsp.+1/2 tsp. extra virgin olive oil, divided
- 1 tbsp. balsamic vinegar
- 1/4 tsp. kosher salt
- 1/4 tsp. freshly ground pepper
- 1 (about 1 1/2 lb.) large eggplant, cut into 1/4-inch slices
- 1 red bell pepper, thinly sliced
- 1 yellow bell pepper, thinly sliced

- 1 large sweet onion, halved lengthwise, thinly sliced
- 6 (6-inch) whole-wheat baguettes
- 6 oz. goat cheese softened
- 3/4 cup fresh basil leaves, loosely packed

Directions:
1. Prepare the grill or heat a large grill pan over medium-high heat.
2. Whisk together 2 tbsp. the oil, vinegar, salt, and ground pepper in a large bowl. Set aside.
3. Combine the eggplant, bell peppers, and onion in another large bowl. Drizzle with 1 tbsp. the remaining oil and toss to coat. Brush the grill rack or grill pan with the 1/2 tsp. remaining oil. Place the vegetables on the grill rack or in the grill pan and grill, turning often, until the vegetables are browned, for 8–10 minutes. Place the vegetables in the oil mixture and toss to coat.
4. Cut the baguettes in half lengthwise. Remove and discard the soft inner crumbs from each piece of bread. Spread the bottom halves of the bread with the goat cheese. Top with the basil, then with the vegetables. Cover with the top of each piece of bread and serve at once.

Nutrition:
- Carbs: 38 g.
- Calories: 368
- Fat: 19 g.
- Saturated Fat: 7 g.
- Cholesterol: 22 mg.
- Fiber: 9 g.
- Protein: 13 g.
- Sodium: 460 mg.

Cornbread Stuffing with Sausage and Apples

Preparation time: 10 minutes
Cooking time: 1 hour 10 minutes
Servings: 8
Ingredients:

- 6 cups 1/2-inch Southern Cornbread®

cubes or purchased cornbread cubes
- 3 tsp. extra virgin olive oil, divided
- 2 oz. mild Italian turkey sausage, crumbled
- 1 medium onion, diced
- 2 stalks celery, diced
- 2 Granny Smith® apples, peeled, cored, and chopped
- 1 1/2 tsp. sage, dried, crumbled
- 1/8 tsp. freshly ground pepper
- 2 tbsp. fresh Italian parsley, chopped
- 1 1/2 cups chicken stock or chicken broth, low-sodium

Directions:
1. Preheat the oven to 350°F. Place the bread cubes in a single layer on a large rimmed baking sheet. Bake, stirring once until the cubes are lightly toasted for 20–25 minutes. Set aside. Maintain the oven temperature.
2. Brush a 2-quart baking dish with 1 tsp. the oil.
3. Heat a large nonstick skillet over medium heat. Add the remaining 2 tsp. oil and tilt the pan to coat the bottom evenly. Add the sausage, onion, and celery and cook, stirring often, until the sausage is browned, 5 minutes. Stir in the apples and cook, stirring occasionally, until they begin to soften, 5 minutes. Stir in the sage and pepper. Transfer the mixture to a large bowl and stir in the bread cubes and parsley. Add the stock and stir until it is absorbed.
4. Spoon the stuffing into the prepared baking dish, cover with foil, and bake for 20 minutes. Uncover and bake until the top of the stuffing is lightly browned, about 15 minutes longer. Serve at once.

Nutrition:
- Carbs: 24 g. Calories: 174
- Fat: 6 g. Saturated Fat: 1 g.
- Cholesterol: 33 mg. Fiber: 2 g.
- Protein: 6 g. Sodium: 402 mg.

Peanut Chicken with Green Beans

Preparation time: 10 minutes
Cooking time: 10 minutes
Servings: 4
Ingredients:

- 8 oz. trimmed green beans
- 1/4 cup peanut butter, natural creamy
- 2 tbsp. soy sauce, reduced-sodium
- 2 tbsp. rice vinegar
- 1 tbsp. water
- 4 tsp. canola oil, divided
- 1 lb. chicken breast, boneless skinless, cut into thin strips
- 2 garlic cloves, minced
- 1 red bell pepper, small, thinly sliced
- 2 scallions, thinly sliced
- 1/4 cup fresh cilantro, chopped

Directions:

1. Fill a medium saucepan half full with water and bring to a boil over high heat. Add the green beans, return to a boil, and cook just until crisp-tender, about 3 minutes. Drain, let cool slightly, and pat dry with paper towels.
2. Whisk together the peanut butter, soy sauce, vinegar, and water in a small bowl until smooth.
3. Heat a large wok or nonstick skillet over medium-high heat. Add 2 tsp. the oil and tilt the pan to coat the bottom evenly. Add the chicken and cook, stirring constantly, until lightly browned, for 2–3 minutes. Transfer the chicken to a plate and wipe out the wok with paper towels.
4. Add the remaining 2 tsp. oil to the wok over medium-high heat. Add the garlic and cook, stirring constantly, until fragrant, for 30 seconds. Add the green beans, bell pepper, and scallions and cook, stirring constantly, until crisp-tender, for 3 minutes. Stir in the chicken and the peanut butter mixture and cook until the sauce is thickened, for 30 seconds. Remove from the heat and stir in the cilantro. Divide evenly among 4 plates and serve at once.

Nutrition:

- Carbs: 10 g.
- Calories: 294
- Fat: 15 g.
- Saturated Fat: 2 g.
- Cholesterol: 63 mg.
- Fiber: 3 g.
- Protein: 28 g.
- Sodium: 422 mg.

Lasagna with Greens and Ricotta

Preparation time: 15 minutes
Cooking time: 40 minutes
Servings: 6
Ingredients:

- 2 cups marinara sauce
- 9 whole-wheat lasagna noodles
- 1 lb. Swiss chard, tough stems removed, leaves chopped
- 1/2 cup water
- 2 tsp. canola oil, divided
- 4 oz. Mozzarella cheese, shredded, part-skim (about 1 cup)
- 1 cup ricotta, part-skim
- 1 oz. (about 1/4 cup) plus 2 tbsp. Parmesan cheese, freshly grated, divided
- 1/8 tsp. freshly ground pepper

Directions:

1. Heat the sauce in a saucepan over medium heat until hot, if necessary.

2. Cook the lasagna noodles according to the package directions. Drain in a colander and rinse with cold water.

3. Meanwhile, combine the chard and water in a large saucepan and bring to a boil over high heat. Cover, reduce the heat to low, and simmer until the chard is tender, for 5 minutes. Drain and let cool. Squeeze the chard dry and transfer to a medium bowl.

4. Preheat the oven to 375°F. Brush an 8-inch square baking dish with 1 tsp. the oil.

5. Add the Mozzarella, ricotta, 1/4 cup of the Parmesan cheese, and the pepper to the chard and stir until well mixed.

6. Spread 1/2 cup of the sauce in the bottom of the baking dish. Place 3 noodles over the sauce, trimming them as needed to fit the dish. Top the noodles with 1 1/2 cups of the chard mixture and 3/4 cup of the remaining sauce. Repeat the layering, ending with the noodles.

7. Brush one side of a sheet of foil with the remaining 1 tsp. oil. Cover the lasagna with the foil, oiled side down, and place the dish on a large rimmed baking sheet. Bake until the noodles are tender, 30 minutes. Uncover, sprinkle the lasagna with the remaining 2 tbsp. Parmesan cheese, and bake until the Parmesan cheese melts for 5 minutes. Let stand 10 minutes. Cut the lasagna into 6 pieces and serve.

Nutrition:
- Carbs: 32 g.
- Calories: 320
- Fat: 12 g.
- Saturated Fat: 6 g.
- Cholesterol: 27 mg.
- Fiber: 7 g.
- Protein: 20 g.
- Sodium: 423 mg.

Carb Choices: 2
Exchanges:
- Starch: 1 1/2
- Vegetables: 1

CHAPTER 10:

Salad Recipes

Asparagus and Bacon Salad

Preparation time: 5 minutes
Cooking time: 5 minutes
Servings: 1
Ingredients:

- 1 egg, hard-boiled, peeled, sliced
- 1 2/3 cups asparagus, chopped
- 2 bacon slices, cooked crisp, crumbled
- 1 tsp. extra virgin olive oil
- 1 tsp. red wine vinegar
- 1/2 tsp. Dijon mustard
- Pinch salt and pepper, to taste

Directions:

1. Bring a pot of water to a boil. Add the asparagus and cook for 2–3 minutes or until tender-crisp. Drain and add cold water to stop the cooking process.
2. In a small bowl, whisk together, mustard, oil, vinegar, and salt and pepper to taste.
3. Place the asparagus on a plate, top with egg and bacon. Drizzle with vinaigrette and serve.

Nutrition:

- Calories: 356
- Total Carbs 10 g.
- Net Carbs 5 g.
- Protein: 25 g.
- Fat: 25 g.
- Sugar 5 g.
- Fiber: 5 g.

Broccoli and Mushroom Salad

Preparation time: 10 minutes
Cooking time: 0 minutes
Servings: 4
Ingredients:

- 4 sun-dried tomatoes, cut in half
- 3 cups torn leaf lettuce
- 1 1/2 cup broccoli florets
- 1 cup mushrooms, sliced
- 1/3 cup radishes, sliced
- 2 tbsp. water

- 1 tbsp. balsamic vinegar
- 1 tsp. vegetable oil
- 1/4 tsp. chicken bouillon granules
- 1/4 tsp. parsley
- 1/4 tsp. dry mustard
- 1/8 tsp. cayenne pepper

Directions:

1. Place tomatoes in a small bowl and pour boiling water over, just enough to cover. Let stand 5 minutes, drain.
2. Chop tomatoes and place them in a large bowl. Add lettuce, broccoli, mushrooms, and radishes.
3. In a jar with a tight-fitting lid, add the remaining ingredients and shake well. Pour over salad and toss to coat. Serve.

Nutrition:

- Calories: 54
- Total Carbs 9 g.
- Net Carbs 7 g.
- Protein: 3 g.
- Fat: 2 g.
- Sugar: 2 g.
- Fiber: 2 g.

Celery Apple Salad

Preparation time: 5 minutes
Cooking time: 10 minutes
Servings: 4
Ingredients:

- 2 green onions, diced
- 2 Medjool dates, pitted and finely diced
- 1 honey crisp apple, thinly sliced
- 2 cup celery, sliced
- 1/2 cup celery leaves, diced
- 1/4 cup walnuts, chopped
- Maple shallot vinaigrette

Directions:

1. Heat oven to 375°F. Place walnuts on a cookie sheet and bake 10 minutes, stirring every few minutes, to toast.
2. In a large bowl, combine all ingredients and toss to mix.

3. Drizzle vinaigrette over and toss to coat. Serve immediately.

Nutrition:
- Calories: 171
- Total Carbs 25 g.
- Net Carbs 21 g.
- Protein: 3 g.
- Fat: 8 g.
- Sugar: 15 g.
- Fiber: 4 g.

Healthy Taco Salad

Preparation time: 15 minutes
Cooking time: 10 minutes
Servings: 4
Ingredients:
- 2 whole Romaine hearts, chopped
- 1 lb. lean beef, ground
- 1 whole avocado, cubed
- 3 oz. grape tomatoes halved
- 1/2 cup Cheddar cheese, cubed
- 2 tbsp. red onion, sliced
- 1/2 batch tangy Mexican salad dressing
- 1 tsp. cumin, ground
- Salt and pepper to taste

Directions:
1. Cook ground beef in a skillet over medium heat. Break the beef up into little pieces as it cooks. Add seasonings and stir to combine. Drain grease and let cool for 5 minutes.
2. To assemble the salad, place all ingredients into a large bowl. Toss to mix then add dressing and toss. Top with reduced-fat sour cream and/or salsa if desired.

Nutrition:
- Calories: 449 Total Carbs 9 g.
- Net Carbs 4 g.
- Protein: 40 g.
- Fat: 22 g.
- Sugar: 3 g.
- Fiber: 5 g.

Pecan Pear Salad

Preparation time: 15 minutes
Cooking time: 0 minutes
Servings: 8
Ingredients:
- 10 oz. mixed greens
- 3 pears, chopped
- 1/2 cup blue cheese, crumbled
- 2 cup pecan halves
- 1 cup cranberries, dried
- 1/2 cup olive oil
- 6 tbsp. champagne vinegar
- 2 tbsp. Dijon mustard
- 1/4 tsp. salt

Directions:
1. In a large bowl combine greens, pears, cranberries, and pecans.
2. Whisk remaining ingredients, except blue cheese, together in a small bowl. Pour over salad and toss to coat. Serve topped with blue cheese crumbles.

Nutrition:
- Calories: 325
- Total Carbs 20 g.
- Net Carbs 14 g.
- Protein: 5 g.
- Fat: 26 g.
- Sugar: 10 g.
- Fiber: 6 g.

Shrimp and Avocado Salad

Preparation time: 20 minutes
Cooking time: 5 minutes
Servings: 4
Ingredients:
- 1/2 lb. raw shrimp, peeled, deveined
- 3 cups romaine lettuce, chopped
- 1 cup napa cabbage, chopped
- 1 avocado, pit removed, sliced
- 1/4 cup red cabbage, chopped
- 1/4 cucumber, julienned
- 2 tbsp. green onions, finely diced
- 2 tbsp. fresh cilantro, diced

- 1 tsp. fresh ginger, finely diced
- 2 tbsp. coconut oil
- 1 tbsp. sesame seeds
- 1 tsp. Chinese 5-spice
- Ranch dressing, fat-free

Directions:
1. Toast sesame seeds in a medium skillet over medium heat. Shake the skillet to prevent them from burning. Cook until they start to brown, about 2 minutes. Set aside.
2. Add the coconut oil to the skillet. Pat the shrimp dry and sprinkle with 5-spice. Add to hot oil. Cook 2 minutes per side, or until they turn pink. Set aside.
3. Arrange lettuce and cabbage on a serving platter. Top with green onions, cucumber, and cilantro. Add shrimp and avocado.
4. Drizzle with the desired amount of dressing and sprinkle sesame seeds over top. Serve.

Nutrition:
- Calories: 306
- Total Carbs: 20 g.
- Net Carbs: 15 g.
- Protein: 15 g.
- Fat: 19 g.
- Sugar: 4 g.
- Fiber: 5 g.

Strawberry and Avocado Salad

Preparation time: 10 minutes
Cooking time: 0 minutes
Servings: 6
Ingredients:
- 6 oz. baby spinach
- 2 avocados, chopped
- 1 cup strawberries, sliced
- 1/4 cup feta cheese, crumbled
- Creamy poppy seed dressing
- 1/4 cup almonds, sliced

Directions:
1. Add spinach, berries, avocado, nuts, and cheese to a large bowl and toss to combine.
2. Pour 1/2 recipe of creamy poppy seed dressing over salad and toss to coat. Add more dressing if desired. Serve.

Nutrition:
- Calories: 253
- Total Carbs 19 g.
- Net Carbs 13 g.
- Protein: 4 g.
- Fat: 19 g.
- Sugar: 9 g.
- Fiber: 6 g.

Grilled Tuna Salad

Preparation time: 15 minutes
Cooking time: 15 minutes
Servings: 4
Ingredients:
- 4 oz. tuna fish, 4 steaks
- 3/4 lb. red potatoes, diced
- 1/2 lb. green beans, trimmed
- 16 Kalamata olives, chopped
- 4 cups baby spinach leaves

For vinaigrette:
- 2 tbsp. canola oil
- 2 tbsp. red wine vinegar
- 1/8 tsp. salt
- 1 tbsp. water
- 1/8 tsp. red pepper flakes

Directions:
1. Steam the green beans and potatoes to make them tender.
2. Drain, rinse to shake off the excess water.
3. Bring together the vinaigrette ingredients in your jar while the vegetables are cooking. Close the lid and shake well. Everything should blend well.
4. Brush the vinaigrette over your fish.
5. Coat canola oil on your pan. Heat over medium temperature.
6. Grill each side of the tuna for 3 minutes.
7. Now divide the greens on your serving plates.
8. Arrange the green beans, olives, and potatoes over the greens.

9. Drizzle the vinaigrette on the salad. Top with tuna.

Nutrition:

- Calories: 345
- Carbs: 26 g.
- Fiber: 5 g.
- Cholesterol: 40 mg.
- Total Fat: 14 g.
- Protein: 29 g.
- Sodium: 280 mg.

Marinated Beet Salad

Preparation time: 10 minutes
Cooking time: 10 minutes
Servings: 2
Ingredients:

- 1 can (16 oz.) whole beets
- 1/4 cup white sugar
- 1 tsp. mustard, prepared
- 1/4 cup white wine vinegar
- 1/4 cup red onion, diced

Directions:

1. At first, beets should be washed properly. Now cut the beet into 1/4–1/2-inch slivers. Now take the slivers of beets and mix with onion in a mixing bowl.
2. To prepare the dressing for the salad, take a saucepan. Put the saucepan on a medium flame and add 1/4 cup liquid which was used to wash the beets.
3. Now add mustard and sugar to the liquid and stir well until the sugar and mustard get dissolved into the liquid. In this mixture, vinegar should be added, and keep the mixture on medium flame until it is boiling. After the mixture reaches boiling point, remove it from the flame and set it aside to cool down.
4. Now put this dressing on the mix of onion and beets and give it a gentle toss to coat the salad properly with dressing.
5. Now keep the salad in the refrigerator and let it chill. Serve the salad when it's completely chilled.

Nutrition:

- Calories: 87
- Protein: 1.63 g.
- Fat: 5 g.
- Carbs: 8.84 g.

Chickpea Salad

Preparation time: 15 minutes
Cooking time: 0 minutes
Servings: 2
Ingredients:

- 1 can (15 oz.) chickpeas (garbanzo beans), drained
- 1/2 onion, chopped
- 1/2 cucumber, sliced
- 1 small tomato, chopped
- 1/2 cup red wine vinegar
- 1/2 cup balsamic vinegar

Directions:

1. Take a medium-sized bowl. To prepare this salad to take cucumber, onion, chickpeas, and tomato and mix all these vegetables well.
2. Now put some red wine and balsamic vinegar into the vegetable mix and toss well to coat the vegetables.
3. Now the salad is ready to be served.

Nutrition:

- Calories: 131
- Protein: 4.98 g.
- Fat: 1.81 g.
- Carbs: 21.95 g.

Grilled Okra Salad

Preparation time: 10 minutes
Cooking time: 5 minutes
Servings: 4
Ingredients:

- 1/4 cup white wine vinegar
- 1 orange tomato, cubed
- 1/2 red onion, diced
- Salt to taste
- 16 pods fresh okra

Directions:

1. An outdoor grill should be heated to prepare this salad. The grill should be heated in medium-high heat and the grate should be oiled lightly.
2. Now take a large mixing bowl. In this bowl mix onion, tomato, and put some vinegar and salt over it. Now keep this mixture aside.
3. Not it's time to cook the okra. Cook it on the grill for 5 minutes and check if the okra has developed black marks on the skin.
4. Now take the cooked okra and mix with tomato and onion mixture, and give all the ingredients a gentle toss to mix properly. Now it's completely ready to serve.

Nutrition:

- Calories: 29
- Protein: 1.39 g.
- Fat: 0.16 g.
- Carbs: 5.85 g.

Mojito Salad

Preparation time: 15 minutes
Cooking time: 0 minutes
Servings: 2
Ingredients:

- 2 limes, zested, juiced
- 2 Romaine hearts, chopped
- 2 Granny Smith® apples, peeled, cored, cut into chunks
- 1/2 cup cucumber, chopped
- 1/3 cup fresh mint, chopped
- 1/4 cup simple syrup
- 2 tbsp. lemon juice, or to taste (optional)

Directions:

1. A large mixing bowl is needed to prepare this dish. Now take romaine lettuce, cucumber, and apple in the bowl and mix well.
2. Now put mint, lemon juice, lime zest, and simple syrup in the bowl and give the mixture a toss to mix properly.

Nutrition:

- Calories: 97
- Protein: 2.59 g.
- Fat: 1.13 g.
- Carbs: 20.29 g.

Piña Colada Fruit Salad

Preparation time: 15 minutes
Cooking time: 0 minutes
Servings: 2
Ingredients:

- 6 fresh strawberries, hulled and sliced
- 1 peach, sliced
- 1 banana, sliced
- 1/2 cup watermelon chunks
- 1/2 cup fresh blueberries
- 1/2 cup fresh pineapple chunks
- 1/4 cup *piña colada* mix

Directions:

1. Take a large mixing bowl. Now take pineapple, watermelon, blueberries in the bowl and mix well.
2. Nod adds banana and peach to this mixture and gives it a gentle toss to mix properly.
3. Now sprinkle some *piña colada* mix over the fruits and toss the mixture to evenly coat the fruits with *piña colada* mix.

Nutrition:

- Calories: 105
- Protein: 0.67 g.
- Fat: 1.46 g.
- Carbs: 21.19 g.

Southwestern Cactus Salad

Preparation time: 1 hour 5 minutes
Cooking time: 0 minutes
Servings: 4
Ingredients:

- 1 jar (16 oz.) no pales, drained, rinsed, dried
- 2 cups tomatoes, chopped
- 1/2 cup onion, diced
- 5 jalapeño peppers, seeded, minced

- 1/2 cup fresh cilantro leaves
- 2 lemons
- 1/2 tsp. garlic salt (optional)

Directions:
1. A medium-sized mixing bowl is needed to make this salad. Not put cactus, onions, tomatoes, and jalapeno in this bowl and mix well all the ingredients.
2. Now sprinkle some cilantro over the mix and squeeze the lemon juice over this mixture. Now give this mixture a gentle toss to mix properly.
3. Now cover the bowl and keep it in the refrigerator for at least 1 hour. Before serving sprinkle garlic salt over the salad. Here garlic salt is optional.

Nutrition:
- Calories: 118
- Protein: 5.59 g.
- Fat: 1.87 g.
- Carbs: 21.75 g.

Taco Slaw

Preparation time: 20 minutes
Cooking time: 0 minutes
Servings: 4
Ingredients:
- 1/2 head cabbage, small, chopped
- 1 jalapeño pepper, seeded, minced
- 1/2 red onion, minced
- 1 carrot, chopped
- 1 tbsp. fresh cilantro, chopped
- 1 lime, juiced

Directions:
1. Take a mixing bowl. Now take the red onion, carrot, cabbage, and jalapeno in the bowl and mix well.
2. Now add some cilantro and lime juice to this mixture and toss well to mix all the ingredients properly.

Nutrition:
- Calories: 38
- Protein: 1.39 g.
- Fat: 0.19 g.
- Carbs: 9.13 g.

Lime Fruit Salad

Preparation time: 20 minutes
Cooking time: 0 minutes
Servings: 6
Ingredients:
- 2 large bananas, sliced
- 1 pkg (16 oz.) fresh strawberries, hulled, sliced
- 1/2 lb. fresh blueberries
- 2 tbsp. honey (optional)
- 1 lime, juiced
- 1/3 cup pine nuts

Directions:
1. Take a large bowl to prepare the salad. Now take strawberries, blueberries, and banana in the bowl and mix well.
2. Prepare the dressing for the salad with honey and lemon juice. Sprinkle the dressing over the fruit mixture and toss well to evenly coat the fruits with the dressing.
3. Garnish the salad with pine nuts.
4. The salad is ready to be served.

Nutrition:
- Calories: 95
- Protein: 1.09 g.
- Fat: 3.18 g.
- Carbs: 17.99 g.

Gingery Carrot Salad

Preparation time: 20 minutes
Cooking time: 2 minutes
Servings: 2
Ingredients:
- 1 lb. carrots, cut diagonally into thin slices
- 2 tbsp. cider vinegar
- 1 tbsp. olive oil
- 2 tbsp. Splenda®
- 1 garlic clove, grated
- 1/4 tsp. cumin, ground
- 1/4 tsp. cinnamon
- 1 tsp. fresh ginger, grated
- 1/8 tsp. seasoned salt

- 1 dash cayenne pepper
- 1/2 cup raisins

Directions:

1. Take a large pot and fill the pot with water. Put the pot on high flame and bring the water to a boil. Now add carrots to the boiling water and let it boil for 2 minutes.
2. After 2 minutes the carrot will be tenderized. Now switch off the flame and take out the carrots. Rinse the carrots with cold water and set them aside.
3. Now take a large mixing bowl. Take vinegar, garlic, Splenda®, and olive oil in the bowl and give the mixture a whisk. The dressing is ready now. Season this mixture with cinnamon, ginger, salt, cumin, and cayenne pepper.
4. Now add the carrots and raisins to the mixture and give it a toss to properly coat the salad with the dressing.
5. Now cover the bowl and keep it in the refrigerator for at least 4 hours. Serve when the salad is chilled.

Nutrition:

- Calories: 78
- Protein: 1.18 g.
- Fat: 3.64 g.
- Carbs: 11.05 g.

Salad with Cilantro and Lime

Preparation time: 10 minutes
Cooking time: 0 minutes
Servings: 6
Ingredients:

- 2 lb. jicama, peeled, julienned
- 1/4 cup cilantro leaves, chopped
- Salt and pepper to taste
- 1/4 cup lime juice

Directions:

1. A large mixing bowl is needed to prepare the salad. Now take the chopped cilantro, lime juice, salt, and pepper in the bowl and mix well.
2. Now add the julienned jicama to this

mixture and give this mixture a good toss to properly mix all the ingredients.
3. Now refrigerate this salad and serve when it's completely chilled.

Nutrition:

- Calories: 67
- Protein: 1.34 g.
- Fat: 0.17 g.
- Carbs: 15.72 g.

Colorful Bulgur Salad

Preparation time: 15 minutes
Cooking time: 10 minutes
Servings: 2
Ingredients:

- 1/2 cup cracked bulgur wheat
- 1/2 cup chicken broth
- 1 small cucumber, seeded and chopped
- 1 tomato, chopped
- 1 carrot, shredded
- 3 green onions, thinly sliced
- 3 tbsp. fresh lime juice
- 3/4 tbsp. chili powder
- 1 pinch garlic powder

Directions:

1. A colander is needed to rinse the bulgur. Rinse the bulgur under cold running water and keep it in a small bowl.
2. Take a small saucepan. Put the chicken broth and the bulgur into the saucepan and bring it to a boil.
3. Now remove the pan from the heat and keep it aside to cool down at room temperature for at least 1 hour.
4. Take the chicken broth and bulgur mix and add cucumber, carrots, tomatoes, and onions one by one. Stir this mixture well to properly mix all these ingredients.
5. Take a small mixing bowl. Add chili powder, garlic powder, and lime juice into the small bowl and whisk well to mix properly.
6. Now add this mixture to the chicken broth mixture and give it a good stir to mix all the ingredients properly.

7. Now, this mix should be covered and kept in a refrigerator for at least 2 hours. Serve when it's completely chilled.

Nutrition:
- Calories: 180
- Protein: 16.16 g.
- Fat: 5.03 g.
- Carbs: 19.34 g.

Dandelion Salad

Preparation time: 10 minutes
Cooking time: 0 minutes
Servings: 2
Ingredients:
- 1/2 lb. torn Dandelion greens
- 1/2 red onion, chopped
- 2 tomatoes, chopped
- 1/2 tsp. basil, dried
- Salt and pepper to taste

Directions:
1. A medium-sized bowl is needed to mix all the vegetables.
2. Now put Dandelion greens, tomatoes, and red onion in the mixing bowl and give the vegetables a good mix. Season this mixture with salt, pepper, and basil. Toss all the ingredients to mix properly. The salad is now ready to be served.

Nutrition:
- Calories: 32
- Protein: 1.58 g.
- Fat: 0.3 g.
- Carbs: 7.01 g.

Warm Chicken and Mango Salad

Preparation time: 15 minutes
Cooking time: 15 minutes
Servings: 4
Ingredients:
- 1/3 cup vanilla yogurt, low-fat
- 1 1/2 tbsp. lime juice
- 1 1/2 tbsp. mango chutney
- 1 tbsp. seasoned rice vinegar
- 1 tsp. honey (optional)
- 1/4 tsp. cumin, ground
- 1/4 tsp. coriander, ground
- 1/4 tsp. paprika, ground
- 1 tsp. olive oil
- 4 chicken breast halves, skinless, boneless, cut into strips
- 2 tsp. fresh ginger, grated
- 1 garlic clove, peeled, minced
- 1 1/2 cups mango, peeled, seeded, chopped
- 1 cup red bell pepper, sliced
- 1/3 cup green onion, chopped
- 8 cups torn Romaine lettuce

Directions:
1. A small mixing bowl is needed. Now put the lime juice, vanilla yogurt, mango chutney, honey, cumin, rice vinegar, coriander, coriander, and paprika into the bowl and blend all these ingredients. Now keep this mixture aside.
2. Now take a medium-sized skillet. Put the skillet on a medium flame. When the skillet is hot, add olive oil. Now sauté ginger and garlic. Now add the chicken and cook it for 7–10 minutes. To check the chicken is done or not put a fork inside the chicken, if the juices of the chicken run clear and the skin of the chicken turns pink then the chicken is ready.
3. Now add mango, green onions, and red bell pepper to the chicken and cook all these ingredients for another 5 minutes. After 5 minutes the pepper and the mangoes will be tenderized. Now add the vanilla yogurt and lemon juice mixture to the skillet and mix all these ingredients. Garnish the meal with romaine lettuce and it's ready to be served.

Nutrition:
- Calories: 99
- Protein: 3.29 g.
- Fat: 1.99 g.
- Carbs: 19.68 g.

Baby Rocket Salad

Preparation time: 10 minutes
Cooking time: 0 minutes
Servings: 2
Ingredients:

- 1 bunch rocket
- 1/4 cup Parmesan cheese, shaved
- 1 tbsp. olive oil
- 1 tsp. red wine vinegar
- 1 sprinkle oregano

Directions:

1. Start by throwing all the ingredients into a bowl.
2. Toss them well then serve fresh.

Nutrition:

- Calories: 239
- Total Fat: 6 g.
- Saturated Fat: 4.3 g.
- Cholesterol: 228 mg.
- Total Carbs: 39 g.
- Fiber: 0 g.
- Sugar: 12 g.
- Protein: 13 g.

Almond Asian Coleslaw

Preparation time: 10 minutes
Cooking time: 0 minutes
Servings: 6
Ingredients:

- 1/2 small head Savoy cabbage, shredded
- 1 carrot, julienned
- 3 shallots, sliced thinly, diagonally
- 6 oz. snow peas, trimmed and sliced diagonally
- 4 radishes, thinly sliced
- 1/2 bunch coriander, picked
- 3 birds eye chili, thinly sliced
- 1/4 cup slivered almonds, toasted

Dressing:

- 2 tbsp. rice wine vinegar
- 2 tbsp. fresh lime juice
- 1 orange, zested
- 2 tbsp. sesame oil

- 1 garlic clove, minced
- 2 tsp. ginger, grated
- 3 twists freshly ground pepper

Directions:

1. Add cabbage, carrot, shallots, radishes, chili, and snow peas to a salad bowl.
2. Separately, mix all the ingredients for the dressing in a bowl.
3. Pour this dressing onto the cabbage mixture then toss well.
4. Garnish with coriander and toasted almonds.
5. Serve.

Nutrition:

- Calories: 113
- Total Fat: 0.7 g.
- Saturated Fat: 4.3 g.
- Cholesterol: 228 mg.
- Sodium: 160 mg.
- Total Carbs 1.5 g.
- Fiber: 0 g.
- Sugar: 0.5 g.
- Protein: 3.4 g.

Pasta Salad

Preparation time: 15 Minutes
Cooking time: 15 Minutes
Servings: 4
Ingredients:

- 8 oz. whole-wheat pasta
- 2 tomatoes
- 1 pkg. (5 oz.) spring mix
- 9 slices bacon
- 1/3 cup mayonnaise (reduced-fat)
- 1 tbsp. Dijon mustard
- 3 tbsp. apple cider vinegar
- 1/4 tsp. salt
- 1/2 tsp. pepper

Directions:

1. Cook pasta.
2. Chilled pasta, chopped tomatoes, and spring mix in a bowl.
3. Crumble cooked bacon over pasta.

4. Combine mayonnaise, mustard, vinegar, salt, and pepper in a small bowl.
5. Pour dressing over pasta, stirring to coat.
6. Understanding diabetes is the first step in curing.

Nutrition:
- Calories: 200
- Protein: 15 g.
- Fat: 3 g.
- Carbs: 6 g.

Chicken, Strawberry, and Avocado Salad

Preparation time: 10 Minutes
Cooking time: 5 Minutes
Ingredients:
- 1 1/2 cups chicken, skinless
- 1/4 cup almonds
- 2 pkg. (5 oz.) salad greens
- 1 (16 oz.) pkg. strawberries
- 1 avocado
- 1/4 cup green onion
- 1/4 cup lime juice
- 3 tbsp. extra virgin olive oil
- 2 tbsp. honey (optional)
- 1/4 tsp. salt
- 1/4 tsp. pepper

Directions:
1. Toast almonds until golden and fragrant.
2. Mix lime juice, oil, honey, salt, and pepper.
3. Mix greens, sliced strawberries, chicken, diced avocado, and sliced green onion and almonds; drizzle with dressing. Toss to coat.
4. Yummy!

Nutrition:
- Calories: 150
- Protein 15 g.
- Fat 10 g.
- Carbs 5 g.

Spinach Salad with Bacon

Preparation time: 15 Minutes
Cooking time: 0 Minutes
Servings: 4
Ingredients:
- 8 slices center-cut bacon
- 3 tbsp. extra virgin olive oil
- 1 pkg. (5 oz.) baby spinach
- 1 tbsp. apple cider vinegar
- 1 tsp. Dijon mustard
- 1/2 tsp. honey (optional)
- 1/4 tsp. salt
- 1/2 tsp. pepper

Directions:
1. Mix vinegar, mustard, honey, salt, and pepper in a bowl.
2. Whisk in oil. Place spinach in a serving bowl; drizzle with dressing, and toss to coat.
3. Sprinkle with cooked and crumbled bacon.

Nutrition:
- Calories: 110
- Protein: 6 g.
- Fat: 2 g.
- Carbs: 1 g.

Zucchini Salmon Salad

Preparation time: 15 minutes
Cooking time: 20 minutes
Servings: 2
Ingredients:
- 400 g. zucchini
- 100 g. smoked salmon
- 6 basil leaves
- 2 tbsp. lemon juice
- 2 tbsp. olive oil
- Salt and pepper to taste

Directions:
1. Peel the zucchini and cut it into strips with a spiral cutter.
2. Heat olive oil in a pan. Add the zucchini and fry for 2 minutes.
3. Cut the salmon into strips.

4. Wash basil, shake dry, and chop finely.
5. Fold the basil and salmon into the zucchini and cook over low heat. M spice its lemon juice, salt, and pepper to taste.

Nutrition:
- Calories: 300
- Carbs: 5 g.
- Protein: 18 g.
- Fat: 23 g.

Beef Salad

Preparation time: 15 minutes
Cooking time: 20 minutes
Servings: 2
Ingredients:
- 2 tbsp. lemon juice
- 800 g. green beans
- 1 avocado
- 600 g. roast beef
- 8 cocktail tomatoes
- 1 tbsp. mustard
- 1 tbsp. soy sauce
- 2 tbsp. linseed oil
- Salt and pepper to taste

Directions:
1. Mix the lemon juice, mustard, and soy sauce in a cup. Add linseed oil.
2. Wash the beans, clean them and cook them al dente in boiling salted water. Then drain, quench and drain.
3. Cut the avocado open. Take out the core. Cut out the pulp and wet it with lemon.
4. Wash the tomatoes. Remove the stems and cut them in half. Put in a bowl with the beans. Mix in the avocado. Season with salt and pepper and season to taste. Mix everything well.
5. Place the roast beef rolled up on a plate and add the salad.

Nutrition:
- Calories: 415 Kcal
- Carbs: 15 g.
- Protein: 46 g.
- Fat: 19 g.

Roasted Pepper Salad

Preparation time: 10 minutes
Cooking time: 10 minutes
Servings: 4
Ingredients:
- 1 lettuce cut into broad strips
- 1 red bell pepper
- 1 tbsp. lemon juice
- 3 tbsp. rocket leaves
- Black pepper to taste
- 2 tbsp. olive oil
- 3 tbsp. plain yogurt

Directions:
1. Preheat your air fryer to 200°F.
2. Cut bell pepper into 4 parts and remove the seeds and skin. Chop the bell pepper into strips. Place the bell pepper in the air fryer basket and roast for 10 minutes. Add pepper to a bowl, cover with a lid, and set aside for 10 minutes.
3. Add lemon juice, yogurt, and oil to a bowl. Season with black pepper. Add lettuce and rocket leaves and toss.
4. Garnish the salad with red bell pepper strips. Serve and enjoy!

Nutrition:
- Calories: 91
- Total Fat: 7 g.
- Carbs: 3 g.
- Protein: 2 g.

Snapper with Tahini Salad

Preparation time: 5–10 minutes
Cooking time: 20 minutes
Servings: 4
Ingredients:
- 1/2 bunch flat parsley, trimmed and finely chopped
- 3 tbsp. olive oil
- 1 tbsp. tahini
- 4 wild-caught snapper fillets
- 8 sticks celery, white parts trimmed and sliced into 1/8-inch sticks
- 1 lemon juice

- 1/2 tbsp. honey (optional)
- Salt and pepper to taste
- Cooking spray

Directions:
1. Preheat the oven to 350°F (175°C). Grease a baking sheet with some cooking spray or olive oil.
2. Season the fish fillets with salt and pepper; place them over the baking sheet.
3. Bake for around 15 minutes, or until the fish is easy to flake. Bake for 2–3 minutes more if needed.
4. Add the parsley and celery sticks to a mixing bowl. Mix well.
5. To another mixing bowl, add the tahini, olive oil, lemon juice, and honey. Combine well.
6. Place the fillets on a serving platter; top with the celery salad and dressing.
7. Serve fresh with some lemon wedges (optional).

Nutrition:
- Calories: 313
- Fat: 15.5 g.
- Total Carbs: 6.5 g.
- Sugar: 3.5 g.
- Protein: 35 g.
- Sodium: 292 mg.

Pita Salad Sandwich

Preparation time: 5 minutes
Cooking time: 0 minutes
Servings: 4
Ingredients:

- 2 whole-wheat pita pockets cut in half
- 1 cup hummus spread
- 1 can black beans, rinsed and drained
- 1/2 cup tomatoes, chopped or sliced
- 1 cup broccoli
- 1/2 tbsp. lemon juice
- 2 tsp. celery salt
- 1 basil leaf, finely chopped or 1 tsp. dried basil

Directions:
1. Set out pitas. In a medium-sized bowl mix black beans, tomatoes, broccoli, lemon juice, celery salt, and basil. Spread a layer of hummus on the inside of the pitas. Fill each pocket with salad mix; can stay refrigerated for 5 hours in an air-tight container.

Nutrition:
- Calories: 165 Carbs: 33 g.
- Protein: 9 g. Fat: 2.8 g.

Quinoa Salad and Ginger Cod

Preparation time: 10 minutes
Cooking time: 15–30 minutes
Servings: 2
Ingredients:

- 1 cup quinoa
- 1/2 can red kidney beans, rinsed and drained
- 1/2 cup low-sodium whole kernel corn
- 1 cup scallions
- 1/2 cup mushrooms, cleaned and sliced
- 1 tsp. celery salt
- 1/4 tsp. thyme, dried
- 2 fillet cod
- 2 tsp. soy sauce
- 2 tsp. ginger
- 1 tsp. red flakes
- 1/2 tsp. orange peel

Directions:
1. Cook quinoa according to package directions and add kidney beans, corn, scallions, mushrooms, salt, and thyme. Turn heat down to low. Turn on the broiler and coat the broiler pan or baking sheet covered in tin foil. In a small bowl mix soy sauce, ginger, red pepper flakes, and orange peel. Lay 2 fillets of fish on the tray and pour the half mix on one and half of the mix on the other. Broil 8–12 minutes.

Nutrition:
- Calories: 140 Carbs: 47 g.
- Protein: 23 g. Fat: 10 g.

Southwestern Barley and Avocado Salad

Preparation time: 10 minutes
Cooking time: 1 hour
Servings: 6
Ingredients:

- 3 cups water
- 1 cup pearl barley
- 1 1/4 tsp. kosher salt, divided
- 1 tsp. orange zest, grated
- 1/4 cup orange juice
- 1 1/2 tbsp. white wine vinegar
- 1 tbsp. canola oil
- 1/2 tsp. chipotle in adobo sauce, minced
- 1/2 tsp. cumin, ground
- 1 cup grape tomatoes, halved
- 1 avocado, pitted, peeled, and chopped
- 1/2 hothouse (English) cucumber, peeled, chopped
- 1/4 cup red onion, minced
- 1/4 cup fresh cilantro, chopped

Directions:

1. Combine the water, barley, and 1/2 tsp. the salt in a medium saucepan and bring to a boil over high heat. Reduce the heat to low, cover, and simmer until the barley is tender, yet firm to the bite, 25–30 minutes. Drain and rinse under cold running water until cool.
2. Meanwhile, whisk together the orange zest, orange juice, vinegar, oil, chipotle, cumin, and the remaining 3/4 tsp. salt in a large bowl. Stir in the cooked barley, tomatoes, avocado, cucumber, onion, and cilantro. Serve at room temperature. The salad tastes best on the day it is made, but it can be refrigerated, covered, for up to 1 day. Let stand at room temperature 30 minutes before serving.

Nutrition:

- Carbs: 32 g. Calories: 207
- Fat: 8 g. Saturated Fat: 1 g.
- Cholesterol: 0 mg. Fiber: 8 g.
- Protein: 5 g. Sodium: 241 mg.

Tuna Salad

Preparation time: 5 minutes
Cooking time: 10 minutes
Servings: 4
Ingredients:

- 1 can of tuna, drained
- 1 cup onion, minced
- 1 celery, minced
- Fresh herbs of choice
- 6 tbsp. mayonnaise
- 100 gram Salmon fillet
- ¼ cup Pickled relish

Directions:

1. In a salad bowl, put together salmon, mayonnaise, onion, pickle relish, celery, and fresh herbs of choice.
2. Mix all the ingredients until well combined. Serve.

Nutrition:

- Protein: 21.89 g. (40%),
- Potassium: (K) 284 mg. (6 %)
- Sodium: (Na) 222 mg. (15%)

Chicken-Broccoli Salad with Buttermilk Dressing

Preparation time: 20 minutes
Cooking time: 0 minutes
Servings: 4
Ingredients:

- 3 cups broccoli slaw mix, packaged and shredded
- 2 cups chicken breast, coarsely chopped and cooked
- 1/2 cup cherries, dried
- 1/3 cup celery, sliced
- 1/4 cup red onion, chopped
- 1/3 cup buttermilk
- 1/3 cup light mayonnaise
- 1 tbsp. honey (optional)
- 1 tbsp. cider vinegar
- 1 tsp. dry mustard
- 1/2 tsp. salt
- 1/8 tsp. black pepper
- 4 cups fresh baby spinach

Directions:

1. Combine the first 5 ingredients in a bowl (through onion). In a small bowl, whisk together the next 7 ingredients (through pepper). Pour buttermilk mixture over broccoli mixture. Toss to gently mix.
2. Cover and chill for 2–24 hours.
3. Add baby spinach and serve.

Nutrition:

- Calories: 278
- Fat: 7 g.
- Carbs: 29 g.
- Protein: 26 g.

Country-Style Wedge Salad with Turkey

Preparation time: 10 minutes
Cooking time: 0 minutes
Servings: 4
Ingredients:

- 1 head bibb or butterhead lettuce, quartered
- 1 recipe buttermilk-avocado dressing (see below)
- 2 cups turkey breast, cooked and shredded
- 1 cup halved grape or cherry tomatoes
- 2 eggs, hard-cooked and chopped
- 4 slices low-sodium, less-fat bacon, crisp-cooked, and crumbled
- 1/4 cup red onion, finely chopped
- Black pepper, cracked

Directions:

1. Arrange one lettuce quarter on each plate. Drizzle half of the dressing over wedges. Top with turkey, eggs, and tomatoes. Drizzle with the remaining dressing. Sprinkle with onion, bacon, and pepper.
2. To make the buttermilk-avocado dressing: in a blender, combine 3/4 cup buttermilk, 1/2 avocado, 1 tbsp. parsley, 1/4 tsp. each salt, onion powder, dry mustard, and black pepper, and 1 garlic clove, minced. Cover and blend until smooth.

Nutrition:

- Calories: 228 Fat: 9 g.
- Carb: 8 g. Protein: 29 g.

Steak and Arugula Salad with Lemon and Dill

Preparation time: 10 minutes
Cooking time: 5 minutes
Servings: 4
Ingredients:

- 2 tbsp. lemon juice
- 1 1/2 tbsp.+2 tsp. extra virgin olive oil, divided
- 3/4 tsp. kosher salt, divided
- 1/4 tsp. freshly ground pepper
- 2 tbsp. fresh dill, chopped
- 4 (4-oz.) filets mignons
- 8 cups baby arugula or torn regular arugula, loosely packed

Directions:

1. To make the dressing, whisk the lemon juice, 1 1/2 tbsp. the oil, 1/2 tsp. the salt, and 1/8 tsp. the pepper in a large bowl. Stir in the dill.
2. Sprinkle the steaks with the remaining 1/4 tsp. salt and 1/8 tsp. pepper. Heat a large heavy-bottomed skillet over medium-high heat. Add the remaining 2 tsp. oil and tilt the pan to coat the bottom evenly. Add the steaks and cook, turning once, 2 minutes on each side for medium-rare, or to the desired degree of doneness.
3. Add the arugula to the dressing and toss to coat. Divide the salad among 4 plates and top each one with a steak. Serve at once.

Nutrition:

- Carbs: 2 g. Calories: 222
- Fat: 13 g. Saturated Fat: 3 g.
- Cholesterol: 52 mg. Fiber: 1 g.
- Protein: 23 g. Sodium: 268 mg.

Braised Plum Tomatoes

Preparation time: 10 minutes
Cooking time: 10 minutes
Servings: 4
Ingredients:

- 2 tsp. extra virgin olive oil
- 1 garlic clove, minced
- 4 plum tomatoes, halved lengthwise
- 2 tbsp. sherry vinegar
- 1/2 tsp. kosher salt
- Pinch of freshly ground pepper
- 1 tbsp. fresh basil, chopped or 2 tsp. fresh rosemary or thyme, chopped

Directions:

1. Heat a large nonstick skillet over medium-high heat. Add the oil and tilt the pan to coat the bottom evenly. Add the garlic and cook, stirring constantly, until fragrant, 30 seconds.
2. Add the tomatoes, cut side down, and cook until lightly browned for 2 minutes. Turn the tomatoes. Add the vinegar and sprinkle with salt and pepper. Reduce the heat to low, cover, and cook until the tomatoes are softened, for 2–3 minutes.
3. Transfer the tomatoes to a serving dish. Drizzle with any juices remaining in the skillet and sprinkle with basil. Serve hot, warm, or at room temperature.

Nutrition:

- Carbs: 3 g.
- Calories: 37
- Fat: 3 g.
- Saturated Fat: 0 g.
- Cholesterol: 0 mg.
- Fiber: 1 g.
- Protein: 1 g.
- Sodium: 118 mg.

CHAPTER 11:

Soup and Stew Recipes

Carrot and Ginger Soup

Preparation time: 10 minutes
Cooking time: 15 minutes
Servings: 4
Ingredients:
- 3/4 lb. carrots, peeled and quartered
- 1 onion, chopped - 1 garlic, chopped
- 3 cm ginger, chopped
- 4 cups vegetable stock

Directions:
1. Start by adding all the vegetables and stock to a casserole dish.
2. Place this dish in a microwave and cook for 15 minutes on high heat.
3. Now, puree this mixture with a handheld blender. Serve warm.

Nutrition:
- Calories: 244 Fat: 11.7 g.
- Cholesterol: 321 mg. Sodium: 432 mg.
- Carbs: 2.5 g. Fiber: 0 g. Protein: 7.4 g.

Zucchini Noodle Egg Soup

Preparation time: 10 minutes
Cooking time: 10 minutes
Servings: 2

Ingredients:
- 2 thin slices fresh ginger, cut into strips
- 1 tsp. olive oil
- 2 shallots, chopped
- 2 button mushrooms, thinly sliced
- 1/2 tsp. chili flakes
- 2 cups vegetable stock
- 1 egg
- 1 tbsp. soy sauce
- 1/2 zucchini, made into noodles

Directions:
1. Start by adding and heating oil in a small saucepan. Stir in ginger and shallots then sauté on medium heat for 1 minute.
2. Toss in mushroom slices and sauté for 1 minute. Stir in chili flakes and stock then continue cooking it to a boil.
3. Meanwhile, beat egg with soy sauce in a small bowl.
4. Pour this mixture slowly into the soup with constant stirring.
5. Add zucchini noodles into the soup and cook for another 2 minutes.
6. Garnish with shallots.
7. Serve warm.

Nutrition:
- Calories: 331 Fat: 7.7 g. Carbs: 14.5 g.
- Fiber: 0 g. Sugar: 0.5 g. Protein: 27.4 g.

Prawn Bisque

Preparation time: 10 minutes
Cooking time: 25 minutes
Servings: 4
Ingredients:
- 1 pinch saffron

- 12 prawn heads and shells
- 1 tbsp. olive oil
- 1 tbsp. Pernod
- 1 carrot, finely sliced
- 1/2 fennel bulb, diced
- 1 tbsp. tomato paste
- 1 orange, juiced and peeled
- 2 cups fish stock

Optional:
- 2 tbsp. butter
- 1 tbsp. almond flour

Directions:
1. Start by cleaning the prawns by chopping off the head and removing the shell and digestive tube.
2. Add 1 tbsp. olive oil to a large skillet and heat it.
3. Toss in prawn shells, prawn heads, fennel, and carrot.
4. Sauté until the carrot turns soft then add tomato paste.
5. Stir cook for 2 minutes then adds saffron, orange peel, pernod, and stock.
6. First, bring this soup to a boil then let it simmer for 20 minutes.
7. Drain the cooked bisque soup through a chinois.
8. Add this soup to a saucepan and place it over medium heat.
9. Whisk melted butter with flour into the soup.
10. Continue cooking the soup until it thickens.
11. Stir in the prawn meat and cook for 1 minute.
12. Serve warm.

Nutrition:
- Calories: 173 Total Fat: 12.7 g.
- Saturated Fat: 8.3 g. Cholesterol: 311 mg.
- Sodium: 213 mg.
- Total Carbs: 12.5 g.
- Fiber: 0 g.
- Sugar: 0.5 g.
- Protein: 7.4 g.

Vegetable and *Zoodle* Soup

Preparation time: 10 minutes
Cooking time: 10 minutes
Servings: 4
Ingredients:
- 3 cups vegetable stock, prepared
- 1/4 cup chicken, poached and shredded
- 1 carrot, diced
- 1 zucchini, julienned
- 2 mushrooms, sliced
- Handful cauliflower florets
- Handful broccoli florets
- 3-inch leek, thinly sliced
- 1 stalk celery, chopped
- 1 squash, chopped
- A handful of baby spinach leaves

Directions:
1. Start by throwing all the ingredients into a saucepan.
2. Cook this mixture on a simmer for approximately 10 minutes.
3. Serve warm.

Nutrition:
- Calories: 324 Fat: 9.7 g.
- Sodium: 240 mg. Carbs: 0.5 g.
- Fiber: 0 g. Sugar: 0.5 g. Protein: 31.4 g.

Broccoli Turmeric Soup

Preparation time: 10 minutes
Cooking time: 15 minutes
Servings: 3
Ingredients:
- 1/2 onion, chopped
- 1 garlic clove, sliced

- 1/2 stalk celery, chopped
- 1 head broccoli, florets
- 1/2 tsp. turmeric
- 1/4 tsp. ginger, grated
- 1 bay leaf
- 2 whole black peppercorns
- 2 cups vegetable stock

Directions:
1. Start by throwing all the ingredients into a saucepan.
2. Cook this mixture on a simmer for approximately 15 minutes.
3. Serve warm.

Nutrition:
- Calories: 114
- Fat: 9.7 g.
- Cholesterol: 281 mg.
- Carbs: 4.5 g.
- Fiber: 0 g.
- Protein: 13.2 g.

Mushroom and Porcini Soup

Preparation time: 10 minutes
Cooking time: 15 minutes
Servings: 3
Ingredients:
- 2 cups prepared vegetable stock
- 12 oz. lean chicken breast
- 1/2 carrot, diced
- 1/4 leek, sliced thick
- 3 mushrooms, thinly sliced
- 4 small pieces of porcini, dried
- Parsley, chopped for garnish

Directions:
1. Start by throwing all the ingredients into a saucepan.
2. Cook this mixture on a simmer for approximately 15 minutes or until the chicken is done.
3. Remove the cooked chicken and shred it.
4. Return the chicken to the soup.
5. Serve warm.

Nutrition:
- Calories: 335
- Fat: 19.8 g.
- Cholesterol: 139 mg.
- Sodium: 396 mg.
- Carbs: 1.7 g.
- Fiber: 0 g.
- Protein: 35.8 g.

Beef Pho

Preparation time: 10 minutes
Cooking time: 20 minutes
Servings: 4
Ingredients:
- 2 cups beef stock
- 2 cups water
- 1 onion, thinly sliced into rounds
- 2 tbsp. fish sauce
- 1 garlic cloves, thinly sliced
- 1/2 cinnamon quill
- 3 cardamom pods, slightly bruised
- 3 star anise
- 1.5-inch piece ginger
- 1/2 tsp. sugar

- 14 oz. eye fillet, sliced very thin
- 1 zucchini, spiralized

For the garnish:

- 1/4 cup bean sprouts
- Thai basil
- Mint
- Coriander
- 1 lemon, cut into segments
- 1 fresh chili, thinly sliced

Directions:

1. Toss bean sprouts with lemon wedges, chili, herbs, and coriander in a bowl.
2. Add the stock and the remaining soup ingredients to a saucepan.
3. First, cook this soup to a boil then let it simmer for 20 minutes.
4. Add zucchini pasta then serve the soup.
5. Garnish with bean sprouts mixture on top.
6. Serve warm.

Nutrition:

- Calories: 302 Fat: 12.1 g.
- Cholesterol: 137 mg.
- Carbs: 1 g. Fiber: 0.1 g.
- Protein: 45.2 g.

Flavorful Broccoli Soup

Preparation time: 10 minutes
Cooking time: 4 hours and 15 minutes
Servings: 6
Ingredients:

- 20 oz. broccoli florets
- 4 oz. cream cheese

- 8 oz. cheddar cheese, shredded
- 1/2 tsp. paprika
- 1/2 tsp. mustard, ground
- 3 cups chicken stock
- 2 garlic cloves, chopped
- 1 onion, diced
- 1 cup carrots, shredded
- 1/4 tsp. baking soda
- 1/4 tsp. salt

Directions:

1. Add all ingredients except cream cheese and cheddar cheese to a crockpot and stir well.
2. Cover and cook on "Low" for 4 hours.
3. Purée the soup using an immersion blender until smooth.
4. Stir in the cream cheese and cheddar cheese. Cover and cook on "Low" for 15 minutes longer.
5. Season with pepper and salt.
6. Serve and enjoy.

Nutrition:

- Calories: 275 Fat: 19.9 g.
- Carbs: 11.9 g. Sugar: 4 g.
- Protein: 14.4 g. Cholesterol: 60 mg.

Healthy Chicken Kale Soup

Preparation time: 10 minutes
Cooking time: 6 hours and 15 minutes
Servings: 6
Ingredients:

- 2 lb. chicken breasts, skinless and boneless
- 1/4 cup fresh lemon juice

- 5 oz. baby kale
- 32 oz. chicken stock
- 1/2 cup olive oil
- 1 large onion, sliced
- 14 oz. chicken broth
- 1 tbsp. extra virgin olive oil
- Salt to taste

Directions:
1. Heat the extra virgin olive oil in a pan over medium heat.
2. Season chicken with salt and place in the hot pan.
3. Cover the pan and cook the chicken for 15 minutes.
4. Remove chicken from the pan and shred it using forks.
5. Add shredded chicken to a crockpot.
6. Add sliced onion, olive oil, and broth to a blender and blend until combined.
7. Pour blended mixture into the crockpot.
8. Add the remaining ingredients to the crockpot and stir well.
9. Cover and cook on "Low" for 6 hours.
10. Stir well and serve.

Nutrition:
- Calories: 493 Fat: 31.3 g.
- Carbs: 5.8 g. Sugar: 1.9 g.
- Protein: 46.7 g. Cholesterol: 135 mg.

Spicy Chicken Pepper Stew

Preparation time: 10 minutes
Cooking time: 6 hours
Servings: 6

Ingredients:
- 3 chicken breasts, skinless and boneless, cut into small pieces
- 1 tsp. garlic, minced
- 1 tsp. ginger, ground
- 2 tsp. olive oil
- 2 tsp. soy sauce
- 1 tbsp. fresh lemon juice
- 1/2 cup green onions, sliced
- 1 tbsp. red pepper, crushed
- 8 oz. chicken stock
- 1 bell pepper, chopped
- 1 green chili pepper, sliced
- 2 jalapeño peppers, sliced
- 1/2 tsp. black pepper
- 1/4 tsp. sea salt

Directions:
1. Add all ingredients to a large mixing bowl and mix well. Place in the refrigerator overnight.
2. Pour marinated chicken mixture into a crockpot.
3. Cover and cook on "Low" for 6 hours.
4. Stir well and serve.

Nutrition:
- Calories: 171
- Fat: 7.4 g.
- Carbs: 3.7 g.
- Sugar: 1.7 g.
- Protein: 22 g.
- Cholesterol: 65 mg.

Beef Chili

Preparation time: 10 minutes
Cooking time: 8 hours
Servings: 6
Ingredients:
- 1 lb. beef, ground
- 1 tsp. garlic powder
- 1 tsp. paprika
- 3 tsp. chili powder
- 1 tbsp. Worcestershire sauce
- 1 tbsp. fresh parsley, chopped

- 1 tsp. onion powder
- 25 oz. tomatoes, chopped
- 4 carrots, chopped
- 1 onion, diced
- 1 bell pepper, diced
- 1/2 tsp. sea salt

Directions:

1. Brown the ground meat in a pan over high heat until the meat is no longer pink.
2. Transfer meat to a crockpot.
3. Add bell pepper, tomatoes, carrots, and onion to the crockpot and stir well.
4. Add the remaining ingredients and stir well.
5. Cover and cook on "Low" for 8 hours.
6. Serve and enjoy.

Nutrition:

- Calories: 152
- Fat: 4 g.
- Carbs: 10.4 g.
- Sugar: 5.8 g.
- Protein: 18.8 g.
- Cholesterol: 51 mg.

Tasty Basil Tomato Soup

Preparation time: 10 minutes
Cooking time: 6 hours
Servings: 6
Ingredients:

- 28 oz. can whole tomatoes, peeled

- 1/2 cup fresh basil leaves
- 4 cups chicken stock
- 1 tsp. red pepper flakes
- 3 garlic cloves, peeled
- 2 onions, diced
- 3 carrots, peeled and diced
- 3 tbsp. olive oil
- 1 tsp. salt

Directions:

1. Add all ingredients to a crockpot and stir well.
2. Cover and cook on "Low" for 6 hours.
3. Purée the soup until smooth using an immersion blender.
4. Season soup with pepper and salt.
5. Serve and enjoy.

Nutrition:

- Calories: 126
- Fat: 7.5 g.
- Carbs: 13.3 g.
- Sugar: 7 g.
- Protein: 2.5 g.
- Cholesterol: 0 mg.

Healthy Spinach Soup

Preparation time: 10 minutes
Cooking time: 3 hours
Servings: 8
Ingredients:

- 3 cups frozen spinach, chopped, thawed, and drained
- 8 oz. cheddar cheese, shredded
- 1 egg, lightly beaten
- 10 oz. can cream of chicken soup

- 8 oz. cream cheese, softened

Directions:
1. Add spinach to a large bowl. Purée the spinach.
2. Add egg, chicken soup, cream cheese, and pepper to the spinach purée and mix well.
3. Transfer the spinach mixture to a crockpot.
4. Cover and cook on "Low" for 3 hours.
5. Stir in cheddar cheese and serve.

Nutrition:
- Calories: 256 Fat: 21.9 g.
- Carbs: 4.1 g. Sugar: 0.5 g.
- Protein: 11.1 g.
- Cholesterol: 84 mg.

Mexican Chicken Soup

Preparation time: 10 minutes
Cooking time: 4 hours
Servings: 6
Ingredients:
- 1 1/2 lb. chicken thighs, skinless and boneless
- 14 oz. chicken stock
- 14 oz. salsa
- 8 oz. Monterey Jack cheese, shredded

Directions:
1. Place chicken into a crockpot.
2. Pour the remaining ingredients over the chicken.
3. Cover and cook on "High" for 4 hours.
4. Remove chicken from crockpot and shred using forks.
5. Return shredded chicken to the crockpot and stir well.
6. Serve and enjoy.

Nutrition:
- Calories: 371
- Fat: 19.5 g.
- Carbs: 5.7 g.
- Sugar: 2.2 g.
- Protein: 42.1 g.
- Cholesterol: 135 mg.

Beef Stew

Preparation time: 10 minutes
Cooking time: 5 hours 5 minutes
Servings: 8
Ingredients:
- 3 lb. beef stew meat, trimmed
- 1/2 cup red curry paste
- 1/3 cup tomato paste
- 13 oz. can coconut milk
- 2 tsp. ginger, minced
- 2 garlic cloves, minced
- 1 medium onion, sliced
- 2 tbsp. olive oil
- 2 cups carrots, julienned
- 2 cups broccoli florets
- 2 tsp. fresh lime juice
- 2 tbsp. fish sauce
- 2 tsp. sea salt

Directions:
1. Heat 1 tbsp. of oil in a pan over medium heat.
2. Brown the meat on all sides in the pan.
3. Add brown meat to a crockpot.
4. Add the remaining oil to the same pan and sauté the ginger, garlic, and onion over medium-high heat for 5 minutes.
5. Add coconut milk and stir well.
6. Transfer pan mixture to the crockpot.
7. Add the remaining ingredients except for carrots and broccoli.
8. Cover and cook on "High" for 5 hours.
9. Add carrots and broccoli during the last 30 minutes of cooking.

10. Serve and enjoy.

Nutrition:

- Calories: 537
- Fat: 28.6 g.
- Carbs: 13 g.
- Sugar: 12.6 g.
- Protein: 54.4 g.
- Cholesterol: 152 mg.

Creamy Broccoli Cauliflower Soup

Preparation time: 10 minutes
Cooking time: 6 hours
Servings: 6
Ingredients:

- 2 cups cauliflower florets, chopped
- 3 cups broccoli florets, chopped
- 3 1/2 cups chicken stock
- 1 large carrot, diced
- 1/2 cup shallots, diced
- 2 garlic cloves, minced
- 1 cup plain yogurt
- 6 oz. cheddar cheese, shredded
- 1 cup coconut milk
- Salt and Pepper to taste

Directions:

1. Add all ingredients except milk, cheese, and yogurt to a crockpot and stir well.
2. Cover and cook on "Low" for 6 hours.
3. Purée the soup using an immersion blender until smooth.
4. Add cheese, milk, and yogurt. Blend until smooth and creamy.
5. Season with pepper and salt.
6. Serve and enjoy.

Nutrition:

- Calories: 281
- Fat: 20 g.
- Carbs: 14.4 g.
- Sugar: 6.9 g.
- Protein: 13.1 g.
- Cholesterol: 32 mg.

Squash Soup

Preparation time: 10 minutes
Cooking time: 8 hours
Servings: 6
Ingredients:

- 2 lb. butternut squash, peeled, chopped into chunks
- 1 tsp. ginger, minced
- 1/4 tsp. cinnamon
- 1 tbsp. curry powder
- 2 bay leaves
- 1 tsp. black pepper
- 1/2 cup heavy cream
- 2 cups chicken stock
- 1 tbsp. garlic, minced
- 2 carrots, cut into chunks
- 2 apples, peeled, cored, and diced
- 1 large onion, diced
- 1 tsp. salt

Directions:

1. Spray a crockpot inside with cooking spray.
2. Add all ingredients except the cream to the crockpot and stir well.
3. Cover and cook on "Low" for 8 hours.
4. Purée the soup using an immersion blender until smooth and creamy.
5. Stir in heavy cream and season soup with pepper and salt.

6. Serve and enjoy.

Nutrition:
- Calories: 170
- Fat: 4.4 g.
- Carbs: 34.4 g.
- Sugar: 13.4 g.
- Protein: 2.9 g.
- Cholesterol: 14 mg.

Herb Tomato Soup
Preparation time: 10 minutes
Cooking time: 6 hours
Servings: 8
Ingredients:
- 55 oz. can tomato, diced
- 1/2 onion, minced
- 2 cups chicken stock
- 1 cup half and half
- 4 tbsp. butter
- 1 bay leaf
- 1/2 tsp. black pepper
- 1/2 tsp. garlic powder
- 1 tsp. oregano
- 1 tsp. thyme, dried
- 1 cup carrots, diced
- 1/4 tsp. black pepper
- 1/2 tsp. salt

Directions:
1. Add all ingredients to a crockpot and stir well.
2. Cover and cook on "Low" for 6 hours.
3. Discard bay leaf and purée the soup using an immersion blender until smooth.
4. Serve and enjoy.

Nutrition:
- Calories: 145
- Fat: 9.4 g.
- Carbs: 13.9 g.
- Sugar: 7.9 g.
- Protein: 3.2 g.
- Cholesterol: 26 mg.

Easy Beef Mushroom Stew
Preparation time: 10 minutes
Cooking time: 8 hours
Servings: 8
Ingredients:
- 2 lb. stewing beef, cubed
- 1 packet dry onion soup mix
- 4 oz. can mushroom, sliced
- 14 oz. can cream of mushroom soup
- 1/2 cup water
- 1/4 tsp. black pepper
- 1/2 tsp. salt

Directions:
1. Spray a crockpot inside with cooking spray.
2. Add all ingredients into the crockpot and stir well.
3. Cover and cook on "Low" for 8 hours.
4. Stir well and serve.

Nutrition:
- Calories: 237
- Fat: 8.5 g.
- Carbs: 2.7 g.
- Sugar: 0.4 g.
- Protein: 35.1 g.
- Cholesterol: 101 mg.

Lamb Stew
Preparation time: 10 minutes
Cooking time: 8 hours
Servings: 2
Ingredients:
- 1/2 lb. lean lamb, boneless and cubed
- 2 tbsp. lemon juice
- 1/2 onion, chopped
- 2 garlic cloves, minced
- 2 fresh thyme sprigs
- 1/4 tsp. turmeric
- 1/4 cup green olives, sliced
- 1/2 tsp. black pepper
- 1/4 tsp. salt

Directions:
1. Add all ingredients to a crockpot and stir well.

2. Cover and cook on "Low" for 8 hours.
3. Stir well and serve.

Nutrition:
- Calories: 297
- Fat: 20.3 g.
- Carbs: 5.4 g.
- Sugar: 1.5 g.
- Protein: 21 g.
- Cholesterol: 80 mg.

Leek and Cauliflower Soup

Preparation time: 10 minutes
Cooking time: 20 minutes
Servings: 2
Ingredients:
- 2 1/2 cups leeks, chopped (2–3 leeks)
- 2 1/2 cups cauliflower florets
- 1 garlic clove, peeled
- 1/3 cup low-sodium vegetable broth
- 1/2 cup half-and-half
- Avocado oil cooking spray
- 1/4 tsp. salt
- 1/4 tsp. freshly ground black pepper

Directions:
1. Heat a large stockpot over medium-low heat. When hot, coat the cooking surface with cooking spray. Put the leeks and cauliflower into the pot.
2. Increase the heat to medium and cover the pan. Cook for 10 minutes, stirring halfway through.
3. Add the garlic and cook for 5 minutes.

4. Add the broth and deglaze the pan, stirring to scrape up the browned bits from the bottom.
5. Transfer the broth and vegetables to a food processor or blender and add the half-and-half, salt, and pepper. Blend well.

Nutrition:
- Calories: 174 Fat: 7.1 g.
- Protein: 6.1 g.
- Carbs: 23.9 g.
- Fiber: 5.1 g.
- Sugar: 8 g.
- Sodium: 490 mg.

Vegetable Chicken Soup

Preparation time: 10 minutes
Cooking time: 6 hours
Servings: 6
Ingredients:
- 4 cups chicken, boneless, skinless, cooked, and diced
- 4 tsp. garlic, minced
- 2/3 cups onion, diced
- 1 1/2 cups carrot, diced
- 6 cups chicken stock
- 2 tbsp. lime juice
- 1/4 cup jalapeño pepper, diced
- 1/2 cup tomatoes, diced
- 1/2 cup fresh cilantro, chopped
- 1 tsp. chili powder
- 1 tbsp. cumin
- 1 3/4 cups tomato juice
- 2 tsp. sea salt

Directions:
1. Add all ingredients to a crockpot and stir well.
2. Cover and cook on "Low" for 6 hours.
3. Stir well and serve.

Nutrition:
- Calories: 192 Fat: 3.8 g.
- Carbs: 9.8 g. Sugar: 5.7 g.
- Protein: 29.2 g. Cholesterol: 72 mg.

Vegan Cream Soup with Avocado and Zucchini

Preparation time: 15 minutes
Cooking time: 20 minutes
Servings: 2
Ingredients:

- 3 tsp. vegetable oil
- 1 leek, chopped
- 1 rutabaga, sliced
- 3 cups zucchinis, chopped
- 1 avocado, chopped
- Salt and black pepper to taste
- 4 cups vegetable broth
- 2 tbsp. fresh mint, chopped

Directions:

1. In a pot, sauté leek, zucchini, and rutabaga in warm oil for about 7–10 minutes. Season with black pepper and salt. Pour in broth and bring to a boil. Lower the heat and simmer for 20 minutes.
2. Lift from the heat. In batches, add the soup and avocado to a blender. Blend until creamy and smooth. Serve in bowls topped with fresh mint.

Nutrition:

- Calories: 378 Fat: 24.5 g.
- Net Carbs: 9.3 g.
- Protein: 8.2 g.

Chinese Tofu Soup

Preparation time: 5 minutes
Cooking time: 10 minutes
Servings: 2
Ingredients:

- 2 cups chicken stock
- 1 tbsp. soy sauce, sugar-free
- 2 spring onions, sliced
- 1 tsp. sesame oil, softened
- 2 eggs, beaten
- 1-inch piece ginger, grated
- Salt and black ground, to taste
- 1/2 lb. extra-firm tofu, cubed
- A handful of fresh cilantro, chopped

Directions:

1. Boil in a pan over medium heat, soy sauce, chicken stock, and sesame oil. Place in eggs as you whisk to incorporate completely. Change heat to low and add salt, spring onions, black pepper, and ginger; cook for 5 minutes. Place in tofu and simmer for 1–2 minutes.
2. Divide into soup bowls and serve sprinkled with fresh cilantro.

Nutrition:

- Calories: 163
- Fat: 10 g.
- Net Carbs: 2.4 g.
- Protein: 14.5 g.

Awesome Chicken Enchilada Soup

Preparation time: 20 minutes
Cooking time: 30 minutes
Servings: 4
Ingredients:

- 2 tbsp. coconut oil
- 1 lb. chicken thighs, boneless and skinless
- 3/4 cup red enchilada sauce, sugar-free
- 1/4 cup water
- 1/4 cup onion, chopped
- 3 oz. green chilies, canned and diced
- 1 avocado, sliced
- 1 cup cheddar cheese, shredded
- 1/4 cup pickled jalapeños, chopped
- 1/2 cup sour cream
- 1 tomato, diced

Directions:

1. Put a large pan over medium heat. Add coconut oil and warm. Place in the chicken and cook until browned on the outside. Stir in onion, chilies, water, and enchilada sauce, then close with a lid.
2. Allow simmering for 20 minutes until the chicken is cooked through.

3. Spoon the soup in a serving bowl and top with the sauce, cheese, sour cream, tomato, and avocado.

Nutrition:

- Calories: 643
- Fat: 44.2 g.
- Net Carbs: 9.7 g.
- Protein: 45.8 g.

Curried Shrimp and Green Beans Soup

Preparation time: 10 minutes
Cooking time: 10 minutes
Servings: 4
Ingredients:

- 1 onion, chopped
- 2 tbsp. red curry paste
- 2 tbsp. butter
- 1 lb. jumbo shrimp, peeled and deveined
- 2 tsp. ginger-garlic puree
- 1 cup coconut milk
- Salt and chili pepper to taste
- 1 bunch green beans, halved
- 1 tbsp. cilantro, chopped

Directions:

1. Add the shrimp to melted butter in a saucepan over medium heat, season with salt and pepper, and cook until they are opaque, 2–3 minutes. Remove to a plate. Add in the ginger-garlic puree, onion, and red curry paste and sauté for 2 minutes until fragrant.
2. Stir in the coconut milk; add the shrimp, salt, chili pepper, and green beans. Cook for 4 minutes. Reduce the heat to a simmer and cook an additional 3 minutes, occasionally stirring. Adjust taste with salt, fetch soup into serving bowls, and serve sprinkled with cilantro.

Nutrition:

- Calories: 351 Fat: 32.4 g.
- Net Carbs: 3.2 g.
- Protein: 7.7 g.

Spinach and Basil Chicken Soup

Preparation time: 5 minutes
Cooking time: 10 minutes
Servings: 4
Ingredients:

- 1 cup spinach
- 2 cups chicken, cooked and shredded
- 4 cups chicken broth
- 1 cup cheddar cheese, shredded
- 4 oz.' cream cheese
- 1/2 tsp. chili powder
- 1/2 tsp. cumin, ground
- 1/2 tsp. fresh parsley, chopped
- Salt and black pepper, to taste

Directions:

1. In a pot, add the chicken broth and spinach, bring to a boil and cook for 5–8 minutes. Transfer to a food processor, add in the cream cheese, and pulse until smooth. Return the mixture to a pot and place over medium heat. Cook until hot, but do not bring to a boil.
2. Add chicken, chili powder, and cumin and cook for about 3–5 minutes, or until it is heated through.
3. Stir in cheddar cheese and season with salt and pepper. Serve hot in bowls sprinkled with parsley.

Nutrition:

- Calories: 351
- Fat: 22.4 g.
- Net Carbs: 4.3 g.
- Protein: 21.6 g.

Rhubarb Stew

Preparation time: 5 minutes
Cooking time: 10 minutes
Servings: 3
Ingredients:

- 1 tsp. lemon zest, grated
- 1 1/2 cup coconut sugar
- 1 lemon juice
- 1 1/2 cup water
- 4 1/2 cup rhubarbs, roughly chopped

Directions:
1. In a pan, combine the rhubarb while using water, fresh lemon juice, lemon zest, and coconut sugar, toss, bring using a simmer over medium heat, cook for 5 minutes, and divide into bowls and serve cold.
1. Enjoy!

Nutrition:
- Calories: 108
- Fat: 1 g.
- Carbs: 8 g.
- Protein: 5 g.
- Sugar: 2 g.
- Sodium: 0 mg.

Spiced Tomato Lentil Soup

Preparation time: 5 minutes
Cooking time: 25 minutes
Servings: 8
Ingredients:
- 1 cup yellow lentils
- 3 medium carrots, peeled and chopped
- 3 stalks celery, chopped
- 28 oz. crushed tomatoes, no salt added
- 1 medium white onion, peeled and chopped
- 1 tbsp. garlic, minced
- 1/2 tsp. salt
- 1/4 tsp. black pepper, ground
- 1 tbsp. cumin, ground
- 1 bay leaf
- 1 tbsp. olive oil

- 1 tbsp. tomato paste
- 4 cups vegetable broth
- 2 cups water

Directions:
1. Plugin instant pot, insert the inner pot, press sauté/simmer button, add oil, and when hot, add chopped carrots, celery, onion, and garlic and cook for 2 minutes or until fragrant.
2. Press the cancel button, add the remaining ingredients, stir well, then shut the instant pot with its lid and turn the pressure knob to seal the pot.
3. Press the "Beans/Chili" button, then press the "Timer" to set the cooking time to 15 minutes and cook at "High Pressure," instant pot will take 5 minutes or more for building its inner pressure.
4. When the timer beeps, press the "Cancel" button and do a quick pressure release until the pressure nob drops down.
5. Open the instant pot and puree lentils with an immersion blender until smooth.
6. Ladle soup into bowls and serve.

Nutrition:
- Calories: 156 Carbs: 27 g.
- Fat: 2 g. Protein: 8 g. Fiber: 6 g.

Vegetable Lentil Soup

Preparation time: 5 minutes
Cooking time: 6 hours
Servings: 10
Ingredients:
- 1/4 cup soy protein

- 1/2 cup lentils, dried and rinsed
- 1 large potato, peeled and diced
- 1 cup carrots, chopped
- 1/2 cups green beans, diced
- 1 cup zucchini, chopped
- 1 medium tomato, chopped
- 1/2 cup white onion, diced
- 1 tsp. garlic, minced
- 1 tsp. salt
- 1/4 tsp. black pepper, ground
- 2 basil leaves
- 1/4 cup tomato sauce
- 4 cups vegetable stock

Directions:
1. Plugin instant pot, insert the inner pot, add all the ingredients, and stir until mixed.
2. Shut the instant pot with its lid and turn the pressure knob to seal the pot.
3. Press the "Slow cook" button, then press the "Timer" to set the cooking time to 6 hours at a "Low" heat setting.
4. When the timer beeps, press the "Cancel" button and do natural pressure release for 10 minutes, and then do quick pressure release until pressure nob drops down.
5. Open the instant pot, then ladle soup into bowls and serve.

Nutrition:
- Calories: 48.2
- Carbs: 8.9 g.
- Fat: 0.2 g.
- Protein: 3.3 g.
- Fiber: 2.6 g.

Split Pea Soup
Preparation time: 20 minutes
Cooking time: 28 minutes
Servings: 8
Ingredients:

- 1 lb. green split peas, rinsed
- 1 medium white onion, peeled and diced
- 3 medium carrots, peeled and chopped

- 3 stalks celery, diced
- 2 tsp. garlic, minced
- 1/2 tsp. salt
- 1/4 tsp. black pepper, ground
- 2 bay leaves
- 1/4 tsp. thyme, dried
- 2 tbsp. olive oil
- 6 cups vegetable broth

Directions:
1. Plugin instant pot, insert the inner pot, press the "sauté/simmer" button, add oil, and when hot, add onion and celery along with thyme and bay leaves.
2. Cook for 5 minutes or until onion begins to tender, then add the remaining ingredients and stir until mixed.
3. Press the "Cancel" button, shut the instant pot with its lid, and turn the pressure knob to seal the pot.
4. Press the "Manual" button, then press the "Timer" to set the cooking time to 18 minutes and cook at "High Pressure," instant pot will take 5 minutes or more for building its inner pressure.
5. When the timer beeps, press the "Cancel" button and do natural pressure release for 10 minutes, and then do quick pressure release until pressure nob drops down.
6. Open the instant pot, remove and discard bay leaves and ladle soup into bowls.
7. Serve straight away.

Nutrition:
- Calories: 122.7 Carbs: 15 g.
- Fat: 4 g.Protein: 11.8 g.
- Fiber: 5.2 g.

Chicken Tortilla Soup
Preparation time: 5 minutes
Cooking time: 6 hours
Servings: 4
Ingredients:

- 2 cups chicken, cooked and shredded
- 2 cups mixed vegetables, stir-fry

- 14.5 oz. stewed tomatoes, Mexican-style
- 1 tsp. garlic, minced
- 2 1/2 cups water
- 1 cup chicken broth
- 1 cup bag tortilla chips
- 1 jalapeño chili peppers, sliced

Directions:
1. Plugin instant pot, insert the inner pot, add all the ingredients except for chips and stir until mixed.
2. Shut the instant pot with its lid and turn the pressure knob to seal the pot.
3. Press the "Slow cook" button, then press the "Timer" to set the cooking time to 6 hours at a "Low" heat setting.
4. When the timer beeps, press the "Cancel" button and do natural pressure release for 10 minutes, and then do quick pressure release until pressure nob drops down.
5. Open the instant pot, ladle soup into bowls, top with tortilla chips, and serve.

Nutrition:
- Calories: 212 Carbs: 17 g.
- Fat: 5 g.
- Protein: 23 g.
- Fiber: 1 g.

Butternut Squash and Carrot Soup

Preparation time: 5 minutes
Cooking time: 20 minutes
Servings: 6
Ingredients:
- 1 medium butternut squash, peeled and cubed

- 3 medium carrots, peeled and chopped
- 1 medium white onion, peeled and diced
- 1 tsp. garlic, minced
- 1 tbsp. ginger, grated
- 2 cups vegetable broth
- 1 tbsp. curry powder
- 1/2 tsp. garam masala
- 1/4 tsp. turmeric powder
- 1 tsp. salt
- 1/4 tsp. cayenne
- 1 lime juice

Directions:
1. Plugin instant pot, insert the inner pot, add all the ingredients, and stir until mixed.
2. Shut the instant pot with its lid and turn the pressure knob to seal the pot.
3. Press the "Manual" button, then press the "Timer" to set the cooking time to 15 minutes and cook at "High Pressure," instant pot will take 5 minutes or more for building its inner pressure.
4. When the timer beeps, press the "Cancel" button and do a quick pressure release until the pressure nob drops down.
5. Open the instant pot, stir the soup and ladle into serving bowls.
6. Drizzle soup with lime juice and serve.

Nutrition:
- Calories: 166
- Carbs: 19 g.
- Fat: 10 g.
- Protein: 2 g.
- Fiber: 3 g.

Irish Beef Stew

Preparation time: 20 minutes
Cooking time: 35 minutes
Servings: 4
Ingredients:
- 1 lb. beef, cut into 1-inch pieces
- 1 large white onion, peeled and diced
- 2 stalks celery, sliced

- 2 medium potatoes, cut into 1-inch pieces
- 2 medium carrots, peeled and sliced
- 1 tsp. garlic, minced
- 1 tsp. salt
- 1/2 tsp. black pepper, ground
- 1 tsp. thyme, dried
- 1 tbsp. parsley, dried
- 1 bay leaf
- 1 tbsp. olive oil
- 1 cup beef stock
- 2 tbsp. cornstarch
- 2 tbsp. warm water

Directions:

1. Plugin instant pot, insert the inner pot, press sauté/simmer button, add oil, and when hot, add onion, celery, carrot, and garlic and cook for 5 minutes or until softened.
2. Add the remaining ingredients, except for cornstarch and warm water, stir until mixed, and press the cancel button.
3. Shut the instant pot with its lid, turn the pressure knob to seal the pot, press the "Manual" button, then press the "Timer" to set the cooking time to 20 minutes and cook at "High Pressure," instant pot will take 5 minutes or more for building its inner pressure.
4. When the timer beeps, press the "Cancel" button and do natural pressure release for 10 minutes, and then do quick pressure release until pressure nob drops down.
5. Open the instant pot, stir together cornstarch and water, add into the stew, stir well and let stew rest for 5 minutes or until slightly thick.
6. Ladle stew into the bowls and serve.

Nutrition:

- Calories: 392.8 Carbs: 61.6 g.
- Fat: 4.1 g.
- Protein: 29.1 g.
- Fiber: 9.8 g.

Zucchini Soup

Preparation time: 5 minutes
Cooking time: 12 minutes
Servings: 2
Ingredients:

- 2 medium zucchinis, chopped
- 1/2 tsp. onion powder
- 1/2 tsp. garlic powder
- 1/2 tsp. salt
- 1/4 tsp. black pepper, ground
- 1/2 tsp. curry powder
- 1 cup coconut milk, reduced-fat and unsweetened
- 1 cup water

Directions:

1. Plugin instant pot, insert the inner pot, pour in water, then insert steamer basket and place zucchini pies on it.
2. Shut the instant pot with its lid and turn the pressure knob to seal the pot.
3. Press the "Steam" button, then press the "Timer" to set the cooking time to 2 minutes and cook at "High pressure," instant pot will take 5 minutes or more for building its inner pressure.
4. When the timer beeps, press the "Cancel" button and do natural pressure release for 5 minutes, and then do quick pressure release until pressure nob drops down.
5. Open the instant pot, transfer zucchini to a plate to cool for 5 minutes, then place zucchini pieces in a food processor and add the remaining ingredients.

6. Pulse zucchini for 1–2 minutes or until smooth and then evenly divide between bowls.
7. Serve straight away.

Nutrition:
- Calories: 141
- Carbs: 7 g.
- Fat: 11 g.
- Protein: 3.5 g.
- Fiber: 3 g.

Rutabaga Stew

Preparation time: 5 minutes
Cooking time: 25 minutes
Servings: 6
Ingredients:
- 2 medium rutabagas, peeled and diced
- 1 stalk celery, diced
- 2 medium beets, peeled and diced
- 2 medium carrots, peeled and diced
- 1/2 small red onion, peeled and diced
- 1 tsp. salt
- 1/3 tsp. black pepper, ground
- 1 1/4 tsp. olive oil
- 2 1/2 cups chicken stock

Directions:
1. Plugin instant pot, insert the inner pot, press sauté/simmer button, add oil and when hot, add celery, onion, and garlic and cook for 5 minutes or until tender.
2. Add remaining ingredients, stir until mixed, then press the cancel button, shut the instant pot with its lid, and turn the pressure knob to seal the pot.
3. Press the "Manual" button, then press the "Timer" to set the cooking time to 15 minutes and cook at "High Pressure," instant pot will take 5 minutes or more for building its inner pressure.
4. When the timer beeps, press the "Cancel" button and do a quick pressure release until the pressure nob drops down.

5. Open the instant pot, stir the soup and then puree using an immersion blender until smooth.
6. Ladle soup into bowls and serve.

Nutrition:
- Calories: 85.3
- Carbs: 12.9 g.
- Fat: 2.1 g.
- Protein: 3.7 g.
- Fiber: 3.9 g.

Clam Chowder

Preparation time: 5 minutes
Cooking time: 10 minutes
Servings: 8
Ingredients:
- 2 cups clams, chopped
- 2 medium potatoes, peeled and chopped
- 1 cup green bell pepper, chopped
- 14.5 oz. tomatoes, diced
- 1/4 cup green onions, chopped
- 1 tsp. salt
- 1/4 tsp. black pepper, ground
- 1 cup tomato and clam juice cocktail
- 1/2 cup water

Directions:
1. Plugin instant pot, insert the inner pot, add all the ingredients, and stir until mixed.
2. Shut the instant pot with its lid, turn the pressure knob to seal the pot, press the "Manual" button, then press the "Timer" to set the cooking time to 5 minutes and cook at "High Pressure," instant pot will take 5 minutes or more for building its inner pressure.
3. When the timer beeps, press the "Cancel" button and do a quick pressure release until the pressure nob drops down.
4. Open the instant pot and stir the chowder, if the chowder is thin then press the "Sauté/simmer" button and cook soup until it reaches to desired thickness.

5. Ladle chowder into bowls and serve.

Nutrition:
- Calories: 82 Carbs: 15.8 g.
- Fat: 0.2 g. Protein: 3.9 g.
- Fiber: 2.1 g.

Mediterranean Stew

Preparation time: 5 minutes
Cooking time: 10 hours
Servings: 5
Ingredients:

- 1/2 medium butternut squash, peeled, seeded, and cubed
- 1 cup eggplant, cubed
- 1 cup zucchini, cubed
- 5 oz. okra
- 1/2 medium carrot, peeled and sliced
- 1/2 medium tomato, chopped
- 1/2 cup white onion, chopped
- 1/2 tsp. garlic, minced
- 1 tsp. salt
- 1/8 tsp. paprika
- 1/8 tsp. red pepper, crushed
- 1/8 tsp. turmeric, ground
- 1/4 tsp. cumin, ground
- 2 tbsp. raisins
- 4-oz. tomato sauce
- 1/2 cup vegetable broth

Directions:

1. Plugin instant pot, insert the inner pot, add all the ingredients, and stir until mixed.
2. Press the cancel button, shut the instant pot with its lid, and turn the pressure knob to seal the pot.
3. Press the "Slow cook" button, then press the "Timer" to set the cooking time to 10 hours at a low heat setting.
4. When the timer beeps, press the "Cancel" button and do natural pressure release until the pressure nob drops down.
5. Open the instant pot, then ladle stew into bowls and serve.

Nutrition:
- Calories: 122 Carbs: 30.5 g.Fat: 0.5 g.
- Protein: 3.4 g. Fiber: 8 g.

Spicy Crockpot Black Bean Soup

Preparation time: 15 minutes
Cooking time: 6 hours
Servings: 2
Ingredients:

- 1 lb. dry black beans, soaked overnight
- 4 tsp. jalapeno peppers, diced
- 6 cups reduced-sodium chicken broth
- 1/2 tsp. garlic powder
- 1 tbsp. chili powder
- 1 tsp. cumin, ground
- 1 tsp. cayenne pepper
- 3/4 tsp. black pepper, ground
- 1/2 tsp. hot pepper sauce

Directions:

1. Drain black beans, and rinse. Combine beans, jalapenos, and chicken broth in a slow cooker. Season mixture with garlic powder, chili powder, cumin, cayenne, pepper, and hot pepper sauce.
2. Cook on High for 4 hours. Reduce heat to Low, and continue cooking for 2 hours.

Nutrition:
- Calories: 281 Total Fat: 2 g.
- Saturated Fat: 0.3 g.
- Cholesterol: 5 mg. Carbs: 50 g.
- Fiber: 12 g. Protein: 18 g.
- Sodium: 530 mg;

Beef and Barley Soup

Preparation time: 10 minutes
Cooking time: 70 minutes
Servings: 4
Ingredients:

- 8 cups water
- 8 sodium-free beef bouillon cubes
- 6 carrots, diced
- 4 onions, chopped
- 1 lb. mushrooms, thinly sliced
- 1 lb. stew beef, cut into small cubes
- 1/2 tsp. salt
- 1/2 tsp. black pepper
- 1 cup quick-cooking barley

Directions:

1. In a large soup pot, combine the water, bouillon cubes, carrots, onions, mushrooms, stew beef, salt, and black pepper. Bring to a boil over medium-high heat, stirring occasionally.
2. Reduce the heat to low and simmer partially covered for 40 minutes, stirring occasionally. Add the barley, and cook partially covered for 10–20 minutes, or until the barley is tender.

Nutrition:

- Calories: 226 Total Fat: 4.6 g.
- Saturated Fat: 1.7 g. Cholesterol: 5 mg.
- Carbs: 30 g. Fiber: 6 g. Protein: 17 g.
- Sodium: 530 mg.

Vegetable Turkey Soup

Preparation time: 10 minutes
Cooking time: 130 minutes
Servings: 2

Ingredients:

- 2 large onions, diced
- 2 carrots, diced
- 2 stalks celery, diced
- 2 cloves garlic, minced
- 1 tsp. poultry seasoning
- 1 tsp. rosemary, dried
- 1 tsp. onion powder
- 2 cups brown rice, cooked

For the stock:

- 1 turkey carcass
- 1 large onion, halved and skin left on
- 1 large carrot, roughly chopped
- 1 stalk celery, roughly chopped
- 1 head garlic, halved
- 1 tsp. rosemary, dried
- 1 tsp. thyme, dried
- 2 bay leaves
- Salt and ground black pepper to taste
- Water to cover

Directions:

1. Combine turkey carcass, halved onion, roughly chopped carrot, roughly chopped celery, halved garlic head, 1 tsp. rosemary, thyme, bay leaves, salt, and pepper in a stockpot; pour in enough water to cover. Bring mixture to a boil, cover pot, reduce heat, and simmer until flavors have blended for about 1 hour.
2. Remove turkey carcass and pull remaining meat from bones; reserve meat and discard the carcass. Remove vegetables and bay leaves from stock using a slotted spoon and discard.
3. Stir diced onions, diced carrots, diced celery, minced garlic, poultry seasoning, 1 tsp. rosemary, and onion powder into stock; bring to a boil. Reduce heat, cover pot, and simmer until vegetables are very tender, 20–30 minutes.
4. Add cooked rice and turkey meat to soup; season with salt and pepper.

5. Cook until rice and turkey meat are warmed, about 5 minutes.

Nutrition:
- Calories: 115 Total Fat: 1.7 g.
- Saturated Fat: 0 g. Cholesterol: 0 mg.
- Carbs: 22.4 g.
- Fiber: 2.3 g.
- Protein: 3.2 g.
- Sodium: 56 mg.

Chili Chicken Soup

Preparation time: 10 minutes
Cooking time: 50 minutes
Servings: 4
Ingredients:
- 1 3/4 lb. chicken breast, diced
- 2 green bell peppers, diced
- 2 red bell peppers, diced
- 1 onion, diced
- 1 onion, diced
- 1/2 cup frozen corn kernels
- 4 (15 oz.) cans kidney beans with liquid
- 2 (14.5 oz.) cans tomatoes, diced
- 1 (15 oz.) can reduced-sodium tomato sauce
- 2 cups water
- 2 tsp. chili powder
- 1 tbsp. parsley, dried
- 1 tsp. garlic powder
- 1/2 tsp. cayenne pepper, ground
- 1/2 tsp. cumin, ground
- Cooking spray

Directions:
1. Coat a large pot with cooking spray and place over medium-high heat. Cook and stir chicken, bell peppers, and onion until chicken is brown and peppers are just tender.
2. Stir in corn, beans, tomatoes, tomato sauce, and water. Season mixture with chili powder, parsley, garlic powder, cayenne, and cumin.
3. Reduce heat, cover, and simmer for 30 minutes.

Nutrition:
- Calories: 159
- Total Fat: 1 g.
- Saturated Fat: 0 g.
- Cholesterol: 25 mg.
- Carbs: 21 g.
- Fiber: 7 g.
- Protein: 16.5 g.
- Sodium: 427 mg.

Quick and Easy Onion Soup

Preparation time: 10 minutes
Cooking time: 80 minutes
Servings: 2
Ingredients:
- 6 yellow onions, thinly sliced
- 1/4 tsp. thyme, dried
- 2 tbsp. sherry cooking wine or dry sherry
- 4 cups water
- 4 (4 g.) packets sodium-free beef broth seasoning
- Cooking spray

Directions:
1. Coat a large saucepan with cooking spray. Over medium heat, cook onions and thyme for about 15 minutes, or until onions begin to brown.
2. Reduce heat to low and continue cooking about 25 additional minutes, or until onions turn a rich brown color, stirring frequently. Add wine and bring to a boil.
3. When wine is evaporated, add water and broth packets and bring to a boil.

4. Reduce heat to low and simmer for about 25 additional minutes.

Nutrition:

- Calories: 42
- Total Fat: 0 g.
- Cholesterol: 5.7 mg.
- Carbs: 8.5 g.
- Fiber: 1 g.
- Protein: 1 g.
- Sodium: 9.6 mg.

Lentil Lemon Soup

Preparation time: 10 minutes
Cooking time: 50 minutes
Servings: 2
Ingredients:

- 6 cups low-sodium chicken stock
- 2 tbsp. lemon juice
- 2 tbsp. fresh parsley, finely chopped
- 2 tsp. canola oil
- 1 onion, chopped
- 2 garlic cloves, finely chopped
- A pinch hot red pepper flakes
- 1 tsp. cumin
- 1 1/2 cups dry split red lentils, cleaned and rinsed
- Salt and pepper to taste

Directions:

1. Heat oil in a large saucepan or Dutch oven.
2. Add onion, garlic, and hot pepper flakes and cook on low heat for 5 minutes.

3. Add cumin and lentils, combine well. Add stock, salt, and pepper. Bring to a boil.
4. Reduce heat, cover, and simmer until lentils are tender and soup is beginning to thicken about 30 minutes.
5. Add extra stock or water to thin if necessary. Add lemon juice and serve sprinkled with parsley.

Nutrition:

- Calories: 193
- Total Fat: 3.4 g.
- Cholesterol: 5.7 mg.
- Carbs: 27.6 g.
- Fiber: 9 g.
- Protein: 3.4 g.
- Sodium: 273.4 mg.

Classic Minestrone Soup

Preparation time: 10 minutes
Cooking time: 40 minutes
Servings: 2
Ingredients:

- 3 cans (14.5 oz.) ready-to-use, sodium-free beef broth
- 1 can (15 oz.) red kidney beans, undrained
- 1 can (20 oz.) cannellini beans, undrained
- 1 can (28 oz.) crush tomatoes
- 1 pkg. (10 oz.) frozen spinach, chopped and thawed
- 1 pkg. (10-oz.) frozen vegetables, mixed and thawed
- 1 small onion, chopped

- 1 tsp. garlic powder
- 1 tsp. salt
- 1/2 tsp. black pepper
- 1 cup elbow macaroni, uncooked

Directions:

1. In a large soup pot, combine all ingredients except macaroni. Bring to a boil over medium-high heat then stir in macaroni.
2. Reduce heat to low and simmer 30 minutes, or until macaroni is tender, stirring occasionally.

Nutrition:

- Calories: 244
- Total Fat: 1 g.
- Saturated Fat: 0.2 g.
- Cholesterol: 5.7 mg.
- Carbs: 27.6 g.
- Fiber: 9 g.
- Protein: 3.4 g.
- Sodium: 273.4 mg.

Potato Cauliflower Soup

Preparation time: 10 minutes
Cooking time: 50 minutes
Servings: 2
Ingredients:

- 1/2 yellow onion, chopped
- 1 leek, diced
- 3 cloves garlic, minced
- 1 head cauliflower, cut into florets
- 1/2 head broccoli, cut into florets
- 3 red potatoes, cut into bite-size pieces

- 1 (32 oz.) carton low-sodium vegetable broth
- 1 cup water to cover
- 1 tbsp. nutritional yeast, or more to taste
- 1/2 tsp. turmeric, ground
- 1 bay leaf
- 1 pinch salt and ground black pepper to taste
- 1 pinch cayenne pepper, or to taste
- 1 (12 fluid oz.) can fat-free evaporated milk
- 3 tbsp. whole wheat flour, or as needed
- 1 tbsp. curry powder
- 1 tsp. extra virgin olive oil, or as needed

Directions:

1. Heat olive oil in a stockpot over medium-low heat; cook and stir onion, leek, and garlic until fragrant, 3–5 minutes. Add cauliflower, broccoli, and potatoes to onion mixture; cook and stir until potatoes are lightly browned about 5 minutes.
2. Increase heat to medium-high; stir broth and enough water to cover vegetables into the mixture. Stir curry powder, turmeric, bay leaf, salt, black pepper, and cayenne pepper into a broth-vegetable mixture. Loosely cover the pot with a lid and bring soup to a boil; reduce heat and simmer until vegetables are softened, 20–25 minutes.
3. Whisk milk and flour together in a bowl until smooth and thickened; stir into soup along with nutritional yeast until soup is slightly thickened, about 5 minutes. Remove soup from heat and allow to slightly cool and thicken.

Nutrition:

- Calories: 74 Total Fat: 0.7 g.
- Saturated Fat: 0.1 g. Cholesterol: 1.2 mg.
- Carbs: 13.5 g.
- Fiber: 2.5 g.
- Protein: 3.4 g.
- Sodium: 137 mg.

Chicken Cabbage Soup

Preparation time: 10 minutes
Cooking time: 40 minutes
Servings: 2
Ingredients:

- 3 chicken breast halves, boneless and skinless
- 8 cups reduced-sodium chicken broth
- 2 leeks, sliced
- 6 carrots, cut into 1-inch pieces
- 1 medium head cabbage, shredded
- 1 pkg. (8 oz.) egg noodles, uncooked
- 1 tsp. Thai chili sauce (to taste)

Directions:

1. Place chicken breasts and broth into a stockpot or Dutch oven. Bring to a boil and let simmer for about 20 minutes, or until chicken is cooked through. Remove the chicken from the broth and set aside to cool.
2. Put the leeks and carrots into the pot and simmer them for 10 minutes, or until tender. Shred the cooled chicken into bite-sized pieces and return it to the pot. Add the cabbage and egg noodles and cook for another 5 minutes or until the noodles are soft. Serve hot and flavor to taste with Thai chili sauce.

Nutrition:

- Calories: 275
- Total Fat: 3 g.
- Saturated Fat 0.7 g.
- Cholesterol: 61 mg.
- Carbs: 42 g.
- Fiber: 7 g.
- Protein: 20.8 g.
- Sodium: 118 mg.

Zucchini and Herb Soup

Preparation time: 10 minutes
Cooking time: 40 minutes
Servings: 2
Ingredients:

- 21 oz. zucchini, sliced
- 2 onions, chopped
- 2 garlic cloves, crushed
- 3 cups water, divided
- Salt to taste
- 1 bunch chives, chopped

Directions:

1. Combine zucchini, onions, garlic, and 2 tbsp. water in a non-stick pan over medium heat; cook until zucchini is softened, 5–10 minutes. Add remaining water and bring to a boil. Reduce heat and simmer for 5 minutes. Remove from heat and cool.
2. Pour zucchini mixture into a food processor no more than half full. Cover and pulse a few times before leaving on to blend. Puree in batches until smooth. Season soup with salt, then garnish with chives if desired.

Nutrition:

- Calories: 56
- Total Fat: 0.5 g.
- Saturated Fat: 0 g.
- Cholesterol: 0 mg.
- Carbs: 11.8 g.
- Fiber: 3.3 g.
- Protein: 3.4 g.
- Sodium: 62 mg.

Crockpot Chicken and Rice Soup

Preparation time: 10 minutes
Cooking time: 6 hours
Servings: 4
Ingredients:

- 3 carrots, peeled and sliced
- 3 stalks celery, sliced
- 1/2 cup onion, chopped
- 1 tsp. garlic powder
- 1/2 tsp. sage, ground
- 1/2 tsp. black pepper
- 3/4 cup wild rice, uncooked
- 3 (about 1 1/2 lb.) chicken breasts, boneless and skinless

- 6 cups reduced-sodium fat-free chicken broth
- 2 tbsp. fresh parsley, chopped

Directions:

1. In a 6-quart slow cooker, combine carrots, celery, onion, garlic powder, sage, pepper, and wild rice. Top with chicken and pour chicken broth over chicken.
2. Place the lid on the slow cooker and cook on "Low" heat for 6–6 1/2 hours, or on high heat for 3 hours. Carefully remove chicken and shred with forks. Return to the slow cooker, add parsley, and stir.

Nutrition:

- Calories: 127 Total Fat: 1.5 g.
- Saturated Fat: 0.3 g. Cholesterol: 27 mg.
- Carbs: 15 g. Fiber: 2 g.
- Protein: 3.4 g. Sodium: 124 mg.

Creamy Butternut Squash Soup

Preparation time: 10 minutes
Cooking time: 4 hours 10 minutes
Servings: 4
Ingredients:

- 2 large butternut squashes, seeded and sliced into rounds
- 4 carrots, peeled and cut into chunks
- 1 large yellow onion, quartered
- 8 cubes vegetable bouillon
- 1 white potato, peeled and cut into chunks
- 8 cups water

- 1 bay leaf
- 1 tsp. garlic powder
- 1/2 tsp. nutmeg, ground
- 1 pinch salt and ground black pepper to taste

Directions:

1. Preheat an oven to 500°F (260°C). Line a baking sheet with aluminum foil.
2. Spread squash, carrots, and onion out into a single layer on the prepared baking sheet.
3. Bake in the preheated oven until slightly browned, about 10 minutes. Cut rind from squash and discard.
4. Place bouillon cubes in a slow cooker. Pour peeled squash pieces, carrots, onions, and potato into a slow cooker. Pour water over vegetables and stir in bay leaf, garlic powder, nutmeg, salt, and black pepper.
5. Cook on High for 4 hours, stirring once. After 4 hours, discard bay leaf and puree soup with an immersion blender until smooth.

Nutrition:

- Calories: 194 Total Fat: 0.5 g.
- Saturated Fat: 0 g. Cholesterol: 0 mg.
- Carbs: 49 g. Fiber: 8.5 g.
- Protein: 4 g. Sodium: 73 mg.

Italian Vegetable Soup

Preparation time: 10 minutes
Cooking time: 40 minutes
Servings: 2
Ingredients:

- 2 cups water

- 3 1/2 cups low-sodium beef broth
- 1 can (15-oz.) red kidney beans
- 1 can (14–16 oz.) cannellini (white kidney) beans
- 1 can (28 oz.) tomatoes, crushed
- 1 pkg. (10 oz.) frozen spinach, chopped
- 1 small onion, chopped
- 1 (10 oz.) package frozen vegetables, mixed
- 1 tsp. garlic powder
- 1/2 tsp. black pepper
- 1 cup elbow macaroni, uncooked

Directions:

1. In a soup pot, combine all the ingredients except the macaroni. Bring to a boil over high heat then add the macaroni.
2. Reduce the heat to low and simmer for 20–30 minutes, or until the macaroni is tender.

Nutrition:

- Calories: 154 Total Fat: 1 g.
- Saturated Fat: 0.2 g. Cholesterol: 0 mg.
- Carbs: 29 g.
- Fiber: 7 g. Protein: 9 g.
- Sodium: 471 mg.

Creamy Zucchini Dill Soup

Preparation time: 10 minutes
Cooking time: 40 minutes
Servings: 2
Ingredients:

- 2 tbsp. margarine
- 2 onions, chopped

- 2 medium potatoes, peeled and diced
- 8 zucchinis, chopped
- 1/4 tsp. thyme, dried
- 1/4 tsp. rosemary, dried
- 1/2 tsp. basil, dried
- 1/4 tsp. white pepper, ground
- 4 cups reduced-sodium chicken broth
- 1 cup skim milk
- 1/4 cup dry potato flakes
- 1 tbsp. low-sodium soy sauce
- 4 tbsp. fresh dill weed, chopped

Directions:

1. In a large frying pan, melt butter or margarine; add onion and sauté until translucent. Add diced potato, zucchini, thyme, rosemary, basil, and white pepper, and cook for 5 minutes.
2. In a medium-sized cooking pot, add broth and bring them to boil. Add zucchini/potato mixture; reduce heat and simmer for about 15 minutes.
3. When cooked, puree in a food processor or blender in batches. Return to the cooking pot, add milk, and bring just to boil, but do not boil.
4. Add instant mashed potato flakes and soy sauce and stir well. Adjust seasonings to taste. Garnish with dill weed. Soup may be served hot or chilled.

Nutrition:

- Calories: 133 Total Fat: 4 g.
- Saturated Fat: 1 g. Cholesterol: 3 mg.
- Carbs: 21.5 g.
- Fiber: 8.5 g.
- Protein: 5 g.
- Sodium: 182 mg.

Easy Spinach Soup

Preparation time: 10 minutes
Cooking time: 45 minutes
Servings: 4
Ingredients:

- 1 tsp. garlic, minced
- 1/2 cup scallions, thinly sliced

- 3 1/2 cups vegetable broth
- 2 pkg. (10 oz.) frozen spinach, thawed and well-drained
- 3 tbsp. cornstarch
- 3 cups low-fat milk
- 1/2 tsp. nutmeg, ground
- 1/8 tsp. salt
- 1/2 tsp. black pepper
- Nonstick vegetable spray

Directions:

1. Coat a large saucepan with nonstick vegetable spray. Add the garlic and scallions and sauté over medium heat for 3–4 minutes or until tender. Stir in the broth and spinach. Cover and reduce the heat to low; simmer for 20 minutes.
2. In a measuring cup, combine the cornstarch and milk and stir until smooth and the cornstarch is dissolved. Pour into the soup and stir until well combined. Add the remaining ingredients and stir constantly for 6–8 minutes or until the soup has thickened. Serve immediately.

Nutrition:

- Calories: 117 Total Fat: 2.5 g.
- Saturated Fat: 0.8 g. Cholesterol: 5 mg.
- Carbs: 19 g.
- Fiber: 8.5 g.
- Protein: 8 g.
- Sodium: 530 mg.

Spiced Lentil Tomato Soup

Preparation time: 10 minutes
Cooking time: 30 minutes
Servings: 2
Ingredients:

- 4 cups low-sodium vegetable broth, divided
- 1 small yellow onion, finely chopped
- 1 (14.5 oz.) can no-salt-added tomatoes, diced and undrained
- 1 garlic clove, finely chopped
- 1 tsp. coriander, ground
- 1/2 tsp. cinnamon, ground

- 1/8 tsp. turmeric, ground
- 1/8 tsp. garam masala
- 1/8 tsp. cayenne pepper
- 1 cup red lentils
- 1 tbsp. fresh lemon juice
- 1 tbsp. feta cheese, crumbled

Directions:

1. Bring 1/2 cup broth to a boil in a pot; reduce heat and simmer. Add onion and garlic and simmer until the onion is translucent and tender about 5 minutes. Stir coriander, cinnamon, turmeric, garam masala, and cayenne pepper into onion mixture; simmer for 1 minute.
2. Stir lentils into spiced onion mixture; cook, stirring constantly, for 30 seconds. Add remaining 3 1/2 cups broth and tomatoes; bring to a boil.
3. Reduce heat to low, cover, and simmer until lentils are tender, 10–12 minutes. Stir lemon juice into the soup and garnish with feta cheese.

Nutrition:

- Calories: 179 Total Fat: 1 g.
- Saturated Fat: 0 g. Cholesterol: 2 mg.
- Carbs: 32.5 g. Fiber: 13.1 g.
- Protein: 11.1 g. Sodium: 194 mg.

Creamy Broccoli Soup

Preparation time: 10 minutes
Cooking time: 30 minutes
Servings: 2
Ingredients:

- 1 potato, peeled and chopped
- 4 cups low-sodium chicken broth

- 1 tbsp. olive oil
- 1 large onion, chopped
- 3 garlic cloves, peeled and chopped
- 2 pkg. (10 oz.) frozen broccoli, chopped and thawed
- 1/4 tsp. nutmeg, ground

Directions:

1. Heat olive oil in a large saucepan, and sauté onion, and garlic until tender. Mix in broccoli, potato, and chicken broth. Bring to a boil, reduce heat, and simmer 15 minutes, until vegetables are tender.
2. With a hand mixer or in a blender, puree the mixture until smooth. Return to the saucepan, and reheat. Season with nutmeg.

Nutrition:

- Calories: 63.5
- Total Fat: 3.4 g.
- Saturated Fat: 0.3 g.
- Cholesterol: 0 mg.
- Carbs: 10.2 g.
- Fiber: 9 g.
- Protein: 2.8 g.
- Sodium: 19.6 mg.

Simple Buttercup Squash Soup

Preparation time: 15 minutes
Cooking time: 33 minutes
Servings: 6
Ingredients:

- 1 medium onion, chopped
- 1 1/2 lb. (680 g.) buttercup squash, peeled, deseeded, and cut into 1-inch chunks
- 4 cups vegetable broth
- Ground nutmeg, to taste
- 2 tbsp. extra virgin olive oil
- 1/2 tsp. kosher salt
- 1/4 tsp. ground white pepper

Directions:

1. Heat the olive oil in a pot over medium-high heat until shimmering.
2. Add the onion and sauté for 3 minutes or until translucent.

3. Add the buttercup squash, vegetable broth, salt, and pepper. Stir to mix well. Bring to a boil.
4. Reduce the heat to low and simmer for 30 minutes or until the buttercup squash is soft.
5. Pour the soup in a food processor, then pulse to purée until creamy and smooth.
6. Pour the soup in a large serving bowl, then sprinkle with ground nutmeg and serve.

Nutrition:

- Calories: 110
- Fat: 5 g.
- Protein: 1 g.
- Carbs: 18 g.
- Fiber: 4 g.
- Sugar: 4 g.
- Sodium: 166 mg.

Sweet Potato, Kale, and White Bean Stew

Preparation time: 15 minutes
Cooking time: 25 minutes
Servings: 4
Ingredients:

- 1 can (15 oz.) low-sodium cannellini beans, rinsed and drained, divided
- 1 tbsp. olive oil
- 1 medium onion, chopped
- 2 garlic cloves, minced
- 2 stalks celery, chopped
- 3 medium carrots, chopped
- 2 cups low-sodium vegetable broth
- 1 tsp. apple cider vinegar
- 2 medium (about 1 1/4 lb.) sweet potatoes
- 2 cups kale, chopped
- 1 cup edamame, shelled
- 1/4 cup quinoa
- 1 tsp. thyme, dried
- 1/2 tsp. cayenne pepper
- 1/2 tsp. salt
- 1/4 tsp. freshly ground black pepper

Directions:

1. Put half the beans into a blender and blend until smooth. Set aside.
2. In a large soup pot over medium heat, heat the oil. When the oil is shining, include the onion and garlic, and cook until the onion softens and the garlic is sweet about 3 minutes. Add the celery and carrots, and continue cooking until the vegetables soften about 5 minutes.
3. Add the broth, vinegar, sweet potatoes, unblended beans, kale, edamame, and quinoa, and bring the mixture to a boil. Reduce the heat and simmer until the vegetables soften about 10 minutes.
4. Add the blended beans, thyme, cayenne, salt, and black pepper, increase the heat to medium-high, and bring the mixture to a boil. Reduce the heat and simmer, uncovered, until the flavors combine, about 5 minutes.
5. Into each of 4 containers, scoop 1 3/4 cups of stew.

Nutrition:

- Calories: 373
- Total Fat: 7 g.
- Saturated Fat: 1 g.
- Protein: 15 g.
- Total Carbs: 65 g.
- Fiber: 15 g.
- Sugar: 13 g.
- Sodium: 540 mg.

Spanish Stew

Preparation time: 10 Minutes
Cooking time: 25 Minutes
Servings: 4
Ingredients:

- 1 1/2 pkg. (12 oz.) smoked chicken sausage links
- 1 pkg. (5 oz.) baby spinach
- 1 can (15 oz.) chickpeas
- 1 can (14 1/2 oz.) tomatoes with basil, garlic, and oregano
- 1/2 tsp. smoked paprika
- 1/2 tsp. cumin
- 3/4 cup onions
- 1 tbsp. extra virgin olive oil

Directions:

1. Cook sliced the sausage in hot oil until browned. Remove from pot.
2. Add chopped onions; cook until tender.
3. Add sausage, drained and rinsed chickpeas, diced tomatoes, paprika, and ground cumin. Cook 15 minutes.
4. Add in spinach; cook 1–2 minutes.
5. This dish is ideal for every day and a festive table.

Nutrition:

- Calories: 200
- Protein: 10 g.
- Fat: 20 g.
- Carbs: 1 g.

Fish Stew

Preparation time: 30 minutes
Cooking time: 20 minutes
Servings: 2
Ingredients:

- 400 g. potatoes
- 400 g. carrots
- 1 medium onion
- 400 ml. vegetable broth
- 400 g. ling fish fillet
- 4 stalks dill
- 150 g. sour cream
- 1 tbsp. capers
- Salt and pepper to taste

Directions:

1. Prepare the vegetable stock. Peel the potatoes and cut them into small cubes. Peel the carrots and dice them too. Peel and cut the onion.
2. Put the oil in a pan and sauté the onion. Add the potatoes and carrots. Let everything cook for 12 minutes. Deglaze with the vegetable stock.
3. Wash and chop the dill. Rinse the fish, pat dry with kitchen paper, and cut into large pieces. Season the fish with salt and pepper, add to the vegetables and cook for 3–5 minutes over low heat. Add dill, sour cream, and capers. Season to taste with salt and pepper. Bring everything to the boil briefly and then serve fresh.

Nutrition:

- Calories: 520
- Carbs: 45 g.
- Protein: 47 g.
- Fat: 14 g

Salmon and Shrimp Stew

Preparation time: 10 minutes
Cooking time: 20 minutes
Servings: 6
Ingredients:

- 2 tbsp. olive oil
- 1/2 cup onion, chopped finely
- 2 garlic cloves, minced
- 1 Serrano pepper, chopped
- 1 tsp. smoked paprika
- 4 cups fresh tomatoes, chopped
- 4 cups low-sodium chicken broth
- 1 lb. salmon fillets, cubed
- 1 lb. shrimp, peeled and deveined
- 2 tbsp. fresh lime juice
- 1/4 cup fresh basil, chopped
- 1/4 cup fresh parsley, chopped
- Black pepper, ground, as required
- 2 scallions, chopped
- 1 tbsp. coconut oil
- 1 tsp. Sea salt

Directions:

1. In a large soup pan, melt coconut oil over medium-high heat and sauté the onion for 5–6 minutes.
2. Add the garlic, Serrano pepper, and smoked paprika, and sauté for 1 minute.
3. Add the tomatoes and broth and bring to a gentle simmer over medium heat.
4. Simmer for 5 minutes.
5. Add the salmon and simmer for 3–4 minutes.
6. Stir in the remaining seafood and cook for 4–5 minutes.
7. Stir in the lemon juice, basil, parsley, sea salt, and black pepper, and remove from heat.
8. Serve hot with the garnishing of scallion.

Nutrition:

- Calories: 271
- Total Fat: 11 g.
- Saturated Fat: 1.8 g.
- Cholesterol: 193 mg.
- Total Carbs 8.6 g.
- Sugar 3.8 g.
- Fiber: 2.1 g.
- Sodium: 273 mg.
- Potassium: 763 mg.
- Protein: 34.7 g.

Spicy Coconut Fish Stew

Preparation time: 10 minutes
Cooking time: 6 hours 20 minutes
Servings: 6
Ingredients:

- 1 1/2 lb. white fish fillets
- 14 oz. coconut milk
- 1 can (14 oz.) tomato, crushed
- 1 green bell pepper, chopped
- 1 red bell pepper, chopped
- 2 garlic cloves, minced
- 1 onion, chopped
- 1 tbsp. butter
- ½ tsp. Pepper
- ¼. Salt

Directions:

1. In a crockpot combine the butter, coconut milk, tomatoes, peppers, garlic, and onion.
2. Cover and cook on "Low" for 6 hours.
3. About 30 minutes before the time is up, open and add the fish fillets to the crockpot. Season with pepper and salt.
4. Cover and cook on "High" for 30 minutes longer.
5. Serve and enjoy.

Nutrition:

- Calories: 398
- Fat: 26.3 g.
- Carbs: 11.6 g.
- Sugar: 6.9 g.
- Protein: 30.5 g.
- Cholesterol: 92 mg.

Mediterranean Shrimp Soup

Preparation time: 15 minutes
Cooking time: 5 hours
Servings: 6
Ingredients:

- 1 lb. medium shrimp, peeled, veined, uncooked
- 14 oz. tomatoes, diced
- 14 oz. low-sodium chicken broth
- 1 medium onion, chopp
- ed
- 8 oz. tomato sauce
- 1/2 cup orange juice
- 1 medium green bell pepper, chopped
- 2 1/2 oz. mushrooms, sliced
- 1/2 cup dry white wine (optional)

- 2 garlic cloves, minced
- 1/4 cup ripe olives, sliced
- 2 bay leaves
- 1 tsp. basil, dried
- 1/4 tsp. fennel seeds, crushed
- 1/4 tsp. black pepper

Directions:

1. In a slow cooker and add diced tomatoes, low-sodium chicken broth, chopped onion, tomato sauce, orange juice, chopped green bell pepper, dry white wine, orange juice, sliced ripe olives, sliced mushrooms, bay leaves, dried basil, minced garlic, black pepper, and crushed fennel seeds. Combine the ingredients thoroughly.
2. Cover the slow cooker and slow cook for 4 1/2 hours until the vegetables become tender.
3. Afterward, stir the shrimp into the slow cooker.
4. Cover the cooker and again slow cook for 30 minutes.
5. Discard the bay leaves before serving.

Nutrition:

- Calories: 162
- Carbs: 12 g.
- Protein: 21 g.
- Fat: 3 g.
- Dietary Fiber: 2 g.
- Cholesterol: 129 mg.
- Sodium: 678 mg.

Slow-Cooker Seafood Stew

Preparation time: 20 minutes
Cooking time: 5 hours and 5 minutes
Servings: 8
Ingredients:

- 1 lb. white fish, cut into 1-inch size
- 3/4 lb. medium shrimp, shelled, uncooked, veined
- 6 oz. tined crab meat, drained
- 2 cups onions, sliced
- 28 oz. tinned tomatoes, diced with liquid

- 5 garlic cloves, grated
- 6 oz. tomato paste
- 8 oz. clam juice
- 1 tbsp. red wine vinegar
- 1/2 cup dry white wine
- 2 1/2 tsp. Italian seasoning, dried
- 1 tbsp. olive oil
- 1/4 tsp. red pepper flakes, crushed
- 1/4 tsp. sugar
- 2 stalks celery, finely chopped
- 1 bay leaf
- 6 1/2 oz. clams with juice, chopped
- 1/4 cup fresh parsley, chopped

Directions:
1. Combine celery, onions, clam juice, tomatoes, wine, tomato paste, Italian seasoning, vinegar, pepper flakes, bay leaf, and sugar in a 6-quart slow cooker.
2. Close the slow cooker and cook on low heat for 8 hours.
3. Stir in shrimp, fish, crabmeat, and clams with juice into the stew.
4. Continue slow cooking for 2 hours.
5. Remove the bay leaf before serving.
6. For seasoning, stir in parsley.
7. Serve hot.

Nutrition:
- Calories: 215
- Carbohydrate: 15 g.
- Protein: 30 g.
- Sugars: 5 g.
- Fat: 4 g.
- Dietary Fiber: 3 g.
- Cholesterol: 125 mg.
- Sodium: 610 mg.

Hearty Pumpkin Chicken Soup

Preparation time: 15–20 minutes
Cooking time: 30 minutes
Servings: 6
Ingredients:
- 1 small onion, thinly sliced
- 2 garlic cloves, minced
- 1 lb. chicken breast, thinly sliced

- 1 tbsp. vegetable oil or coconut oil
- 1 medium zucchini, diced
- 1-inch piece ginger, peeled and minced
- 3/4 lb. pumpkin, cubed into 1/2-inch pieces
- 1 small chili or jalapeno pepper, seeded and thinly sliced
- 1 red bell pepper, seeded and thinly sliced
- 2 cups chicken broth
- 1 can (14 oz.) light coconut milk
- A handful of cilantro leaves
- 1 lime juice
- Salt and pepper to taste

Directions:
1. Season the chicken slices with salt and pepper.
2. Heat the oil over medium-high heat in a large cooking pot.
3. Add the chicken and stir cook for 4–5 minutes to evenly brown.
4. Add the onion, ginger, and garlic and stir cook for 2–3 minutes until softened and translucent.
5. Add the zucchini and cubed pumpkin; stir well.
6. Add the chicken broth, coconut milk, bell pepper, chili or jalapeño pepper, and lime juice; stir again.
7. Bring to a boil, cover, and simmer over low heat for about 20 minutes, until the pumpkin is cooked well and softened.
8. Season with additional salt and pepper, if required.
9. Serve warm with cilantro leaves on top.

Note: You can store leftovers in an airtight container in the refrigerator for up to 3–4 days. Simply re-heat in a cooking pot and serve.

Nutrition:
- Calories: 231 Fat: 13 g.
- Total carbs: 11.5 g.
- Sugar: 5 g
- Protein: 17 g.
- Sodium: 1207 mg.

Chicken Bone Soup

Preparation time: 10 minutes
Cooking time: 1 hour
Servings: 5
Ingredients:

- 1 lb. chicken bones
- 1 tsp. onion powder
- 1 tsp. garlic powder
- 1 tsp. ginger powder
- 1/2 tsp. chili powder
- 2 oz. ghee
- 1 oz. squash
- 2 oz. soy sauce
- 3 cups chicken broth
- 2 oz. cream cheese
- 1 tsp. cumin powder
- Salt and Pepper to taste

Directions:

1. Break the chicken bones into chunks and drop them in a pot and add all the rest of the ingredients to the cooking pot except the cream cheese.
2. Set the cooking pot on heat for 60 minutes and cook completely. Once everything is cooked, remove the chicken from the cooking pot and shred using a fork.
3. Add cream cheese to the cooking pot. Using an immersion blender, emulsify all of the liquids together (remove the bones before you do this). This will keep the soup from separating while you are eating
4. Place the chicken back into the cooking pot. Taste and season with extra salt, pepper, cumin, and soy sauce, if needed. Serve and enjoy the taste.

Nutrition:

- Calories: 402
- Protein: 51.57 g.
- Fat: 17.64 g.
- Carbs: 6.25 g.

Creamy Vegetable Soup

Preparation time: 5 minutes
Cooking time: 15 minutes
Servings: 2
Ingredients:

- 1 1/2 cup vegetable broth
- 1 oz. mixed vegetables
- 2 bouillon cubes
- 1 tbsp. olive oil
- 2 large eggs, hard-boiled
- 2 tbsp. rosemary leaves
- 1 oz. Mascarpone cheese
- 1/2 tsp. chili paste
- 1/2 tsp. garlic paste

Directions:

1. Place a pan over medium heat and add vegetable broth, vegetables, bouillon cubes, and olive oil.
2. Bring the broth to a boil and stir everything together, then add the chili paste and garlic paste, and stir again. Turn the stove off.
3. Chop the boiled eggs and add them to the steaming broth. Add mascarpone cheese and stir together well. Let the soup sit for a moment and add chopped

rosemary leaves. Serve up some awesome tasting soup in just 5 minutes!

Nutrition:
- Calories: 327
- Protein: 8.79 g
- Fat: 30.99 g
- Carbs: 4.81 g

Spicy Chick Pea Stew

Preparation time: 15 minutes
Cooking time: 6–8 hours
Servings: 4
Ingredients:
- 1 tbsp. vegetable oil
- 2 onions, peeled and finely chopped
- 4 garlic cloves, finely chopped
- 2 tbsp. fresh ginger root, minced
- 2 tsp. coriander, ground
- 1 tsp. cumin seed
- 1 tsp. salt
- 1/2 tsp. black pepper, fresh ground
- 1/2 tsp. cayenne pepper
- 2 tsp. balsamic vinegar
- 2 cups tomatoes, coarsely chopped (canned or fresh)
- 2 (19 oz.) cans chickpeas, rinsed and drained

Directions:
1. In a skillet over medium heat, cook onions, stirring, just until they begin to brown; then add garlic and all spices and cook, stirring, for 1 minute.
2. Add vinegar and tomatoes and bring to a boil, then place mixture in your slow cooker; add chickpeas and combine well.
3. Cover and cook on "Low" for 6–8 hours or on "High" for 3–4 hours, or until the mixture is hot and bubbling.

Nutrition:
- Calories: 269
- Fat: 5 g.
- Carbs: 48 g.
- Protein: 10 g.

Easy Salsa Chicken Stew

Preparation time: 15 minutes
Cooking time: 6–8 hours
Servings: 4
Ingredients:
- 4 chicken breasts, boneless and skinless
- 32 oz. salsa
- 1 can (14 1/2 oz.) corn, drained
- 1 can (14 1/2 oz.) black beans, drained

Directions:
1. Place ingredients in the slow cooker and cook on "Low" for 6–8 hours.
2. About 30–60 minutes before serving, remove chicken, shred it and return to slow cooker.

Nutrition:
- Calories: 157
- Fat: 2 g.
- Carbs: 21 g.
- Protein: 15 g.
- Sodium: 599 mg.

Chicken and Potato Stew

Preparation time: 15 minutes
Cooking time: 6 hours 10 minutes
Servings: 4
Ingredients:
- 1 1/2 cups russet potatoes, peeled cut into bite-size pieces, washed
- 1 1/2 cups carrots, peeled, cut into bite-size pieces, and washed
- 1/2 cup onion, finely chopped
- 1/4 tsp. garlic powder
- 1/2 tsp. salt
- 3/4 tsp. black pepper, ground
- 1/2 tsp. sage
- 1/4 tsp. thyme
- 2 chicken breast halves, boneless and skinless
- 1 can (10 3/4 oz.) cream of chicken soup

Directions:
1. Place vegetables in the bottom of a 2 1/2-quart slow cooker. Sprinkle seasonings evenly over the vegetables.

2. Top with chicken, then cover with soup. Cook on "Low" for 6 hours.

Nutrition:

- Calories: 278
- Fat: 8 g.
- Carbs: 29 g.
- Protein: 21 g.

Butternut Squash Stew

Preparation time: 15 minutes
Cooking time: 8–10 hours
Servings: 4
Ingredients:

- 1 butternut squash, peeled, seeded, diced
- 2 cups eggplant, diced, with peel
- 2 cups zucchini, diced
- 1 pkg. (10 oz.) frozen okra, thawed
- 1 can (8 oz.) tomato sauce
- 1 cup onion, chopped
- 1 ripe tomato, chopped
- 1 carrot, thinly sliced
- 1/2 cup vegetable broth
- 1/3 cup raisins
- 1 garlic clove, chopped
- 1/2 tsp. cumin, ground
- 1/2 tsp. turmeric, ground
- 1/4 tsp. red pepper, crushed
- 1/4 tsp. cinnamon, ground
- 1/4 tsp. paprika

Directions:

1. In a slow cooker, combine butternut squash, eggplant, zucchini, okra, tomato sauce, onion, tomato, carrot, broth,

raisins, and garlic. Season with cumin, turmeric, red pepper, cinnamon, and paprika.
2. Cover, and cook on "Low" for 8–10 hours, or until vegetables are tender.

Nutrition:

- Calories: 122
- Fat: 1 g.
- Carbs: 30 g.
- Protein: 3 g.
- Sodium: 157 mg.

Tuscan Chicken Stew

Preparation time: 15 minutes
Cooking time: 1 hour 30 minutes
Servings: 2
Ingredients:

- medium eggplant, cubed
- 3 zucchinis, cubed
- 1 cup onion, chopped
- 2 cans Great Northern® beans
- 2 cans tomatoes, diced, no salt added
- 1 tsp. sugar
- 2 tbsp. Italian seasoning
- 1 tsp. garlic powder
- Salt and pepper to taste
- 2 lbs. chicken breasts, boneless and skinless
- 3 cups chicken stock

Directions:

1. Put tomatoes, chicken, broth seasonings, and sugar into the slow cooker. Cook on "Low" for 6–8 hours if using frozen chicken breasts.
2. During the last 1 1/2 hours, add eggplant, zucchini, and beans in, and stir.

Nutrition:

- Calories: 304
- Fat: 2 g.
- Carbs 36 g.
- Protein: 35 g. per 1/8 of recipe

Zucchini Vegetable Stew

Preparation time: 10 minutes
Cooking time: 15 minutes
Servings: 4
Ingredients:

- 1 (1 lb.) eggplant, peeled, cubed
- 1 zucchini, sliced
- 1/2 cup pasta sauce, reduced-sodium
- 1 pkg. (12 oz.) frozen mixed stew vegetables (celery, onion, peppers)

Directions:

1. Combine eggplant, vegetable blend, zucchini, and 2 tbsp. water in a large heavy pan. Heat until mixture boils, then reduce heat to low, and cover.
2. Cook for 10–15 minutes or until vegetables are tender and drain.
3. Return eggplant mixture to pan. Add pasta sauce and stir until sauce heats through.

Nutrition:

- Calories: 50
- Fat: 5 g.
- Carbs: 10 g.
- Protein: 1 g.

Root Vegetable Soup

Preparation time: 10 minutes
Cooking time: 40 minutes
Servings: 6
Ingredients:

- 2 tsp. extra virgin olive oil
- 1 medium onion, chopped
- 2 garlic cloves, minced
- 3 1/2 cups vegetable stock, or vegetable broth, low-sodium
- 3 celery roots (about 1 lb.), small, peeled, chopped
- 1 rutabaga (about 1 lb.), medium, peeled, chopped
- 1/4 tsp. kosher salt
- 1/8 tsp. freshly ground pepper
- 2 Yukon Gold or red-skinned potatoes (about 1 lb.), medium, peeled, chopped

- 1/2 cup milk, 1% low-fat
- Fresh Italian parsley, chopped

Directions:

1. Heat a large pot over medium heat. Add the oil and tilt the pan to coat the bottom evenly. Add the onion and cook, stirring often, until softened, 5 minutes. Add the garlic and cook, stirring constantly, until fragrant, 30 seconds. Add the stock, celery roots, rutabaga, salt, and pepper, and bring to a boil over high heat. Cover, reduce the heat to low, and simmer for 15 minutes. Add the potatoes, cover, and simmer until all the vegetables are very tender, 15–20 minutes longer.
2. Ladle about 2 cups of the vegetable mixture into a medium bowl and mash with a potato masher until smooth. Return the mixture to the pot. Stir in the milk and cook just until heated through for 1 minute. Ladle the soup into 6 bowls, sprinkle with parsley, and serve at once. The soup can be refrigerated, covered, for up to 4 days.

Nutrition:

- Carbs: 29 g.
- Calories: 144
- Fat: 2 g.
- Saturated Fat: 0 g.
- Cholesterol: 0 mg.
- Fiber: 4 g.
- Protein: 4 g.
- Sodium: 277 mg.

White Bean and Roasted Tomato Soup

Preparation time: 15 minutes
Cooking time: 2 hours
Servings: 8
Ingredients:

- 8 plum tomatoes, halved lengthwise
- 4 tsp. extra virgin olive oil, divided
- 3/4 tsp. kosher salt, divided
- 1/4 tsp. freshly ground pepper
- 2 stalks celery, chopped

- 2 carrots, peeled and chopped
- 1 onion, large, chopped
- 2 garlic cloves, minced
- 8 cups chicken stock or chicken broth, low-sodium
- 1 lb. cannellini beans or navy beans, dried, picked over, rinsed
- 1 tsp. basil, dried
- 1 tsp. oregano, dried

Directions:

1. Preheat the oven to 400°F.
2. Place the tomatoes on a large rimmed baking sheet. Drizzle with 2 tsp. the oil and sprinkle with 1/4 tsp. the salt and 1/8 tsp. the pepper and turn to coat. Arrange the tomatoes skin side down in a single layer. Bake until the tomatoes are soft and the bottoms are well browned for 40–45 minutes. Let the tomatoes stand until cool enough to handle. Coarsely chop the tomatoes.
3. Meanwhile, heat a large pot over medium-high heat. Add the remaining 2 tsp. oil and tilt the pot to coat the bottom evenly. Add the celery, carrots, and onion and cook, stirring often, until the vegetables are softened, 5 minutes. Add the garlic and cook, stirring constantly, until fragrant, 30 seconds.
4. Add the stock, beans, basil, oregano, remaining 1/2 tsp. salt, and remaining 1/8 tsp. pepper and bring to a boil over high heat. Cover, reduce the heat to low and simmer until the beans are tender, for 1 hour. Stir in the tomatoes and cook until heated through, for 2 minutes. Ladle the soup into 8 bowls and serve at once. The soup can be refrigerated, covered, for up to 4 days, or frozen for up to 3 months.

Nutrition:

- Carbs: 31 g. Calories: 240
- Fat: 4 g. Saturated Fat: 1 g.
- Cholesterol: 5 mg. Fiber: 11 g.
- Protein: 17 g. Sodium: 272 mg.

Shrimp and Chicken Dumpling Soup

Preparation time: 10 minutes
Cooking time: 5 minutes
Servings: 6
Ingredients:

- 1 pkg. (6 oz.) frozen shrimp, cooked, peeled, thawed, and finely chopped
- 1/2 cup cooked chicken, chopped
- 1/2 cup fresh mushrooms, chopped
- 2 tbsp. reduced-sodium soy sauce
- 1/2 cup green onions, sliced
- 1/4 cup fresh cilantro, snipped
- 24 wonton wrappers
- 6 cups low-sodium chicken broth
- 3/4 cup red sweet pepper, chopped
- 1/2 cup frozen edamame
- 1/4 tsp. salt
- 2 cups fresh baby spinach
- 2 tsp. sesame oil, toasted

Directions:

1. For the filling, combine the first 4 ingredients (through soy sauce), 1/4 cup of green onions, and 2 tsp. Cilantro.
2. Working with 2 wonton wrappers at a time, top each with a rounded tsp. of the filling. Brush edges of the wrappers with water. Fold and seal edges. Repeat with the remaining.
3. In a saucepan, combine the next 4 ingredients (through salt) and the remaining green onions and cilantro.
4. Bring to a boil. Slowly add wontons to the boiling broth mixture. Boil gently until tender, about 2–3 minutes. Stirring occasionally.
5. Stir in sesame oil and spinach.
6. Top with additional snipped fresh cilantro and serve.

Nutrition:

- Calories: 189
- Fat: 3 g. Carb: 24 g.
- Protein: 17 g.

Pea and Collards Soup

Preparation time: 10 Minutes
Cooking time: 50 Minutes
Servings: 4
Ingredients:

- 1/2 pkg. (16 oz.) black-eyed peas
- 1 onion
- 2 carrots
- 1 1/2 cups low-sodium ham
- 1 lb. bunch collard greens, trimmed
- 1 tbsp. extra virgin olive oil
- 2 garlic cloves
- 1/2 tsp. black pepper
- 1 tbsp. hot sauce
- 3 cups water

Directions:

1. Cook chopped onion and carrots for 10 minutes.
2. Add peas, diced ham, collards, and minced garlic. Cook 5 minutes.
3. Add broth, 3 cups water, and pepper. Bring to a boil; simmer 35 minutes, adding water if needed.
4. Serve with hot sauce.

Nutrition:

- Calories: 86 Protein: 15 g.
- Fat: 2 g. Carbs: 9 g.

Creamy Shrimp

Preparation time: 10 minutes
Cooking time: 2 hours 10 minutes
Servings: 4
Ingredients:

- 1 lb. shrimp, cooked
- 1 cup sour cream

- 1 can (16 oz.) cream of mushroom soup
- 1 tsp. curry powder
- 1 onion, chopped
- Nonstick cooking spray

Directions:

1. Spray a medium pan with cooking spray and heat over medium heat.
2. Add onion to the hot pan and sauté until the onion is soft.
3. Transfer sautéed onion to a crockpot along with the shrimp, curry powder, and cream of mushroom soup.
4. Cover and cook on low for 2 hours.
5. Stir in sour cream and serve.

Nutrition:

- Calories: 302
- Fat: 16.2 g.
- Carbs: 9.5 g.
- Sugar: 1.8 g.
- Protein: 28.6 g.
- Cholesterol: 264 mg.

Broccoli Soup

Preparation time: 15 minutes
Cooking time: 30 minutes
Servings: 2
Ingredients:

- 1 lb. fresh broccoli (1 medium-sized head)
- 14 oz. chicken broth, low-sodium, fat-free
- 2 tbsp. margarine
- 2 tbsp. all-purpose flour
- 2 cups skim milk
- 1/4 tsp. pepper
- 1 cup Cheddar cheese, reduced-fat, shredded

Directions:

1. Clean the broccoli, then chop the florets and thinly slice the stems.
2. In a medium-sized saucepan, combine the broccoli and chicken broth; heat to a boil. Reduce heat and simmer, covered, for 7 minutes or until the broccoli is fork-tender.

3. Transfer to a food processor or blender. Process until fairly smooth.
4. In the same saucepan, melt the margarine over medium heat; add the flour. Cook, stirring constantly until it starts to bubble. Add the milk and pepper; heat to a boil, stirring constantly.
5. Reduce heat to medium and add the broccoli purée. Stir in the cheese; heat just until the cheese melts—do not boil, keep stirring constantly.

Nutrition:

- Calories: 294
- Fat: 12 g.
- Carbs: 18 g.
- Protein: 28 g.

CHAPTER 12:

Sauce, Dip, and Dressing Recipes

Barbecue Sauce

Preparation time: 10 minutes
Cooking time: 20 minutes
Servings: 2
Ingredients:

- 1 onion, small, minced
- 1 can (8 oz.) tomato sauce
- 2 cups water
- 1/4 cup wine vinegar
- 1/4 cup Worcestershire sauce
- 1 tsp. salt (optional)
- 2 tsp. paprika
- 2 tsp. chili powder
- 1 tsp. pepper
- 1/2 tsp. cinnamon
- 1/8 tsp. cloves

Directions:

1. Combine all; bring to a full boil. Simmer 20 minutes.

Nutrition:

- Calories: 71
- Protein: 1.56 g.
- Fat: 0.77 g.
- Carbs: 15.28 g.

Spaghetti Sauce

Preparation time: 10 minutes
Cooking time: 60 minutes
Servings: 6
Ingredients:

- 1 tsp. vegetable oil
- 1 1/4 lb. lean round, ground
- 3 cans (8 oz.) tomato sauce
- 1 can (6 oz.) tomato paste
- 4 cups water
- 1/4 tsp. salt (optional)
- 1 tsp. pepper
- 1 tsp. oregano
- A dash garlic
- 1 onion chopped

Directions:

1. Brown onions in oil
2. Add meat and brown. Drain fat; add rest of ingredients.
3. Simmer 1 hour uncovered.

Nutrition:

- Calories: 131
- Protein: 14.32 g.
- Fat: 6.59 g.
- Carbs: 4.64 g.

Chocolate Sauce with Dry Milk

Preparation time: 10 minutes
Cooking time: 20 minutes
Servings: 2
Ingredients:

- 3 tbsp. cocoa
- 4 tsp. cornstarch
- 1/3 cup instant dry milk

- 1/3 cup. Splenda®
- 1/8 tsp. salt
- 1 tbsp. margarine
- 2 tsp. vanilla

Directions:
1. Stir cocoa, cornstarch, dry milk, and salt to blend in a small saucepan. Stir water into the dry mixture until smooth. Add margarine and cook and stir over low heat. Bring to a boil and simmer for 2 minutes, stirring constantly.
2. Remove from heat. Add vanilla and Splenda® to the sauce. Stir lightly to mix. Pour into a glass jar and refrigerate until used. Return to room temperature before serving over ice cream, or it may be heated gain to serve over cake or pudding.

Nutrition:
- Calories: 141
- Protein: 5.43 g.
- Fat: 6.84 g.
- Carbs: 16.04 g.

Chocolate Sauce

Preparation time: 10 minutes
Cooking time: 10 minutes
Servings: 4
Ingredients:
- 1 tbsp. butter
- 2 tbsp. cocoa
- 1 tbsp. cornstarch

- 1 cup skim milk
- 2 tsp. Splenda®
- 1/8 tsp. salt

Direction:
1. Melt butter. Combine cocoa, cornstarch, and salt; blend with melted butter until smooth. Add milk and Splenda® and cook over moderate heat, constantly stirring until slightly thickened, remove from heat. Stir in vanilla. Set pan in ice water and stir until completely cold. (Sauce thickens as it cools.)

Nutrition:
- Calories: 78
- Protein: 2.46 g.
- Fat: 3.29 g.
- Carbs: 11.35 g.

Creamed Sauce

Preparation time: 10 minutes
Cooking time: 10 minutes
Servings: 4
Ingredients:
- 1 box frozen cauliflower or fresh
- 1 can (4 oz.) stem and pieces of mushrooms
- 1/2 tsp. onion flakes
- 1/2 tsp. garlic powder
- Salt and pepper to taste
- 1 cup water

Directions:

1. Cook cauliflower in water. Put in blender, using water it's cooked in. Add mushrooms using water they are packed in. Add onion flakes, garlic powder, salt, and pepper. Blend until smooth.

Nutrition:

- Calories: 23
- Protein: 1.67 g.
- Fat: 0.22 g.
- Carbs: 4.73 g.

Salad Dressing

Preparation time: 10 minutes
Cooking time: 0 minutes
Servings: 4
Ingredients:

- 46 oz. low-sodium V-8 juice
- 1 tbsp. wine vinegar
- 1/4 tsp. oregano
- 1/4 tsp. garlic powder
- 1/2 tsp. onion powder
- 1 tsp. Splenda®

Directions:

1. Mix them and chill. Shake before using it.

Nutrition:

- Calories: 43
- Protein: 2.03 g.
- Fat: 0.7 g.
- Carbs: 8.62 g.

Zero Salad Dressing

Preparation time: 10 minutes
Cooking time: 0 minutes
Servings: 2
Ingredients:

- 1/2 cup tomato juice
- 1 tbsp. onion, finely chopped
- 2 tbsp. lemon juice or vinegar
- Salt and pepper to taste
- Parsley or green pepper, chopped
- Horseradish or mustard may be added if desired.

Directions:

1. Combine in a jar with a tightly fitted top. Shake well before using. Use as desired.

Nutrition:

- Calories: 32
- Protein: 1.52 g.
- Fat: 0.53 g.
- Carbs: 6.47 g.

No Calorie Dressing

Preparation time: 10 minutes
Cooking time: 0 minutes
Servings: 2
Ingredients:

- 1/2 cup water
- 1/2 cup white vinegar
- 1/2 tsp. salt
- 1/2 tsp. dry mustard
- 1/8 tsp. pepper
- 1/16 tsp. paprika
- 4 tsp. Splenda®

Directions:

1. Combine all and refrigerate.

Nutrition:

- Calories: 15 Protein: 0.11 g.
- Fat: 0.05 g.
- Carbs: 0.93 g.

Low-Calorie Tomato Dressing

Preparation time: 10 minutes
Cooking time: 0 minutes
Servings: 2
Ingredients:

- 1 cup tomato juice

- 1/4 cup salad oil
- 1/4 cup vinegar
- 1 tsp. salt
- 1 tsp. dry mustard
- 1/4 tsp. garlic salt
- 1/4 tsp. onion salt
- 1 tbsp. steak sauce

Directions:
1. Combine all and beat well to mix thoroughly. Chill. Good on salad greens.

Nutrition:
- Calories: 138 Protein: 0.59 g.
- Fat: 13.83 g.
- Carbs: 3.32 g.

Low-Calorie Salad Dressing
Preparation time: 10 minutes
Cooking time: 0 minutes
Servings: 6
Ingredients:
- 1/2 cup cottage cheese
- 1/2 cup buttermilk
- 1/2 lemon, peeled, seeded
- 1 tsp. salt
- 1/2 tsp. paprika
- 1/2 green pepper
- 4 radishes
- Dash salt

Directions:
1. Put all the ingredients in a blender and blend until the green pepper and the radishes are finely chopped.

Nutrition:
- Calories: 69 Protein: 4.09 g.
- Fat: 1.2 g. Carbs: 11.55 g.

Pineapple Salad Dressing
Preparation time: 10 minutes
Cooking time: 0 minutes
Servings: 2
Ingredients:
- 1 cup pineapple juice
- 1/2 cup Splenda®

- 1 tbsp. cornstarch
- 1 egg white, beaten
- A pinch salt
- 2 tbsp. lemon juice
- 1/4 tsp. lemon rind, grated

Directions:
1. Cook pineapple juice, lemon juice, lemon rind, cornstarch, Splenda, and salt until thickened. Fold in stiffly beaten egg white last. Whipping cream can be added if a richer dressing is desired.

Nutrition:
- Calories: 51 Protein: 1.19 g.
- Fat: 0.08 g. Carbs: 12.21 g.

Yogurt Salad Dressing

Preparation time: 10 minutes
Cooking time: 0 minutes
Servings: 4
Ingredients:
- 2 cups yogurt
- 3–4 tbsp. soy sauce
- 1/4 cup sesame seeds, toasted
- 2 tbsp. celery seeds
- 2 tbsp. dill weed
- 1 tbsp. onion, chopped

Directions:
1. Combine and blend in a blender.

Nutrition:
- Calories: 178
- Protein: 7.53 g.
- Fat: 11.24 g.
- Carbs: 13.7 g.

Low-Calorie Cooked Dressing

Preparation time: 10 minutes
Cooking time: 10 minutes
Servings: 4
Ingredients:

- 1/3 cup instant non-fat dry milk
- 1 1/4 tsp. dry mustard
- 1 tsp. salt
- 1/8 tsp. freshly ground pepper
- 1 tbsp. all-purpose flour
- 1 egg, medium
- 1 cup water
- 2 tbsp. white vinegar
- 1 tbsp. margarine
- 6 tsp. Splenda®

Directions:

1. Combine dry ingredients on top of a double boiler. Beat egg slightly and combine with water and vinegar. Add to dry slowly, stirring to blend well.
2. Cook over simmering water, constantly stirring until thick and smooth. Remove from heat; add margarine and Splenda® blend well. Pour into a 1-pint jar, cover. Store in refrigerator.

Nutrition:

- Calories: 76
- Protein: 2.32 g.
- Fat: 4.38 g.
- Carbs: 6.54 g.

Buttermilk Dressing

Preparation time: 10 minutes
Cooking time: 0 minutes
Servings: 2
Ingredients:

- 1/3 cup yogurt, low-fat
- 1/2 cup buttermilk
- 3 tbsp. mayonnaise, reduced-calorie
- 1 tbsp. dry Ranch-style dressing mix

Directions:

1. Combine, cover tightly, and keep for 5 days.

Nutrition:

- Calories: 106 Kcal
- Protein: 4.61 g.
- Fat: 5.28 g.
- Carbs: 10.48 g.

Fruit Dip

Preparation time: 10 minutes
Cooking time: 0 minutes
Servings: 4
Ingredients:

- 1 cup plain yogurt
- 8 oz. light cream
- 1/3 cup Splenda®
- 1 tsp. vanilla.

Directions:

1. Mix all together.

Nutrition:

- Calories: 151 Kcal
- Protein: 3.66 g.
- Fat: 12.94 g.
- Carbs: 5.06 g.

Liteer's Dip

Preparation time: 10 minutes
Cooking time: 0 minutes
Servings: 4
Ingredients:

- 1 (8 oz.) cottage cheese
- 1 (6–7 oz.) white tuna, packed in water
- 3 tbsp. pimento, chopped
- 2 tsp. onion, grated
- Salt and pepper to taste

Directions:
1. Blend cottage cheese until smooth and soft. Use a blender or electric mixer: drain and flake tuna. Combine with cottage cheese and seasonings.

Nutrition:
- Calories: 60
- Protein: 1.65 g.
- Fat: 0.18 g.
- Carbs: 14.02 g.

Onion Dip

Preparation time: 10 minutes
Cooking time: 0 minutes
Servings: 2
Ingredients:
- 6 oz. cottage cheese
- 2 1/2 tbsp. lemon juice
- 2 tbsp. buttermilk
- Dash onion flakes
- 1/2 tsp. garlic salt
- Cake coloring for looks

Directions:
1. Blend until creamy. Serve with celery sticks or raw cauliflower.

Nutrition:
- Calories: 95
- Protein: 10.08 g.
- Fat: 3.84 g.
- Carbs: 5.15 g.

Lemon Sauce

Preparation time: 10 minutes
Cooking time: 10 minutes
Servings: 2
Ingredients:
- 2 cups water
- 2 tbsp. cornstarch
- 1/8 tsp. salt
- 1 lemon rind, grated
- 2 tbsp. margarine
- 2 tbsp. lemon juice
- 1 drop yellow food coloring
- 1/3 cup Splenda®

Directions:
1. Combine water, cornstarch, and salt. Stir until smooth in a small saucepan. Cook and stir over medium heat until thickened and clear, then continue to simmer, constantly stirring for another 2 minutes.
2. Remove from heat and add remaining ingredients to the sauce, stir lightly to mix well. Serve warm over cake or pudding.

Nutrition:
- Calories: 140 Kcal
- Protein: 0.19 g.
- Fat: 11.48 g.
- Carbs: 10.12 g.

Green Pepper Salsa

Preparation time: 10 minutes
Cooking time: 30 minutes
Servings: 4
Ingredients:
- 1 onion, chopped
- 1 green pepper, chopped
- 1/3 cup whole coriander leaves, chopped
- 2 tomatoes, seeds removed, finely chopped
- 1 garlic clove, minced
- 1/2 lime, freshly squeezed
- 1 tbsp. olive oil
- Salt to taste

Directions:

1. Start by throwing all the ingredients into a bowl.
2. Toss them well then refrigerate for approximately 30 minutes.
3. Serve fresh.

Nutrition:

- Calories: 132
- Total Fat: 1.7 g.
- Saturated Fat: 0.3 g.
- Cholesterol: 121 mg.
- Sodium: 321 mg.
- Total Carbs: 3.5 g.
- Fiber: 0 g.
- Sugar: 0.5 g.
- Protein: 7.4 g.

CHAPTER 13:

Dessert Recipes

Greek Yogurt Berry Smoothie Pops

Preparation time: 5 minutes
Cooking time: 0 minutes
Servings: 6
Ingredients:

- 2 cups frozen berries, mixed
- 1/2 cup plain almond milk, unsweetened
- 1 cup plain nonfat Greek yogurt
- 2 tbsp. hemp seeds

Directions:

1. Place all the ingredients in a blender and process until finely blended.
2. Pour into 6 clean ice pop molds and insert sticks.
3. Freeze for 3–4 hours until firm.

Nutrition:

- Calories: 70
- Fat: 2 g.
- Protein: 5 g.
- Carbs: 9 g.
- Sugar: 2 g.
- Fiber: 3 g.
- Sodium: 28 mg.

Grilled Peach and Coconut Yogurt Bowls

Preparation time: 5 minutes
Cooking time: 10 minutes
Servings: 4
Ingredients:

- 2 peaches, halved and pitted
- 1/2 cup plain nonfat Greek yogurt
- 1 tsp. pure vanilla extract

- 1/4 cup coconut flakes, dried and unsweetened
- 2 tbsp. unsalted pistachios, shelled and broken into pieces

Directions:

1. Preheat the broiler to high. Arrange the rack in the closest position to the broiler.
2. In a shallow pan, arrange the peach halves, cut-side up. Broil for 6–8 minutes until browned, tender, and hot.
3. In a small bowl, mix the yogurt and vanilla.
4. Spoon the yogurt into the cavity of each peach half.
5. Sprinkle 1 tbsp. of coconut flakes and 1 1/2 tsp. of pistachios over each peach half. Serve warm.

Nutrition:

- Calories: 102
- Fat: 5 g.
- Protein: 5 g.
- Carbs: 11 g.
- Sugars: 8 g.
- Fiber: 2 g.
- Sodium: 12 mg.

Frozen Chocolate Peanut Butter Bites

Preparation time: 5 minutes
Cooking time: 0 minutes
Servings: 32
Ingredients:

- 1 cup coconut oil, melted

- 1/4 cup cocoa powder
- 1/4 cup honey (optional)
- 1/4 cup natural peanut butter

Directions:
1. Pour the melted coconut oil into a medium bowl. Whisk in the cocoa powder, honey, and peanut butter.
2. Transfer the mixture to ice cube trays in portions about 1 1/2 tsp. each.
3. Freeze for 2 hours or until ready to serve.

Nutrition:
- Calories: 80
- Fat: 8 g.
- Protein: 1 g.
- Carbs: 3 g.
- Sugars: 2 g.
- Fiber: 0 g.
- Sodium: 20 mg.

No-Bake Carrot Cake Bites

Preparation time: 15 minutes
Cooking time: 0 minutes
Servings: 20
Ingredients:
- 1/2 cup old-fashioned oats
- 2 medium carrots, chopped
- 6 dates, pitted
- 1/2 cup walnuts, chopped
- 1/2 cup coconut flour
- 2 tbsp. hemp seeds
- 2 tsp. pure maple syrup
- 1 tsp. cinnamon, ground
- 1/2 tsp. nutmeg, ground

Directions:
1. In a blender jar, combine the oats and carrots, and process until finely ground. Transfer to a bowl.
2. Add the dates and walnuts to the blender and process until coarsely chopped. Return the oat-carrot mixture to the blender and add the coconut flour, hemp seeds, maple syrup, cinnamon, and nutmeg. Process until well mixed.

3. Using your hands, shape the dough into balls about the size of a tbsp.
4. Store in the refrigerator in an airtight container for up to 1 week.

Nutrition:
- Calories: 68
- Fat: 3 g.
- Protein: 2 g.
- Carbs: 10 g.
- Sugars: 6 g.
- Fiber: 2 g.
- Sodium: 6 mg.

Creamy Strawberry Crepes

Preparation time: 10 minutes
Cooking time: 10 minutes
Servings: 4
Ingredients:
- 1/2 cup old-fashioned oats
- 1 cup plain almond milk, unsweetened
- 1 egg
- 3 tsp. honey, divided (optional)
- Nonstick cooking spray
- 2 oz. (57 g.) low-fat cream cheese
- 1/4 cup low-fat cottage cheese
- 2 cups strawberries, sliced

Directions:
1. In a blender jar, process the oats until they resemble flour. Add the almond milk, egg, and 1 1/2 tsp. honey, and process until smooth.

2. Heat a large skillet over medium heat. Spray with nonstick cooking spray to coat.

3. Add 1/4 cup of oat batter to the pan and quickly swirl around to coat the bottom of the pan and let cook for 2–3 minutes. When the edges begin to turn brown, flip the crepe with a spatula and cook until lightly browned and firm, about 1 minute. Transfer to a plate. Continue with the remaining batter, spraying the skillet with nonstick cooking spray before adding more batter. Set the cooked crepes aside, loosely covered with aluminum foil, while you make the filling.

4. Clean the blender jar, then combine the cream cheese, cottage cheese, and remaining 1 1/2 tsp. honey, and process until smooth.

5. Fill each crepe with 2 tbsp. of the cream cheese mixture, topped with 1/4 cup of strawberries. Serve.

Nutrition:
- Calories: 149 Fat: 6 g.
- Protein: 6 g.
- Carbs: 20 g.
- Sugar: 10 g.
- Fiber: 3 g.
- Sodium: 177 mg.

Swirled Cream Cheese Brownies

Preparation time: 10 minutes
Cooking time: 20 minutes
Servings: 12
Ingredients:
- 2 eggs
- 1/4 cup applesauce, unsweetened
- 1/4 cup coconut oil, melted
- 3 tbsp. pure maple syrup, divided
- 1/4 cup cocoa powder, unsweetened
- 1/4 cup coconut flour
- 1/4 tsp. salt
- 1 tsp. baking powder
- 2 tbsp. low-fat cream cheese

Directions:
1. Preheat the oven to 350°F (180°C). Grease an 8x8-inch baking dish.

2. In a large mixing bowl, beat the eggs with the applesauce, coconut oil, and 2 tbsp. of maple syrup.

3. Stir in the cocoa powder and coconut flour, and mix well. Sprinkle the salt and baking powder evenly over the surface and mix well to incorporate. Transfer the mixture to the prepared baking dish.

4. In a small, microwave-safe bowl, microwave the cream cheese for 10–20 seconds until softened. Add the remaining 1 tbsp. of maple syrup and mix to combine.

5. Drop the cream cheese onto the batter, and use a toothpick or chopstick to swirl it on the surface. Bake for 20 minutes, until a toothpick inserted in the center comes out clean. Cool and cut into 12 squares.

6. Store refrigerated in a covered container for up to 5 days.

Nutrition:
- Calories: 84 Fat: 6 g.
- Protein: 2 g. Carbs: 6 g.
- Sugar: 4 g. Fiber: 2 g. Sodium: 93 mg.

Maple Oatmeal Cookies

Preparation time: 5 minutes
Cooking time: 15 minutes
Servings: 16
Ingredients:
- 3/4 cup almond flour

- 3/4 cup old-fashioned oats
- 1/4 cup coconut, shredded and unsweetened
- 1 tsp. baking powder
- 1 tsp. cinnamon, ground
- 1/4 tsp. salt
- 1/4 cup applesauce, unsweetened
- 1 large egg
- 1 tbsp. pure maple syrup
- 2 tbsp. coconut oil, melted

Directions:
1. Preheat the oven to 350°F (180°C).
2. In a medium mixing bowl, combine the almond flour, oats, coconut, baking powder, cinnamon, and salt, and mix well.
3. In another medium bowl, combine the applesauce, egg, maple syrup, and coconut oil, and mix. Stir the wet mixture into the dry mixture.
4. Form the dough into balls a little bigger than a tbsp. and place on a baking sheet, leaving at least 1-inch between them. Bake for 12 minutes until the cookies are just browned. Remove from the oven and let cool for 5 minutes.
5. Using a spatula, remove the cookies and cool on a rack.

Nutrition:
- Calories: 76
- Fat: 6 g.
- Protein: 2 g.
- Carbs: 5 g.
- Sugar: 1 g.
- Fiber: 1 g.
- Sodium: 57 mg.

Ambrosia

Preparation time: 10 minutes
Cooking time: 0 minutes
Servings: 8
Ingredients:

- 3 oranges, peeled, divided, and quartered

- 2 (4 oz./113 g.) cups peaches in water, drained and diced
- 1 cup coconut, shredded and unsweetened
- 1 (8 oz./227 g.) container fat-free crème Fraiche

Directions:
1. In a large mixing bowl, combine the oranges, peaches, coconut, and crème Fraiche. Gently toss until well mixed. Cover and refrigerate overnight.

Nutrition:
- Calories: 111
- Fat: 5 g.
- Protein: 2 g.
- Carbs: 12 g.
- Sugar: 8 g.
- Fiber: 3 g.
- Sodium: 7 mg.

Banana Pudding

Preparation time: 30 minutes
Cooking time: 20 minutes
Servings: 10
Ingredients:
For the pudding:

- 3/4 cup erythritol or other sugar replacement
- 5 tsp. almond flour
- 1/4 tsp. salt
- 2 1/2 cups fat-free milk
- 6 tbsp. egg replacement, prepared
- 1/2 tsp. vanilla extract
- 2 (8 oz./227 g.) containers sugar-free spelled hazelnut biscuits, crushed
- 5 medium bananas, sliced

For the meringue:

- 5 medium egg whites (1 cup)
- 1/4 cup erythritol or other sugar replacement
- 1/2 tsp. vanilla extract

Directions:

Make the Pudding

1. In a saucepan, whisk the erythritol, almond flour, salt, and milk together. Cook over medium heat until the sugar is dissolved.
2. Whisk in the egg replacement and cook for about 10 minutes, or until thickened.
3. Remove from the heat and stir in the vanilla.
4. Spread the thickened pudding onto the bottom of a 3x6-inch casserole dish.
5. Arrange a layer of crushed biscuits on top of the pudding.
6. Place a layer of sliced bananas on top of the biscuits.

Make the Meringue

1. Preheat the oven to 350°F (180°C).
2. In a medium bowl, beat the egg whites for about 5 minutes, or until stiff.
3. Add the erythritol and vanilla while continuing to beat for about 3 more minutes.
4. Spread the meringue on top of the banana pudding.
5. Transfer the casserole dish to the oven, and bake for 7–10 minutes, or until the top is lightly browned.

Nutrition:
- Calories: 323
- Fat: 14 g.
- Protein: 12 g.
- Carbs: 42 g.
- Sugar: 11 g.
- Fiber: 3 g.
- Sodium: 148 mg.

Air Fryer Apples

Preparation time: 5 minutes
Cooking time: 15 minutes
Servings: 6–8
Ingredients:
- 4 Pink Lady apples, quartered
- 1/4 cup erythritol or other brown sugar replacement

Directions:

1. In a small mixing bowl, toss the apples in the erythritol. Working in batches, place in the basket of an air fryer.
2. Set the air fryer to 390°F (199°C), close, and cook for 15 minutes.
3. Once cooking is complete, transfer the apples to a plate. Repeat until no apples remain.

Nutrition:
- Calories: 47
- Fat: 0 g.
- Protein: 0 g.
- Carbs: 11 g.
- Sugar: 8 g.
- Fiber: 2 g.
- Sodium: 0 mg.

Pineapple Nice Cream

Preparation time: 10 minutes
Cooking time: 0 minutes
Servings: 6
Ingredients:
- 2 cups frozen pineapple
- 1 cup peanut butter (no added sugar, salt, or fat)
- 1/2 cup almond milk, unsweetened

Directions:

1. In a blender or food processor, combine the frozen pineapple and peanut butter and process.
2. Add the almond milk, and blend until smooth. The result should be a smooth paste.

Nutrition:
- Calories: 301
- Fat: 22 g.
- Protein: 14 g.
- Carbs: 15 g.
- Sugars: 8 g.
- Fiber: 4 g.
- Sodium: 39 mg.

Apple Crunch

Preparation time: 13 minutes
Cooking time: 2 minutes
Servings: 4
Ingredients:

- 3 (about 1 1/2 lb./680 g.) apples, peeled, cored, and sliced
- 1 tsp. pure maple syrup
- 1 tsp. apple pie spice or ground cinnamon
- 1/4 cup unsweetened apple juice, apple cider, or water 1/4 cup low-sugar granola

Directions:

1. In the electric pressure cooker, combine the apples, maple syrup, apple pie spice, and apple juice. Close and lock the lid of the pressure cooker. Set the valve to sealing. Cook on "High Pressure" for 2 minutes. When the cooking is complete, hit Cancel and quickly release the pressure.
2. Once the pin drops, unlock and remove the lid.
3. Spoon the apples into 4 serving bowls and sprinkle each with 1 tbsp. of granola.

Nutrition:

- Calories: 103 Fat: 1 g.
- Protein: 1 g. Carbs: 26 g. Sugar: 18 g.
- Fiber: 4 g. Sodium: 13 mg.

Tapioca Berry Parfaits

Preparation time: 10 minutes
Cooking time: 6 minutes
Servings: 4
Ingredients:

- 2 cups almond milk, unsweetened
- 1/2 cup small pearl tapioca, rinsed and still wet
- 1 tsp. almond extract
- 1 tbsp. pure maple syrup
- 2 cups berries
- 1/4 cup almonds, slivered

Directions:

1. Pour the almond milk into the electric pressure cooker. Stir in the tapioca and almond extract. Close and lock the lid of the pressure cooker. Set the valve to sealing. Cook on "High Pressure" for 6 minutes. When the cooking is complete, hit "Cancel." Allow the pressure to release naturally for 10 minutes, then quickly release any remaining pressure.
2. Once the pin drops, unlock and remove the lid. Remove the pot to a cooling rack.
3. Stir in the maple syrup and let the mixture cool for about an hour.
4. In small glasses, create several layers of tapioca, berries, and almonds. Refrigerate for 1 hour.
5. Serve chilled.

Nutrition:

- Calories: 174 Fat: 5 g.
- Protein: 3 g. Carbs: 32 g.
- Sugar: 11 g. Fiber: 3 g. Sodium: 77 mg.

Coffee and Cream Pops

Preparation time: 10 minutes
Cooking time: 5 minutes
Servings: 4
Ingredients:

- 2 tsp. espresso powder (or to taste)

- 2 cups canned coconut milk
- 1/2 tsp. vanilla extract
- 1/2 tsp. cinnamon
- 3 (1 g.) packets Stevia

Directions:
1. In a medium saucepan over medium-low heat, heat all of the ingredients, stirring constantly, until the espresso powder is completely dissolved, about 5 minutes.
2. Pour the mixture into 4 ice pop molds. Freeze for 6 hours before serving.

Nutrition:
- Calories: 225 Fat: 24 g.
- Protein: 2 g. Carbs: 7 g.
- Sugar: 1 g.
- Fiber: 3 g.
- Sodium: 15 mg.

Cinnamon Spiced Baked Apples

Preparation time: 10 minutes
Cooking time: 15 minutes
Servings: 4
Ingredients:
- 2 apples, peeled, cored, and chopped
- 2 tbsp. pure maple syrup
- 1/2 tsp. cinnamon
- 1/2 tsp. ginger, ground
- 1/4 cup pecans, chopped

Directions:
1. Preheat the oven to 350°F (180°C).
2. In a bowl, mix the apples, syrup, cinnamon, and ginger. Pour the mixture into a 9-inch square baking dish. Sprinkle the pecans over the top.
3. Bake until the apples are tender, about 15 minutes.

Nutrition:
- Calories: 122
- Fat: 5 g.
- Protein: 1 g.
- Carbs: 21 g.
- Sugar: 13 g.
- Fiber: 3 g.
- Sodium: 2 mg.

Broiled Pineapple

Preparation time: 5 minutes
Cooking time: 5 minutes
Servings: 4
Ingredients:
- 4 large slices fresh pineapple
- 2 tbsp. canned coconut milk
- 2 tbsp. coconut, unsweetened, shredded
- 1/4 tsp. sea salt

Directions:
1. Preheat the oven broiler on high.
2. On a rimmed baking sheet, arrange the pineapple in a single layer. Brush lightly with the coconut milk and sprinkle with coconut.
3. Broil until the pineapple begins to brown, for 3–5 minutes.
4. Sprinkle with sea salt.

Nutrition:
- Calories: 78
- Fat: 4 g.
- Protein: 1 g.
- Carbs: 13 g.
- Sugars: 16 g.
- Fiber: 2 g.
- Sodium: 148 mg.

Cottage Cheese Almond Pancakes

Preparation time: 10 minutes
Cooking time: 20 minutes
Servings: 4
Ingredients:
- 2 cups cottage cheese, low-fat

- 4 egg whites
- 2 eggs
- 1 tbsp. pure vanilla extract
- 1 1/2 cups almond flour
- Nonstick cooking spray

Directions:

1. Place the cottage cheese, egg whites, eggs, and vanilla in a blender and pulse to combine.
2. Add the almond flour to the blender and blend until smooth.
3. Place a large nonstick skillet over medium heat and lightly coat it with cooking spray.
4. Spoon 1/4 cup of batter per pancake, 4 at a time, into the skillet. Cook the pancakes until the bottoms are firm and golden, about 4 minutes.
5. Flip the pancakes over and cook the other side until they are cooked through for 3 minutes.
6. Remove the pancakes to a plate and repeat with the remaining batter.
7. Serve with fresh fruit.

Nutrition:

- Calories: 344
- Fat: 22 g.
- Protein: 29 g.
- Carbs: 11 g.
- Sugars: 5 g.
- Fiber: 4 g.
- Sodium: 559 mg.

Pumpkin Apple Waffles

Preparation time: 10 minutes
Cooking time: 20 minutes
Servings: 6
Ingredients:

- 2 1/4 cups whole-wheat pastry flour
- 2 tbsp. granulated sweetener
- 1 tbsp. baking powder
- 1 tsp. cinnamon, ground
- 1 tsp. nutmeg, ground
- 4 eggs

- 1 1/4 cups pure pumpkin purée
- 1 apple, peeled, cored, finely chopped
- Melted coconut oil, for cooking

Directions:

1. In a large bowl, stir together the flour, sweetener, baking powder, cinnamon, and nutmeg.
2. In a small bowl, whisk together the eggs and pumpkin.
3. Add the wet ingredients to the dry and whisk until smooth.
4. Stir the apple into the batter.
5. Cook the waffles according to the waffle maker manufacturer's directions, brushing your waffle iron with melted coconut oil, until all the batter is gone.
6. Serve.

Nutrition:

- Calories: 231
- Fat: 4 g.
- Protein: 11 g.
- Carbs: 40 g.
- Sugars: 5 g.
- Fiber: 7 g.
- Sodium: 51 mg.

Buckwheat Crêpes with Fruit and Yogurt

Preparation time: 20 minutes
Cooking time: 20 minutes
Servings: 5
Ingredients:

- 1 1/2 cups skim milk
- 3 eggs
- 1 tsp. extra virgin olive oil, plus more for the skillet

- 1 cup buckwheat flour
- 1/2 cup whole-wheat flour
- 1/2 cup Greek yogurt, 2% plain
- 1 cup strawberries, sliced
- 1 cup blueberries

Directions:

1. In a large bowl, whisk together the milk, eggs, and 1 tsp. oil until well combined.
2. Into a medium bowl, sift together the buckwheat and whole-wheat flours. Add the dry ingredients to the wet ingredients and whisk until well combined and very smooth.
3. Allow the batter to rest for at least 2 hours before cooking.
4. Place a large skillet or crêpe pan over medium-high heat and lightly coat the bottom with oil.
5. Pour about 1/4 cup of batter into the skillet. Swirl the pan until the batter completely coats the bottom.
6. Cook the crêpe for 1 minute, then flip it over. Cook the other side of the crêpe for another minute, until lightly browned. Transfer the cooked crêpe to a plate and cover with a clean dish towel to keep warm.
7. Repeat until the batter is used up; you should have about 10 crêpes.
8. Spoon 1 tbsp. yogurt onto each crêpe and place 2 crêpes on each plate.
9. Top with berries and serve.

Nutrition:

- Calories: 329
- Fat: 7 g.
- Protein: 16 g.
- Carbs: 54 g.
- Sugars: 11 g.
- Fiber: 8 g.
- Sodium: 102 mg.

Apple Cinnamon Cake

Preparation time: 10 minutes
Cooking time: 35 minutes
Servings: 4
Ingredients:

- 2/3 cup flour
- 1/2 cup whole-wheat flour
- 1 tsp. baking soda
- 1 tsp. cinnamon
- 1/4 tsp. salt
- 1 1/2 cups apples, peeled, cored, finely chopped
- 1/4 cup liquid egg product, fat-free
- 1/2 cup Splenda® + 1/4 cup brown sugar
- 1/2 cup walnuts, chopped, or pecans
- 1/4 cup applesauce

To make topping:

- 1 tbsp. flour
- 1 tbsp. whole-wheat flour
- 1/2 tsp. cinnamon
- 1 tbsp. butter
- 1/4 cup walnuts or 1/4 cup pecans

Directions:

1. Lightly coat a 9-inch baking pan with cooking spray; set aside.
2. In a medium bowl combine the 2/3 cup flour, 1/2 cup whole-wheat flour, soda, 1 tsp. cinnamon, and salt, set aside.

3. In a large mixing bowl toss together the chopped apple and egg product; stir in the 1/2 cup Splenda®, the 1/2 cup nuts, and applesauce. Add flour mixture and stir until just combined.

4. Pour batter into prepared pan.

To make topping:

1. Stir together the brown sugar, the remaining flour, whole-wheat flour, and cinnamon; cut in butter until crumbly, stir in remaining nuts, sprinkle topping over batter in pan.

2. Bake in 350°F oven for 30–35 minutes or until a toothpick comes out clean; cool in pan for 10 minutes, serve warm.

Nutrition:

- Calories: 217
- Fat: 7 g.
- Carbs: 37 g.
- Protein: 3 g.

Chocolate Apple Cake

Preparation time: 10 minutes
Cooking time: 3 minutes
Servings: 4
Ingredients:

- 3/4 cup whole-wheat flour
- 3/4 cup flour
- 1 tsp. baking soda
- 1/4 cup cocoa
- 1/2 tsp. salt
- 1 cup water
- 1/4 cup applesauce
- 1 tsp. lemon juice
- 1 tsp. vanilla
- 1 apple (1 cup), chopped, peeled
- 3/4 cup Splenda®
- 1/2 tsp. cinnamon
- Nonstick spray and oil

Directions:

1. Preheat the oven to 350°F.
2. Spray a square pan with nonstick spray, I used a glass pan. Combine the first 5 ingredients in a bowl.
3. In another bowl, combine water, oil,

lemon juice, apple sauce, and vanilla. Add to dry ingredients, stir until just combined.

4. Toss apples with Splenda® and cinnamon, fold into batter. Pour into a prepared pan.

5. Bake for 30–35 minutes or until done.

Nutrition:

- Calories: 141
- Fat: 1 g.
- Carbs: 32 g.
- Protein: 3 g. per 1/9 of recipe

Walnut Apple Cake

Preparation time: 10 minutes
Cooking time: 3 minutes
Servings: 4
Ingredients:

- 1 1/2 cups buttermilk, low-fat
- 1 cup organic rolled oats
- 1/2 cup applesauce
- 2 eggs, beaten (or 1/2 cup eggbeaters)
- 1/4 cup honey or 1/4 cup Splenda® granular
- 1 cup whole-wheat flour
- 1/2 cup self-rising flour, unbleached
- 1 1/4 tsp. baking powder
- 3/4 tsp. cinnamon, ground (or to taste)
- 1/4 cup walnuts, roughly chopped
- 2 tbsp. sultanas

Directions:

1. Combine the buttermilk and rolled oats in a bowl and set aside for 15–20 minutes until the oats have softened.
2. While the buttermilk and oats are standing, preheat your oven to 350°F and line a standard baking tin with greaseproof paper.
3. Beat the eggs and add to the oatmeal mixture along with the applesauce.
4. If using honey add to wet ingredients. It using Splenda® add to dry ingredients.
5. Mix the dry ingredients, stirring to combine, and add to the wet, mixing well.

6. Transfer the solid batter into the prepared baking tin. Using a wooden spoon, spread the batter to even it out.

7. Sprinkle the cake with roughly chopped walnuts and sultanas and let it sit for 20 minutes before baking.

8. Bake cake for approximately 1 hour or until a skewer inserted into the cake comes out clean.

Nutrition:
- Calories: 141
- Fat: 1 g.
- Carbs: 32 g.
- Protein: 3 g. per 1/9 of recipe

Apple Pie

Preparation time: 10 minutes
Cooking time: 3 minutes
Servings: 4
Ingredients:
- 1 cup dry rolled oats
- 1/4 cup whole-wheat pastry flour
- 1/4 cup almonds, ground
- 2 tbsp. brown sugar, packed
- 3 tbsp. canola oil
- 1 tbsp. water

Filling:
- 6 cups tart apples, sliced, peeled (about 4 large apples)
- 1/3 cup frozen apple juice concentrate
- 2 tbsp. tapioca, quick-cooking
- 1 tsp. cinnamon

Directions:
1. To prepare pie crust, mix dry ingredients in a large mixing bowl. In a separate bowl, mix oil and water with a whisk. Add oil and water mixture to dry ingredients. Mix until dough holds together. Add a bit more water if needed. Press dough into a 9-inch pie plate. Set aside until filling is prepared.

2. To prepare the filling, combine all ingredients in a large bowl. Let stand for 15 minutes. Stir and then spoon into prepared pie crust.

3. Bake at 425°F for 15 minutes. Reduce heat to 350°F and bake 40 minutes, or until apples are tender.

Nutrition:
- Calories: 204
- Fat: 8 g.
- Carbs: 29 g.
- Protein: 4 g. per cookie

Cranberry Pound Cake

Preparation time: 10 minutes
Cooking time: 40 minutes
Servings: 4
Ingredients:
- 2 cups all-purpose flour
- 1 1/4 tsp. baking powder
- 1/2 tsp. baking soda
- 3 tbsp. butter softened
- 1/2 cup Splenda®, sugar blend for baking
- 2 eggs
- 1/4 tsp. orange extract (optional)
- 2/3 cup yogurt, plain nonfat
- 2 cups fresh cranberries

- 1/4 cup water or 1/4 cup orange juice
- 1 1/2 tsp. orange zest, finely grated

Directions:

1. Preheat the oven to 350°F. Prepare Bundt or tube pan with a light coat of cooking spray.
2. In a medium bowl, sift together the flour, baking soda, and baking powder.
3. In a large bowl, cream the butter with an electric mixer. Add Splenda® blend and beat until pale, light, and fluffy. Add the eggs, one at a time, mixing after each addition for a total of 2–3 minutes. If you want more orange flavor, mix in the orange extract and orange zest at this step.
4. Mix the yogurt and water or orange juice.
5. Add in the cranberries, folding them in to distribute throughout the batter.
6. Pour batter into the prepared tube pan and bake for 40 minutes or until an inserted toothpick comes out clean.
7. Cool cake in pan for 10 minutes until turning onto cake rack or plate.

Nutrition:

- Calories: 161
- Fat: 4 g.
- Carbs: 27 g.
- Protein: 4 g. per 1/12 of recipe

Chocolate Fudge Nut Cake

Preparation time: 10 minutes
Cooking time: 35 minutes
Servings: 4
Ingredients:

- 1/2 cup whole-wheat pastry flour

- 1/2 cup all-purpose flour
- 1/3 cup sugar or 3 tbsp. Splenda® sugar blend for baking
- 1/4 cup cocoa powder, unsweetened, sifted
- 1 1/2 tsp. baking powder
- 1/2 tsp. salt
- 1 egg, large
- 1/2 cup milk, 1% fat
- 2 tbsp. canola oil
- 2 tsp. vanilla extract
- 3/4 cup chocolate chips, semisweet
- 1 1/3 cups coffee, hot brewed
- 2/3 cup packed light brown sugar, or Splenda® granular
- 1/4 cup walnuts, or pecans, toasted, chopped
- Confectioner's sugar, for dusting

Directions:

1. Preheat the oven to 350°F. Coat a 1 1/2 to 2-quart baking dish with cooking spray. Whisk whole-wheat flour, all-purpose flour, sugar or Splenda® sugar blend, cocoa, baking powder, and salt in a large bowl.
2. Whisk egg, milk, oil, and vanilla in a glass measuring cup. Add to the flour mixture; stir with a rubber spatula until just combined.
3. Fold in chocolate chips, if using. Scrap the batter into the prepared baking dish. Mix hot coffee and brown sugar or Splenda® granular in the measuring cup and pour over the batter.
4. Sprinkle with nuts.
5. Bake the pudding cake until the top springs back when touched lightly, for 30–35 minutes. Let cool for at least 10 minutes. Dust with confectioner's sugar and serve hot or warm.

Nutrition:

- Calories: 162 Carbs: 22 g.
- Fat: 7 g.
- Protein: 4 g. per 1/8 of recipe

Crustless Pumpkin Pie

Preparation time: 10 minutes
Cooking time: 0 minutes
Servings: 4
Ingredients:

- 1 (15 oz.) can pumpkin puree
- 1/2 cup skim milk
- 1 (1 oz.) package instant vanilla pudding mix, sugar-free
- 1 tsp. pumpkin pie spice
- 1 (8 oz.) container whipped topping, fat-free, frozen

Directions:

1. In a medium bowl, mix the pumpkin, milk, and instant pudding mix. Stir in the pumpkin pie spice, and fold in half of the whipped topping.
2. Pour into an 8-inch pie plate, and spread remaining whipped topping over the top. Chill for 1 hour, or until set.

Nutrition:

- Calories: 110
- Fat: 0 g.
- Carbs: 23 g.
- Protein: 1.5 g. per 1/6 of the recipe

Applesauce Raisin Cake

Preparation time: 10 minutes
Cooking time: 1 hour
Servings: 4
Ingredients:

- 2 cups all-purpose flour
- 1 tsp. baking powder
- 1 tsp. baking soda
- 1/2 tsp. cinnamon, ground
- 1/2 tsp. nutmeg, ground
- 1/2 tsp. salt
- 1 1/2 cups applesauce, unsweetened
- 3/4 cup brown sugar twin
- 2 eggs
- 1 tsp. vanilla extract
- 1/2 cup raisins
- Cooking spray

Directions:

1. Preheat the oven to 350°F (175°C). Spray an 8x4-inch loaf pan with cooking spray.
2. Sift together flour, baking powder, baking soda, cinnamon, nutmeg, and salt. Set aside.
3. Beat the eggs until light and add sugar twin. Add applesauce and vanilla.
4. Add flour mixture and beat until smooth. Fold in raisins.
5. Pour batter into loaf pan. Bake at 350°F (175°C) for 1 hour, or until a toothpick inserted into the cake comes out clean.

Nutrition:

- Calories: 125
- Fat: 1 g.
- Carbs: 26 g.
- Protein: 3 g. per 1/12 of recipe

Chocolate Walnut Brownies

Preparation time: 10 minutes
Cooking time: 30 minutes
Servings: 4
Ingredients:

- 1/2 cup margarine

- 1/4 cup cocoa powder, unsweetened
- 2 eggs
- 1 cup granular sucralose sweetener
- 1/4 tsp. baking powder
- 1/2 tsp. vanilla
- 3/4 cup all-purpose flour
- 1/8 tsp. salt
- 1/4 cup milk, 2%
- 1/2 cup walnuts, chopped

Directions:

1. Preheat the oven to 350°F (175°C). Grease and flour an 8x8-inch pan.
2. In a small saucepan over medium heat, melt margarine and cocoa together, stirring occasionally until smooth. Remove from heat and set aside to cool. In a large bowl, beat eggs until frothy. Stir in the sucralose sweetener. Combine the flour, baking powder, and salt; stir into the egg mixture then mix in the vanilla, cocoa, and margarine.
3. Finally, stir in the 1/4 cup of milk and the walnuts. Pour into the prepared pan.
4. Bake for 25–30 minutes in the preheated oven, until a toothpick inserted into the center, comes out clean.

Nutrition:

- Calories: 129 Fat: 4 g.
- Carbs: 24 g.
- Protein: 2 g. per 1/12 of recipe

Banana Peanut Butter Cookies

Preparation time: 10 minutes
Cooking time: 14 minutes
Servings: 6
Ingredients:

- 1 1/2 cups all-purpose flour
- 2 tsp. baking powder
- 1/2 tsp. baking soda
- 1/8 tsp. tartar cream
- 1/8 tsp. salt
- 1/2 cup all-natural peanut butter
- 1/2 cup butter, unsalted
- 1 egg, large
- 1 ripe medium banana, mashed
- 1/2 cup Splenda® brown sugar substitute
- 1/4 cup Splenda®
- 2 tsp. vanilla

Directions:

1. Preheat the oven to 350°F.
2. Sift together the first 5 dry ingredients.
3. In a large mixer bowl, cream together the peanut butter and unsalted butter until fluffy. At low speed, mix in the egg, pureed banana, Splenda®, tartar, and vanilla.
4. With the mixer at low speed, slowly add the sifted dry ingredients until fully mixed.
5. Shape dough into 1-inch balls. Place on ungreased cookie sheet 1-inch (2.5 cm.) apart. Flatten cookies with the palm of your hand.
6. Bake for 12–14 minutes or until bottoms are golden brown.
7. Remove cookies from cookie sheets to a wire rack, and cool completely.

Nutrition:

- Calories: 46
- Fat: 3 g.
- Carbs: 5 g.
- Protein: 1 g. per cookie

Pumpkin Cinnamon Cookies

Preparation time: 10 minutes
Cooking time: 5 minutes
Servings: 14
Ingredients:

- 3/4 cup Splenda® Granular
- 1 cup rolled oats
- 1 cup whole-wheat flour
- 1/2 cup soy flour
- 1 3/4 tsp. baking soda
- 1/2 tsp. baking powder
- 1/2 tsp. salt
- 2 tsp. cinnamon, ground
- 1 tsp. nutmeg, ground
- 1/2 cup pumpkin puree
- 1 tbsp. canola oil
- 2 tsp. water
- 2 egg whites
- 1 tsp. molasses
- 1 tbsp. flax seeds (optional)

Directions:

1. Preheat the oven to 350°F.
2. In a large bowl, whisk together Splenda®, oats, wheat flour, soy flour, baking soda, baking powder, salt, cinnamon, and nutmeg. Stir in pumpkin, canola oil, water, egg whites, and molasses. Stir in flax seeds, if desired. Roll into 14 large balls, and flatten on a baking sheet.
3. Bake for 5 minutes in preheated oven. Careful not to over bake or the cookies will be too dry.

Nutrition:

- Calories: 85
- Fat: 2 g.
- Carbs: 13 g.
- Protein: 4 g.

Almond Cookies

Preparation time: 10 minutes
Cooking time: 20 minutes
Servings: 30 cookies
Ingredients:

- 1 1/2 cups almond flour
- 1/2 cup flax seed meal
- 1/4 cup artificial sweetener
- 2 oz. walnuts, chopped
- 1 tsp. baking powder
- 4 egg whites
- 1 oz. butter softened

Directions:

1. Preheat the oven to 350°F. Combine and mix all dry ingredients.
2. Add softened butter and rub into dry ingredients until even and produces a slightly grainy texture. Add egg whites and mix well.
3. Using a leveled tbsp., add dough onto parchment paper. Press each cookie down with a fork.
4. Bake for 18–20 minutes. Remove and cool on a wire rack.

Nutrition: per cookie

- Calories: 31 Fat: 3 g.
- Carbs: 1 g. Protein: 1 g.

No-Added Sugar Strawberry Shortcake

Cooking time: 10 minutes
Preparation time: 15 minutes
Servings: 1
Ingredients:

- 1 cup skim milk
- 1 packet artificial sweetener
- 6 cups fresh strawberries, sliced
- Cooking spray, refrigerated, butter-flavored
- 1 1/4 cups biscuit and baking mix, low-fat
- 12 tbsp. whipped topping, frozen, thawed, fat-free, no sugar added

Directions:

1. Preheat the oven to 400°F.
2. Coat a nonstick baking sheet lightly using cooking spray.
3. Combine the milk, biscuit mix, and sweetener in a bowl, mixing until just combined.
4. Roll dough out on a floured surface into a circle 1/3-inch thick.
5. Cut out 6 biscuits using a 2-inch biscuit cutter, reusing scraps as needed.
6. On your prepared baking sheet, place the biscuits.
7. Spray the tops of the biscuits lightly using cooking spray and bake until nicely browned and done, for 10 minutes.
8. Split the biscuits in half horizontally, placing half in each of 12 dessert dishes.
9. Top each with 1/2 cup of strawberries and 1 tbsp. whipped topping.
10. Serve immediately and enjoy it.

Nutrition:

- Fat: 1 g.
- Protein: 2 g.
- Fiber: 2 g.
- Sodium: 159 mg.
- Sugar: 0 g.

Carrot Cake

Preparation time: 20 minutes
Cooking time: 45 minutes
Servings: 1
Ingredients:

- Cooking spray
- 2 tsp. baking powder
- 1/2 tsp. baking soda
- 1/4 tsp. salt
- 1 tsp. cinnamon, ground
- 1/2 tsp. nutmeg, ground
- 2 large egg whites, at room temperature
- 1/2 cup yogurt, plain non-fat
- 3 tbsp. canola oil
- 3/4 cup applesauce, unsweetened
- 1/3 cup dark brown sugar, packed
- 2 tsp. vanilla extract
- 2 1/2 cups all-purpose flour
- 4 oz. pineapple with juice, unsweetened crushed
- 1/4 cup dark raisins
- 1/4 cup sugar substitute

Directions:

1. Preheat the oven to 400°F. Position the top rack in the center of the oven. Coat a 9-inch cake pan lightly using cooking spray. Dust with flour, then tap out excess. Whisk together yogurt, oil, egg

whites, brown sugar, applesauce, vanilla, pineapple with juice in a large bowl.

2. Sift together the baking powder, sugar substitute, salt (if using), baking soda, flour, nutmeg, and cinnamon in a bowl.

3. Add to egg-applesauce mixture gradually, stirring until the cake batter, then add dark raisins. Spoon the batter into the prepared pan, smoothing the top using the back of a spoon. Bake until a toothpick inserted in the center comes out clean, for 30–40 minutes.

4. Cool in the pan on a rack for 10 min.

5. Slide a thin knife just around the edges to loosen the cake from the pan. Invert onto a rack to cool.

6. Transfer cake into a serving platter when ready to serve.

7. Serve and enjoy.

Nutrition:
- Calories: 103 Kcal
- Carbs: 19 g.
- Fat: 2 g.
- Protein: 3 g.
- Fiber: 1 g.
- Sodium: 123 mg.

Frozen Ice Cream Pecan Cake

Preparation time: 10 minutes
Cooking time: 0 minutes
Servings: 2
Ingredients:
- 1 (6 1/2 oz.) package chocolate sandwich cookies, sugar-free, crushed
- 1/3 cup pecans, chopped
- 3 tbsp. margarine, melted, reduced-calorie
- 1-quart vanilla ice cream, softened, no-sugar-added, fat-free

Directions:
1. Combine the first 3 ingredients; reserve 1 cup mixture. Press the remaining crumb mixture firmly in the bottom of a 9-inch square pan. Freeze 10 minutes.

2. Spread ice cream over crumb mixture in pan. Sprinkle reserved crumb mixture over ice cream; gently press mixture into ice cream. Cover and freeze for at least 8 hours.

3. To serve, let stand at room temperature for 5 minutes; cut into 9 squares.

Nutrition:
- Calories: 232
- Fat: 10 g.
- Fiber: 0 g.
- Carbs: 34 g.
- Protein: 6 g.

Cafe Mocha Smoothies

Preparation time: 5 minutes
Cooking time: 0 minutes
Servings: 3
Ingredients:
- 1 avocado, remove the pit, cut in half
- 1 1/2 cup almond milk, unsweetened
- 1/2 cup canned coconut milk
- 3 tbsp. Splenda®
- 3 tbsp. cocoa powder, unsweetened
- 2 tsp. instant coffee
- 1 tsp. vanilla

Directions:
1. Place everything but the avocado in the blender. Process until smooth.

2. Add the avocado and blend until smooth and no chunks remain.

3. Pour into glasses and serve.

Nutrition:
- Calories: 109 Total Carbs 15 g.
- Protein: 6 g. Fat: 1 g.
- Sugar 13 g.
- Fiber: 0 g.

Diabetic Friendly Brownies

Preparation time: 10 minutes
Cooking time: 40 minutes
Servings: 2
Ingredients

- 2 cups and 2 tbsp. Truvia (equivalent to 1 2/3 cup granulated sugar)
- 3/4 cup butter, salted
- 2 tbsp. water
- 1 tbsp. instant coffee
- 2 tsp. vanilla extract
- 1 1/3 cup quinoa flour
- 1 1/2 cup cocoa unsweetened (24 tbsp.)
- 1/2 tsp. baking powder
- 1/4 tsp. sea salt
- 3 eggs

Directions

1. Preheat the oven to 350°F. Grease 13x9-inch baking pan.
2. Combine Truvia, butter, water, and instant coffee in a large bowl. Stir in eggs and vanilla extract.
3. Combine quinoa flour, cocoa, baking powder, and sea salt in a medium bowl; stir into the wet mixture.
4. Spread into a prepared baking pan.
5. Bake for 18–25 minutes or until wooden pick inserted in center comes out slightly sticky.
6. Cool completely in a pan on a wire rack then cut into bars.

Nutrition:

- Calories: 119 Fat: 9 g.
- Fiber: 0 g. Carbs: 8 g. Protein: 3 g.

Raspberry Chocolate Cake

Preparation time: 10 minutes
Cooking time: 50 minutes
Servings: 2
Ingredients:

- 2 (8-oz.) packages chocolate cake mix, sugar-free, low-fat
- 1 1/2 cups chocolate-almond flavored coffee, strongly brewed
- 1/4 cup raspberry spreadable fruit, melted
- 2 (0.53-oz.) packages instant cocoa mix, sugar-free
- 1 (1.3-oz.) envelope whipped topping mix, sugar-free, reduced-calorie
- 1/2 cup cold milk, fat-free
- 1/2 tsp. vanilla extract

Directions:

1. Preheat the oven to 375°F.
2. Prepare cake mix according to package directions, substituting coffee for water.
3. Pour batter into 2 (8-inch) round cake pans. Bake at 375°F for 20–25 minutes or until a wooden pick inserted into the center comes out clean. Cool cakes in pans for 10 minutes on a wire rack.
4. Remove cakes from pans. Poke several holes in each cake layer with a wooden pick. Brush warm cake layers with melted raspberry spread. Let cool completely on wire racks.
5. Combine cocoa mix and whipped topping mix in a large bowl. Add milk

and vanilla; beat with a mixer at low speed until blended. Beat at high speed for 4 minutes or until soft peaks form.

6. Place 1 cake layer on a serving plate; top with half of the frosting. Top first layer with second cake layer; spread remaining frosting on sides and top of the cake. Chill frosted cake until ready to serve.

Nutrition:
- Calories: 133
- Fat: 2.5 g.
- Fiber: 0 g.
- Carbs: 28 g.
- Protein: 2 g.

Angel Food Cake

Preparation time: 10 minutes
Cooking time: 60 minutes
Servings: 2
Ingredients:
- 1 cup cake flour, sifted
- 1 1/2 cups sugar, divided (or equivalent artificial sweetener)
- 12 large egg whites
- 1 tsp. cream of tartar
- 1/4 tsp. salt
- 1 1/2 tsp. vanilla extract
- 1 1/2 tsp. fresh lemon juice
- 1/2 tsp. almond extract

Directions:
1. Preheat the oven to 325°F.
2. To prepare cake, lightly spoon flour into a dry measuring cup; level with a knife. Combine flour and 3/4 cup sugar, stirring with a whisk.
3. Place egg whites in a large bowl; beat with a mixer at high speed until foamy. Add cream of tartar and salt; beat until soft peaks form. Add 3/4 cup sugar, 2 tbsp. at a time, beating until stiff peaks form. Beat in vanilla, juice, and almond extract.
4. Sift 1/4 cup flour mixture over egg white mixture; fold in. Repeat with the remaining flour mixture, 1/4 cup at a

time.

5. Spoon the batter into an ungreased 10-inch tube pan, spreading evenly. Break air pockets by cutting through the batter with a knife.
6. Bake at 325°F for 55 minutes or until cake springs back when lightly touched. Invert pan; cool completely.
7. Loosen the cake from the sides of the pan using a narrow metal spatula. Invert the cake onto a plate.

Nutrition:
- Calories: 146
- Fat: 0 g.
- Fiber: 0 g.
- Carbs: 31 g.
- Protein: 4 g.

Diabetic Friendly Cream Cheese Brownies

Preparation time: 15 minutes
Cooking time: 30 minutes
Servings: 4
Ingredients:
- 3/4 cup sugar
- 1/4 cup plus 2 tbsp. stick margarine, softened, reduced-calorie
- 1 egg, large
- 1 egg white, large
- 1 tbsp. vanilla extract
- 1/2 cup all-purpose flour
- 1/4 cup cocoa, unsweetened
- Cooking spray
- 1 (8-oz.) block cream cheese, softened, 1/3-less-fat
- 1/4 cup sugar substitute, calorie-free, measures-like-sugar
- 3 tbsp. milk, 1% low-fat

Directions:
1. Preheat the oven to 350°F.
2. Beat sugar and margarine with a mixer at medium speed until light and fluffy. Add egg, egg white, and vanilla; beat well. Gradually add flour and cocoa, beating

well. Pour into an 8-inch square pan coated with cooking spray.

3. Beat cream cheese and sweetener with a mixer at high speed until smooth. Add milk; beat well. Pour cream cheese mixture over chocolate mixture; swirl together using the tip of a knife to create a marbled effect.

4. Bake at 350°F for 30 minutes. Cool completely in a pan on a wire rack. Cut into squares.

Nutrition:
- Calories: 127 Fat: 7 g.
- Fiber: 0 g.
- Carbs: 8 g.
- Protein: 3 g.

Moist Chocolate Cake

Preparation time: 15 minutes
Cooking time: 25 minutes
Servings: 4
Ingredients:
- 2/3 cup Splenda®, no-calorie, granulated
- 2/3 cup all-purpose flour
- 1 tsp. baking powder
- 1 pinch salt
- 6 oz. chocolate, semisweet
- 1/2 cup hot water
- 4 egg whites
- 1 tsp. vanilla

Directions:
1. Preheat the oven to 350°F. Butter and flour an 8-inch square cake pan.
2. Stir together Splenda®, flour, baking

powder, and salt. Set aside.

3. In a large heatproof bowl set over hot (not boiling) water, melt chocolate with water, stirring until smooth. Remove from heat. Let cool slightly. Whisk in egg whites and vanilla.

4. Stir the dry ingredients into the chocolate batter just until combined. Pour into an 8-inch square prepared cake pan.

5. Bake on the top rack of a 350°F oven for 15–20 minutes or until edges pull away from pan check at 15 minutes. Do not overcook.

6. Let cool on a rack.

Nutrition:
- Calories: 76 Fat: 3 g.
- Fiber: 0 g. Carbs: 10 g. Protein: 1 g.

Crustless Cheesecake

Preparation time: 15 minutes
Cooking time: 45–60 minutes
Servings: 4
Ingredients:
- 1/2 cup Splenda®
- 4 egg whites
- 2 tbsp. cornstarch
- 2 packages (8 oz. each) *Neufchatel* cheese, reduced fat
- 1 package (8 oz.) cream cheese, fat-free
- 1 cup sour cream, fat-free
- 2 tsp. vanilla
- Cinnamon for sprinkling

Directions:
1. Soften the cream cheese and *Neufchatel* cheese in the microwave and stir. Stir in Splenda®, cornstarch, and sour cream and egg whites'/egg beaters.
2. Beat until smooth and pour into the cheesecake pan. Bake at 300°F for 45–60 minutes.
3. Sprinkle with cinnamon.

Nutrition:
- Calories: 169 Fat: 10 g.
- Fiber: 0 g. Carbs: 10 g.
- Protein: 8 g.

Apple Cheddar Muffins

Preparation time: 10 minutes
Cooking time: 20 minutes
Servings: 4
Ingredients:

- 1 egg
- 3/4 cup tart apple, peel, and chopped
- 2/3 cup Cheddar cheese, grated, reduced fat
- 2/3 cup skim milk
- 2 cup baking mix, low-carb
- 2 tbsp. vegetable oil
- 1 tsp. cinnamon

Directions:

1. Heat oven to 400°F. Line a 12 cup muffin pan with paper liners.
2. In a medium bowl, lightly beat the egg. Stir in remaining ingredients just until moistened. Divide evenly between prepared muffin cups.
3. Bake for 17–20 minutes or until golden brown. Serve warm.

Nutrition:

- Calories: 162
- Total Carbs 17 g.
- Net Carbs 13 g.
- Protein: 10 g.
- Fat: 5 g.
- Sugar 8 g.
- Fiber: 4 g.

Apple Cinnamon Muffins

Preparation time: 15 minutes
Cooking time: 25 minutes
Servings: 12
Ingredients:

- 1 cup apple, finely diced
- 2/3 cup skim milk
- 1/4 cup margarine, melted, reduced-calorie
- 1 egg, lightly beaten
- 1 2/3 cups flour
- 1 tbsp. Stevia
- 2 1/2 tsp. baking powder
- 1 tsp. cinnamon
- 1/2 tsp. sea salt
- 1/4 tsp. nutmeg
- Nonstick cooking spray

Directions:

1. Heat oven to 400°F. Spray a 12-cup muffin pan with cooking spray.
2. In a large bowl, combine dry ingredients and stir to mix.
3. In another bowl, beat milk, margarine, and egg to combine.
4. Pour wet ingredients into dry ingredients and stir just until moistened. Gently fold in apples.
5. Spoon into prepared muffin pan. Bake for 25 minutes, or until tops are lightly browned.

Nutrition:

- Calories: 119 Total Carbs 17 g.
- Net Carbs 16 g. Protein: 3 g.
- Fat: 4 g. Sugar 3 g. Fiber: 1 g.

Raspberry Smoothie

Preparation time: 10 minutes
Cooking time: 0 minutes
Servings: 2
Ingredients:

- 1 avocado, pitted, peeled
- 3/4 cup raspberry juice
- 3/4 cup orange juice
- 1/2 cup raspberries

Directions:

1. In your blender, mix the avocado with raspberry juice, orange juice, and raspberries. Pulse well, divide into 2 glasses, and serve.
2. Enjoy!

Nutrition:

- Calories: 125 Fat: 11 g. Fiber: 7 g.
- Carbs: 9 g. Protein: 3 g.

Coconut and Berry Smoothie

Preparation time: 5 minutes
Cooking time: 0 minutes
Servings: 2
Ingredients:

- 1/2 cup mixed berries (blueberries, strawberries, blackberries)
- 1 tbsp. flaxseed, ground
- 2 tbsp. coconut flakes, unsweetened
- 1/2 cup coconut milk, plain, unsweetened
- 1/2 cup leafy greens like kale or spinach
- 1/4 cup vanilla yogurt, unsweetened, non-fat
- 1/2 cup ice

Directions:

1. In a blender jar, combine the berries, flaxseed, coconut flakes, coconut milk, greens, yogurt, and ice.
2. Process until smooth. Serve.

Nutrition:

- Calories: 182
- Fat: 14.9 g.
- Protein: 5.9 g.
- Carbs: 8.1 g.
- Fiber: 4.1 g.
- Sugar: 2.9 g.
- Sodium: 25 mg.

Grapefruit-Hibiscus Cooler

Preparation time: 10 minutes
Cooking time: 10 minutes
Servings: 8
Ingredients:

- 4 cups water, divided
- 6 hibiscus tea bags
- 1/2 cup fresh mint leaves, loosely packed
- 2 cups pink grapefruit juice
- 2 cups apple juice, unsweetened
- Mint sprigs

Directions:

1. Bring 2 cups of the water to a boil in a small saucepan over high heat. Remove from the heat, add the tea bags and mint, and let stand 10 minutes.
2. Set a fine wire mesh strainer over a 2-quart pitcher. Pour the tea mixture

through the strainer. Discard the solids. Stir in the remaining 2 cups of water, the grapefruit juice, and apple juice. Refrigerate until chilled, at least 2 hours, and up to 4 days. Serve over ice and garnish each serving with a mint sprig.

Nutrition:

- Carbs: 13 g.
- Calories: 53
- Fat: 0 g.
- Saturated Fat: 0 g.
- Cholesterol: 0 mg.
- Fiber: 0 g.
- Protein: 0 g.
- Sodium: 2 mg.

Fruit-and-Nut-Stuffed Baked Apples

Preparation time: 15 minutes
Cooking time: 45 minutes
Servings: 4
Ingredients:

- 1 tsp. canola oil
- 1/2 cup cranberries, dried
- 2 tbsp. walnuts, chopped
- 1/2 tsp. cinnamon, ground
- 4 Granny Smith® or Rome® apples, medium
- 1/2 cup apple cider or apple juice, unsweetened
- 1/2 cup water
- 2 tsp. all-purpose flour, unbleached

Directions:

1. Preheat the oven to 350°F. Brush an 8-inch square glass baking dish with oil.
2. Combine the cranberries, walnuts, and cinnamon in a small bowl and toss to coat. Set aside.
3. Core the apples, cutting to, but not through, the bottoms. Cutaway 1-inch of the peel from the tops of the apples. Divide the cranberry mixture evenly among the apples, pressing the mixture into each cavity. Arrange the apples upright in the prepared baking dish.

4. Combine the apple cider, water, and flour in a medium bowl and whisk until smooth. Pour over the apples.
5. Bake, uncovered, basting twice, until the apples are tender, for 40–45 minutes.
6. To serve, place the apples in shallow bowls and drizzle evenly with the sauce. Serve hot, warm, or at room temperature.

Nutrition:

- Carbs: 37 g.
- Calories: 175
- Fat: 4 g.
- Saturated Fat: 0 g.
- Cholesterol: 0 mg.
- Fiber: 5 g.
- Protein: 1 g.
- Sodium: 5 mg.

Pear Butter

Preparation time: 10 minutes
Cooking time: 15 minutes
Servings: 1 1/2 cups
Ingredients:

- 2 1/2 lb. ripe pears, peeled, cored, coarsely chopped
- 1/2 cup sugar
- 1 tsp. fresh ginger, grated
- 1/8 tsp. nutmeg, ground
- 1/2 tsp. lemon zest, grated
- 1 tbsp. lemon juice

Directions:

1. Place the pears in a food processor and process until smooth. Transfer the puree to a medium saucepan. Add the sugar, ginger, and nutmeg and bring to a boil over high heat.
2. Reduce the heat to low and simmer, uncovered, stirring occasionally, until the mixture is very thick, about 45 minutes (stir more often as the mixture thickens). Remove from the heat and stir in the lemon zest and lemon juice.
3. Transfer the pear butter to a bowl and let them stand to cool to room temperature.

The butter can be refrigerated in an airtight container for up to 2 weeks.

Nutrition:

- Carbs: 23 g.
- Calories: 90
- Fat: 1 g.
- Saturated Fat: 0 g.
- Cholesterol: 0 mg.
- Fiber: 0 g.
- Protein: 1 g.
- Sodium: 0 mg.

CHAPTER 14:

28-Day Meal Plan

Days	Breakfast	Lunch	Dinner	Dessert
1	Apple cinnamon scones	Spaghetti squash and chickpea Bolognese	Mustard-crusted sole	Greek yogurt berry smoothie pops
2	Apple filled Swedish pancake	Zucchini and pinto bean casserole	Almond crusted cod with chips	Grilled peach and coconut yogurt bowls
3	Apple topped French toast	Eggplant-zucchini parmesan	Lemon snapper with fruit	Frozen chocolate peanut butter bites
4	Apple walnut pancakes	Grilled Portobello and zucchini burger	Easy tuna wraps	No-bake carrot cake bites
5	"Bacon" and egg muffins	Lemon wax beans	Asian-inspired swordfish steaks	Creamy strawberry crepes
6	Berry breakfast bark	Wilted dandelion greens with sweet onion	Salmon with fennel and carrot	Swirled cream cheese brownies
7	Blueberry cinnamon muffins	Asparagus with scallops	Ranch tilapia fillets	Maple oatmeal cookies
8	Blueberry English muffin loaf	Butter cod with asparagus	Chilean sea bass with green olive relish	Ambrosia
9	Blueberry stuffed French toast	Creamy cod fillet with quinoa and asparagus	Ginger and green onion fish	Banana pudding
10	Breakfast pizza	Asparagus and scallop skillet with lemony	Asian sesame cod	Air fryer apples
11	Cauliflower breakfast hash	Butter-lemon grilled cod on asparagus	Roasted shrimp and veggies	Pineapple nice cream
12	Cheese spinach waffles	Lemon parsley white fish fillets	Lemon scallops with asparagus	Apple crunch
13	Cinnamon apple granola	Cilantro lime shrimp	Fish tacos	Tapioca berry parfaits
14	Cinnamon rolls	Cajun catfish	Spicy Cajun shrimp	Coffee and cream pops

15	Coconut breakfast porridge	Lamb and mushroom cheeseburgers	General Tso's chicken	Cinnamon spiced baked apples
16	Cottage cheese pancakes	Pulled pork sandwiches with apricot jelly	Balsamic meatloaf	Broiled pineapple
17	Crab and spinach frittata	Parmesan golden pork chops	Beef pot pie	Cottage cheese almond pancakes
18	Walnut and oat granola	Chipotle chili pork	Lobster bisque	Pumpkin apple waffles
19	Crispy pita with Canadian bacon	Leek and cauliflower soup	Chicken casserole	Buckwheat crêpes with fruit and yogurt
20	Coconut and chia pudding	Simple buttercup squash soup	Beef and broccoli	Apple cinnamon cake
21	Blueberry muffins	Pumpkin, Bean, and Chicken Enchiladas	Garlic shrimp	Chocolate apple cake
22	Apple and bran muffins	Mu Shu chicken	Curried shrimp	Walnut apple cake
23	Coconut and berry oatmeal	Stove-top chicken, macaroni, and cheese	Chicken and vegetable stir fry	Apple pie
24	Spanakopita frittata	Chicken sausage omelets with spinach	Blackened salmon	Cranberry lb. cake
25	Ratatouille egg bake	Chicken-broccoli salad with buttermilk dressing	Coconut shrimp curry	Chocolate fudge nut cake
26	Cottage pancakes	Country-style wedge salad with turkey	Delicious fish curry	Crustless pumpkin pie
27	Greek yogurt and oat pancakes	Turkey kabob pitas	Lemon dill salmon	Applesauce raisin cake
28	Apple and pumpkin waffles	Caribbean fish with mango-orange relish	Creamy shrimp	Easy peanut butter squares

Leftovers Idea

If you have leftover food, there are many ways to fix it for a diabetic diet. For example, if you cook a roast, make 2 or more servings and put them in separate containers. One container will be eaten for dinner and the other can be used the next day as lunch. Soups and stews can also be made ahead of time in large quantities so that they are prepared quickly when needed. Another good idea is to plan a menu for the week and make double the amount of each meal. For example, if you are making meatballs, make 2 packages so that one can be used immediately and the other can be frozen. If you are ready to use the frozen meatballs, simmer them in spaghetti sauce for a meatball sub. The next day, they can be sliced and used in a meatball soup or stew. This way, you will have 2 meals at your disposal without taking up extra time in cooking and preparation.

Food is also prepared in a way that it can be used in multiple ways. For example, if you are making spaghetti sauce from scratch, cook extra tomatoes so that the sauce can be put on scrambled eggs for a quick breakfast or used to top pizza for lunch.

This is a great way to save time when planning your meals. Also, there will be less of a chance that you will have to skip a meal because it was not prepared. You might also consider using fresh vegetables in your meals instead of canned vegetables. Canned vegetables will be more convenient, but fresh vegetables do not have a lot of the preservatives that canned foods have.

Another great idea for busy people is to cook extra portions and freeze them. Then you can use them in another meal or for snacks. These portions can be made from leftovers. If you do not like the way something tastes, all you need to do is add some spices and ingredients to make a different dish. You can also use this technique to make a familiar dish into something new and interesting. This type of cooking is a great way to save time, money and never have the same meal twice. All you need to do is access your freezer more often. This way, you can enjoy delicious meals and still eat healthy even with a reduced income budget.

Another main rule for a diabetic diet is to prepare plenty of fruits and vegetables at the beginning of the week. This way you will have an abundance of food available for snacks or meals. You should also eat fruit for dessert at least once a week. You can store fresh or canned fruits in your refrigerator. Some of the fruit that you can use as a snack are raspberries, blueberries, blackcurrants, peeled peaches, and cut-up potatoes. You should also avoid fast food while on a diabetic diet. If you do not have the time or the energy to prepare your meals, then it is better to eat out and purchase food that is prepared more healthily. If you are on the go a lot during the day, it is better to eat food that will not make you gain weight. For example, if you have a busy schedule and do not have time to cook breakfast then it is better to eat breakfast bars. They are easy and quick to prepare. You can also eat fruit during the day instead of grabbing a muffin from your local coffee shop. You can even put some fruit in a carrying bag and take it with you when you leave home. You will also be able to avoid gaining weight if you practice portion control. Refrain from eating too fast and put the food that is on your plate away so that you do not eat as much when you are finished. Try not to view food as being forbidden or limiting. If you see a piece of cake, for example, and think that it is off-limits, you will most likely overeat once you get it in your hands. If you crave sweets, then it is better to have low-fat frozen yogurt instead of ice cream. You can also take some of your favorite fruit and mix it in a blender with some ice and frozen yogurt. This will give you a delicious dessert without too much sugar. You should also not feel guilty if you sometimes want to eat junk food. You can now have this type of food on a limited basis, and the weight will remain the same since you are now being more conscious of your choices and monitoring yourself more often.

Conclusion

The Diabetic Diet is popular because it focuses on the elimination of carbohydrates. While this is not an easy endeavor, it can be extremely beneficial in maintaining your health. This study was done to see if there was a significant difference between a diabetic diet and a normal diet when it comes to blood sugar levels.

Diabetics are at particular risk of developing health problems in their feet, as well as in their hands. Taking care of your feet is important to protect the rest of your body. Taking care of your body is important to prevent all kinds of health issues. So, what can you do to better protect yourself from developing Diabetes? To protect yourself from developing diabetes, you need to take good care of yourself.

Everyone can benefit from diabetic recipes because these dishes keep you healthy while making your family happy at the same time. Whatever your feelings about the benefits of diabetic recipes, they have become an important part of many people's lives. That is because the recipes in this cookbook can help you provide your family with healthy, accessible dishes that can help improve their diabetes management.

Diabetes can affect many aspects of your physical health. Everyone knows that your blood sugar levels need to be properly regulated. Diabetes affects the way you think, feel, and react to food because of your changed understanding of how certain foods affect your body. You might not think that certain foods affect your blood sugar, but they can make you feel tired or anxious if consumed in large quantities or quickly.

A well-balanced diet is crucial for maintaining a diabetic lifestyle and preventing high blood sugar levels. Make sure that you find out which foods are best for pre-diabetics without conversion as well as for diabetics, who should be on special diets.

To protect yourself from developing diabetes, you need to take good care of yourself.

Made in the USA
Las Vegas, NV
25 August 2022

53984623R00155